THE CAMBRIDGE COMPANION TO
ATHEISM

In *The Cambridge Companion to Atheism*, eighteen of the world's leading scholars present original essays on various aspects of atheism: its history, both ancient and modern, defense, and implications. The topic is examined in terms of its implications for a wide range of disciplines, including philosophy, religion, feminism, postmodernism, sociology, and psychology. In its defense, both classical and contemporary theistic arguments are criticized, and the argument from evil and impossibility arguments, along with a non-religious basis for morality, are defended. These essays give a broad understanding of atheism and a lucid introduction to this controversial topic.

Michael Martin is Professor of Philosophy Emeritus at Boston University. He is the author of more than 150 articles and reviews as well as several books, including *Atheism, Morality and Meaning*; *The Impossibility of God* (with Ricki Monnier) and *Atheism: A Philosophical Justification*.

CAMBRIDGE COMPANIONS TO PHILOSOPHY

VOLUMES IN THE SERIES OF CAMBRIDGE COMPANIONS:

Continued after the Index

The Cambridge Companion to
ATHEISM

Edited by Michael Martin
Boston University

CAMBRIDGE
UNIVERSITY PRESS

CAMBRIDGE UNIVERSITY PRESS
Cambridge, New York, Melbourne, Madrid, Cape Town, Singapore, São Paulo, Delhi

Cambridge University Press
32 Avenue of the Americas, New York, NY 10013-2473, USA

www.cambridge.org
Information on this title: www.cambridge.org/9780521842709

First published 2007
Reprinted 2007, 2008

Printed in the United States of America

A catalog record for this publication is available from the British Library.

Library of Congress Cataloging in Publication Data

The Cambridge companion to atheism / edited by Michael Martin.
p. cm. – (Cambridge companions to philosophy)
Includes bibliographical references.
ISBN 0-521-84270-0 (hardback) – ISBN 0-521-60367-6 (pbk.)
1. Atheism. I. Martin, Michael, 1932 Feb. 3– II. Title. III. Series.
BL2747.3.C36   2007
211'.8–dc22   2006005949

ISBN 978-0-521-84270-9 hardback
ISBN 978-0-521-60367-6 paperback

CONTENTS

vii

CONTRIBUTORS

More extensive biographical material about the contributors can usually be obtained from the Web page of their respective academic departments or, if available, from the contributor's own personal Web page or on the Secular Web.

BENJAMIN BEIT-HALLAHMI is Professor of Psychology, University of Haifa, and author of *Prologomena to the Psychology of Religion* (1989) and *The Psychology of Religious Behaviour* (1997).

JAN N. BREMMER is Professor of the General History of Religion and the Comparative Science of Religion, the University of Groningen, the Netherlands, and the author of *Greek Religion* (1999) and *The Rise and Fall of the Afterlife* (2002).

DAVID O. BRINK is Professor of Philosophy, University of California at San Diego, and the author of *Moral Realism and the Foundations of Ethics* (1989) and *Perfectionism and the Common Good: Themes in the Philosophy of T. H. Green* (2003).

JOHN D. CAPUTO is Thomas J. Watson Professor of Religion and Humanities, Syracuse University, and author of *On Religion* (2001) and *The Weakness of God: A Theology of the Event* (2006).

WILLIAM LANE CRAIG is Research Professor of Philosophy, Talbot School of Theology, and author of *The Kalam Cosmological Argument* (1979) and *God, Time, and Eternity* (2001).

DANIEL C. DENNETT is Director of the Center for Cognitive Studies, University Professor, Austin B. Fletcher Professor of Philosophy, Tufts University, and author of *Darwin's Dangerous Idea* (1995) and *Freedom Evolves* (2003).

EVAN FALES is Associate Professor of Philosophy, the University of Iowa, and author of *Causation and Universals* (1990) and *A Defense of the Given: Studies in Epistemology and Cognitive Theory* (1996).

RICHARD M. GALE is Professor of Philosophy Emeritus, University of Pittsburgh, and author of *On the Nature and Existence of God* (1991) and *The Divided Self of William James* (1999).

STEVEN G. GEY is David and Deborah Fonvielle and Donald and Janet Hinkle Professor, College of Law, Florida State University, and author of *Cases and Material on Religion and the State* (2001).

PATRICK GRIM is Professor of Philosophy, SUNY at Stony Brook, and author of *The Incomplete Universe* (1991) and *The Philosophical Computer* (with Gary Mar and Paul St. Denis, 1998) and editor of *The Philosopher's Annual*.

STEWART E. GUTHRIE is Professor of Anthropology Emeritus, Fordham University, and author of *A Japanese New Religion: Rissho Kosei-Kai in a Mountain Hamlet* (1988) and *Faces in the Clouds: A New Theory of Religion* (1993).

GAVIN HYMAN is Lecturer in Religious Studies, University of Lancaster, and author of *The Predicament of Postmodern Theology: Radical Orthodoxy or Nihilist Textualism?* (2001) and editor of *New Directions in Philosophical Theology: Essays in Honour of Don Cupitt* (2004).

MICHAEL MARTIN is Professor of Philosophy Emeritus, Boston University, and author of *Atheism: A Philosophical Justification* (1990) and *The Case against Christianity* (1991).

CHRISTINE OVERALL is a Professor of Philosophy, Queen's University, Kingston, Ontario, and author of *Thinking Like a Woman: Personal Life and Political Ideas* (2001) and *Aging, Death, and Human Longevity: A Philosophical Inquiry* (2003).

KEITH PARSONS is Associate Professor of Philosophy, University of Houston, Clear Lake, and author of *God and the Burden of Proof* (1990) and *Drawing Out Leviathan* (2001).

QUENTIN SMITH is Professor of Philosophy, Western Michigan University, and coauthor of *Theism, Atheism, and Big Bang Cosmology* (with

William Lane Craig, 1993) and *Ethical and Religious Thought in Analytic Philosophy of Language* (1997).

ANDREA M. WEISBERGER was Chair of Philosophy and Religious Studies at Jacksonville University and author of *Suffering Belief: Evil and the Anglo-American Defense of Theism* (1999) and various articles in professional journals on philosophy, religion, and the sciences.

PHIL ZUCKERMAN is Associate Professor of Sociology, Pitzer College, and author of *Strife in the Sanctuary: Religious Schism in a Jewish Community* (1999) and *Invitation to the Sociology of Religion* (2003).

PREFACE

It has been a distinct honor to edit *The Cambridge Companion to Atheism*. To help bring to fruition a volume of original essays published by one of world's great university presses on one of the world's most controversial topics was an unforgettable and thrilling experience. I am grateful to Andy Beck, my editor at Cambridge University Press, who offered me the job as editor and who was patient and willing to answer my questions. I am deeply beholden to the seventeen other contributors to this volume whose essays provide novel insights to various aspects of atheism. It was a pleasure to work with them.

My wife, Jane Roland Martin, provided warm encouragement and wise advice. In addition, many nonbelieving friends and colleagues provided their support and help. In particular, I would like to thank my friend and fellow collaborator on other books on atheism, Dr. Ricki Monnier, whose encyclopedic knowledge on things atheistic was an enormous help and inspiration. I am also grateful to Dr. Tyler Wunder for his comments on chapter 6 and Dr. Wiebke Denecke for her comments on chapter 13.

GLOSSARY

For further definitions of the terms found in the volume, see Robert Audi (ed.), *The Cambridge Dictionary of Philosophy*, 2nd ed. (Cambridge: Cambridge University Press, 1999), and Bill Cooke (ed.), *Dictionary of Atheism, Skepticism, and Humanism* (Amherst, N.Y.: Prometheus Books, 2005).

a posteriori argument: an argument based on experience. *See also* teleological argument

a priori argument: an argument not based on experience. *See also* impossibility argument; ontological argument

Anselmian conception of God: the view attributed to St. Anselm that God is a being such that no greater being can be conceived

anthropomorphism: the ascription of human traits to God

apostasy: disaffection, defection, alienation, disengagement, or disaffiliation from a religious group

argument from design. *See* teleological argument

argument from evil: an argument that purports to show that the existence of evil is either incompatible with the existence of God or makes God's existence improbable. *See also* problem of evil

argument from indexicals: a type of impossibility argument that maintains that, although allegedly all-knowing, God cannot have certain knowledge expressed in indexicals. *See also* indexical

argument from miracles: an argument that purports to show that the existence of God is the most plausible explanation of miracles. *See also* miracle

argument from religious experience: an argument that purports to show that the existence of God or other supernatural beings provides the best explaination of religious experience. *See also* mystical experience; religious experience

autonomy of ethics: the view that ethics is not based on theology. *Cf.* divine command theory. *See also* ethical naturalism

Big Bang cosmology: a theory that holds that the universe originated approximately 15 billion years ago from the violent explosion of a very small agglomeration of matter of extremely high density and temperature. *See also* Kalam cosmological argument for atheism; Kalam cosmological argument for God

cancellation agnosticism: the view that the arguments for and against belief in God are equally strong and cancel each other out. *Cf.* skeptical agnosticism

clairvoyance: the power to see objects or events that cannot be perceived by the senses. *See also* paranormal phenomena

cosmological argument: an argument that seeks to give a causal explanation of why some universe exists

deism: the view that God created the world and then had no further interaction with it; also, a view of God based on reason and not revelation. *Cf.* pantheism; theism

devas: the finite and impermanent gods described by some Eastern religions

divine command theory: the theory that ethical propositions are based on what God commands. *Cf.* autonomy of ethics; ethical naturalism. *See also* voluntarism

eliminative materialism: the view that despite appearances, there are no mental entities or processes. *Cf.* reductive materialism

empiricism: the theory that all knowledge is based on experience. *Cf.* rationalism

epicureanism: a leading Hellenistic philosophical school that advocated an atomistic metaphysics and a hedonistic ethics

epistemological naturalism: the thesis that the supernatural lies beyond the scope of what we can know, hence theology is rejected as a source of knowledge

epistemology: the theory of knowledge

ethical naturalism: the theory that the ethical properties of situations depend on the nature of those situations. *Cf.* divine command theory. *See also* autonomy of ethics

Euthyphro problem: a dilemma posed in the Platonic dialogue *The Euthyphro* and used as a critique of religiously based ethics. *See also* autonomy of ethics; divine command theory; voluntarism

fine-tuning argument: a teleological argument based on the alleged improbability that the fundamental physical constants in the universe are compatible with life. *See also* teleological argument

free-will defense: the response to the argument from evil that evil is the result of free will and cannot be blamed on God. *See also* argument from evil; theodicy

impossibility argument: an a priori argument against the existence of God that purports to show that the concept of God is inconsistent. *See also* argument from indexicals; paradox of the stone

indexical: a type of expression whose meaning varies with the context; e.g., "I," "here," "now." *See also* argument from indexicals

intelligent design theory: a theory that does not reject Darwin's theory completely but maintains that evolution needs to be explained in terms of the working out of some intelligent design

Kalam cosmological argument for atheism: an argument that purports to show that according to the latest scientific cosmology, the origin of the universe is incompatible with the existence of God. *Cf.* Kalam cosmological argument for god

Kalam cosmological argument for God: an argument that maintains that the most plausible explanation for the universe coming into being is that God brought it into existence. *Cf.* Leibniz cosmological argument

knowledge by acquaintance: knowledge based on direct experience. *Cf.* propositional knowledge

Leibniz cosmological argument: an argument attributed to Leibniz that the whole series of contingent beings that make up the universe requires an external cause that is not contingent but necessary and that this cause is God

logical positivism: a philosophical movement in Anglo-American philosophy in the 1930s and '40s advocating the rejection of metaphysics because it is unverifiable and hence meaningless. Both belief in God and disbelief in God are thought to be meaningless. *See also* metaphysics; negative atheism

metaphysics: the philosophical investigation of the nature, composition, and structure of ultimate reality

miracle: an event that is not explainable by laws of nature known or unknown. *See also* argument from miracles

modus ponens: the argument form: If A, then B; A therefore B

modus tollens: the argument form: If A, then B; not-B therefore not-A

mystical experience: religious experience that transcends ordinary sense perception and purports to be a direct experience of ultimate reality

naturalism: the view that everything that exists is composed of natural entities and processes that can in principle be studied by science

naturalized epistemology: an approach that views human beings as natural entities and uses the methods of science to study epistemological processes; sometimes considered a branch of cognitive science

negative atheism: absence of belief in any god or gods. More narrowly conceived, it is the absence of belief in the theistic God. *Cf.* positive atheism. *See also* logical positivism

neo-Darwinian theory: a synthesis of Darwin's theory and genetic theory

Occam's razor: a methodological principle advocating simplicity in theory construction

omnibenevolence: the property attributed to God of being all good

omnipotence: the property attributed to God of being all powerful

omniscience: the property attributed to God of being all knowing

ontological argument: an a priori argument that maintains that God's existence is true by definition

ontology. *See* metaphysics

out-of-body experiences: the experience of floating free of one's body; used by believers as evidence of an immaterial soul

pantheism: the view that God is identical with nature. *Cf.* deism; theism

paradox of the stone: if God can make a stone that he cannot lift, he is not all-powerful; but if he cannot make such a stone, he is also not all-powerful. *See also* impossibility argument

paranormal phenomena: phenomena such an ESP, clairvoyance, and psychokinesis that at the present time are unexplainable in terms of science

physicalism: the claim that minds are not distinct from matter and hence cannot exist apart from it. *See also* reductive materialism; supervenience theory

polytheism: the view that there are many gods

positive atheism: disbelief in any God or gods. More narrowly conceived, it is disbelief in the theistic God. *Cf.* negative atheism

postmodernism: a complex set of reactions to modern philosophy and its assumption that typically opposes foundationalism, fixed binary categories that describe rigorously separable regions, and essentialism and affirms a radical and irreducible pluralism

problem of evil: the problem of why there appears to be gratuitous evil although God is all-powerful and all-good. *See also* argument from evil

procedural knowledge: knowing how to do something. *Cf.* knowledge by acquaintance; propositional knowledge

propositional knowledge: factual knowledge that something is, was, or will be the case. *Cf.* knowledge by acquaintance; procedural knowledge

psychokinesis: the ability to affect physical objects without physical contact by using powers of the mind

rationalism: the theory that reason is the primary source of knowledge. *Cf.* empiricism

reductive materialism: the theory that mental states and processes are identical with brain states and processes. *Cf.* eliminative materialism; supervenience theory

religious experience: a wide variety of experiences, such as hearing voices and having visions, of supernatural beings such as God, angels, and Satan

skeptical agnosticism: the rejection of both belief and disbelief in God because there are no good arguments for or against such belief. *Cf.* cancellation agnosticism

Sophists: a group of itinerant teachers of rhetoric and philosophy in ancient Greece

supervenience theory: the theory that when a certain physical state obtains, so does a certain mental state. *Cf.* eliminative materialism; reductive materialism

teleological argument: an argument for the existence of God based on the apparent design and order in the universe. Also called the argument from design. *See also* fine-tuning argument. *Cf.* cosmological argument

theism: belief in an omnipotent, omniscient, omnibenevolent, personal God who created the universe, takes an active interest in the world, and has given a special revelation to humans. *Cf.* deism

theodicy: a theory attempting to explain the problem of evil and answer the argument from evil. *See also* argument from evil; free-will defense

verificationism: the theory that the meaning of a statement consists in its method(s) of verification; usually associated with logical positivism

voluntarism: the view that something's being good depends on God's will. *See also* Euthyphro problem

General Introduction

The purpose of this volume is to provide general readers and advanced students with an introduction to atheism: its history, present social context, legal implications, supporting arguments, implications for morality, and relation to other perspectives. This general introduction will set the stage for the chapters that follow.

ATHEISM, AGNOSTICISM, AND THEISM

The concept of atheism was developed historically in the context of Western monotheistic religions, and it still has its clearest application in this area. Applied, for example, to premodern non-Western contexts, the concept may be misleading. Moreover, even in the modern Western context "atheism" has meant different things depending on changing conceptions of God. Nevertheless, it will be assumed in this volume that, if applied cautiously outside its clearest historical context, the concept of atheism can be illuminating for contemporary Western readers.

If you look up "atheism" in a dictionary, you will find it defined as the belief that there is no God. Certainly, many people understand "atheism" in this way. Yet this is not what the term means if one considers it from the point of view of its Greek roots. In Greek "a" means "without" or "not," and "theos" means "god."[1] From this standpoint, an atheist is someone without a belief in God; he or she need not be someone who believes that God does not exist.[2] Still, there is a popular dictionary meaning of "atheism" according to which an atheist is not simply one who holds no belief in the existence of a God or gods but is one who believes that there is no God or gods. This dictionary use of the term should not be overlooked. To avoid confusion, let us call it *positive atheism* and let us call the type of atheism derived from the original Greek roots *negative atheism*.

No general definition of "God" will be attempted here,[3] but it will prove useful to distinguish a number of different concepts of God that have figured in the traditional controversies and debates about religion. In modern times "theism" has usually come to mean a belief in a personal God who takes an active interest in the world and who has given a special revelation to humans. So understood, theism stands in contrast to deism, the belief in a God that is based not on revelation but on evidence from nature. The God assumed by deists is usually considered to be remote from the world and not intimately involved with its concerns. Theism is also to be contrasted with polytheism, the belief in more than one God, and with pantheism, the belief that God is identical with nature.

Negative atheism in the broad sense[4] is then the absence of belief in any god or Gods, not just the absence of belief in a personal theistic God, and negative atheism in the narrow sense is the absence of belief in a theistic God. Positive atheism in the broad sense is, in turn, disbelief in all gods, with positive atheism in the narrow sense being the disbelief in a theistic God. For positive atheism in the narrow sense to be successfully defended, two tasks must be accomplished. First, the reasons for believing in a theistic God must be refuted; in other words, negative atheism in the narrow sense must be established. Second, reasons for disbelieving in the theistic God must be given.

These categories should not be allowed to mask the complexity and variety of positions that atheists can hold, for a given individual can take different atheistic positions with respect to different concepts of God. Thus, a person might maintain that there is good reason to suppose that anthropomorphic gods such as Zeus do not exist and therefore be a positive atheist with respect to Zeus and similar gods. However, he or she could, for example, be only a negative atheist with respect to Paul Tillich's God.[5] In addition, people can and often do hold different atheistic positions with respect to different conceptions of a theistic God. For example, someone could be a positive atheist with respect to Aquinas' God and only a negative atheist with respect to St. Teresa's God.

Agnosticism, the position of neither believing nor disbelieving that God exists, is often contrasted with atheism. However, this common opposition of agnosticism to atheism is misleading. Agnosticism and positive atheism are indeed incompatible: if atheism is true, agnosticism is false and conversely. But agnosticism is compatible with negative atheism in that agnosticism *entails* negative atheism. Since agnostics do not believe in God, they are by definition negative atheists. This is not to say that negative atheism entails agnosticism. A negative atheist *might* disbelieve in God but need not.

Elsewhere I have evaluated the main arguments for agnosticism.[6] Here I will explore what is at issue between positive atheism and agnosticism. An agnostic, one might suppose, is skeptical that good grounds exist, whereas an atheist is not. However, this is not the only way the difference between these positions can be construed. An agnostic might think that there are good grounds for disbelieving that God exists but *also* believe that there are equally good grounds for believing that God exists. These opposing reasons would offset one another, leaving no overall positive reason to believe or disbelieve.

Let us call the view that there are no good reasons for believing that God exists and none for believing that God does not exist skeptical agnosticism and the view that that are equally good reasons for believing both theism and atheism that offset one another cancellation agnosticism.

Arguments that are intended to establish both negative and positive atheism refute both skeptical and cancellation agnosticism. Showing that negative atheism is justified undermines cancellation agnosticism, for it assumes that both atheism and theism have good grounds that cancel each other out, and negative atheism entails that there are no good grounds for theistic belief. Moreover, arguments showing that there are good grounds for the nonexistence of God undermine skeptical agnosticism since skeptical agnosticism assumes that there are no good grounds for either atheism or theism.

BACKGROUND, THE CASE AGAINST THEISM, AND IMPLICATIONS

Atheism has a long and distinguished history as several of the background chapters in this volume attest. Jan Bremmer in "Atheism in Antiquity" argues, on the one hand, that the Greeks discovered theoretical atheism, which some scholars maintain is one of the most important events in the history of religion. On the other hand, Bremmer maintains, "Greeks and Romans, pagans and Christians, soon discovered the utility of the term 'atheist' as a means to label opponents. The invention of atheism would open a new road to intellectual freedom, but also enabled people to label opponents in a new way. Progress rarely comes without a cost." Gavin Hyman in "Atheism in Modern History" outlines the development of atheistic thought in the Western world, arguing that atheism and modernity are so linked that modernity seems almost necessarily to culminate in atheism. He concluded that we can be sure of one thing: "the fate of atheism would seem to be inescapably bound up with the fate of modernity." And Paul Zuckerman in "Atheism: Contemporary Numbers and Patterns" brings together a vast amount of data on the number and distribution of atheists throughout the world. Among other things, he shows that atheists make up a signification portion of the world's population, that nonbelief tends to be associated with social health, and that the pattern and distribution of atheists in the world calls into question the now fashionable theory that belief in God is innate.

Needless to say, many contemporary philosophers have defended theism against the criticisms of atheists.[7] In this volume William Lane Craig in "Theistic Critiques of Atheism" presents the theistic position. Readers must decide for themselves whether his defense of theism succeeds or whether atheism has been successfully defended by the arguments put forward in other chapters in this volume.[8]

Several chapters in this book contribute to the task of defending negative atheism. Richard Gale in "The Failure of Classical Theistic Arguments" brings up objections to such classical arguments for the existence of God as the ontological argument. Keith Parsons in "Some Contemporary Theistic Arguments" criticizes the arguments for God defended by two leading contemporary Christian philosophers, Alvin Plantinga and Richard Swinburne. Daniel Dennett offers criticisms of creationism and intelligent design theories, both of which are often associated with theism. Evan Fales in "Naturalism and Physicalism" raises objections to supernaturalism, of which theism is a special case, and David Brink in "The Autonomy of Ethics" argues that ethics is independent of belief in God, although theists often claim that ethics is dependent on God.[9]

Other chapters contribute to the task of defending positive atheism. In "The Argument from Evil," Andrea Weisberger defends the traditional argument from evil – the attempt to show that the large amount of evil in the world makes the existence of the theistic God either false or improbable. Quentin Smith in "Kalam Cosmological Argument for Atheism" maintains that cosmology has atheistic implications. Patrick Grim in "Impossibility Arguments" attempts to show that the concept of God is inconsistent.[10] It should be noted, however, that many other arguments also contribute to the second task that are not considered in this volume.[11] Elsewhere, for example, Ted Drange has defended positive atheism by attempting to show that the large amount of nonbelief in the world makes the existence of a theistic God improbable.[12] John Schellenberg[13] has attempted to demonstrate that the belief in the existence of nontheistic religions makes a theistic God's existence improbable. In addition, Schellenberg has argued that the existence of reasonable nonbelief is itself grounds for supposing that God does not exist.[14]

Several chapters in this volume draw out some of atheism's important and exciting implications. Atheism has been accused of being antireligious, but Michael Martin in "Atheism and Religion" shows that although atheism is not a religion, there are atheistic religions. Christine Overall in "Feminism and Atheism" concludes, "Being a feminist also requires that one be an atheist." According to Steve Gey in "Atheism and the Freedom of Religion," "the religious liberty of atheists has come a long way since the days in which serious political theorists could argue that atheists should be put to death, denied the ability to give evidence in court, or prohibited from becoming a Member of Parliament.... [But] atheists will not enjoy the same religious liberty as religious adherents unless the government under which they live is comprehensively secularized." John Caputo in "Atheism, A/theology, and the Postmodern Condition" reviews some of the important challenges postmodernism poses for theism and atheism and maintains that "postmodernism turns out to be not a particularly friendly environment for atheism, either, not if atheism is a metaphysical or an otherwise fixed and decisive denial of God."

An important, although not primary, part of the case for atheism is to show that religion can be explained as a natural phenomenon. Stewart Guthrie in "Anthropological Theories of Religion " reviews different types of naturalistic explanations of religion and advocates a cognitive explanation of religion in which animism and anthropomorphism are central notions. Finally, Benjamin Beit-Hallahmi in "Atheists: A Psychological Profile" reviews the psychological data and concludes that atheists tend to be more intelligent and better educated than believers; less authoritarian, less suggestible, less dogmatic, and less prejudiced than believers; and more tolerant of others, law-abiding, compassionate, and conscientious. "In short, they are good to have as neighbors."

BIBLIOGRAPHIC NOTE

For introductions to atheism, see Douglas Krueger, *What Is Atheism?* (Amherst, N.Y.: Prometheus Books, 1998), and Julian Baggini, *Atheism: A Very Short Introduction* (Oxford: Oxford University Press, 2003). Excellent references to atheistic literature can be found in the bibliographies and end notes of the chapters in this volume. In addition, extensive bibliographies can be found in Nicholas Everett, *The Non Existence of God* (London: Routledge, 2004); Finngeir Hiorth, *Atheism in the World* (Oslo, Norway: Human-Etisk Forbund, 2003), *Ethics for Atheists* (Mumbia, India: Indian Secular Society, 1998), and Hiorth, *Introduction to Atheism* (Oslo, Norway: Human-Etisk Forbund, 2002); S. T. Joshi (ed.), *Atheism* (Amherst, N.Y.: Prometheus Books, 2000); and Gordon Stein (ed.), *The Encyclopedia of Unbelief*, vols. 1 and 2 (Buffalo, N.Y.: Prometheus Books, 1985). For more on feminism and atheism, see Annie Laurie Gaylord (ed.), *Women without Superstition: No God – No Masters* (Madison, Wis.: Freedom from Religion Foundation, 1997), and *Woe to the Women: The Bible Tells Me So* (Madison, Wis.: Freedom from Religion Foundation, 1981). Moreover, a Google search of the Secular Web (http://www.infidel.org) turns up over 700 items on atheism and related topics.

6   GENERAL INTRODUCTION

NOTES

1. Gordon Stein, "The Meaning of Atheism and Agnosticism," in Gordon Stein (ed.), *An Anthology of Atheism and Rationalism* (Buffalo, N.Y.: Prometheus, 1980), p. 3.

2. This negative sense of "atheism" should be distinguished from the sense of "atheism" introduced by Paul Edwards. According to Edwards, an atheist is a person who rejects a belief in God. This rejection may be because the person believes that the statement "God exists" is false, but it may be for other reasons. The negative sense of "atheism" used here is broader than Edwards's definition since on the present definition someone can be an atheist if he or she has no belief in God, although the lack of belief is not the result of rejection. See Paul Edwards, "Atheism," in Paul Edwards (ed.), *The Encyclopedia of Philosophy* (New York: Macmillan and Free Press, 1967), vol. 1, p. 175.

3. However, the definition of "God" proposed by Beardsley and Beardsley has considerable merit. On their view, for a being to be a god it must meet four criteria: it must have supernatural powers; be free from so many of the natural limitations of inanimate objects, subhuman organisms, and humans that it cannot be classified as belonging to any of these groups; have some kind of mental life; and be regarded as superior to human beings. See Monroe Beardsley and Elizabeth Beardsley, *Philosophical Thinking: An Introduction* (New York: Harcourt, Brace and World, 1965), pp. 46–50.

4. I owe the distinction between the broad and narrow senses of "atheism" to William L. Rowe, "The Problem of Evil and Some Varieties of Atheism," *American Philosophical Quarterly* 16 (1979): 335–41.

5. This seems to be the position of Kai Nielsen. He rejects a nonanthropomorphic God as meaningless and an anthropomorphic God as false. See, e.g., Kai Nielsen, "Introduction: How Is Atheism to Be Characterized?" in Karl Nielsen, ed., *Philosophy and Atheism* (Buffalo, N.Y.: Prometheus Press, 1985).

6. Michael Martin, "Atheism v. Agnosticism," *Philosophers' Magazine* 19 (Summer 2002): 17–19; see also Michael Martin, "On an Argument for Agnosticism," Aug. 27, 2001, http://www.infidels.org/library/modern/michael_martin/martinag.html.

7. For example, see Alvin Plantinga, *Warranted Christian Belief* (Oxford: Oxford University Press, 2000) and *God, Freedom and Evil* (Grand Rapids, Mich.: Eerdmans, 1977), and Richard Swinburne, *The Coherence of Theism* (Oxford: Oxford University Press, 1977) and *The Existence of God* (Oxford: Oxford University Press, 1979).

8. For further critiques of Craig, see Stan Wallace (ed.), *Does God Exist?* (Burlington, Vt.: Ashgate Publishing, 2003); William Lane Craig and Quentin Smith (eds.), *Theism, Atheism, and Big Bang Cosmology* (Oxford: Clarendon, 1993); Erik J. Wielenberg, *Values and Virtue in a Godless Universe* (Cambridge: Cambridge University Press, 2005); and Jeffrey Jay Lowder, "Historical Evidence and the Empty Tomb: A Reply to William Lane Craig," in Robert Price and Jeffrey Jay Lowder (eds.), *The Empty Tomb* (Amherst, N.Y.: Prometheus Books, 2005). Also see the critical papers

on Craig at http://www.infidels.org/library/modern/theism/christianity/
craig.html.

9. For arguments against theism that are not included in this volume see
Michael Martin, *Atheism: A Philosophical Justification* (Philadelphia:
Temple University Press, 1990); Nicholas Everett, *The Non Existence of
God* (London: Routledge, 2004); and Richard Gale, *On the Nature and Exis-
tence of God* (Cambridge: Cambridge University Press, 1991).

10. See Michael Martin and Ricki Monnier (eds.), *The Impossibility of God*
(Amherst, N.Y.: Prometheus Books, 2004).

11. See Martin, *Atheism*; Everett, *The Non Existence of God*.

12. Theodore Drange, *Nonbelief and Evil* (Amherst, N.Y.: Prometheus Books,
1998).

13. J. L. Schellenberg, "Pluralism and Probability," *Religious Studies* 33 (1997):
143–59.

14. J. L. Schellenberg, *Hiddenness and Human Reason* (Ithaca, N.Y.: Cornell
University Press, 1993).

I. Background

1   Atheism in Antiquity

In 1942 the French historian Louis Febvre published his epoch-making study of Rabelais, in which he noted the absence of atheism in the Middle Ages.[1] Febvre explained this absence as a kind of *blocage mental*. In the life of society and the individual, Christianity was of overriding importance. Its festivals constituted the rhythm of the year; important transitions in the life of the individual – birth, marriage, and death – were completely integrated into religious life, as were everyday activities. Churches, whose bells would always remind the forgetful believer of their existence, often dominated the landscape. It was simply impossible to think Christianity away from medieval society.[2]

Subsequent research has modified Febvre's findings to some extent,[3] but his main findings still stand. Antiquity was not that different from the Middle Ages in this respect. The ancient Greeks and Romans also moved in a landscape where temples were everywhere, where gods adorned their coins, where the calendar went from religious festival to festival, and where religious rites accompanied all major transitions in life. Consequently, atheism never developed into a popular ideology with a recognizable following. All we have in antiquity is the exceptional individual who dared to voice his disbelief or bold philosophers who proposed intellectual theories about the coming into existence of the gods without, normally, putting their theories into practice or rejecting religious practice altogether. If we find atheism at all, it is usually a "soft" atheism or the imputation of atheism to others as a means to discredit them.

Even if we may assume that mankind always has known its sceptics and unbelievers, the expression of that scepticism and unbelief is subject to historical circumstances. Some periods were more favorable to dissenters than other times, and later times may interpret as atheism what earlier times permitted as perhaps only just acceptable theories about the gods or the origin of religion. This means that we must be attentive to the different periods in which atheism more or less flourished, to the interpretations by later Greeks and Romans of their predecessors, and to the reasons why contemporaries impute atheism to people who differ from them in religious opinion.

The Epicurean Philodemus (ca. 110–35 B.C.) classified the various kinds of atheists in antiquity as follows:

(1) Those who say that it is unknown whether there are any gods or what they are like;
(2) Those who say openly that the gods do not exist;
(3) Those who clearly imply it.[4]

Although this classification is a fairly acceptable one, it stays at the level of ideas and neglects practicing atheists. More seriously, it does not mention atheism as a labeling device to slander your opponents, be they religious or philosophical ones. That is why we do not follow Philodemus but divide our evidence into three periods: (1) the classical period, (2) the Hellenistic period, which started to label earlier thinkers as atheists and developed a "soft" atheism that tried to save the existence of the gods, and (3) the Roman period when the Christians were called *atheoi* by the pagans and vice versa. Given its interest for the history of atheism, we will concentrate on the classical period. In all cases, we will use the term "atheism" rather loosely for those thinkers and people who denied the existence of the gods or put forward theories to explain the existence of the gods.[5]

It is not our intention to give an exhaustive listing of all people that have been called atheists in antiquity. This has already been done in a very competent manner and needs not to be redone.[6] Atheism itself has also been studied repeatedly.[7] Yet recent publications of new papyri and new editions of already published texts enable us to take a fresh look at the older Greek evidence and thus to sketch a better picture than was possible in most of the twentieth century.

I. THE CLASSICAL PERIOD

Atheism in Greece became visible especially in Athens in the second half of the fifth century, although the first "atheist" was not from Athens. The first prominent philosopher that was later categorized as such was Protagoras (ca. 490–420 B.C.) from Abdera, a city in the northeast of Greece, where Democritus (ca. 460–400? B.C.), who could have developed into an atheist but apparently did not, was born. He was famous for what probably was the opening sentence of his work called "Concerning the Gods," as in antiquity the titles of prose works often consisted of the opening words: "Concerning the gods I am unable to discover whether they exist or not, or what they are like in form; for there are many hindrances to knowledge, the obscurity of the subject and the brevity of human life."[8] It is clear from this quote that Protagoras was an agnostic rather than an atheist, as Cicero in his *De natura deorum* (I.1.2) and Galen in his *De propriis placitis* (2, ed. Boudon-Millot and Pietrobelli) still recognized. And indeed, during his life he was highly respected: Pericles, the leading Athenian politician in the middle of the fifth century, invited him to write the constitution of the panhellenic colony Thurii in Southern Italy (Heraclides Ponticus, fragment 150 Wehrli[2]) and Plato even noted in his *Meno* (91e) that Protagoras had lived out his life in high repute. Yet his fame soon took a turn for the worse, and already in the Hellenistic period notices started to appear that he had been condemned to death and that his book with the famous opening words had been burned in the marketplace.[9] Although these reports are probably fictitious, they developed into accusations of straightforward atheism in, at the latest, the second century A.D. in the writings of the empiricist Sextus Empiricus (*Adversus Mathematicos* 9.50–1, 56) and the Epicurean Diogenes of Oenoanda (fragment 16 Smith), who may have derived his accusation from Epicurus himself.[10]

Protagoras' agnosticism can be explained only in the most general of terms. There is little known about his life and hardly anything about his intellectual formation. Yet we can say something about the intellectual climate he grew up in and the preconditions for his agnosticism. Protagoras belonged to the so-called sophistic movement, a loose term that denotes the critical intellectuals, in particular, the philosophers of the second half of the fifth century B.C. The sophists were connected to books by their contemporaries,[11] and this points to literacy as an important condition for the development of critical philosophy. Its importance for philosophy becomes visible around 500 B.C. when Pythagoras (ca. 560–495 B.C.) was criticized by Xenophanes (B 7 DK: ca. 570–495 B.C.) in writing; and Heraclitus (B 129 DK: ca. 500 B.C.) even reproached him for having plundered many writings.[12]

The latter two influential philosophers also fiercely attacked the anthropomorphic gods of Homer and Hesiod, the authoritative Greek poets. Xenophanes even proclaimed "the one god, greatest among gods and humans" (fragment B 23 DK). In other words, he and his contemporaries tried to introduce new ideas of the divine rather than abolishing the idea of the divine altogether. The situation started to change with Anaxagoras (ca. 500–428 B.C.), who was the first philosopher known to have settled in Athens, at the time the center of intellectual life in Greece, probably in the middle of the 450s. According to the third-century A.D. Diogenes Laertius (2.7 = fragment A 1 DK), "he said that the sun was a red-hot mass of metal." We may not think this revolutionary, but for the Athenians the sun was a god, Helios, and Anaxagoras' observation stripped the sun from its divine nature.

When did Anaxagoras pronounce this statement? Unfortunately, his chronology is not at all assured.[13] Much of our evidence points to the years he came to Athens, but later accounts connect him with attempts to harm Pericles, and speak of a legal case caused by his "impiety."[14] The trouble with these accounts is that mockery of the views of natural philosophers starts to appear in texts only in the 420s. In his *Panoptai* (fragment 167 Kassel/Austin), which must have appeared shortly before 423 B.C., the playwright Cratinus mocks the philosopher Hippon, who is later pictured as impious, because he had stated that the sky is a baking-cover.[15] In 423 B.C., Aristophanes put on the *Clouds* and mocked the inhabitants of the "Reflectory" (*phrontistêrion*) for espousing the same idea; Socrates even says: "I walk the air and contemplate the sun."[16] In 421, another playwright of comedies, Eupolis, implicated even Protagoras in these ideas in his *Flatterers* of 421 B.C. by representing him as pontificating "about the heavens" (fragment 157 Kassel/Austin), and in 414 Aristophanes let the chorus of his *Birds* say that people have to pay attention to them so that "you may hear correctly from us all about the things on high" (690), which in the text seems connected with the briefly mentioned Prodicus (below).[17]

But it was not only the authors of comedy who took a jibe at the new philosophy. The tragedian Euripides, too, contributed to the general resentment by letting the chorus of an unknown play recite: "who, seeing this, does not teach beforehand that his soul is considered a god, and does not hurl far from him the crooked deceits of talkers about the heavens, whose mad tongues make random throws about what is hidden, devoid of understanding."[18] It is this connection between atheism and speculating about the nature of the heavens that also comes to the fore in Plato's *Apology* (18bc), where Socrates says that his accusers state:

There is a wise man called Socrates who has theories about the heavens and has investigated everything below the earth, and can make the weaker argument defeat the stronger. It is these people, gentlemen of the jury, the disseminators of these rumours, who are my dangerous accusers, because those who hear them suppose that anyone who inquires into such matters must be an atheist.[19]

This testimony from an early dialogue of Plato is most valuable, as it shows that speculating about the heavens was indeed already connected with atheism by Socrates' contemporaries.

We move in a different direction with the sophist Prodicus of Keos (ca. 465–395 B.C.). Unfortunately, next to nothing is known about the title, content, and scope of the work in which he expounded his views. The best candidate is perhaps his *Horai*, or seasons personified,[20] which must have appeared around 420 B.C., as Prodicus' theory was parodied in Aristophanes' *Birds* of 414 B.C. and echoed by Euripides' *Bacchae* of 406 B.C.[21] Although Prodicus was also one of those philosophers with the reputation of speculating "about the heavens" (above), this was not his main claim to fame. In fact, his ideas were much more radical, as, according to Philodemus, he maintained "that the gods of popular belief do not exist nor do they know, but primitive man, [out of admiration, deified] the fruits of the earth and virtually everything that contributed to his existence." The highly stylized character of the language suggests that this passage reflects rather closely Prodicus' very words.[22] But what did Prodicus actually mean?

Renewed attention to the fragmentary papyri that are our best source for Prodicus' ideas has shown that Prodicus proposed a two-stage theory of the origin of polytheism. First, primitive man started to call "gods" those elements of nature on which he was most dependent, such as sun and moon, rivers, and fruits. Subsequently, those humans who had been the main benefactors as inventors of the proper usage of the fruits of the earth, namely, bread and wine, Demeter and Dionysos, were likewise called "gods" and worshipped as such. Evidently, there had been a time without gods yet for Prodicus, even though man was already there.

Comparison with other cultural theories of his time suggests that Prodicus located the beginning of religion in agriculture. Now the advent of Demeter and Dionysos with their gifts of bread and wine was part of Attic mythology. In fact, Athens prided itself as having given agriculture to the Greek world.[23] Prodicus may well have heard about this claim on his island Keos, which was in easy reach of Attica, but he may also have been influenced by his frequent stays in Athens, where he did not forget his own interests while being ambassador of his island. The fact that he had appeared before the Athenian Council and had impressed them by his eloquence almost certainly guarantees that he had well prepared his case by studying Attic mythology.[24]

In addition to Prodicus, the only other fifth-century intellectuals in whose work clear atheistic statements can be found are Euripides and Critias. Unfortunately, ancient biographical evidence for Euripides' atheism is based primarily on inferences from his poetry, which were elaborated, often with a degree of malice, by writers of the fourth century and after. Even the tradition of Euripides' trial for atheism is probably either derived from comedy or invented in analogy of the trial of Socrates.[25] On the other hand, these inferences had some material to work from.[26] In the end, though, there is only one passage with a clear atheistic content, and it pays to quote it in full. In a fragment that has been handed down in Christian times from the *Bellerophon*, a tragedy that was probably performed around 430 B.C., Bellerophon himself states early in the play:

Does someone say there are indeed gods in heaven? There are not, there are not, if a man is willing not to rely foolishly on the antiquated reasoning. Consider for yourselves, do not base your opinion on words of mine. I say myself that tyranny kills very many men and deprives them of their possessions; and that tyrants break their oaths to ransack cities, and in doing this they are more prosperous under heaven than men who live quietly in reverence from day to day. I know too of small cities doing honour to the gods that are subject to larger, more impious ones, because they are overcome by a more numerous army. I think that, if a man were lazy and prayed to the gods and did not go gathering his livelihood with his hand, you would [here is a lacuna in the text] fortify religion, and ill-fortune.[27]

The statement is a radical expression of a feeling encountered more often in Euripides that the irreligious prosper, whereas the pious suffer.[28] Consequently, the gods have no power and religion is imaginary. Such a radical stance must be one of those that elicited Aristophanes' scorn,[29] but at the end of the play the traditional order was re-established and Bellerophon's atheistic declaration is more than outweighed by his pitiable lot. In other words, the statement is the expression of a character in the play, not the opinion of the playwright himself.[30]

There could be a second passage, but its authorship is highly debated. It used to be ascribed to the sophist Critias (ca. 450–403 B.C.), who was one of the most unscrupulous members of the Thirty Tyrants, a group of aristocrats that had seized power at the end of the Peloponnesian War and was remembered for its rule of terror. As such, the cynical tone of the piece seemed to fit perfectly the image of its author in the historiographical tradition. On the other hand, Critias is mentioned only once as the author of this passage, whereas Euripides is mentioned twice. In fact, several recent studies have persuasively argued that it is completely out of character of the genre of the satyr play that a character would develop here a highly provocative theory for the very first time instead of parodying it, as indeed seems to be the case here – the more so when the passage does not reflect the opinion of just one philosopher but those of several. Moreover, a character that tries to persuade somebody that a crime without witnesses will remain unpunished fits a satyr play much better than a tragedy. Finally, the passage contains a number of words that occur only in Euripides' work. Consequently, the passage could have belonged to either Euripides' *Sisyphus* (415 B.C.) or, perhaps more attractively, his *Autolykos A* (date unknown).[31] Yet the recent authoritative edition of Euripides' fragments has not accepted these arguments and once again ascribes the fragment to Critias.[32] This is probably correct, since the new edition of Philodemus' *On Piety* (519–41) shows that Epicurus already concluded that what Critias himself had said about the gods "made it impossible for them as generally conceived to exist"; in fact, lines 539–40 and 1185–1217 of *On Piety* exhibit vestigial echoes of the *Sisyphus* account. In other words, Critias' reputation as an atheist predates the Hellenistic biographers.[33] Given its interest for the history of atheism I will quote the piece in full:

Once there was a time when the life of human beings was disordered, and similar to that of animals and ruled by force, when there was no reward for the virtuous nor any punishment for the wicked. And then I think that humans decided to establish laws as punishers so that Justice (*Dikê*) might be ruler [lacuna] and keep Crime and Violence (*Hybris*) as slave. And they punished only those who kept doing wrong. Then, since the laws held open deeds of violence in check, they continued to commit them in secret; then, I believe, a wise and clever-minded man invented for mortals a fear of the gods, so that there might be a deterrent for the wicked, even if they act or say or think anything in secret. Hence from this source he explained the divine: there is a deity (*daimôn*) who enjoys imperishable life, hearing and seeing with his mind, his thought and attention on all things, bearer of a divine nature. He will hear whatever is said among mortals and be able to see whatever is done. If you silently plot evil, this will not escape the gods. For they [lacuna] have knowledge. With these words he explained the most delightful part of the teaching and hid the truth with a false tale. He said the gods dwell there where he – by placing them there – could frighten human beings most, whence, as he knew, fears come to mortals and troubles for their wretched life; that is, from the vault on high, where they beheld the lightnings and fearful blows of thunder and heaven with its starry eyes, the beautiful, brilliantly decorated building of Time, the wise craftsman. Whence too the brilliant mass of the sun strides and the liquid rain falls on the earth. [4 interpolated lines] It was thus, I think, that someone first persuaded mortals to believe that there exists a race of gods.[34]

In this long passage, which most probably was pronounced by Sisyphus, the cleverest Greek in mythology, we see the first occurrence of the theory that religion (here: the gods) was invented to ensure good behavior of humans. It is unique in its time, but it is hardly imaginable that a playwright would put forward such a theory in a play meant to entertain his audience without any previous knowledge of it among its spectators. Now it is clear that several aspects of this passage must have been familiar to the audience. First, the picture of an animal-like situation at the beginning of humankind was a recurrent topos in descriptions and parodies of the primeval situation by contemporaries of Euripides.[35] Second, the opposition between public assent to laws but private freedom from restraint can be paralleled in the work of the contemporary sophist Antiphon, who stated that justice would be most advantageous

to a man if "he were to regard the laws as great in the presence of witnesses, but nature as great when deprived of witnesses" (F 44(a), I, 13–23
Pendrick). Third, Democritus' (A 75 DK) institutors of religion relied
on human fear of celestial phenomena, and, fourth, Prodicus had also
advanced a two-stage theory of the development of religion (above). Yet
the theory espoused in our passage goes further and is more cynical than
anything proposed in our surviving texts.

Critias' (or Euripides') drama well illustrates a gradual change in mood
regarding the gods in Athens in the later fifth century. There was worse
to come. In 415 the Athenians undertook a major expedition to Sicily
to conquer Syracuse, and our sources enable us to observe the ner-
vous mood of the Athenian population at that time.[36] It was at this
precarious moment that the highly guarded secrecy of the Eleusinian
Mysteries twice came under attack. One morning, shortly before the
Athenian fleet was due to sail to Sicily, it was discovered that nearly
all the images of the god Hermes in public places had been mutilated.
Those denounced were also accused of having profaned the Eleusinian
Mysteries.[37] Whereas the mutilators had parodied the Mysteries (if they
actually had done so) in private circumstances, around the same time
Diagoras, a citizen of the island Melos, mocked the Mysteries openly
after the Athenians had treated his home island badly.[38] Consequently,
as the eleventh-century Arab Mubashshir, whose account – directly or
indirectly – seems to derive from the erudite Athenian Apollodorus
(*ca.* 180–120 B.C.), notes:

When he [viz., Dhiyaghuras *al-mariq*, or "Diagoras the heretic, or apostate"]
persisted in his hypocrisy [or "dissimulation"], his unbelief and his atheism, the
ruler, the wise men [or philosophers, *hukama*] and leaders of Attica sought to
kill him. The ruler Charias the Archon [Khariyus al-Arkun (415–4)] set a price
on his head [literally: "spent money," *badhal*] and commanded that it should
be proclaimed among the people: "He who apprehends Diagoras from Melos
[*Maylun*] and kills him will be rewarded with a large sum [*badra*, traditionally a
leather bag containing 1,000 or 10,000 dirhams]."[39]

This is a pretty exact report of the events, since the Athenians
promised one talent of silver to anyone who killed Diagoras, and two
to anyone who caught him alive. Now Diagoras is already mocked in
Hermippus' comedy *Moirai* (fragment 43 Kassel-Austin), which was
written before 430. In Aristophanes' *Clouds* (830), which even in its
revised version cannot be later than ca. 418 B.C., Socrates is called the
"Melian" for espousing "atheistic" views. This must mean that Diagoras
had been living safely in Athens for many years despite his irreligious
views – a fact that also shines through in the Arab report. However, his
mocking went too far, and Epicurus already mentions Diagoras together

with Critias and Prodicus as the arch-atheists.[40] In that capacity Diagoras would remain notorious all through antiquity.[41]

More famous than Diagoras, if less for his atheism, was Socrates
(469–399 B.C.). It is clear from Arisptophanes' portrait of Socrates in the
Clouds that already in that time the latter was considered to be something like an atheist; this is also suggested by his frequent association
with Euripides in comedy.[42] It is therefore not wholly surprising that
in 399 B.C. the Athenians charged Socrates as follows: "Socrates does
wrong by not acknowledging the gods the city acknowledges, and introducing other, new powers (*daimonia*). He also does wrong by corrupting
the young."[43] The trial of Socrates still poses many questions, but it is
certain that for many Athenians Socrates had moved too close to those
who questioned the traditional gods.[44]

It is only about a decade after Socrates' death, in Plato (ca. 429–
347 B.C.), that we start to find the Greek word *atheos*, which originally
was used in the meaning "godless, without gods, godforsaken," denot-
ing intellectuals who denied the gods of the city or any form of deity.
This particular meaning may of course be slightly older, but its date fits
our impression of the intellectual climate of the last decades of the fifth
century.[45] The increasing criticism of the gods by philosophers and poets
had eroded the traditional beliefs in the gods, and some intellectuals
drew the inevitable consequence. Yet the combined power of traditional
belief and Plato's influential theism made it that "real" atheists would
always remain a rare phenomenon in the Greek world.

2. THE HELLENISTIC PERIOD

The death of Socrates constituted the end of an era. Most philosophers had got the message and remained careful in expounding their
views. There was the occasional exception, such as Theodorus of Cyrene
(ca. 340–250 B.C.), who is mentioned most with Diagoras as the atheist
par excellence. However, our evidence mainly exists of anecdotes, and
it is hard to reconstruct his theology.[46]

In the Hellenistic period two important developments are noticeable.
First, we now start to find a listing of atheists in an *index atheorum*. The
earliest example is by Epicurus (341–270 B.C.) in the twelfth book of his
On Nature, which must have been written around 300 B.C.[47] He probably included his criticisms of Protagoras, Prodicus, Critias, and possibly
Diagoras, as "raving lunatics" in the context of how men first came
to believe in and worship the gods. Epicurus himself was not an atheist, but later philosophers, probably the Stoics, attacked the premises
of his physical system, inferred that the gods had no necessary place in
his system, and happily labeled him as an atheist.[48] After Epicurus, at

the end of the second century B.C., the list was extended by the Academic sceptic Clitomachus in his treatise *Concerning Atheism*.[49] He was an adherent of the most important representative of the sceptical Academy, Carneades (ca. 214–128 B.C.), who probably had alleged that Epicurus did not really mean what he said about the gods.[50] He, in turn was followed by Cicero in his *De natura deorum* (I.1.63), Pseudo-Aëtius (ca. A.D. 50–100),[51] and, toward the end of the second century A.D., by Sextus Empiricus (*Adversus mathematicos* 9.50–8).

The second development was the instant success of Prodicus' theory about the gods; witness its reflection after Euripides (above) in later poets and historians. Yet his most famous follower lived a good deal later.[52] In the first quarter of the third century B.C., the Alexandrian Euhemerus wrote his *Sacred Record* in which he turned the Hesiodic succession of Ouranos, Kronos, and Zeus into a dynasty of mortal kings that inhabited a fictitious island called Panchaea.[53] It was the aim of Euhemerus to keep the gods but to present them in a form in which sophisticated people could believe. We have only a few fragments left,[54] but Sextus Empiricus seems to summarize his work in saying that "the traditional gods were important mortals and therefore deified by their contemporaries and considered gods."[55] Euhemerus was particularly successful in Rome where the poet Ennius (239–169 B.C.) translated his work around 200 B.C. into Latin prose, perhaps in preparation of a spiritual climate favorable to the deification of Scipio Africanus, the victor of Carthage and Hannibal. Ennius did not make a literal translation, but he expanded the original somewhat and explained the Greek names to his Roman public, where his work proved to be highly successful and was read by Varro (116–27 B.C.) and Cicero and, eventually, furnished ammunition to the Christians.

The ever-expanding lists with atheists should not conceal the fact that in historical reality no practicing atheists are mentioned in our sources for the period. In the first two centuries of our era, atheism had mainly become a label to be used against philosophical opponents but not to be taken too seriously. Even the Jews knew how to play the game and reproached the Egyptians for their atheism.[56] A new development becomes visible in the middle of the second century A.D. In his *Life of Alexander of Abonouteichos*, the biography of a religious entrepeneur who had founded a new cult in Abonouteichos, a small town in Pontus in Asia Minor, the malicious satirist Lucian mentions that Alexander had excluded from his cult the "atheist, Christian and Epicurean" (25, 38). The grave consequences of such an attitude become visible in Smyrna. In the *Martyrdom of Polycarp*, which probably dates from about A.D. 160, a member of a group of Christian martyrs, the youth Germanicus, dragged the animal that was supposed to kill him, perhaps a leopard, on top of him. In reaction, the crowd shouted, "Away with these atheists. Go and get Polycarp!" – the old bishop of the Christians (3.2). When Polycarp was caught and interrogated by the Roman governor, the latter tried to save him and told him to "Recant. Say, 'Away with the atheists!'." Polycarp looked at the crowd, shook his fist at them, and said: "Away with the atheists!" (9.2). He was not the only martyr confronted with the charge. When in A.D. 177 a group of martyrs was executed in Lyon, one of them, the youth Vettius Epagathus, requested a hearing from the prefect in order that he could explain that the Christians were "innocent of atheism and impiety."[57]

The accusation of "atheism" must have been very widespread, since the Christian apologists often did their best to rebut the charge.[58] Toward the end of the second century A.D., Tatian (*Oratio ad Graecos* 27.1) even mentions that the pagans called the Christians *atheotatous*, "the most atheist ones"! Only Justinus in his *Apology* (1.6), written about A.D. 154–55, tells us which opponent had made the charge. It was the Cynic Crescens, who would also be responsible for his martyrdom. Justinus admitted that the Christians were indeed atheists regarding their attitude toward the pagan gods. It is indeed hard to see how the pagans could have thought differently, given that the Christians had no temples or statues of deities and did not perform sacrifices. In the eyes of the pagan philosopher Celsus (ca. 180), quoted by Origen (184–254) in his *Contra Celsum* (7.62: written ca. 249), this made the Christians comparable to other uncivilised peoples who had no gods either, such as the barbaric Scythians or nomadic Lybians. The charge had a long life and survived even into the fourth century.[59] It is hardly surprising that the Jews suffered from the same accusations, even though they had a temple.[60] Yet their separate position made them vulnerable too, and Julian the Apostate (*Contra Galileos* 43) even stated that the Christians had inherited their atheism from the Jews.

3. THE CHRISTIAN PERIOD

The Christians were not slow in taking up the possibility of labeling opponents, as Justinus already called fellow Christians with whom he disagreed, "atheist[s] and impious heretics."[61] Yet it took them some time before they were able to develop a strategy to refute the accusation of atheism. In his *Apologeticus* (24) of about A.D. 200, Tertullian (ca. 160–240) tried to refute the charge by arguing that the pagan gods were no gods at all but demons. Consequently, the Christians could not possibly be atheists! Some Christians now even tried to turn the tables. Origen charged the pagans of an "atheist polytheism" or an "polytheist atheism."[62] Clement of Alexandria (ca. 150–215) went even further and stated that the real atheists were those who did not believe in God or his Providence,[63] the prime example of those being Epicurus. Rather surprisingly, he tried to rehabilitate the "canonical" atheists, such as Diagoras, Euhemerus, and Theodorus, by claiming that they had at least recognized the foolishness of the pagan ideas.[64]

It is time to come to a close. Our survey has shown that antiquity is important for the history of atheism, in at least three respects. First, the Greeks discovered theoretical atheism, which "can be seen to be one of the most important events in the history of religion."[65] Second, the Greeks invented the term *atheos*, which was taken over by the Romans as *atheus*, which gave rise to the words "atheist" and "atheism" in early modern times. Third, Greeks and Romans, pagans and Christians, soon discovered the utility of the term "atheist" as a means to label opponents. The invention of atheism would open a new road to intellectual freedom, but also enabled people to label opponents in a new way. Progress rarely comes without a cost.

NOTES

1. In this chapter I limit the notes as much as possible to the most recent, accessible literature and to matters pertaining to ancient atheism. For more information on the various "atheists" discussed, see the relevant literature, which is now easily consulted in *Der neue Pauly* (Tübingen, 1996–2003).

2. L. Febvre, *Le problème de l'incroyance au XVIe siècle: La religion de Rabelais* (Paris, 1942), but also note P. Dinzelbacher, "Etude sur l'incroyance à l'époque de la foi," *Revue des sciences religieuses* 73 (1999): 42–79.

3. K. Thomas, *Religion and the Decline of Magic* (Harmondsworth, 1973), pp. 198–206, notes that skeptics were often aliens and strangers to the district.

4. *P. Herc.* 1428 cols. 14, 32–15, 8, cf. A. Henrichs, "Die Kritik der stoischen Theologie im *P. Hercul.* 1428," *Cronache Ercolanesi* 4 (1974): 5–32 at 25; D. Obbink, *Philodemus: On Piety*, vol. 1 (Oxford, 1996), 1f.

5. Cf. M. Winiarczyk, "Methodisches zum antiken Atheismus," *Rheinisches Museum* 133 (1900): 1–15, and "Antike Bezeichnungen der Gottlosigkeit und des Atheismus," *Rheinisches Museum* 135 (1992): 216–25.

6. M. Winiarczyk, "Wer galt im Altertum als Atheist?" *Philologus* 128 (1984): 157–83, and, with supplements and addenda, "Wer galt im Altertum als Atheist? II," *Philologus* 136 (1992): 306–10.

7. P. Decharme, *La critique des traditions religieuses chez les grecs* (Paris, 1904); A. B. Drachman, *Atheism in Pagan Antiquity* (Gyldendal, 1922); W. Nestle, "Atheismus," *Reallexicon für Antike und Christentum*, vol. 1 (Stuttgart, 1950), pp. 866–70; W. Fahr, *Theous nomizein: Zum Problem der Anfänge des Atheismus bei den Griechen* (Hildesheim and New York, 1969); W. K. C. Guthrie, *The Sophists* (Cambridge, 1971), pp. 226–49; and M. Winiarczyk, "Bibliographie zum antiken Atheismus," *Elenchos* 10 (1989): 103–92.

8. Protagoras B 4 Diels/Kranz (hereafter DK). All fragments are quoted from their standard editions.

9. For the development of this legend, see K. J. Dover, *The Greeks and Their Legacy* (Oxford, 1988), pp. 142–45, 158, and R. Parker, *Athenian Religion* (Oxford, 1996), p. 207 n. 36.

10. Obbink, *Philodemus: On Piety*, p. 355.

11. Bremmer, "Literacy and the Origins and Limitations of Greek Atheism," in J. den Boeft and A. Kessels (eds.), *Actus: Studies in Honour of H. L. W. Nelson* (Utrecht, 1982), pp. 43–56, and J. Mansfeld, *Studies in the Historiography of Greek Philosophy* (Assen and Maastricht, 1990), p. 305.

12. Bremmer, "Rationalization and Disenchantment in Ancient Greece: Max Weber among the Pythagoreans and Orphics?" in R. Buxton (ed.), *From Myth to Reason?* (Oxford, 1999), pp. 71–83 at 78.

13. For Anaxagoras' chronology, see Parker, *Athenian Religion*, 209; D. Sider, *The Fragments of Anaxagoras* (Sankt Augustine, 2005), pp. 1–11.

14. See, esp., Ephorus *FGrH* 70 F 196.

15. S. Shapiro, "Hippon the Atheist: The Surprisingly Intelligent Views of Hippon of Samos," *Journal of Ancient Civilisation* 14 (1999): 111–23; note also Aristophanes, *Birds* 1000f.

16. Aristophanes, *Clouds* 225–9, 360, 490, 1284.

17. N. Dunbar, *Aristophanes: Birds* (Oxford, 1995), 436, who compares Aristophanes, *Clouds* 360, and the Christian Epiphanius, *Against Heretics* 3.21.

18. Euripides, fragment 913 Kannicht, trans. Parker, *Athenian Religion*, 209, adapted in the light of Kannicht's revised text.

19. Plato's *Apology* 18bc, see also *Apology* 26d and *Laws* 967a.

20. A. Henrichs, "The Sophists and Hellenistic Religion: Prodicus as the Spiritual Father of the Isis Aretologies," *Harvard Studies in Classical Philology* 88 (1984): 139–58.

21. Euripides, *Bacchae* 274–85, where the seer Teiresias hails Demeter and Dionysos as the respective inventors of bread and wine; cf. A. Henrichs, "Two Doxographical Notes: Democritus and Prodicus on Religion," *Harvard Studies in Classical Philology* 79 (1975): 93–123 at 110 n. 64.

22. Philodemus, *PHerc.* 1428, fragment 19, trans. Henrichs; cf. Henrichs, "Two Doxographical Notes," 107–15, whose interpretation I here follow, including Henrichs's second thoughts about the translation in his "The Atheism of Prodicus," *Cronache Ercolanesi* 6 (1976): 15–21.

23. F. Graf, *Eleusis und die orphische Dichtung Athens in vorhellenistischer Zeit* (Berlin, 1974), pp. 22–39, and Parker, *Athenian Religion*, p. 99.

24. Plato, *Cratylus* 384b, *Hippias major* 282c.

25. For the texts, see R. Kannicht, *Tragicorum graecorum fragmenta*, vol. 5.1 (Göttingen, 2004), T 98–100, 166c, 170–171ab.

26. A. Dihle, "Das Satyrspiel 'Sisyphos,'" *Hermes* 105 (1977): 28–42 at 33, and M. R. Lefkowitz, "Was Euripides an Atheist?" *Studi Italiani di Filologia Classica* 3, no. 5 (1987): 149–66, and "'Impiety' and 'Atheism' in Euripides' Dramas," *Classical Quarterly* 39 (1989): 70–82.

27. Euripides, fragment 286 Kannicht, trans. Collard, slightly adapted. The last line of the fragment may not originally belong to it. For the date see C. Collard et al., *Euripides: Selected Fragmentary Plays*, vol. 1 (Warminster, 1995), p. 101.

28. Euripides, *Hippolytus* 1102ff., *Scyrii*, fragment 684 Kannicht.

29. Aristophanes, *Thesmophoriazusai* 448–52, *Frogs* 888–94.

30. C. Riedweg, "The 'Atheistic' Fragment from Euripides' Bellerophontes (286 N)," *Illinois Classical Studies* 15 (1990): 39–53.

31. See the very detailed discussion of N. Pechstein, *Euripides satyrographos* (Stuttgart and Leipzig, 1998), pp. 289–343; note also M. Davies, "Sisyphus and the Invention of Religion," *Bulletin of the Institute of Classical Studies* 36 (1989): 16–32; M. C. Santoro, "Sisifo e il presunto ateismo di Crizia," *Orpheus* 15 (1994) 419–29, and "Il fr. 19 Snell del 'Sisifo' di Crizia come testimonianza della concezione socratica del divino: Crizia 'accusatore' di Socrate?" *Elenchos* 18 (1997): 257–76; R. Krumeich et al., *Das griechische Satyrspiel* (Darmstadt, 1999), pp. 552–61 (text, commentary, and German translation by N. Pechstein).

32. See Kannicht, *Tragicorum graecorum fragmenta*, 2.658f.

33. Obbink, *Philodemus: On Piety*, p. 355.

34. Critias, *TGrF* 43 F 19I, trans. Ch. Kahn, "Greek Religion and Philosophy in the Sisyphus Fragment," *Phronesis* 42 (1997): 247–62 at 247–48, adapted in the light of Pechstein's translation and commentary (note 32).

35. See most recently Pechstein, *Euripides satyrographos*, p. 323f.

36. For the mood, see also Bremmer, "Prophets, Seers, and Politics in Greece, Israel, and Early Modern Europe," *Numen* 40 (1993): 150–83 at 170.

37. Parker, *Athenian Religion*, 206; F. Graf, "Der Mysterienprozess," in L. Burckhardt and J. von Ungern-Sternberg (eds.), *Grosse prozesse im antiken Athen* (Munich, 2000), pp. 114–27.

38. As is persuasively argued by C. Auffarth, "Aufnahme und Zurückweisung 'Neuer Götter' im spätklassischen Athen: Religion gegen die Krise, Religion in der Krise?" in W. Eder (ed.), *Die athenische Demokratie im 4. Jahrhundert v. Chr.* (Stuttgart, 1995), pp. 337–65; F. E. Romer, "Atheism, Impiety and the Limos Melios in Aristophanes' *Birds*," *American Journal of Philology* 115 (1994): 351–65, and "Diagoras the Melian (Diod. Sic. 13.6.7)," *Classical Weekly* 89 (1995–96): 393–401.

39. Mubashshir in F. Rosenthal, *Greek Philosophy in the Arab World* (London, 1990), ch. I., p. 33 (= *Orientalia* 6, 1937, 33), trans. Gert Jan van Gelder, whom I thank for his comments and fresh translation of the passage; note also Melanthius *FGrH* 326 F3; Craterus *FGrH* 342 F16. For the date, see Diodorus Siculus 13.6,7 and, independently, Mubashshir.

40. Obbinks, *Philodemus: On Piety*, p. 525.

41. For Diagoras, see most recently M. Winiarczyk, *Diagorae Melii et Theodori Cyrenaei reliquiae* (Leipzig, 1981), to be read with his "Ergänzungen zu Diagoras und Theodoros," *Philologus* 133 (1989): 151–52; Bremmer, "Religious Secrets and Secrecy in Classical Greece," in H. Kippenberg and G. Stroumsa (eds.), *Secrecy and Concealment* (Leiden, 1995), pp. 61–78; Parker, *Athenian Religion*, p. 208; Obbink, *Philodemus: On Piety*, pp. 525–26; and J. Hordern, "Philodemus and the Poems of Diagoras," *Zeitschrift für Papyrologie und Epigraphik* 136 (2001): 33–38. The recent attempts by R. Janko, "The Physicist as Hierophant: Aristophanes, Socrates and the Authorship of the Derveni Papyrus," *Zeitschrift für Papyrologie und Epigraphik* 118 (1997): 61–94, and "The Derveni Papyrus (Diagoras of Melos, 'Apopyrgizontes logoi'?): A New Translation," *Classical Philology* 96 (2001): 1–32,

to make Diagoras into the author of the Derveni papyrus is refuted by
G. Betegh, *The Derveni Papyrus: Cosmology, Theology, and Interpretation*
(Cambridge, 2004), pp. 373–80.

42. Aristophanes, *Frogs* 1491, fragment 392 Kassel/Austin; Telecleides, frag-
    ments 41–42 Kassel/Austin.

43. Favorinus in Diogenes Laertius 2.40, trans. Parker; note also Xenophon,
    Memorabilia 1.1.1, *Apology* 10; Plato, *Apology* 24b8-c1, *Eutyphron* 3b;
    Obbink, *Philodemus: On Piety*, pp. 1696–97.

44. For the charge and the process, see Parker, *Athenian Religion*, pp. 199–207,
    and P. Millett, "The Trial of Socrates Revisited," *European Review of History*
    12 (2005): 23–62.

45. Plato, *Apology* 26c, *Laws* 12.967a, cf. Henrichs, "Atheism of Prodicus,"
    p. 20.

46. M. Winiarczyk, "Theodoros *ho atheos*," *Philologus* 125 (1981): 64–94,
    Diagorae Melii et Theodori Cyrenaei, and "Ergänzungen"; G. Giannantoni,
    Socraticorum reliquiae, 3 vols. (Rome, 1983–85), vol. 1, pp. 301–15, vol. 3,
    pp. 173–76.

47. D. Obbink, "The Atheism of Epicurus," *Greek, Roman, and Byzantine Stud-
    ies* 30 (1989): 187–223; Obbink, *Philodemus: On Piety*, pp. 1–4, 14–17.

48. Cicero, *De natura deorum* 1.123, cf. Obbink, *Philodemus: On Piety*, p. 352.

49. M. Winiarczyk, "Der erste Atheistenkatalog des Kleitomachos," *Philologus*
    120 (1976): 32–46, and "Bibliographie," p. 185f.

50. Obbink, "Atheism of Epicurus," pp. 218–20.

51. D. Runia, "Atheists in Aëtius: Text, Translation and Comments on *De
    placitis* 1, 7, 1–10," *Mnemosyne* 4, no. 49 (1996): 542–76. Note that the
    name Aëtius was attached only later to this treatise; cf. Bremmer, "Aëtius,
    Arius Didymus and the Transmission of Doxography," *Mnemosyne* 4, no. 51
    (1998): 154–60.

52. Henrichs, "The Sophists and Hellenistic Religion," pp. 148–52.

53. M. Winiarczyk, "Ennius' Euhemerus sive Sacra historia," *Rheinisches
    Museum* 137 (1994): 274–91, and *Euhemeros von Messene: Leben, Werk
    und Nachwirkung* (Munich and Leipzig, 2002), and A. Baumgarten, "Euhe-
    merus' Eternal Gods or How Not to Be Embarrassed by Greek Mythology,"
    in *Classical Studies in Honor of David Sohlberg* (Ramat Gan, 1996), pp. 91–
    103.

54. See M. Winiarczyk, *Euhemeri Messenii Reliquiae* (Stuttgart, 1991).

55. Sextus Empiricus, *Adversus mathematicos* 9.51, trans. Henrichs.

56. Philo, *Legatio ad Gaium* 25.

57. Eusebius, *Historia ecclesiastica* 5.1.9–10.

58. Aristides 4; Athenagoras 3–5, 10; Minucius Felix 8.2, 15ff.; Clement of
    Alexandria, *Stromata* 7.1.1.4; E. Fascher, "Der Vorwurf der Gottlosigkeit in
    der Auseinandersetzung bei Juden, Griechen und Christen," in O. Betz et al.
    (eds.), *Abraham unser Vater: Juden und Christen im Gespräch über die Bibel*
    (Leiden, 1963), pp. 78–105; N. Brox, "Zum Vorwurf des Atheismus gegen
    die Alte Kirche," *Trierer Theologische Zeitschrift* 75 (1966): 274–82; P. F.
    Beatrice, "L'accusation d'athéisme contre les chrétiens," in M. Narcy and
    É. Rebillard (eds.), *Hellénisme et christianisme* (Villeneuve d'Ascq, 2004),
    pp. 133–52. Still valuable is A. von Harnack, *Der Vorwurf des Atheismus in
    den drei ersten Jahrhunderten* (Leipzig, 1905).

59. Eusebius, *Praeparatio evangelica* 1.2.2–4, 3.13.4; Arnobius 1.26.3; Athanasius, *Contra gentiles* 1 and *De incarnatione Verbi* 1.2.
60. Flavius Josephus, *Contra Apionem* II.65, 79, 148.
61. Justinus, *Dialogus contra Tryphonem* 80.3 Marcovich.
62. Origen, *Exhortatio ad martyrium* 5, 32 and *Contra Celsum* 1.1, 3.73.
63. Clement of Alexandria, *Stromata* 5.1.6.1, 6.1.1.1, and 15.122.3, 7.1.1.1, and 9.54.3–4; *Protrepticus* 2.23.1.
64. Clement, *Protrepticus* 2.24.2.
65. W. Burkert, *Greek Religion* (Oxford, 1985), p. 315.

2   Atheism in Modern History

In October 1632, the small town of Loudun in mid-France was con-
vulsed by the belief that the nuns of the town's Ursuline convent were
possessed with devils. Over the following months and years, as the cries
and shrieks of the unfortunate nuns became ever louder and their bodily
writhings more obscene, Loudun became a place of celebrity as a pro-
cession of priests, doctors, politicians, and tourists came to witness the
extraordinary spectacle for themselves. The possession was not short-
lived, and the execution of the supposed sorcerer, the parish priest Urbain
Grandier, did not bring the closure that some hoped it would. The exor-
cisms of priests and the ministrations of doctors were to little effect,
and there seemed to be no hope of deliverance until the arrival of the
saintly Father Jean-Joseph Surin in Loudun in December 1634. Within a
few months, the mother superior, Jeanne des Anges, was delivered from
her demons, although the last devil was not reported to have departed
until 1637.

In his extended study of this remarkable episode, the French historian Michel de Certeau is not so facile as to provide a definitive (or even
provisional) "explanation" of these happenings. But he does interpret
them as, among other things, a "symptom" of a trauma – what might
be described as the trauma of the birth of modernity. He says that the
"diabolical crisis" (of which the Loudun possession was just one
instance) "is not merely an object of historical curiosity. It is the con-
frontation (one among others, though more visible than others) of a
society with the certainties it is losing and those it is attempting
to acquire."[1] One of the certainties this society is losing is that of
theism, and de Certeau sees in the possession an indirect expression
of a repressed anxiety and fear of doubt and blasphemy. Such doubt was
becoming a common feature of society at this time, with atheism emerging as a recognized phenomenon, in a way that was unknown a century
earlier.[2] Atheism, it seems, is a feature or symptom of the modernity that
is traumatically coming to birth. It might be said that if theism is one of
the certainties this society is losing, then atheism is one of those certainties it is attempting to acquire. In this sense, atheism is an inescapable

aspect of modernity; atheism and modernity seem to be inextricably linked. It is one of the aims of this chapter to examine the precise nature of this link. But before doing so, some attention must be given to questions of definition.

Disputes about what constitutes the "modern" or "modernity" have been long and tortuous, and no definition is likely to gain universal assent. What does seem fairly uncontroversial, however, is to say that the old understanding of the "modern," which made it virtually synonymous with the "contemporary," has been eclipsed by an understanding of the "modern" as a particular "mode of thought" or "sensibility" having certain distinctive characteristics of its own.[3] What these characteristics actually are vary considerable from one sphere of thought or activity to another. Consequently, the quest for an all-embracing definition of the "modern" that would do justice to the many and various understandings of modernity in art, architecture, literature, philosophy, music, politics, and economics (to name but a few) would seem to be doomed from the start. Any broad-ranging characterization of the modern will therefore inevitably be inadequate. With this in mind, however, I have elsewhere provisionally characterized the modern as a "desire for an all-encompassing mastery of reality by rational and/or scientific means."[4] While by no means doing justice to the nuances that many would rightly feel to be essential to understanding the "modern" in various spheres of thought, such a characterization is at least not misleading about the dominant desire of the modern sensibility. It is a desire that becomes evident and increasingly dominant from the sixteenth century onward and that remains strong until around the middle of the twentieth century, when signs of a crisis in modernity's self-confidence begin to creep in. This understanding of the modern will be refined and qualified as this chapter proceeds, but this will serve as a provisional indication of what I am here taking the modern to mean.

The meaning of "atheism" is only slightly less contentious. At first sight, it would appear to be more straightforward, for the term can (with fewer qualifications than were necessary with the term "modern") be defined as "the belief that God does not exist." But immediately, we see that, like the term "postmodernism," the term "atheism" itself "positions the phenomenon as relational. [Theism] as that from which [atheism] is breaking away remains inscribed into the very word with which [atheists] describe [their] distance from [theism]."[5] Consequently, our understanding of atheism can be straightforward and unambiguous only if our definition of theism is straightforward and unambiguous. For atheism defines itself in terms of that which it is denying. From this it follows that if definitions and understandings of God change and vary, so too our definitions and understandings of atheism will change and vary. This further means that there will be as many varieties of atheism as there are varieties of theism.[6] For atheism will always be a rejection, negation, or denial of a *particular* form of theism. As we shall see, this is more than just a question of nomenclature and definition; the implications are potentially much more far-reaching. For some have argued that modern atheism is dependent on a peculiarly *modern* and innovative form of theism that is in many ways quite different from the theism that prevailed before. If this is so, then it raises some important questions. Was the distinctively modern conception of theism that emerged in the early modern period so much a distortion of premodern theism that it made itself incredible and atheism inevitable? Furthermore, if this same atheism was a reaction against this specific form of theism, what, if any, implications does this atheism have for a different, nonmodern (premodern) form of theism? These are questions I shall pursue in much greater depth later in this chapter. But first it is necessary to examine the phenomenon of atheism as it appeared in modern history.

I. THE "APPEARANCE" OF ATHEISM IN MODERN HISTORY

If, as I have suggested and as is commonly held, there is more than a coincidental relationship between atheism and modernity, one would perhaps expect atheism to have manifested itself somewhat earlier than it did. In fact, it emerges in an explicit and undisguised form relatively late. Certainly, the term itself appears at the precise moment at which philosophers and cultural historians locate the birth of modernity. Michael J. Buckley traces its first use in England to the Greek scholar, Sir John Cheke, in a translation of Plutarch's *On Superstition* in 1540, but here atheism is conceived as a denial of the intervention of divine providence rather than a denial of the existence of God.[7] Indeed, in this period, in both England and France, the term "atheism" usually denoted heresy rather than an outright denial of theism. As Western Europe made its traumatic transition to modernity, however, the term quite quickly transmuted its meaning into a form more familiar to us. Michel de Certeau points out that in France in the early seventeenth century, atheism became the focus of not only a whole body of literature, but also of political measures, judicial sentences, and social precautions against atheists: "The 'atheists' who first occupy the polemic are the 'heretics' of every Church, the nonconformist believers and such. But soon the controversy centers on the existence of God. Around 1630 groups of 'libertines,' erudites and skeptics [s]pring up; they will fade away around 1655...before coming back around 1680. 'Atheism,' which was never spoken of a hundred years earlier, becomes a recognized fact."[8] What is more, de Certeau points out that this phenomenon is not restricted to the learned, but is to be found at all levels in society.

But if, at the outset of modernity, minds in England and France are beginning to be afflicted and plagued with doubts, the term "atheism" is being used here more in the manner of an accusation, a term of abuse. As a term of self-definition, a declaration of one's own belief (or lack thereof), it does not really appear until the mid-eighteenth century when it is found among Parisian intellectuals, particularly Denis Diderot, who is widely recognized as being the first explicit and self-confessedly atheist philosopher. As Buckley puts it, "in many ways, Diderot is the first of the atheists, not simply in chronological reckoning but as an initial and premier advocate and influence."[9] Diderot claimed to be bringing the mathematical physics of Descartes and the universal mechanics of Newton to their logical conclusions. He freed the former from what he considered to be its unwarranted metaphysics, and the latter from an urge to point beyond itself to nonmechanical principles. In so doing, he made "the initial but definitive statement" of atheism: "the principle of everything is creative nature, matter in its self-activity eternally productive of all change and all design."[10] The significance of Diderot also lay in the fact that he could not be dismissed as a malevolent or frivolous mind. On the contrary, Diderot's atheism was a consequence of his intellectual integrity and a disinterested quest for truth. Furthermore, Diderot reached his atheistic conclusions by furthering and intensifying the insights of Descartes and Newton – the very thinkers upon whom Christians depended as modern defenders of the faith.

But Diderot's explicit avowal of atheism was slow to spread. Well into the nineteenth century, the negative connotations of the word – as a term of abuse – persisted and came increasingly to be associated with immorality and lawlessness, two of the great fears of the nineteenth-century mind. This led those who were unable to subscribe to orthodox theism to coin new terms of self-definition, which would allow them to remain uncontaminated by the stigma of atheism. George Jacob Holyoake, for instance, preferred to describe himself as a "secularist," with the need to avoid being regarded as morally suspect uppermost in his mind.[11] But there were also other factors in nontheists' search for a new term. Thomas Huxley, for instance, was unhappy with "atheism" because it was too dogmatic; it made a definitive metaphysical claim about the nonexistence of God, for which Huxley believed there was insufficient evidence. Furthermore, it seems that "atheism" was also being increasingly linked with far-left revolutionary politics, which further tainted the term in polite society.[12] These concerns led Huxley and his associates to coin a new term, "agnosticism," suggesting that the term represented not a new creed, but a metaphysical unknowing.[13] Henceforth, agnosticism would rival atheism as an alternative intellectual disposition for those unable to profess belief in theism. Indeed, Adrian Desmond even goes so far as to say that "as the social axis shifted in late Victorian times, agnosticism was to become the new faith of the West."[14]

If it was the case, however, that atheism was increasingly coming to be associated with far-left revolutionary politics, it is not difficult to find the intellectual source of this connection. In Karl Marx's thought, revolution and atheism went hand in hand. It was not that atheism was a necessary precondition for revolution but, rather, that revolution would necessarily bring atheism in its trail. For Marx, Christianity was an "ideology" that emerged out of society's economic base; it both reflected and reinforced capitalism. When the economic base of capitalism disintegrated (as, for Marx, it inevitably would), then Christianity would simply fade away, so entirely was it a reflection of that base. For both would-be revolutionaries and those for whom revolution was their chief horror, Marx had implanted an indelible connection between left-wing revolution and atheism (the seeds of which had already been sown in human consciousness by the French revolution). The results were considerable and long-lasting. Not only would atheism be tainted with blood, violence, and revolution, but also Christianity came to be regarded as inherently conservative and reactionary, an upholder of the status quo.

In spite of atheism's growing connection with immorality, metaphysical presumption, and left-wing revolution, there were still some who were committed to making it a respectable and acceptable outlook. One of the most prominent of these was Charles Bradlaugh, the first explicitly and self-confessedly atheist member of the British Parliament. He was able to take his seat in parliament only after a lengthy and hard-fought battle of wills. To take their seats, members had to swear an oath of allegiance to the Queen, an oath sworn on the Bible. It was only after several false attempts that Bradlaugh was finally able to overcome this hurdle.[15] He also battled to make atheism acceptable to civic society and, in particular, fought for the right of atheists to give evidence in court.[16] He sought little more than a neutral respectability, and although by the end of the nineteenth century, he had by no means achieved this, he had nevertheless made a considerable advance toward it.

If, by the nineteenth century, atheism was finally beginning to rear its head as a respectable intellectual position, it was still far from widespread as a cultural phenomenon, and remained the preserve of the intellectual elite. This is not to say that all but the intellectual elite were filled with religious fervor. On the contrary, in Victorian England, for instance, the working classes were notoriously irreligious (as Horace Mann's innovative religious census of 1851 made all too clear). But it seems not that the working classes were atheistic or positively anti-religious, but that their collective attitude was one of "indifference."[17] It is not entirely clear how such indifference should be interpreted. Was it the case that they were predominantly theistic believers, who were nonetheless suspicious and distrustful of a class-ridden and intimidating Church? Or was their indifference such that it amounted to a practical agnosticism? It may well be that both interpretations are, to some degree, correct, but either way, it appears that, even among the notoriously irreligious working classes, the avowal of outright atheism was still comparatively rare.

As the nineteenth century turned into the twentieth century, however, the tide began to turn. Two prescient prophets, though unlikely soul mates, were Friedrich Nietzsche and John Henry Newman. Both were aware that a new spirit was stirring, and although people were scarcely aware of it yet, they knew that this new spirit would have far-reaching consequences. As Buckley observes, "What Nietzsche and Newman foresaw was that religious impotence or uninterest would not remain a private or an isolated phenomenon, that it would increasingly characterize the 'educated intellect of England, France and Germany,' and that its influence would eventually tell upon every routine aspect of civilization."[18] And yet Nietzsche's and Newman's prophecies did not come to fruition for at least another sixty years or so. What may be described as the "age of atheism" (to borrow Gerhard Ebeling's phrase) did not become a reality until the last forty years of the twentieth century.[19]

But by the 1960s, the predictions of Newman and Nietzsche came to pass. In the affluent West, at least, there emerged a "radical godlessness" that was, by world historical standards, unique. As Buckley expresses this, "It is critical to notice the historical uniqueness of the contemporary experience: the rise of a radical godlessness which is as much a part of the consciousness of millions of ordinary human beings as it is the persuasion of the intellectual. Atheisms have existed before, but there is a novelty, a distinctiveness about the contemporary denial of god both in its extent and in its cultural establishment."[20] If there is, therefore, a necessary connection between "modernity" and "atheism," we seem now to be in a position to say something provisional about the nature of this link. For it does not seem that the modern sensibility always brings with it a necessary commitment to atheism. On the contrary, the cultural, philosophical, and scientific primacy of "modernity" had been established for several centuries before "atheism" had become a widely recognized fact. In many ways, therefore, it seems better to view "modernity" not as static entity, but as an always onward-moving sensibility or process, the end point of which is atheism.

But this also raises the question of whether this end point itself gives way, in turn, to something else. For it does seem to be the case that at the very moment that atheism reached its "high noon," it also began immediately to crumble. Recent sociological studies have concluded that although modernity has undoubtedly witnessed a turn from tradition-based religious commitment, this has not resulted in the widespread atheism that many had previously predicted. In fact, outright atheism remains a minority confession, and the modern Western world has witnessed the proliferation of alternative "spiritualities" of various kinds.[21] Many, it seems, are dissatisfied with atheism as the "final truth" of the human condition. This would appear to qualify Buckley's analysis of the contemporary situation. But whether or not atheism marks a final *telos* or terminal condition, it does appear that modernity is not only a sensibility but also a process, the eventual and logical culmination of which is atheism. I now want to look at the nature of this progression, and the movement by which modern thought passed from theism to atheism.

2. THE DEVELOPMENT OF ATHEISM IN MODERN THOUGHT

Although it has lately been disputed (as we shall see below), it has long been common to attribute the origins of philosophical and theological modernity to René Descartes. The Cartesian revolution was, in effect, the rejection of a theological methodology. Such a methodology, as most comprehensively expressed by Thomas Aquinas, certainly accorded an indispensable role to human reason, but it was a role that was always to be exercised in the context of, and subject to the authority of, divine revelation. For Aquinas, this had to be the case because human reason was, by its very nature, finite and limited. Truth (and God; for Aquinas, the two were not clearly separable), on the other hand, was neither finite nor limited, and therefore human reason would always fail to articulate it. Only with the supplement of divine revelation could human reason hope to grasp something of the divine truth. Descartes rejected this centuries-old methodology in favor of the development of an epistemology and theology on the basis of reason alone. This revolution did not, of course, appear from nowhere and can be properly understood only in the context of the historical circumstances in which Descartes was writing.

When Descartes' *Meditations* were written, Europe was in a state of religious and political upheaval. The Reformation was less than a century old, and Christendom had not yet recovered from the resulting fracture. For a religion that had always laid such a strong emphasis on the universality of truth, the psychological effects of the Reformation were particularly devastating. The traditional and distinctive Christian aversion to doctrinal pluralism meant that the two sides of the Reformation divide could only regard each other as heretics deeply mired in error. Such attitudes hardly made for an atmosphere of world peace, and the Thirty Years' War was, at least in part, the result. In any attempt to find a peaceful way forward, the solution was not to be found in appealing to revelation, scriptures, and creeds. For these were the very things in dispute, and the disputants appealed to the same sources in articulating their respective positions. The challenge, therefore, was to develop a universal epistemological method that would yield universal assent. Descartes' rationalist epistemology was an attempt to do precisely this. Theological knowledge was not in any sense privileged and was subject to the same method of radical doubt as was every other form of inherited knowledge. Having doubted everything until he arrived at his certain foundation, that which could not be doubted, the *cogito*, Descartes then found himself in the peculiar position of having to invoke God in order to secure certainty of the existence of the external world. Maintaining his prohibition on an appeal to unfounded revelation, he was obliged to establish God's existence on purely rationalistic grounds, rehearsing a decontextualized version of Anselm's ontological argument. In light of this, it may well be argued that Descartes had *already* inaugurated an atheistic framework, and that Descartes' invocation of God was an importation of an alien theological category into a secular rationalist framework. As such, it is an example of what Wittgenstein would later call a "category mistake," that is, the removal of a concept from its natural linguistic home in order to import it into a fundamentally alien linguistic framework, the result of which is to distort the concept and, if the concept is sufficiently at odds with the framework into which it has been imported, to ensure its ultimate demise.

In the late seventeenth century, Descartes' rationalist epistemology came under heavy attack from the English empiricist philosopher John Locke. For Locke, knowledge and truth were to be attained not through the exercise of reason but through the founding of all knowledge on empirical sense data. But like Descartes, he attempted to force the theological concept of God into a framework in which it was ill at ease. In Locke's case, however, the incongruity between the concept of God and the framework into which that concept was being inserted was even more severe than it was for Descartes. For if God is, ultimately, not a "rationalist" concept, then even less so is it an "empirical" concept. Indeed, according to theological discourse, God is precisely that which is nonempirical. If, therefore, God has somehow to be "founded" on empirical grounds, the result promises to be even less fortuitous than it was for Descartes. In the event, Locke not only develops a series of convoluted and tortuous arguments for God's existence on empirical grounds, but he also argues that the concept of God can itself be arrived at from within an empirical framework. He suggests that the attributes of God are all derived from "*Ideas*, received from Sensation and Reflection," and that these "ideas" are then projected into infinity in order to reach a concept of God that would answer to the requirements of the concept that is called forth by his cosmological argument.[22] One consequence of these attempts to transplant a theological concept into fundamentally atheological frameworks was a conception of theism that was susceptible to attack on two particular fronts. First, a consistent rationalism or empiricism seemed to disallow any substantive knowledge of God, and, second, if a concept of God was developed, it seemed to be little more than a hypostatization of rational concepts or empirical realities. Indeed, these vulnerabilities were brought into sharp focus by Hume and Kant in the first place and by Feuerbach and Marx in the second.

The first difficulty was identified by David Hume. The brilliance of Hume lay in the fact that he was willing to confront, unflinchingly, the implications of a thoroughgoing empirical epistemology. He saw that if empiricism were adopted consistently, this would mean reasoning "merely from the known phenomena, and [dropping] every arbitrary supposition or conjecture,"[23] with the result that one could have *knowledge* of nothing that was not derived from sense experience. As that branch of knowledge called metaphysics consisted, by definition, of that which was not empirical, this meant, for Hume, that one could have no knowledge of metaphysics whatsoever. This prohibition extended to, but was not restricted to, theism. Hume saw what Locke had not: that theism was fundamentally incompatible with empiricism.

Also recognizing that Descartes and Locke were attempting to do the impossible, Immanuel Kant saw all too clearly that God would have to be placed *beyond* rather than *within* the limits of human knowing. The stark choice with which he was confronted was therefore between dispensing with God altogether (in the manner of Hume) or leaving God agnostically hovering beyond the limits of human knowing. He opted for the latter, with the result being that the only thing that "saved" God from a spectral existence of sheer possibility was Kant's invocation of his transcendental argument. God was now a "necessary practical postulate," required in order to make sense of the human experience of morality, but pushed into the realm of the unknowable noumenon. For Kant, we must now live *as if* there is a God, but his actual existence is something that can be neither known nor demonstrated. We must necessarily suppose, according that Kant, that God is not mere possibility but actuality, even if this actuality can never be established. If this is theism, it is clearly a "thin-line theism," and although some still hail Kant as a "savior" of Christianity for the modern world, it has to be said that this is a very precarious salvation. It is therefore hardly surprising that Kant's philosophical successors should have veered toward atheism, whether real or virtual.

The "reality" of atheism, in the work of the so-called left Hegelians in the nineteenth century, could not be doubted. Drawing out what they perceived to be the implications of Hegel's philosophy of history, they developed some of the central elements of that system in an explicitly atheistic way. One of the most prominent of these thinkers was Ludwig Feuerbach, whose critique of Christian theism was unsparing. He saw the Christian God as an incoherent amalgam of personal, active, quasi-anthropomorphic attributes, on the one hand, and an impersonal ultimate reality that is perfect, timeless, and changeless, on the other. He reconceived theology as anthropology, regarding the traditional attributes of God as the best and highest attributes of humanity, personified and projected into infinity to produce what has become known as theism. Our doctrine of God, therefore, is really a disguised or coded doctrine of humanity. If, for Feuerbach, theism was a projection of humanity, for Karl Marx, as we have seen, theism, as an "ideology," was a reflection of the economic base. On the one hand, it endorsed the capitalist order by teaching that all worldly authority is ordained of God and, as such, is to be respected and obeyed by humanity. The worldly hierarchy both reflects and participates in the divine hierarchy, with each person being divinely appointed to their appropriate position within this hierarchy. On the other hand, Christian theism also served as a compensation for those who occupied a lowly position within this hierarchy. Its rituals and consolations provided an amelioration of earthly suffering as well as a compensatory promise of eternal bliss. For Marx, the collapse of capitalism would mean that there would no longer be any such functions for religion to fulfill, and so it would naturally and inevitably fade away.

For all their differences, what Feuerbach and Marx share is their conviction that theism is a projection or hypostatization of empirical realities – whether human attributes or the economic base; for them, theism is an unjustified abstraction from such realities. Their diagnoses seem all too pertinent if the theism in question is that represented by, for instance, Locke. For Locke, we have noted, theism is an explicit projection of human "ideas." If, therefore, Locke's theism is representative of modern conceptions of God, then the critiques of Feuerbach and Marx become all the more compelling.[24] To understand atheism properly in modern history and modern thought, it is thus necessary to clarify what conception of God was dominant here. Precisely which God was modern atheism rejecting?

3. THE GOD THAT MODERN ATHEISM REJECTS

It seems a truism to say that modern atheism rejected a modern God. But such a statement has considerable significance if it can be shown that a specifically modern conception of God was distinctive and marked a new departure from that which had prevailed hitherto. Many have claimed that this was indeed the case, to such an extent that the modern God was a "thing" quite different from the premodern God. Indeed, to say that the modern God was a "thing" in many ways captures the distinction; for premodern theology, God was not a "thing" at all. The transition can perhaps best be understood in terms of a corresponding transition in the use of *language*.

We have already made brief mention of Aquinas' high emphasis on the *transcendence* of God. When creatures speak of God, it was believed, there is a constant temptation to "domesticate" God's transcendence, to turn God more into a creature rather than the creator.[25] Much of Aquinas' writing may be understood as a constant attempt to guard against this ever-present temptation and to preserve the most essential characteristic of God: his transcendence. Thus, as we have seen, Aquinas emphasized the limits of human rationality with respect to God and a certain agnosticism with respect to our knowledge of God. But another weapon crucial to Aquinas' battle to defend the citadel of divine transcendence was his doctrine of analogy. Although Aquinas' teaching on analogical language is well known, its centrality and ubiquity with respect to all his other teachings has not always been appreciated.

For Aquinas, the fundamental problem with language is that it has been developed by creatures to refer to creaturely things. It is therefore inadequate – and potentially misleading – when applied to God. If we are to avoid the conclusion that nothing whatsoever can be said about God, then we must at least recognize that our language can be applied to God only in a highly qualified and provisional way. We cannot imagine that our language refers to God in the same way that it refers to things in the world. This conviction lies at the heart of Aquinas' teachings on analogy. He said that whenever we use a word of God, we do so in a way that is *related* to the way in which we use it of finite things, but as to the precise nature of that relation and as to what the word actually means when applied to God, we have to remain silent. To use language in this way, with a constant awareness of this "relation-in-difference" is to use language analogically. It enables the creature to say and know something of God, but this "something" is always tempered by a certain agnosticism or unknowing. And for Aquinas, *all* language predicated of God is analogical; from this linguistic usage, there is no escape if God's transcendence is not to be compromised. As de Certeau puts it, "The weight of [God's] transcendence makes any proposition relative, even to the point that the statement 'God exists' has to be followed by a denial."[26]

In modernity, this understanding of analogy came to be lost. This is not to say that it disappeared altogether, but it became marginal rather than central. Even where it did continue to be invoked as a doctrine, it was considerably less equivocal than its Thomistic predecessor had been.[27] Aquinas' insistence that *all* language of God is analogical came to be forgotten, and it now came to be thought that God shared with creation at least some genuine predicates literally and unequivocally. This has been argued, for instance, by Amos Funkenstein, who refers to "what may be called the transparency of God in the seventeenth century. I do not necessarily mean that seventeenth-century thinkers always claimed to know *more* about God than medieval theologians. To some of them God remained a *deus absconditus* about whom little can be known. What I mean to say is that they claimed what they knew about God, be it much or little, to be precise, 'clear and distinct' ideas."[28] To imagine that one can refer to God in precise, "clear and distinct" ideas is clearly the antithesis of what is taught by the doctrine of analogy, and if Funkenstein is correct, it does seem that there has been a major shift in the understanding of theological language here. But this linguistic shift would not be so significant were it not for the fact that it carried with it a major revolution in how God was *conceived.*

That such a linguistic shift should have implications for the modern conception of God should not surprise us, given that Aquinas had intended his all-pervasive doctrine of analogy to preserve God's transcendence. With the abandonment or marginalization and weakening of the commitment to analogy, it was perhaps inevitable that it would carry with it a dissolution or at least a change in the notion of what it means for God to be "transcendent." If language can now be predicated of God in the same unequivocal way that it is predicated of things in the world, the implication of this is that God is, in some sense, closer to things in the world, indeed, to such an extent that he becomes a "thing" himself. In other words, there is a qualitative change in what God is. But in order to preserve God's transcendence, modern thinkers instead began to stress God's quantitative difference from worldly things. So God's transcendence over the world came to be expressed as a quantitative distance from the world rather than a qualitative difference from it. This meant that God's goodness differed from worldly goodness in the sense that it was much greater (in quantitative terms) rather than a different kind or quality of goodness, as Aquinas would have maintained. Similarly, God's existence came to be understood to differ from human existence in the sense that it was infinitely greater (in quantitative terms) rather than a different kind or quality of existence.

One consequence of this was that God's "being" came to be conceived no longer as an ontologically transcendent mystery but as a specifiable "substance" in the world with an identifiable "location." Thus, there emerged a family of ideas that Funkenstein calls the "body of God." As the scientific elevation of precise, univocal, mechanical language came to infiltrate both philosophical and theological thinking, it became necessary to specify what sort of "thing" God was. Thus, Henry More, for instance, argued that the world is composed of both spiritual and solid bodies. Spiritual bodies are distinct from solid bodies in that they are penetrable and are able to contract and expand. For More, God is the highest spirit, such that all other spirits are dependent on him. As a spirit, God is extended, but his extension is infinite; it is space itself. What is significant about this is that God is here being conceived as having an identifiable place and function within the natural world. As Funkenstein puts it, "More's concept of the divine amounts to the concept of a harmonious sum total of all mechanical and purposive forces in the universe."[29]

More was by no means alone. Although modern theology (along with philosophy and science) was an arena of vigorous disagreement and debate, this was nonetheless conducted against a commonly accepted backdrop where the "domestication" of God seemed to be taken for granted. Buckley, for instance, detects two major strands in the development of modern theism. One was a rationalistic and mathematical strand pioneered by Descartes and developed by Nicolas Malebranche. The other was more empirical and mechanical, deriving from Isaac Newton and pursued by Samuel Clarke. The resulting conceptions of God were quite distinct. But what they had in common was a conception of God as a "thing" in the world with a definable "substance" and identifiable "location" that could be referred to in much the same way as other things. Modern theologians continued to insist on God's transcendence, but this difference was qualitative rather than quantitative, with the result that this transcendence became epistemological rather than ontological. That is to say, because God's "being" was deemed to be of the same quality as human "being" (so that an ontological transcendence was lacking), God's otherness instead came to be preserved by emphasizing his epistemological transcendence, so that God became increasingly hidden and unknowable, thus giving rise to Kant's agnosis and God's gradual but inevitable withdrawal.

The God that atheism rejected, therefore, was a very specific, distinctive, and modern conception of God. If every atheism is a rejection of a specific form of theism, it can be seen that modern atheism was the rejection of a modern form of theism, wherein God was a substance who could be referred to unequivocally and who was accorded a specific place and function in the natural world. For some scholars, such a form of theism not only marked a radical break from much medieval theism, but was also ultimately unsustainable, making atheism almost inevitable. As Funkenstein comments, "It is clear why a God describable in unequivocal terms, or even given physical features and functions, eventually became all the easier to discard. As a scientific hypothesis, he was later shown to be superfluous; as a being, he was shown to be a mere hypostatization of human of rational, social, psychological ideals and images."[30]

But this gives rise to the question of how God came to be reconceived in this distinctively modern fashion in the first place. Was this a secular corruption of an authentic theism? Was theology invaded by the alien powers of secular philosophy and science, giving rise to this quasi-philosophical and quasi-scientific God? Was theism forced to prostitute itself to these external attacks? What such questions imply is that the advent of modernity is marked by the autonomous rise of a rational-scientific world-view that addressed the problematic of an anachronistic theism in its midst by first distorting it and then, ultimately, rejecting it. There is, however, a strong line of argument against such an analysis. Rather than envisaging an "innocent" theology being attacked and undermined by a "malign" secularism, it is argued that within medieval theology itself, certain moves took place that *both* caused the nature of theism to change and laid the epistemological groundwork for an immanent, univocal, and, ultimately, therefore, atheistic world-view. In other words, atheism did not so much provide an *external* challenge to theism, but rather a revolution *within theology itself* is what gave rise to atheism. This is to claim that the origins of modern atheism are ultimately *theological.*

4. THE THEOLOGICAL ORIGINS OF MODERN ATHEISM

We have seen that one of the chief characteristics of the theism against which modern atheism reacted was that God's attributes were believed to be of the same order or quality as human attributes, but that God held them to an infinitely greater degree. As a consequence of this, language could be applied to God univocally. If, as we have also seen, this conception of theism contrasts with that of Aquinas, we are led to ask where, when, and how this distinctively modern conception of theism emerged. This is precisely the question that has been asked by the Swiss theologian Hans Urs von Balthasar and, more recently, by Éric Alliez, Catherine Pickstock, and William C. Placher, among others.[31] For these thinkers, the turning point comes as early as the fourteenth century with the Franciscan priest and theologian John Duns Scotus. For it was Duns Scotus who explicitly rejected the ontological difference between divine being and human being.

For Aquinas, it was essential to stress that "being" is not something shared by God and humanity; rather, "being" only "is" insofar as it emerges from and is created by God. Only thus is God's ontological priority preserved. If both God and humanity shared the same quality of "being," then God and creatures would both be members of a common genus, which Aquinas explicitly rejects. He says that "God is not a measure that is proportionate to what is measured; so it does not follow that he and his creatures belong to the same order."[32] This is why, as we have seen, Aquinas insisted that all language predicated of God was analogical. Duns Scotus questioned this understanding. Incorporating insights from Averroism in the thirteenth century, his fundamental contention was that "being is univocal to the created and uncreated."[33] Hans Urs von Balthasar says that Duns Scotus made this fundamental shift as a result of a concern to secure the place of "reason" in the face of Christian theology. Reason now grasps being alone as its first unlimited concept, and reason thereby transcends the distinction between finite and infinite Being: "The concept has not only logical (expressive) universality, but also metaphysical universality, for it captures Being in its objective ('catholic') generality, so that *it can be univocally applied to infinite and to finite Being*, that is to God and the world, to substance and accidents, to act and potentiality."[34]

As a consequence of this, "being" was no longer something emerging from and created by God, but something in which God and humanity shared, even if God's "share" in this "being" was infinitely greater than that of human beings. As Duns Scotus puts it, "Whatever pertains to 'being,' then, in so far as it remains indifferent to finite and infinite, or as proper to the Infinite Being, does not belong to it as determined to a genus, but prior to any such determination, and therefore as transcendental and outside any genus."[35] With this move, the ontological difference between God's being and human being was destroyed, and for many commentators, this marks the fundamental turning point that laid the foundations not only for the distinctively modern concept of theism, but also for the modern world-view itself. In the context of a discussion of Duns Scotus' work, Éric Alliez, for instance, comments, "What can be seen to be constituted ... is a thought whose moving edges end up leading to that scientific revolution destined to make an 'epoch' of our modernity."[36] Insofar as modern theism ultimately became untenable within the modern world view, a case could perhaps be made for locating the "origin" of modern atheism in Duns Scotus, however much he may have recoiled from such a thought.

There was, of course, a further distance to travel between Duns Scotus and Descartes. We have seen that Aquinas' commitment to analogy was consequent upon his preservation of the ontological difference. When the ontological difference is destroyed, therefore, it is to be expected that this will have a considerable impact on the doctrine of analogy. If Aquinas's conception of the task of analogy was to steer a precarious but necessary middle way between univocity on the one hand and equivocation on the other, in the wake of Duns Scotus, we see conceptions of analogy slowly shifting away from a Thomist middle way toward a more modern univocity. One may observe this shift taking place first in the work of Thomas de Vio, Cardinal Cajetan, especially in his *The Analogy of Names* (1498), and then, subsequently, in that of Francisco Suárez, particularly his *Disputationes metaphysicae* (1597). In both thinkers, we find a rejection of forms of analogy that are "indeterminate," "uncertain," and have "no definite meaning," in favor of forms of analogy that are based on "certain and demonstrable grounds."[37] It is because of these shifts that Jean-Luc Marion has spoken of a "univocist drift that analogy undergoes with Suarez and others."[38] In light of this drift, the modern form of theism observed above, with its conception of God as a "substance" with a "location" in the natural world and who can be referred to univocally with "clear and distinct" ideas, becomes more intelligible. Furthermore, it could be argued that Duns Scotus' abolition of the ontological difference had implications not only for theism, but also for metaphysics and epistemology. With a single level of ontology, the foundations for an "immanent" world-view are being laid, within which an immanent reality may be neutrally observed and "represented." The world is no longer perceived as participating in a higher ontological level, but is self-sufficient and self-explanatory. In such a world, analogy, poetry, narrative, and rhetoric become superfluous (as far as epistemology is concerned), and representation, observation, and the scientific method become epistemologically privileged. It is not difficult to see how, in such a world, atheism becomes inevitable. As there is only a single level of ontology, God cannot be seen to transcend the ontology of this world, but must somehow be fitted in – given a function and location – with the ontology of this world. As such God becomes a "thing" (albeit a supreme "thing") among other things in this world. But such a God is not only liable to appear incredible or unbelievable (a "big thing" that soon becomes too obviously a projection of "ordinary things"), but also, as the world becomes more self-explanatory and self-sufficient, increasingly superfluous. In such a world, atheism becomes almost irresistible.

It should be noted that not all commentators wish to lay the blame (or credit) for these innovations solely at the feet of Duns Scotus.[39] But the identification of the specific innovatory figure(s) is less important than the fact that there is a widespread conviction that the origins of modernity and, by implication, atheism itself, lie within theology. As befitting a negative and parasitic term, "atheism" did not arise autonomously as an independent mode of thought, but emerged as a result of certain intellectual moves within theology and resulting changes in the prevailing conception of theism. Modern atheism was the rejection of a specific form of theism, a form of theism that can be understood only in the context of the ontological and epistemological shifts we have here been discussing. Furthermore, our discussion has helped us to come to a greater understanding of certain observations we noted at the outset. It is now easier to see why atheism and modernity are so inextricably linked. In the light of the analysis here presented, we can see why each is almost inconceivable without the other. It is also now easier to see the significance of "atheism" being a negative and parasitic term; we have seen why it is almost impossible to understand the modern (or any) form of theism without having a proper understanding of the particular form of theism it is reacting against.

5. THE END OF MODERNITY: THE END OF ATHEISM?

If it is the case that atheism and modernity are so linked that modernity seems almost necessarily to culminate in atheism, then what happens when modernity comes to an "end"? Many have been the voices announcing the "end of modernity" during recent decades, and this will no doubt give pause for thought for both theist and atheist alike. Of course, for those who hold that modernity is, uniquely, the culmination of truth, they may well claim that modernity will never "end," that history itself has ended. But for those less apocalyptically minded, the "end" of modernity can at least be contemplated. If modernity is, as we have suggested, less a "period" and more a "sensibility," then talk of its "end" may well be premature and insufficiently nuanced. But we may instead, perhaps, talk more modestly (and more appropriately) of a weakening of modernity's hegemony or, as Jacques Derrida more succinctly puts it, of modernity's "closure." But if we do, the implications for atheism cannot be ignored. As John D. Caputo suggests (in his chapter in this volume), perhaps the "closure" of modernity brings with it also the "closure" of atheism. At any rate, if modernity and atheism are as closely linked as we have been suggesting, the "closure" of modernity cannot leave atheism undisturbed.

There are some who argue that the eclipse of modernity means the eclipse of both modern theism and modern atheism, and allows for the possibility of a return to more medieval (and more authentic) forms of theism. Somewhat paradoxically, they argue that the advent of the "postmodern" allows for the repetition (albeit differently) of the premodern and, specifically, premodern forms of theism.[40] On the other hand, others argue that the "postmodern" is too bound up with the "modern" for any supposed return to the premodern. The way forward, they suggest, is not so much to return to premodern theism but, rather, to make innovative attempts to think *beyond* or *between* theism and atheism, which is, in effect, an attempt to think *beyond* metaphysics.[41] The future, it seems, is open; perhaps more open than has been the case for some time. This makes predictions more than usually perilous. But of one thing we can be sure: the fate of atheism would seem to be inescapably bound up with the fate of modernity.

NOTES

1. Michel de Certeau, *The Possession at Loudun*, trans. Michael B. Smith (Chicago: University of Chicago Press, 2000), p. 2.
2. Ibid., p. 101.
3. See Jean-François Lyotard, *The Lyotard Reader*, ed. Andrew Benjamin (Oxford: Basil Blackwell, 1989), p. 314.
4. Gavin Hyman, *The Predicament of Postmodern Theology: Radical Orthodoxy or Nihilist Textualism?* (Louisville: Westminster John Knox Press, 2001), p. 11.
5. Andreas Huyssen, "Mapping the Postmodern," New *German Critique* 33 (1984): 10. I have replaced the terms "modernism" and "postmodernism" here with the terms "theism" and "atheism."
6. See Denys Turner, *How to Be an Atheist: Inaugural Lecture Delivered at the University of Cambridge* (Cambridge: Cambridge University Press, 2002).
7. Michael J. Buckley, *At the Origins of Modern Atheism* (New Haven: Yale University Press, 1987), pp. 9–10.
8. De Certeau, *Possession at Loudun*, p. 101.
9. Buckley, *Origins of Modern Atheism*, p. 249.
10. Ibid., p. 250.
11. Ibid., p. 10.
12. Adrian Desmond, *Huxley: The Devil's Disciple* (London: Michael Joseph, 1994), p. 373: "Huxley's scientific civil service needed its own brocade banner. 'Atheism' was out, there being no disproof of God; and anyway, it was a red republican flag, a political weapon to smash the spiritual basis of privilege."
13. Ibid., pp. 374–75.
14. Adrian Desmond suggests that the new term had many advantages: "It switched the emphasis to the scientific method and its sensual

limitations....He portrayed agnosticism not as a rival 'creed,' but as a method of inquiry....His was a sect to end all sects: an attempt to clamber on to a higher moral plane, to escape the priests and paupers, Comtists and Christians. Agnosticism was a many-coloured philosophical cloak, allowing him to mask his deep doubt and indulge in moral brinkmanship. The word would push alienated intellectuals off the defensive for the first time since the French revolution." Ibid., p. 375.

15. For a primary account of these events, see the "Judgment on Appeal: The Attorney General v. Bradlaugh, 1885," in James R. Moore (ed.), *Religion in Victorian Britain*, vol. 3: *Sources* (Manchester: Manchester University Press, 1988), pp. 360–69.

16. Buckley, *Origins of Modern Atheism*, pp. 10–11.

17. See Owen Chadwick, *The Victorian Church*, vol. 1 (London: A & C Black, 1966), chap. 5. He points out that "most slum pastors agreed that they were free or almost free of infidelity. They found apathy and indifference and hostility, not unbelief" (p. 333).

18. Buckley, *Origins of Modern Atheism*, pp. 28–29. Quotation from John Henry Newman, *Apologia pro vita sua* (New York: Norton, 1968), p. 188.

19. This has led some commentators to ask why the new spirit detected by Nietzsche and Newman took so long to come to birth. Stephen Toulmin, for instance, has suggested that the intellectual, psychological, and artistic conditions for the emergence of the cultural *Zeitgeist* of the 1960s were already well in place by as early as 1914. But world historical events were such that they delayed the consummation of this world-view for a further fifty years. See Stephen Toulmin, *Cosmopolis: The Hidden Agenda of Modernity* (Chicago: University of Chicago Press, 1990), pp. 157–58.

20. Buckley, *Origins of Modern Atheism*, p. 28.

21. See Paul Heelas and Linda Woodhead, *The Spiritual Revolution: Why Religion Is Givng Way to Spirituality* (Oxford: Blackwell, 2005).

22. John Locke, *An Essay Concerning Human Understanding* (1690) (Oxford: Clarendon, 1975): "when we would frame an *Idea* the most suitable we can to the supreme Being, we enlarge every one of these [simple *Ideas*] with our *Idea* of Infinity; and so putting them together, make our complex *Idea of God*" (p. 314).

23. David Hume, *Dialogues Concerning Natural Religion* (1789), in *Principal Writings on Religion Including Dialogues Concerning Natural Religion and the Natural History of Religion* (Oxford: Oxford University Press, 1993), p. 106.

24. It has been common to present Friedrich Nietzsche as the thinker who brought atheism to its final fruition. But this is misleading. For Nietzsche, "truth" was an effect of theism, and the death of the latter entails also the death of the former. Insofar as atheism represents a truth claim, it is as problematic as theism. Both theism and atheism, therefore, are casualties of Nietzsche's "death of God."

25. See William C. Placher, *The Domestication of Transcendence: How Modern Thinking about God Went Wrong* (Louisville: Westminster John Knox Press, 1996).

26. Michel de Certeau, "Is There a Language of Unity?" *Concilium* 6 (1970): 91.

27. See Don Cupitt, "The Doctrine of Analogy in the Age of Locke," *Journal of Theological Studies* 19 (1968): 186–202.

28. Amos Funkenstein, *Theology and the Scientific Imagination: From the Middle Ages to the Seventeenth Century* (Princeton: Princeton University Press, 1986), p. 25.

29. Ibid., p. 80.

30. Ibid., p. 116.

31. These thinkers – and others – provide detailed analyses of complex developments in intellectual thought, to which I cannot do justice here. What follows is no more than a sketch of some of their key points. For more detail, see, e.g., Hans Urs von Balthasar, *The Glory of the Lord: A Theological Aesthetics*, vol. 5: *The Realm of Metaphysics in the Modern Age*, trans. Oliver Davies et al. (Edinburgh: T & T Clark, 1991); Éric Alliez, *Capital Times: Tales from the Conquest of Time*, trans. Georges Van De Abbeele (Minneapolis: University of Minnesota Press, 1996); Catherine Pickstock, *After Writing: The Liturgical Cosummation of Philosophy* (Oxford: Blackwell, 1997), esp. pp. 135–58, and "Theology and Post-modernity: An Exploration of the Origins of a New Allegiance," in Gavin Hyman (ed.), *New Directions in Philosophical Theology: Essays in Honour of Don Cupitt* (Aldershot: Ashgate, 2004), pp. 67–84; and Placher, *Domestication of Transcendence*.

32. Thomas Aquinas, *Summa theologiae*, vol. 3, trans. Herbert McCabe (London: Blackfriars, 1964), p. 67.

33. John Duns Scotus, *Philosophical Writings*, ed. and trans. Allan Wolter (Edinburgh: Nelson, 1962), p. 5.

34. Balthasar, *Glory of the Lord*, p. 16. Emphasis added.

35. Duns Scotus, *Philosophical Writings*, p. 2.

36. Alliez, *Capital Times*, p. 226.

37. I discuss these developments in more detail in Hyman, *Predicament of Postmodern Theology*, pp. 35–38.

38. Jean-Luc Marion, "The Essential Incoherence of Descartes' Definition of Divinity," in Amélie Oksenberg Rorty (ed.), *Essays in Descartes' Meditations* (Berkeley: University of California Press, 1986), p. 306.

39. For a critique of such an analysis, see Richard Cross, "Where Angels Fear to Tread: Duns Scotus and Radical Orthodoxy," *Antonianum* 76 (2001): 1–36.

40. See, e.g., Jean-Luc Marion, *God without Being*, trans. Thomas A. Carlson (Chicago: University of Chicago Press, 1991), and John Milbank, Catherine Pickstock, and Graham Ward (eds.), *Radical Orthodoxy: A New Theology* (London: Routledge, 1999).

41. See, e.g., Mark C. Taylor, *Erring: A Postmodern A/theology* (Chicago: University of Chicago Press, 1984), and John D. Caputo, *The Prayers and Tears of Jacques Derrida: Religion without Religion* (Bloomington: Indiana University Press, 1997) and also his chapter in this volume, "Atheism, A/theology, and the Postmodern Condition."

3 Atheism

Contemporary Numbers and Patterns

Determining what percentage of a given society believes in God – or doesn't – is fraught with methodological hurdles. First: low response rates; most people do not respond to surveys, and response rates of lower than 50 percent cannot be generalized to the wider society. Second: nonrandom samples. If the sample is not randomly selected – that is, every member of the given population has an equal chance of being chosen – it is nongeneralizable. Third: adverse political/cultural climates. In totalitarian countries where atheism is governmentally promulgated and risks are present for citizens viewed as disloyal, individuals will be reluctant to admit that they do believe in God. Conversely, in societies where religion is enforced by the government and risks are present for citizens viewed as nonbelievers, individuals will be reluctant to admit that they don't believe in Allah, regardless of whether anonymity is "guaranteed." Even in democratic societies without governmental coercion, individuals often feel that it is necessary to say that are religious, simply because such a response is socially desirable or culturally appropriate. For example, the designation "atheist" is stigmatized in many societies; even when people directly claim to *not* believe in God, they still eschew the self-designation of "atheist." Greeley (2003) found that 41 percent of Norwegians, 48 percent of the French, and 54 percent of Czechs claimed to not believe in God, but only 10 percent, 19 percent, and 20 percent of those respondents self-identified as "atheist," respectively. A final methodological problem: terminology. Definitions of specific words seldom translate well cross-culturally. Signifiers such as "religious" or "God" have different meanings in different cultures (Beyer 2003), making cross-national comparisons of beliefs among markedly different societies tenuous. Despite the above methodological limitations, we *can* make reliable estimates. Though methodological flaws persist, in the words of Robert Putnam (2000: 23): "[W]e must make do

For help with this chapter, thanks to Steve Bruce, Russ Dalton, Paul Froese, Ronald Inglehart, Charles Lachman, Peter Nardi, and Marvin Zuckerman.

with the imperfect evidence that we can find, not merely lament its deficiencies."

Below is a presentation of the findings of the most recently available surveys concerning rates of nonbelief in God in various countries worldwide.

AUSTRALIA, CANADA, NEW ZEALAND, AND THE UNITED STATES

According to Norris and Inglehart (2004), 25 percent of Australians do not believe in God. According to Paul (2002), 24 percent Australians are atheist or agnostic.

Guth and Fraser (2001) found that 28 percent of Canadians "show no evidence of religious salience or activity." According to Norris and Inglehart (2004), 22 percent of those in Canada do not believe in God. According to Bibby (2002), when asked, "Do you believe that God exists?" 6 percent of Canadians answered, "No, I definitely do not," and another 13 percent answered, "No, I don't think so," for a total of 19 percent classifiable as either atheist or agnostic. According to Gallup and Lindsay (1999: 121), 30 percent of Canadians do not believe in God or a "Higher Power."

Between 20 percent and 22 percent of those in New Zealand do not believe in God (Inglehart et al. 2004; Paul 2002).

According to Norris and Inglehart (2004), 6 percent of those in the United States do not believe in God. According to a 2004 survey commissioned by the BBC,[1] 9 percent of Americans do not believe in God. Rice (2003) found that 3.8 percent of Americans don't believe in God or "a spirit or life force." According to Hout and Fischer (2002), between 3 percent and 4.5 percent of Americans are either atheist or agnostic; Marwell and Demerath (2003) suggest an estimate of 7 percent. According to Froese (2001), 8 percent of Americans are atheist or agnostic. According to Gallup and Lindsay (1999: 99), 5 percent of Americans do not believe in God or a "Higher Power."

LATIN AMERICA

A 2004 survey commissioned by the BBC found that 7 percent of Mexicans do not believe in God. Inglehart et al. (2004) found that 2 percent of Mexicans do not believe in God.

The 1999 Gallup International Poll[2] found that nearly 7 percent of Argentineans chose "none" as their religion. According to Inglehart et al. (2004), 4 percent of those in Argentina do not believe in God.

According to Inglehart et al. (2004), 12 percent of those in Uruguay do not believe in God, and 3 percent of those in Chile do not believe in God, down from 5 percent in 1990.

According to Inglehart et al. (1998, 2004), the 1999 Gallup International Poll, and Barret et al. (2001), Hiorth (2003), less than 1 percent to 2 percent of those in El Salvador, Guatemala, Bolivia, Brazil, Costa Rica, Colombia, Ecuador, Honduras, Nicaragua, Panama, Peru, Paraguay, and Venezuela are atheist, agnostic, or nonreligious.

EUROPE

Norris and Inglehart (2004) found that 39 percent of those in Britain do not believe in God. According to a 2004 survey commissioned by the BBC, 44 percent of the British do not believe in God. According to Greeley (2003), 31 percent of the British do not believe in God, although only 10 percent self-identify as "atheist." According to Bruce (2002), 10 percent of the British self-identify as an "agnostic person" and 8 percent as a "convinced atheist," with an additional 21 percent choosing "not a religious person." According to Froese (2001), 32 percent of the British are atheist or agnostic. According to Gallup and Lindsay (1999: 121), 39 percent of the British do not believe in God or a "Higher Power."

According to Norris and Inglehart (2004), 44 percent of those in France do not believe in God. According to Greeley (2003), 48 percent of the French do not believe in God, although only 19 percent self-identify as "atheist." According to Froese (2001), 54 percent of the French are atheist or agnostic. According to Davie (1999), 43 percent of the French do not believe in God.

Norris and Inglehart (2004) found that 64 percent of Swedes do not believe in God. According to Bondeson (2003), 74 percent of Swedes said that they did not believe in "a personal God." According to Greeley (2003), 46 percent of Swedes do not believe in God, although only 17 percent self-identify as "atheist." According to Froese (2001), 69 percent of Swedes are either atheist or agnostic. According to Gustafsson and Pettersson (2000), 82 percent of Swedes do not believe in a "personal God." According to Davie (1999), 85 percent of Swedes do not believe in God.

According to Norris and Inglehart (2004), 48 percent of Danes do not believe in God. According to Bondeson (2003), 49 percent of Danes do not believe in "a personal God." According to Greeley (2003), 43 percent of Danes do not believe in God, although only 15 percent self-identify as "atheist." According to Froese (2001), 45 percent of Danes are either atheist or agnostic. According to Gustafsson and Pettersson (2000), 80 percent of Danes do not believe in a "personal God."

According to Inglehart et al. (2004), 31 percent of Norwegians do not believe in God. According to Bondeson (2003), 54 percent of Norwegians said that they did not believe in a "personal God." According to Greeley (2003), 41 percent of Norwegians do not believe in God, although only 10 percent self-identify as "atheist." According to Gustafsson and Pettersson (2000), 72 percent of Norwegians do not believe in a "personal God." According to Froese (2001), 45 percent of Norwegians are either atheist or agnostic.

Norris and Inglehart (2004) found that 28 percent of those in Finland do not believe in God. According to Bondeson (2003), 33 percent of Finns do not believe in "a personal God." According to Gustafsson and Pettersson (2000), 60 percent of Finns do not believe in a "personal God." According to Froese (2001), 41 percent of Finns are either atheist or agnostic.

According to Norris and Inglehart (2004), 42 percent of those in the Netherlands do not believe in God. According to Greeley (2003), 43 percent of the Dutch do not believe in God, although only 17 percent self-identify as "atheist." Houtman and Mascini (2002) found that 39 percent of the Dutch are either agnostic or atheist. According to Froese (2001), 44 percent of the Dutch are either atheist or agnostic.

Norris and Inglehart (2004) found that 31 percent of West Germans do not believe in God. According to Greeley (2003), 35 percent of West Germans do not believe in God. According to Froese (2001), 35 percent of West Germans are either atheist or agnostic. According to Greeley (2003), 75 percent of East Germans do not believe in God. According to Pollack (2002), 74 percent of East Germans and 38 percent of West Germans do not believe in God. According to Shand (1998), 42 percent of West Germans and 72 percent of East Germans are either atheist or agnostic.

Between 17 percent and 27 percent of those in Switzerland do not believe in God (Greeley 2003; Inglehart et al. 2004). Between 18 percent and 26 percent of those in Austria do not believe in God (Froese 2001; Greeley 2003; Norris and Inglehart 2004).

Inglehart et al. (2004) found that 15 percent of those in Spain do not believe in God, and according to Greeley (2003), 18 percent of Spaniards do not believe in God. According to Froese (2001), 24 percent of Spaniards are either atheist or agnostic.

Ingelhart et al. (2004) found that 6 percent of Italians do not believe in God. According to Greeley (2003), 14 percent of Italians do not believe in God. According to Froese (2001), 15 percent of Italians are either atheist or agnostic. According to Davis and Robinson (1999), 23 percent of

Italians disagreed (some strongly) that a God exists who concerns him-self with every human being personally.

According to Norris and Inglehart (2004) and Froese (2001), between 42 percent and 43 percent of Belgians do not believe in God. According Inglehart et al. (2004), 8 percent of Albanians do not believe in God, and 34 percent of Bulgarians do not believe in God. According to Greeley (2003), 40 percent of Bulgarians do not believe in God.

According to Inglehart et al. (2004), 61 percent of Czechs do not believe in God. According to Greeley (2003), 54 percent of Czechs do not believe in God. According to a 1999 Gallup International Poll, over 55 percent of Czechs chose "none" as their religion. Between 10 percent and 28 percent of those in Slovakia do not believe in God (Gall 1998; Greeley 2003; Inglehart et al. 2004).

According to Inglehart et al. (2004), 7 percent of Croatians do not believe in God. According to a 1999 Gallup International Poll, 5.5 per-cent of Croatians and 6.4 percent of those in Bosnia chose "none" as their religion. According to Inglehart et al. (2004), 4 percent of Romanians do not believe in God.

Between 4 percent and 5 percent of those in Ireland do not believe in God (Davie 1999; Greeley 2003; Inglehart et al. 2004). Between 4 percent and 9 percent of those in Portugal do not believe in God (Greeley 2003; Inglehart et al. 2004).

According to Ingelhart et al. (2004) and Greeley (2003), between 35 percent and 38 percent of those in Slovenia do not believe in God. Inglehart et al. (2004) found that 32 percent of Hungarians do not believe in God. According to Greeley (2003), 35 percent of Hungarians do not believe in God. According to Froese (2001), 46 percent of Hungarians are either atheist or agnostic.

According to Inglehart et al. (2004) and Greeley (2003), between 3 per-cent and 6 percent of those in Poland do not believe in God. According to Inglehart et al. (2004), 16 percent of those in Iceland do not believe in God. According to Froese (2001), 23 percent of those in Iceland are either atheist or agnostic.

According to Norris and Inglehart (2004), 16 percent of those in Greece do not believe in God. According to Greeley (2003), 4 percent of those in Cyprus do not believe in God. According to Inglehart et al. (2004) and the 1999 Gallup International Poll, less than 1 percent to 2 percent of those in Turkey are nonreligious.

RUSSIA AND FORMER SOVIET STATES

A 2004 survey commissioned by the BBC found that 24 percent of Russians do not believe in God. According to Inglehart et al. (2004),

30 percent of Russians do not believe in God, but only 5 percent self-identify as "atheist" (Froese 2004). According to Greeley (2003), 48 percent of Russians do not believe in God.

According to Inglehart et al. (2004), 17 percent of those in Belarus do not believe in God. Froese (2004) reports that 5 percent of Ukrainians are self-described atheists. According to Inglehart et al. (2004), 20 percent of Ukrainians do not believe in God. According to Yelensky (2002), 44 percent of Ukrainians claim "none" in terms of religious identification.

Froese (2004) found that 6 percent of those in Latvia are self-described atheists, but according to Inglehart et al. (2004), 20 percent of those in Latvia do not believe in God, far fewer than in 1990, when 42 percent did not believe in God. According to Greeley (2003), 29 percent of those in Latvia do not believe in God.

According to Inglehart et al. (2004), 13 percent of Lithuanians and 49 percent of Estonians do not believe in God, although only 1 percent and 11 percent describe themselves as atheists, respectively (Froese 2004).

According to Inglehart et al. (2004), 14 percent of those in Armenia do not believe in God, although only 7 percent are self-described atheists (Froese 2004). According to a 1999 Gallup International Poll, over 11 percent of Armenians chose "none" as their religion.

According to Froese (2004), less than 1 percent of those in Azerbaijan and 4 percent of those in Georgia are atheist. According to Froese (2004), 12 percent of those in Kazakhstan are atheist. According to Barrett et al. (2001), 29 percent of those in Kazakhstan are nonreligious, with 11 percent claiming to be atheist. According to the 1999 Gallup International Poll, almost 19 percent of Kazakhs chose "none" as their religion.

According to Froese (2004), 7 percent of those in Kyrgyzstan, 6 percent of those in Moldova, 4 percent of those in Uzbekistan, 2 percent of those in Tajikstan, and 2 percent of those in Turkmenistan are atheist. According to Barret et al. (2001), 3.5 percent of Uzbeks are atheist. According to Johnstone (1993), 28 percent of those in Kyrgystan, 27 percent of those in Moldova, 26 percent of Uzbeks, 18 percent of those in Turkmenistan, and 13 percent of those in Tajikstan are nonreligious.

ASIA

Survey data of religious belief in China is extremely unreliable (Demerath 2001: 154; Guest 2003). Estimates of high degrees of atheism are most probably exaggerations (Overmyer 2003). Only recently has sound scholarship begun to emerge (Yang 2004). That said, according to Barrett et al. (2001), 8 percent of the Chinese are atheist. According to O'Brien and Palmer (1993), between 10 percent and 14 percent of those in China are "avowed atheists."

According to Norris and Inglehart (2004), 6 percent of those in India do not believe in God. According to a 2004 survey commissioned by the BBC, less than 3 percent of Indians do not believe in God.

According to Norris and Inglehart (2004), 65 percent of those in Japan do not believe in God. According to Demerath (2001: 138), 64 percent do not believe in God and 55 percent do not believe in Buddha. According to the 1999 Gallup International Poll, nearly 29 percent of the Japanese chose "none" as their religion. According to Johnstone (1993: 323), 84 percent of the Japanese claim no personal religion, but most follow "the customs of Japanese traditional religion."

According to Inglehart et al. (2004), 81 percent of those in Vietnam and 24 percent of those in Taiwan do not believe in God.

Barrett et al. (2001) report that 15 percent of North Koreans are atheist. According to Johnstone (1993), 68 percent of North Koreans are nonreligious; however, for reasons similar to those discussed above concerning China, this high estimate should be met with skepticism.

A 2004 survey commissioned by the BBC found that 30 percent of South Koreans do not believe in God. According to Eungi (2003), 52 percent of South Koreans do not believe in God.

According to Barrett et al. (2001), 9 percent of those in Mongolia are atheist. According to Johnstone (1993), 20 percent of those in Mongolia, 7 percent of Cambodians, and 5 percent of Laotians are nonreligious.

Inglehart et al. (2004) found that 13 percent of those in Singapore do not believe in God. According to the 1999 Gallup International Poll, over 12 percent of those in Singapore chose "none" as their religion.

According to Moaddel and Azadarmaki (2003), less than 5 percent of Iranians do not believe in God. According to a 2004 survey commissioned by the BBC, less than 2 percent of those in Indonesia do not believe in God.

According to Inglehart et al. (2004), Barrett et al. (2001), the 1999 Gallup International Poll, and Johnstone (1993), less than 1 percent of those in Indonesia, Bangladesh, Brunei, Thailand, Sri Lanka, Iran, Malaysia, Nepal, Laos, Afghanistan, Pakistan, and the Philippines are nonbelievers in God.

AFRICA

According to a 2004 survey commissioned by the BBC, Hiorth (2003), Inglehart et al. (1998, 2004), Barrett et al. (2001), the 1999 Gallup International Poll, and Johnstone (1993), less than 1 percent of those in Algeria, Benin, Botswana, Burkina Faso, Burundi, Cameroon, Chad,

Cote D'Ivoire, Ethiopia, Gambia, Ghana, Guinea, Kenya, Liberia, Libya, Madagascar, Malawi, Mali, Mauritania, Morocco, Niger, Nigeria, Rwanda, Senegal, Sierra Leone, Somalia, Sudan, Tanzania, Togo, Tunisia, Uganda, Zimbabwe, and Zambia are atheist, agnostic, or nonreligious.

According to Johnstone (1993), 2.7 percent of those in Congo, 4 percent of those in Zimbabwe, 4 percent of those in Namibia, 1.5 percent of those in Angola and the Central African Republic, and 5 percent of those in Mozambique are nonreligious.

According to a 1999 Gallup International Poll, nearly 11 percent of South Africans chose "none" as their religion. According to Inglehart et al. (2004), 1 percent of South Africans do not believe in God.

THE MIDDLE EAST

According to a 2004 survey commissioned by the BBC, 15 percent of Israelis do not believe in God. According to Yuchtman-Ya'ar (2003), 54 percent of Israelis identify themselves as "secular." According to Dashefsky et al. (2003), 41 percent of Israelis identify themselves as "not religious." According to Kedem (1995), 31 percent of Israelis do not believe in God, with an additional 6 percent choosing "don't know," for a total of 37 percent being atheist or agnostic.

A 2004 survey commissioned by the BBC found that less than 3 percent of those in Lebanon do not believe in God. According to Moaddel and Azadarmaki (2003), less than 5 percent of those in Jordan and Egypt do not believe in God. According to Inglehart et al. (2004), less than 1 percent of those in Jordan and Egypt do not believe in God.

According to Barrett et al. (2001) less than 1 percent of those in Syria, Oman, Kuwait, Saudi Arabia, United Arab Emirates, and Yemen are secular. According to Johnstone (1993), less than 2 percent of Oman, Saudi Arabia, Syria, Yemen, and Kuwait are nonreligious. According to Johnstone (1993), less than 1 percent of those in Iraq are nonreligious.

THE WEST INDIES

According to Hiorth (2003), 40 percent of Cubans claim "none" as their religion. According to Barrett et al. (2001), 30 percent of Cubans are nonreligious, with 7 percent claiming to be atheist. According to Johnstone (1993), 9 percent of those in Trinidad and Tobago and 3 percent of Jamaicans are nonreligious. According to Hiorth (2003) and Johnstone (1993), less than 1 percent of those in Haiti are nonreligious.

According to Inglehart et al. (2004), 7 percent of those in the Dominican Republic do not believe in God, and the 1999 Gallup International

Poll found that almost 10 percent of those in the Dominican Republic chose "none" as their religion.

THE TOP 50

Table 3.1 presents the top fifty countries containing the largest percentage of people who identify as atheist, agnostic, or nonbeliever in a "personal God."

We can also include Mexico (2%–7% do not believe in God), Poland (3%–6%), Moldova (6%), Romania, Georgia, and Uzbekistan (4%), India (2%–6%), Ireland (4%–5%), and Chile (3%). From the fifty-plus countries above, the total worldwide number of atheists, agnostics, and nonbelievers in God is somewhere between 505 million and 749 million. These numbers are conservative; were one to factor in a mere 0.25 percent of such highly populated countries as Egypt, Brazil, Indonesia, Nigeria, Burma, Tanzania, and Iran as nonbelievers in God, estimates would be significantly larger.

Given the above estimates, we can deduce that there are approximately 58 times as many atheists as there are Mormons, 41 times as many atheists as there are Jews, 35 times as many atheists as there are Sikhs, and twice as many atheists as there are Buddhists. Finally, nonbelievers in God as a group come in fourth place after Christianity (2 billion), Islam (1.2 billion), and Hinduism (900 million) in terms of global ranking of commonly held belief systems.

EXPLAINING HIGH RATES OF NONBELIEF

What accounts for the staggering differences in rates of nonbelief between nations? For instance, why do most nations in Africa, South America, and Southeast Asia contain almost no atheists, while many European nations contain an abundance of nonbelievers? There are various explanations (Bruce 1999; Stark and Finke 2000; Paul 2002; Zuckerman 2004). One leading theory comes from Norris and Inglehart (2004), who argue that in societies characterized by plentiful food distribution, excellent public health care, and widely accessible housing, religiosity wanes. Conversely, in societies where food and shelter are scarce and life is generally less secure, religious belief is strong. Through an examination of current global statistics on religiosity as they relate to income distribution, economic inequality, welfare expenditures, and basic measurements of lifetime security (such as vulnerability to famines or natural disasters), Inglehart and Norris (2004) convincingly argue that despite numerous factors possibly relevant for explaining

TABLE 3.1. *Top fifty countries containing the largest percentage of people who identify as atheist, agnostic, or nonbeliever in God*

Country	Total population (2004)	Percentage atheist/ agnostic/nonbeliever in "personal" God
1. Sweden	8,986,000	46–85
2. Vietnam	82,690,000	81
3. Denmark	5,413,000	43–80
4. Norway	4,575,000	31–72
5. Japan	127,333,000	64–65
6. Czech Rep.	10,246,100	54–61
7. Finland	5,215,000	28–60
8. France	60,424,000	43–54
9. South Korea	48,598,000	30–52
10. Estonia	1,342,000	49
11. Germany	82,425,000	41–49
12. Russia	143,782,000	24–48
13. Hungary	10,032,000	32–46
14. Netherlands	16,318,000	39–44
15. Britain	60,271,000	31–44
16. Belgium	10,348,000	42–43
17. Bulgaria	7,518,000	34–40
18. Slovenia	2,011,000	35–38
19. Israel	6,199,000	15–37
20. Canada	32,508,000	19–30
21. Latvia	2,306,000	20–29
22. Slovakia	5,424,000	10–28
23. Switzerland	7,451,000	17–27
24. Austria	8,175,000	18–26
25. Australia	19,913,000	24–25
26. Taiwan	22,750,000	24
27. Spain	40,281,000	15–24
28. Iceland	294,000	16–23
29. New Zealand	3,994,000	20–22
30. Ukraine	47,732,000	20
31. Belarus	10,311,000	17
32. Greece	10,648,000	16
33. North Korea	22,698,000	15[a]
34. Italy	58,057,000	6–15
35. Armenia	2,991,000	14
36. China	1,298,848,000	8–14[a]

Country	Total population (2004)	Percentage atheist/ agnostic/nonbeliever in "personal" God
37. Lithuania	3,608,000	13
38. Singapore	4,354,000	13
39. Uruguay	3,399,000	12
40. Kazakhstan	15,144,00	11–12
41. Estonia	1,342,000	11
42. Mongolia	2,751,000	9
43. Portugal	10,524,000	4–9
44. United States	293,028,000	3–9
45. Albania	3,545,000	8
46. Argentina	39,145,000	4–8
47. Kyrgyzstan	5,081,000	7
48. Dominican Rep.	8,834,000	7
49. Cuba	11,309,000	7[a]
50. Croatia	4,497,000	7

[a] Certainty/validity on these figures is relatively low.

different rates of religiosity worldwide, "the levels of societal and individual security in any society seem to provide the most persuasive and parsimonious explanation" (p. 109).[3] Of course, there are anomalies, such as Vietnam (81% nonbelievers in God) and Ireland (4%–5% nonbelievers in God). But aside from these two exceptions, the correlation between high rates of individual and societal security/well-being and high rates of nonbelief in God remains strong.

ATHEISM AND SOCIETAL HEALTH

When recognizing that countries containing high percentages of nonbelievers are among the healthiest and wealthiest nations on earth (Paul 2004), we must distinguish between nations where nonbelief has been forced upon the society by dictators ("coercive atheism") and nations wherein nonbelief has emerged on its own without governmental coercion ("organic atheism"). Nations marked by coercive atheism – such as North Korea and former Soviet states – are marked by all that comes with totalitarianism: poor economic development, censorship, corruption, depression, and so on. However, nations marked by high levels of organic atheism – such as Sweden or the Netherlands – are among the healthiest, wealthiest, best educated, and freest societies on earth.

Consider the *Human Development Report* (2004), commissioned by the United Nations Development Program. This report ranks 177 nations on a "Human Development Index," which measures societal health through a weighing of such indicators as life expectancy at birth, adult literacy rate, per capita income, and educational attainment. According to the 2004 Report, the five highest ranked nations in terms of total human development were Norway, Sweden, Australia, Canada, and the Netherlands. All five of these countries are characterized by notably high degrees of organic atheism. Of the top twenty-five nations ranked on the "Human Development Index," all but one (Ireland) are top-ranking nonbelief nations, containing very high percentages of organic atheism. Conversely, of those countries ranked at the bottom of the "Human Development Index" – the bottom fifty – *all* are countries lacking statistically significant percentages of atheism.

Concerning the infant mortality rate (number of deaths per 1,000 live births), irreligious countries have the lowest rates, and religious countries have the highest. According to the CIA *World Factbook* (2004), the top twenty-five nations with the *lowest* infant mortality rates were all nations containing significantly high percentages of organic atheism. Conversely, the seventy-five bottom nations with the *highest* infant mortality rates were all nations without any statistically significant levels of organic atheism.

Concerning international poverty rates, the United Nations' *Report on the World Social Situation* (2003) found that of the forty poorest nations on earth, all but one (Vietnam) are highly religious nations with statistically minimal or insignificant levels of atheism. Concerning illiteracy rates, the same report found that of the thirty-five nations with the highest levels of youth illiteracy rates, all are highly religious nations with statistically insignificant levels of organic atheism.

Concerning homicide rates, Fox and Levin (2000) and Fajnzylber et al. (2002) found that the nations with the highest homicide rates are all highly religious nations with minimal or statistically insignificant levels of organic atheism, while nations with the lowest homicide rates tend to be highly secular nations with high levels of atheism.

Concerning suicide rates, religious nations fare better than secular nations. According to the 2003 World Health Organization's report on international male suicide rates, of the top ten nations with the *highest* male suicide rates, all but one (Sri Lanka) are strongly irreligious nations with high levels of atheism. Of the top remaining nine nations leading the world in male suicide rates, *all* are former Soviet/Communist nations, such as Belarus, Ukraine, and Latvia. Of the bottom ten nations with the *lowest* male suicide rates, all are highly religious nations with statistically insignificant levels of organic atheism.

Concerning gender equality, nations marked by high degrees of organic atheism are among the most egalitarian in the world, while highly religious nations are among the most oppressive. According to the 2004 *Human Development Report's* "Gender Empowerment Measure," the top ten nations with the highest degrees of gender equality are *all* strongly organic atheistic nations with significantly high percentages of nonbelief. Conversely, the bottom ten are *all* highly religious nations without any statistically significant percentages of atheists. According to Inglehart (2003), countries with the most female members of Parliament tend to be countries characterized by high degrees of organic atheism (such as Sweden and Denmark), and countries with the fewest female members in Parliament tend to be highly religious countries (such as Pakistan and Nigeria).

In sum, with the exception of suicide, countries marked by high rates of organic atheism are among the most societally healthy on earth, while societies characterized by nonexistent rates of organic atheism are among the most unhealthy. Of course, none of the above correlations demonstrate that high levels of organic atheism *cause* societal health or that low levels of organic atheism *cause* societal ills. Rather, societal health seems to cause widespread atheism, and societal insecurity seems to cause widespread belief in God, as has been demonstrated by Norris and Inglehart (2004), mentioned above.

FUTURE TRENDS

Is worldwide atheism growing or declining? This is a difficult question to answer simply. On the one hand, there are more atheists in the world today than ever before. On the other hand, worldwide atheism overall may be in decline, due to the demographic fact that highly religious nations have the highest birth rates in the world, and highly irreligious nations have the lowest birth rates in the world. As Norris and Inglehart (2004: 25) observe, "the world as a whole now has more people with traditional religious views than ever before – and they constitute a growing proportion of the world's population."

Thus, the picture is complicated, making definite predictions of the future growth or decline of atheism difficult. What is clear is that while most people continue to maintain a firm belief in deities (especially in the most populous countries) in certain societies, nonbelief in God is definitely increasing (Bruce 2002). According to Gallup and Lindsay (1999: 121), 30 percent of Canadians do not believe in God or a "Higher Power," *up from 23 percent in 1985*. According to Beyer (1997), 12.5 percent of Canadians chose "none" when presented with a plethora of religious identity options in 1991, *up from 7 percent in 1981 – a*

90 percent increase in one decade. According to Gallup and Lindsay (1999: 121), 39 percent of the British do not believe in God or a "Higher Power," *up from 24 percent in 1979.* According to Bruce (2002) and Gill et al. (1998), survey data from the 1960s found that *79 percent of the British held a belief in God, but this dropped down to 68 percent in surveys taken in the 1990s;* whereas only 10 percent answered that they "don't believe in God" in the 1960s, *this percentage had almost tripled to 27 percent in the 1990s.* According to Bruce (2001), surveys in the 1950s found that only 2 percent of the British replied they did not believe in God; *that percentage was up to 27 percent in the 1990s.* According to Palm and Trost (2000), when Swedes were asked in 1947, "Do you believe in God?" 83 percent said yes, 9 percent said they didn't know, and 8 percent said no. In the early 1990s, in response to the same question, only 38 percent said yes, 16 percent didn't know, and *46 percent said they did not.* According to CUNY's 2001 American Religious Identification Survey, *14 percent of Americans claim "no religion" in terms of self-identification, up from 8 percent in 1990.* Finally, according to Norris and Inglehart (2004: 90), the percentage of people believing in God over the past fifty years has declined by 33 percent in Sweden, 22 percent in the Netherlands, 20 percent in Australia, 19 percent in Norway, 18 percent in Denmark, 16.5 percent in Britain, 12 percent in Greece, 11 percent in Belgium, 7 percent in Canada, and 3 percent in Japan.

In sum, loss of belief in God has occurred over the course of the twentieth century in Canada, Australia, and various European countries (Davie 2000), including Germany (Greeley 2003; Shand 1998), the United Kingdom (Bruce 2001, 2002), the Netherlands (Grotenhuis and Scheepers 2001), and Scandinavia (Bruce 1999). However, secularization is quite limited to specific advanced industrialized nations (with relatively low birth rates), and has not occurred throughout much of the rest of the world.

ATHEISM AND THE "INNATENESS" OF RELIGIOUS BELIEF

In recent years, a new attempt at explaining religious belief has emerged. Its central tenet is that belief in God is biologically determined, neurologically based, or genetically inborn, growing out of the "natural" processes of the human brain.

Justin Barret (2004) has argued that belief in God is a result of the "way our minds are structured" (p. viii) and is thus "an inevitable consequence of the sorts of minds we are born with" (p. 91). David Wilson (2002) suggests that religion is part of humanity's naturally evolving adaptive strategy and that religious belief represents "the healthy functioning of the biologically and culturally well-adapted human mind" (p. 228). Michael Persinger (1987) has stressed the role of the hippocampus, the amygdala, temporal lobes, and hormonal processes in explaining religious belief in God. Ashbrook and Albright (1997) focus on the neural workings of the brain in explaining belief in God. Newberg and D'Aquili (2001) argue that religiosity is an evolved "neurological process" (p. 9), that the roots of belief in God are to be found in "the wiring of the human brain" (p. 129), and that "as long as our brains are arranged the way they are," belief in God will remain (p. 172).

The data presented in this chapter deliver a heavy blow to this new explanation of theism. First of all, the sheer numbers; with between 500 million and 750 million nontheists living on this planet today, any suggestion that belief in God is natural, inborn, or a result of how our brains are wired becomes difficult to sustain. Second, innate/neural theories of belief in God cannot explain the dramatically different rates of belief among similar countries. Consider Britain (31%–44% atheist) compared with Ireland (4%–5% atheist), the Czech Republic (54%–61% atheist) compared with Poland (3%–6% atheist), and South Korea (30%–52% atheist) compared with the Philippines (less than 1% atheist). It is simply unsustainable to argue that these glaring differences in rates of atheism among these nations is due to different biological, neurological, or other such brain-related properties. Rather, the differences are better explained by taking into account historical, cultural, economic, political, and sociological factors (Verweij et al. 1997; Bruce 1999; Grotenhuis and Scheepers 2001; Zuckerman 2003; Norris and Inglehart 2004).

CONCLUSION

Between 500 million and 750 million humans currently do not believe in God. Such figures render any suggestion that theism is innate or neurologically based manifestly untenable. The nations with the highest degrees of organic atheism include most of the nations of Europe, Japan, Canada, Australia, New Zealand, Taiwan, and Israel. However, atheism is virtually nonexistent in most Africa, South America, the Middle East, and Asia. Most nations characterized by high degrees of individual and societal security have the highest rates of organic atheism, and, conversely, nations characterized by low degrees of individual and societal security have the lowest rates of organic atheism and the highest degrees of belief. High levels of organic atheism are strongly correlated with high levels of societal health, such as low poverty rates and strong gender equality. In many societies atheism is growing; however, throughout much of the rest of the world – particularly among the poorest nations with highest birth rates – atheism is barely discernible.

NOTES

1. This BBC study was posted online by bbcnews.com (U.K. edition) under the heading "What the World Thinks of God."
2. The Gallup International Survey Poll data can be obtained from the Gallup International Association or on the web under their "Millennium Survey."
3. Norris and Inglehart (2004) account for the United States' high degree of religious belief on page 108: "The United States...is one of the most unequal postindustrial societies...relatively high levels of economic insecurity are experienced by many sectors of U.S. society....Many American families...face risks of unemployment, the dangers of sudden ill health without adequate private medical insurance, vulnerability to becoming a victim of crime...."

REFERENCES

Ashbrook, James, and Carol Rausch Albright. 1997. *The Humanizing Brains: Where Religion and Neuroscience Meet.* Cleveland, Ohio: Pilgrim Press.

Ashford, Sheena, and Noel Timms. 1992. *What Europe Thinks.* Brookfield, Vt.: Dartmouth Publishing.

Barret, Justin. 2004. *Why Would Anyone Believe in God?* Walnut Creek, Calif.: AltaMira Press.

Barrett, David, George Kurian, and Todd Johnson. 2001. *World Christian Encyclopedia.* New York: Oxford University Press.

Berger, Peter. 2001. "Reflections on the Sociology of Religion Today." *Sociology of Religion* 62, no. 4:443–54.

Beyer, Peter. 1997. "Religious Vitality in Canada: The Complemetarity of Religious Market and Secularization Perspectives." *Journal for the Scientific Study of Society* 36, no. 2: 272–88.

Beyer, Peter. 2003. "Social Forms of Religion and Religions in Contemporary Global Society." In Michele Dillon (ed.), *Handbook of the Sociology of Religion.* New York: Cambridge University Press, pp. 45–60.

Bibby, Reginald. 2000. "Canada's Mythical Religious Mosaic: Some Census Findings." *Journal for the Scientific Study of Religion* 39, no. 2: 235–39.

Bibby, Reginald. 2002. *Restless Gods: The Renaissance of Religion in Canada.* Toronto, Canada: Stoddart Publishing.

Bondeson, Ulla. 2003. *Nordic Moral Climates.* New Brunswick, N.J.: Transaction.

Bruce, Steve. 1999. *Choice and Religion.* New York: Oxford University Press.

Bruce, Steve. 2001. "Christianity in Britain, R.I.P." *Sociology of Religion* 62, no. 2: 191–203.

Bruce, Steve. 2002. *God Is Dead: Secularization in the West.* Malden, Mass.: Blackwell.

Dashefsky, Arnold, Bernard Lazerwitz, and Ephraim Tabory. 2003. "A Journey of the 'Straight Way' or the 'Roundabout Path': Jewish Identity in the United States and Israel." In Michele Dillon (ed.), *Handbook of the Sociology of Religion.* New York: Cambridge University Press, pp. 240–60.

Davie, Grace. 1999. "Europe: The Exception That Proves the Rule?" In Peter Berger (ed.), *The Desecularization of the World.* Grand Rapids, Mich.: William B. Eerdmans, pp. 65–83.

Davie, Grace. 2000. *Religion in Modern Europe.* New York: Oxford University Press.

Davis, Nancy, and Robert Robinson. 1999. "Religious Cosmologies, Individualism, and Politics in Italy." *Journal for the Scientific Study of Religion* 38, no. 3: 339–53.

Demerath, N. J. 2001. *Crossing the Gods.* New Brunswick, N.J.: Rutgers University Press.

Eungi, Kim. 2003. "Religion in Contemporary Korea: Change and Continuity." *Korea Focus* (July–August): 133–46.

Fajnzylber, Oablo, Daniel Lederman, and Norman Loatza. 2002. "Inequality and Violent Crime." *Journal of Law and Economics* (April): 1–25.

Fox, James, and Jack Levin. 2000. *The Will to Kill.* Boston: Allyn and Bacon.

Froese, Paul. 2001. "Hungary for Religion: A Supply-Side Interpretation of the Hungarian Religious Revival." *Journal for the Scientific Study of Religion* 40, no. 2: 251–68.

Froese, Paul. 2004. "After Atheism: An Analysis of Religious Monopolies in the Post-Communist World." *Sociology of Religion* 65, no. 1: 57–75.

Gall, Timothy. 1998. *Worldmark Encyclopedia of Culture and Daily Life,* vol. 4 (Europe). Cleveland, Ohio: Eastword.

Gallup, George, and Michael Lindsay. 1999. *Surveying the Religious Landscape.* Harrisburg, Pa.: Morehouse.

Gill, Robin, Kirk Hadaywa, and Penny Marler. 1998. "Is Religious Belief Declining in Britain?" *Journal for the Scientific Study of Religion* 37, no. 3: 507–16.

Greeley, Andrew. 2003. *Religion in Europe at the End of the Second Millennium.* New Brunswick, N.J.: Transaction.

Grotenhuis, Manfred, and Peer Scheepers. 2001. "Churches in Dutch: Causes of Religious Disaffiliation in the Netherlands, 1937–1995." *Journal for the Scientific Study of Religion* 40, no. 4: 591–606.

Guest, Kenneth. 2003. *God in Chinatown.* New York: New York University Press.

Gustafsson, Goran, and Thorleif Pettersson. 2000. *Folkkyrk och religios pluraism – den nordiska religiosa modellen.* Stockholm, Sweden: Verbum Forlag.

Guth, James, and Cleveland Fraser. 2001. "Religion and Partisanship in Canada." *Journal for the Scientific Study of Religion* 40, no. 1: 51–64.

Hagevi, Magnus. 2002. "Religiosity and Swedish Opinion on the European Union." *Journal for the Scientific Study of Religion* 41, no. 4: 759–69.

Heritage, Andrew. 2003. *World Reference Atlas.* New York: Dorling Kindersley.

Hiorth, Finngeir. 2003. *Atheism in the World.* Oslo, Norway: Human-Etosk Forbund.

Hout, Michael, and Claude Fischer. 2002. "Why More Americans Have No Religious Preference: Politics and Generations." *American Sociological Review* 67, no. 2: 165–90.

Houtman, Dick, and Peter Mascini. 2002. "Why Do Churches Become Empty, While New Age Grows? Secularization and Religious Change in the Netherlands." *Journal for the Scientific Study of Religion* 41, no. 3: 455–73.

Human Development Report. 2004. United Nations Development Programme. New York: Oxford University Press.

Ingelhart, Ronald, ed. 2003. *Human Values and Social Change.* Boston: Brill.

Inglehart, Ronald, Miguel Basanez, and Alejandro Moreno. 1998. *Human Values and Beliefs: A Cross Cultural Sourcebook.* Ann Arbor: University of Michigan Press.

Inglehart, Ronald, Miguel Basanez, Jaime Diez-Medrano, Loek Halman, and Ruud Luijkx. 2004. *Human Beliefs and Values: A Cross-Cultural Sourcebook Based on the 1999–2002 Value Surveys.* Buenos Aires, Argentina: Siglo Veintiuno Editores.

Johnstone, Patrick. 1993. *Operation World*. Grand Rapids, Mich.: Zondervan Publishing.

Kedem, Peri. 1995. "Dimensions of Jewish Religiosity." In Shlomo Deshen, Charles Liebman, and Mishe Shokeid (eds.), *Israeli Judaism*. London: Transaction, pp. 33–62.

Marwell, Gerald, and N. J. Demerath. 2003. "'Secularization' by Any Other Name." *American Sociological Review* 68, no. 2: 314–18.

Moaddel, Mansoor, and Taqhi Azadarmaki. 2003. "The Worldview of Islamic Publics: The Cases of Egypt, Iran, and Jordan." In Ronald Inglehart (ed.), *Human Values and Social Change*. Boston: Brill, pp. 69–89.

Newberg, Andrew, and Eugene D'Aquili. 2001. *Why God Won't Go Away: Brain Science and the Biology of Belief*. New York: Ballantine Books.

Norris, Pippa, and Ronald Inglehart. 2004. *Sacred and Secular: Religion and Politics Worldwide*. New York: Cambridge University Press.

O'Brien, Joanne, and Martin Palmer. 1993. *The State of Religion Atlas*. New York: Simon and Schuster.

Overmyer, D. L., ed. 2003. *Religion in China Today*. Cambridge, U.K.: Cambridge University Press.

Palm, Irving, and Jan Trost. 2000. "Family and Religion in Sweden." In Sharon Houseknecht and Jerry Pankhurst (eds.), *Family, Religion, and Social Change in Diverse Societies*. New York: Oxford University Press, pp. 107–20.

Paul, Gregory. 2002. "The Secular Revolution of the West." *Free Inquiry* (Summer): 28–34.

Paul, Gregory. 2004. "Testing the Creationist, Secular, and Neutral Hypotheses against Quantifiable Societal Health in the Developed Democracies." Unpublished manuscript.

Persinger, Michael. 1987. *Neuropsychological Bases of God Beliefs*. New York: Praeger.

Pollack, Detlef. 2002. "The Change in Religion and Church in Eastern Germany after 1989: A Research Note." *Sociology of Religion* 63, no. 3: 373–87.

Putnam, Robert. 2000. *Bowling Alone*. New York: Touchstone.

Rice, Tom. 2003. "Believe It or Not: Religious and Other Paranormal Beliefs in the United States." *Journal for the Scientific Study of Religion* 42, no. 1: 95–106.

Shand, Jack. 1998. "The Decline of Traditional Christian Beliefs in Germany." *Sociology of Religion* 59, no. 2: 179–84.

Sherkat, Darren, and Chistopher Ellison. 1999. "Recent Developments and Current Controversies in the Sociology of Religion." *Annual Review of Sociology* 25: 363–94.

Shoemaker, Wesley. 1997. *Russia, Eurasian States, and Eastern Europe*. Harpers Ferry, W.V.: Stryker-Post.

Stark, Rodney, and Roger Finke. 2000. *Acts of Faith*. Berkeley: University of California Press.

United Nations. 2003. *Report on the World Social Situation*. New York: United Nations.

Verweij, Johan, Peter Ester, and Rein Natua. 1997. "Secularization as an Economic and Cultural Phenomenon: A Cross-National Analysis." *Journal for the Scientific Study of Religion* 36, no. 2: 309–24.

Wilson, David Sloan. 2002. *Darwin's Cathedral: Evolution, Religion, and the Nature of Society*. Chicago: University of Chicago Press.

Yang, Fenggang. 2004. "Between Secularist Ideology and Desecularizing Reality: The Birth and Growth of Religious Research in Communist China." *Sociology of Religion* 65, no. 20: 101–19.

Yelensky, Victor. 2002. "Religion, Church, and State in the Post-Communist Era: The Case of Ukraine." *Brigham Young University Law Review* 2: 453–88.

Yuchtman-Ya'ar, Ephraim. 2003. "Value Priorities in Israeli Society: An Examination of Inglehart's Theory of Modernization and Cultural Variation." In Ronald Inglehart (ed.), *Human Values and Social Change*. Boston: Brill, pp. 117–37.

Zuckerman, Phil. 2003. *Invitation to the Sociology of Religion*. New York: Routledge.

Zuckerman, Phil. 2004. "Secularization: Europe – Yes, United States – No." *Skeptical Inquirer* 28, no. 2: 49–52.

II. The Case against Theism

4   Theistic Critiques of Atheism

INTRODUCTION

The last half-century has witnessed a veritable revolution in Anglo-American philosophy. In a recent retrospective, the eminent Princeton philosopher Paul Benacerraf recalls what it was like doing philosophy at Princeton during the 1950s and '60s. The overwhelmingly dominant mode of thinking was scientific naturalism. Metaphysics had been vanquished, expelled from philosophy like an unclean leper. Any problem that could not be addressed by science was simply dismissed as a pseudo-problem. Verificationism reigned triumphantly over the emerging science of philosophy. "This new enlightenment would put the old metaphysical views and attitudes to rest and replace them with the new mode of doing philosophy."[1]

The collapse of verificationism was undoubtedly the most important philosophical event of the twentieth century. Its demise meant a resurgence of metaphysics, along with other traditional problems of philosophy that had been suppressed. Accompanying this resurgence has come something new and altogether unanticipated: a renaissance in Christian philosophy.

The face of Anglo-American philosophy has been transformed as a result. Theism is on the rise; atheism is on the decline.[2] Atheism, though perhaps still the dominant viewpoint at the American university, is a philosophy in retreat. In a recent article in the secularist journal *Philo* Quentin Smith laments what he calls "the desecularization of academia that evolved in philosophy departments since the late 1960s." He complains,

Naturalists passively watched as realist versions of theism...began to sweep through the philosophical community, until today perhaps one-quarter or one-third of philosophy professors are theists, with most being orthodox Christians.... [I]n philosophy, it became, almost overnight, "academically respectable" to argue for theism, making philosophy a favored field of entry for the most intelligent and talented theists entering academia today.[3]

Smith concludes, "God is not 'dead' in academia; he returned to life in the late 1960s and is now alive and well in his last academic stronghold, philosophy departments."

As vanguards of a new philosophical paradigm, theistic philosophers have freely issued various critiques of atheism. In so short a space as this chapter it is impossible to do little more than sketch a few of them. These critiques could be grouped under two basic heads: (1) There are no cogent arguments for atheism, and (2) There are cogent arguments for theism.

NO COGENT ARGUMENTS FOR ATHEISM

Presumption of Atheism

At face value, the so-called presumption of atheism is the claim that in the absence of evidence for God, we should presume that God does not exist. So understood, such an alleged presumption seems to conflate atheism with agnosticism. When one looks more closely at how protagonists of the presumption of atheism use the term "atheist," however, one discovers that they are sometimes redefining the word to indicate merely the absence of belief in God. Such a redefinition trivializes the claim of the presumption of atheism, for on this definition atheism ceases to be a view, and even infants count as atheists. One would still require justification in order to know that God does not exist.

Other advocates of the presumption of atheism use the word in the standard way but insist that it is precisely the absence of evidence for theism that justifies their claim that God does not exist. The problem with such a position is captured neatly by the aphorism, beloved of forensic scientists, that "absence of evidence is not evidence of absence." The absence of evidence is evidence of absence only in cases in which, were the postulated entity to exist, we should expect to have more evidence of its existence than we do. With respect to God's existence, it is incumbent on the atheist to prove that if God existed, he would provide more evidence of his existence than what we have. This is an enormously heavy burden of proof for the atheist to bear, for two reasons: (1) On at least Christian theism the primary way in which we come to know God is not through evidence but through the inner work of his Holy Spirit, which is effectual in bringing persons into relation with God wholly apart from evidence.[4] (2) On Christian theism God has provided the stupendous miracles of the creation of the universe from nothing and the resurrection of Jesus from the dead, for which events there is good scientific and historical evidence – not to mention all the other arguments of natural theology.[5] In this light, the presumption of atheism is presumptuous, indeed!

The contemporary debate has therefore moved beyond the facile presumption of atheism to the so-called hiddenness of God – in effect, a discussion of the probability or expectation that God, if he existed, would leave more evidence of his existence than what we have. Unsatisfied with the evidence we have, some atheists have argued that God, if he existed, would have prevented the world's unbelief by making his existence starkly apparent. But why should God want to do such a thing? On the Christian view it is actually a matter of relative indifference to God whether people believe that he exists or not. For what God is interested in is building a love relationship with us, not just getting us to believe that he exists. There is no reason at all to think that if God were to make his existence more manifest, more people would come into a saving relationship with him. In fact, we have no way of knowing that in a world of free persons in which God's existence is as obvious as the nose on one's face that more people would come to love him and know his salvation than in the actual world. But then the claim that if God existed, he would make his existence more evident, has little or no warrant. Worse, if God is endowed with middle knowledge, so that he knows how any free person would act under any circumstances in which God might place him, then God can have so providentially ordered the world as to provide just those evidences and gifts of the Holy Spirit which he knew would be adequate for bringing those with an open heart and mind to saving faith. Thus, the evidence is as adequate as needs be.

(In)coherence of Theism

During the previous generation the concept of God was often regarded as fertile ground for antitheistic arguments. The difficulty with theism, it was said, was not merely that there are no good arguments for the existence of God, but, more fundamentally, that the notion of God is incoherent.

This antitheistic critique has evoked a prodigious literature devoted to the philosophical analysis of the concept of God. Two controls have tended to guide this inquiry into the divine nature: scripture and perfect being theology. For thinkers in the Judeo-Christian tradition, the Anselmian conception of God as the greatest conceivable being or most perfect being has guided philosophical speculation on the raw data of scripture, so that God's biblical attributes are to be conceived in ways that would serve to exalt God's greatness. Since the concept of God is underdetermined by the biblical data and since what constitutes a "great-making" property is to some degree debatable, philosophers working within the Judeo-Christian tradition enjoy considerable latitude in formulating a philosophically coherent and biblically faithful doctrine of God.

Theists thus find that antitheistic critiques of certain conceptions of God can actually be quite helpful in formulating a more adequate conception. For example, most Christian philosophers today deny that God is simple or impassible or immutable in any unrestricted sense, even though medieval theologians affirmed such divine attributes, since these attributes are not ascribed to God in the Bible and are not clearly great-making.

A coherent doctrine of God's essential attributes can be formulated. Take omnipotence, for example. This attribute stubbornly resisted adequate formulation until Flint and Freddoso's article "Maximal Power" (1983). On their analysis a person S is omnipotent at a time t iff S can at t actualize any state of affairs that is not described by counterfactuals about the free acts of others and that is broadly logically possible for someone to actualize, given the same hard past at t and the same true counterfactuals about free acts of others. Such an analysis successfully sets the parameters of God's omnipotence without imposing any nonlogical limit on His power.

Or consider omniscience. On the standard account of omniscience, any person S is omniscient iff S knows every true proposition and believes no false proposition. On this account God's cognitive excellence is defined in terms of his propositional knowledge. Some persons have charged that omniscience so defined is an inherently paradoxical notion, like the set of all truths. But the standard definition does not commit us to any sort of totality of all truths but merely to universal quantification with respect to truths: God knows every truth. Moreover, adequate definitions of omniscience are possible that make no mention of propositions at all. Charles Taliaferro proposes, for example, that omniscience be understood in terms of maximal cognitive power; to wit, a person S is omniscient iff it is metaphysically impossible for there to be a being with greater cognitive power than S and this power is fully exercised.

Thus, far from undermining theism, the antitheistic critiques of theism's coherence have served mainly to refine and strengthen theistic belief.

Problem of Evil

Traditionally, atheists have presented the so-called problem of evil as an internal problem for theism. That is, atheists have claimed that the statements

A. An omnipotent, omnibenevolent God exists.

and

B. The quantity and kinds of suffering in the world exist.

are either logically inconsistent or improbable with respect to each other. As a result of the work of Christian philosophers such as Alvin Plantinga, it is today widely recognized that the internal problem of evil is a failure as an argument for atheism. No one has ever been able to show that (A) and (B) are either logically incompatible with each other or improbable with respect to each other.

Having abandoned the internal problem, atheists have recently taken to framing evil as an external problem, often called the evidential problem of evil. If we call suffering that is not necessary to achieve some adequately compensating good "gratuitous evil," the argument can be simply summarized:

1. If God exists, gratuitous evil does not exist.
2. Gratuitous evil exists.
3. Therefore, God does not exist.

What makes this an external problem is that the theist is not committed by his world-view to the truth of (2). The atheist claims that the apparently pointless and unnecessary suffering in the world constitutes *evidence* against God's existence.

Now the most controversial premise in this argument is (2). Everybody admits that the world is filled with *apparently* gratuitous suffering. But there are at least three reasons why the inference from apparently gratuitous evil to genuinely gratuitous evil is tenuous.

1. *We are not in a good position to assess with confidence the probability that God lacks morally sufficient reasons for permitting the suffering in the world.* Whether God's existence is improbable relative to the evil in the world depends on how probable it is that God has morally sufficient reasons for permitting the evil that occurs. What makes the probability here so difficult to assess is that we are not in a good epistemic position to make these kinds of probability judgements with any sort of confidence. Only an omniscient mind could grasp the complexities of providentially directing a world of free creatures toward one's pre-visioned goals. One has only to think of the innumerable, incalculable contingencies involved in arriving at a single historical event, say, the enactment of the lend-lease policy by the American Congress prior to the U.S. entry into World War II. We have no idea of the natural and moral evils that might be involved in order for God to arrange the circumstances and free agents in them requisite to such an event.

Ironically, in other contexts atheists recognize these cognitive limitations. One of the most damaging objections to utilitarian ethical theory, for example, is that it is quite simply impossible for us to estimate which action that we might perform will ultimately lead to the greatest amount of happiness or pleasure in the world. Because of our cognitive limitations, actions that appear disastrous in the short term may redound to the greatest good, while some short-term boon may issue in untold misery. Once we contemplate God's providence over the whole of history, then it becomes evident how hopeless it is for limited observers to speculate on the probability that some evil we see is ultimately gratuitous.

2: *Christian theism entails doctrines that increase the probability of the coexistence of God and evil.* The atheist maintains that if God exists, then it is improbable that the world would contain the evils it does. The Christian can try to show that if God exists and certain doctrines are true, then it is not so surprising that evil exists. Four Christian doctrines come to mind:

(i) *The chief purpose of life is not happiness, but the knowledge of God.* One reason that the problem of evil seems so intractable is that people tend naturally to assume that if God exists, then his purpose for human life is happiness in this world. God's role is to provide a comfortable environment for his human pets. But on the Christian view, this is false. We are not God's pets, and the goal of human life is not happiness per se, but the knowledge of God – which in the end will bring true and everlasting human fulfillment. Many evils occur in life that may be utterly pointless with respect to producing human happiness; but they may not be pointless with respect to producing a deeper, saving knowledge of God. To carry his argument, the atheist must show that it is feasible for God to create a world in which the same amount of the knowledge of God is achieved, but with less evil – which is sheer speculation.

(ii) *Mankind has been accorded significant moral freedom to rebel against God and his purpose.* Rather than submit to and worship God, people have freely rebelled against God and go their own way and so find themselves alienated from God, morally guilty before him, and groping in spiritual darkness, pursuing false gods of their own making. The horrendous moral evils in the world are testimony to man's depravity in this state of spiritual alienation from God.

(iii) *God's purpose spills over into eternal life.* In the Christian view God will give those who have trusted Him for salvation an eternal life of unspeakable joy. Given the prospect of eternal life, we should not expect to see in this life God's compensation for every evil we experience. Some may be justified only in light of eternity.

(iv) *The knowledge of God is an incommensurable good.* To know God, the locus of infinite goodness and love, is an incomparable good, the fulfillment of human existence. The sufferings of this life cannot even be compared with it. Thus, the person who knows God, no matter what he or she suffers, no matter how awful his or her pain, can still truly say, "God is good to me!" simply in virtue of the fact that he or she knows God.

These doctrines increase the probability of the coexistence of God and the evils in the world.

3. *There is better warrant for believing that God exists than that the evil in the world is really gratuitous.* It has been said that one man's *modus ponens* is another man's *modus tollens.* Thus, one may argue:

1. If God exists, gratuitous evil does not exist.
2*. God exists.
3*. Therefore, gratuitous evil does not exist.

Thus, if God exists, then the evil in the world is not really gratuitous.

So the issue comes down to which is true: (2) or (2*)? To prove that God does not exist, atheists would have to show that (2) is significantly more probable than (2*). As Howard-Snyder points out, an argument from evil is a problem only for the person "who finds all its premises and inferences compelling and who has lousy grounds for believing theism."[6] But if one has better reasons for believing that God exists, then evil "is not a problem." The Christian theist might maintain that when we take into account the full scope of the evidence, then the existence of God becomes quite probable.

COGENT ARGUMENTS FOR THEISM

The renaissance of Christian philosophy over the last half-century has been accompanied by a new appreciation of the traditional arguments for the existence of God. Space permits mention of only four.

Contingency Argument

A simple statement of the argument might run:

1. Anything that exists has an explanation of its existence (either in the necessity of its own nature or in an external cause).
2. If the universe has an explanation of its existence, that explanation is God.
3. The universe exists.
4. Therefore the explanation of the existence of the universe is God.

Premise (1) is a modest version of the principle of sufficient reason. It circumvents the typical atheist objections to strong versions of that principle. For (1) is compatible with there being brute *facts* about the world. What it precludes is that there could exist things that just exist inexplicably. This principle seems quite plausible, at least more so than its contradictory. One thinks of Richard Taylor's illustration of finding a translucent ball while walking in the woods. One would find the claim quite bizarre that the ball just exists inexplicably; and increasing the size of the ball, even until it becomes coextensive with the cosmos, would do nothing to obviate the need for an explanation of its existence.

Premise (2) is, in effect, the contrapositive of the typical atheist retort that on the atheistic world-view the universe simply exists as a brute contingent thing. Moreover, (2) seems quite plausible in its own right. For if the universe includes all of physical reality, then the cause of the universe must (at least causally prior to the universe's existence) transcend space and time and therefore cannot be temporal or material. But there are only two kinds of things that could fall under such a description: either an abstract object or a mind. But abstract objects do not stand in causal relations. Therefore it follows that the explanation of the existence of the universe is an external, transcendent, personal cause – which is one meaning of "God."

Finally, (3) states the obvious. It follows that God exists.

The atheist might retort that while the universe has an explanation of its existence, that explanation lies in the necessity of its own nature. This retort is, however, so counter to our modal intuitions that atheists have not been eager to embrace it. Moreover, we have good reason to think that the universe does not exist by a necessity of its own nature (see below).

Cosmological Argument

A simple version of this argument is:

1. Whatever begins to exist has a cause.
2. The universe began to exist.
3. Therefore, the universe has a cause.

Conceptual analysis of what it means to be a cause of the universe then helps to establish some of the theologically significant properties of this being.

Premise (1) seems obviously true – at the least, more so than its negation. It is rooted in the metaphysical intuition that something cannot come into being from nothing. If things could really come into being uncaused out of nothing, then it becomes inexplicable why just anything and everything do not come into existence uncaused from nothing. Moreover, the conviction that an origin of the universe requires a causal explanation seems quite reasonable, for on the atheistic view, if the universe began at the Big Bang, there was not even the *potentiality* of the universe's existence prior to the Big Bang, since nothing is prior to the Big Bang. But then how could the universe become actual if there was not even the potentiality of its existence? Finally, the first premise is constantly confirmed in our experience. Atheists who are scientific naturalists thus have the strongest of motivations to accept it.

Premise (2) is supported by both deductive, philosophical arguments and inductive, scientific arguments. Classical proponents of the argument contended that an infinite temporal regress of events cannot exist, since the existence of an actually infinite, as opposed to merely potentially infinite, number of things leads to intolerable absurdities. The best way to support this claim is still by way of thought experiments, like the famous Hilbert's Hotel,[7] which illustrate the various absurdities that would result if an actual infinite were to be instantiated in the real world. It is usually alleged that this sort of argument has been invalidated by Georg Cantor's work on the actual infinite. But Cantorian set theory may be taken to be simply a universe of discourse based on certain adopted axioms and conventions. The argument's defender may hold that while the actual infinite may be a fruitful and consistent concept within the postulated universe of discourse, it cannot be transposed into the spatio-temporal world, for this would involve counterintuitive absurdities. He is at liberty to reject Platonistic views of mathematical objects in favor of non-Platonist views such as fictionalism or divine conceptualism combined with the simplicity of God's cognition.

A second classical argument for (2) is that the temporal series of past events cannot be an actual infinite because a collection formed by successive addition cannot be actually infinite. Sometimes the problem was described as the impossibility of traversing the infinite. In order for us to have "arrived" at today, temporal existence has, so to speak, traversed an infinite number of prior events. But before the present event could arrive, the event immediately prior to it would have to arrive; and before that event could arrive, the event immediately prior to it would have to arrive; and so on ad infinitum. No event could ever arrive, since before it could elapse there will always be one more event that will had to have happened first. Thus, if the series of past events were beginningless, the present event could not have arrived, which is absurd.

It is frequently objected that this sort of argument illicitly presupposes an infinitely distant starting point in the past and then pronounces it impossible to travel from that point to today, whereas in fact from any given point in the past, there is only a finite distance to the present, which is easily traversed. But proponents of the argument have not in fact assumed that there was an infinitely distant starting point in the past. To traverse a distance is to cross every proper part of it. Thus, such traversal does not entail that the distance traversed has a beginning or ending point. To say that the infinite past could have been formed by successive addition is like saying that someone has just succeeded in writing down all the negative numbers, ending at -1. Moreover, to think that because every *finite* segment of the series can be formed by successive addition, the whole *infinite* series can as well, commits the fallacy of composition.

A third argument for (2) is an inductive argument based not on evidence for the expansion of the universe. The big bang model describes not the expansion of the material content of the universe into a preexisting, empty space, but rather the expansion of space itself. As one extrapolates back in time, space-time curvature becomes progressively greater until one arrives at a singularity, at which space-time curvature becomes infinite. It therefore constitutes an edge or boundary to space-time itself.

Twentieth-century cosmology has witnessed a long series of failed attempts to craft plausible models of the expanding universe that avert the absolute beginning predicted by the standard model. While such theories are possible, it has been the overwhelming verdict of the scientific community than none of them is more probable than the big bang theory.[8] There is no mathematically consistent model that has been so successful in its predictions or as corroborated by the evidence as the traditional big bang theory. For example, some theories, such as the oscillating universe or the chaotic inflationary universe, do have a potentially infinite future but turn out to have only a finite past. Vacuum fluctuation universe theories cannot explain why, if the vacuum was eternal, we do not observe an infinitely old universe. The no-boundary universe proposal of Hartle and Hawking, if interpreted realistically, still involves an absolute origin of the universe even if the universe does not begin in a singularity, as it does in the standard big bang theory. Recently proposed ekpyrotic cyclic universe scenarios based on string theory or M-theory have also been shown not only to be riddled with problems but to imply the very origin of the universe that its proponents sought to avoid. There is no doubt that one who asserts the truth of (2) rests comfortably within the scientific mainstream.

A fourth argument for (2) is also an inductive argument, appealing to thermodynamic properties of the universe. According to the second law of thermodynamics, processes taking place in a closed system tend toward states of higher entropy, as their energy is used up. Already in the nineteenth century scientists realized that the application of the law to the universe as a whole implied a grim eschatological conclusion: given sufficient time, the universe would eventually come to a state of equilibrium and suffer heat death. But this projection raised an even deeper question: if, given sufficient time, the universe will suffer heat death, then why, if it has existed forever, is it not now in a state of heat death?

The advent of relativity theory altered the shape of the eschatological scenario but did not materially affect this fundamental question. Astrophysical evidence indicates overwhelmingly that the universe will expand forever. As it does, it will become increasingly cold, dark, dilute, and dead. Eventually, the entire mass of the universe will be nothing but a cold, thin gas of elementary particles and radiation, growing ever more dilute as it expands into the infinite darkness, a universe in ruins.

But if in a finite amount of time the universe *will* achieve a cold, dark, dilute, and lifeless state, then why, if it has existed for *infinite time*, is it not *now* in a such a state? If one is to avoid the conclusion that the universe has not in fact existed forever, then one must find some scientifically plausible way to overturn the findings of physical cosmology so as to permit the universe to return to its youthful condition. But no realistic and plausible scenario is forthcoming.[9] Most cosmologists agree with physicist Paul Davies that whether we like it or not, we seemed forced to conclude that the universe's low entropy condition was simply "put in" as an initial condition at the moment of creation.[10]

We thus have good philosophical and scientific grounds for affirming (2). It is noteworthy that this premise is a religiously neutral statement that can be found in any textbook on astrophysical cosmology, so that facile accusations of "God-of-the-gaps" theology find no purchase. Moreover, since a being that exists by a necessity of its own nature must exist either timelessly or sempiternally, it follows that the universe cannot be metaphysically necessary, which fact closes the final loophole in the contingency argument above.

It follows logically that the universe has a cause. Conceptual analysis of which properties must be possessed by such an ultramundane cause enables us to recover a striking number of the traditional divine attributes, revealing that if the universe has a cause, then an uncaused, personal creator of the universe exists, who sans the universe is beginningless, changeless, immaterial, timeless, spaceless, and enormously powerful.

Teleological Argument

We may formulate a design argument as follows:

1. The fine-tuning of the universe is due to physical necessity, to chance, or to design.
2. It is not due to physical necessity or chance.
3. Therefore, it is due to design.

The physical laws of nature, when given mathematical expression, contain various constants, such as the gravitational constant, whose values are independent of the laws themselves; moreover, there are certain arbitrary quantities that are simply put in as boundary conditions on which the laws operate, for example, the initial low entropy condition of the universe. By "fine-tuning" one means that the actual values assumed by the constants and quantities in question are such that small deviations from those values would render the universe life-prohibiting or, alternatively, that the range of life-permitting values is exquisitely narrow in comparison with the range of assumable values.

Laypeople might think that if the constants and quantities had assumed different values, then other forms of life might well have evolved. But this is not the case. By "life" scientists mean that property of organisms to take in food, extract energy from it, grow, adapt to their environment, and reproduce. The point is that in order for the universe to permit life so defined, whatever form organisms might take, the constants and quantities have to be incomprehensibly fine-tuned. In the absence of fine-tuning, not even matter or chemistry would exist, not to speak of planets where life might evolve.

It has been objected that in universes governed by different laws of nature, such deleterious consequences might not result from varying the values of the constants and quantities. The teleologist need not deny the possibility, for such universes are irrelevant to his or her argument. All he or she needs to show is that among possible universes governed by the same laws (but having different values of the constants and quantities) as the actual universe, life-permitting universes are extraordinarily improbable.

Now (1) states the three alternatives in the pool of live options for explaining cosmic fine-tuning.

The alternative of physical necessity seems extraordinarily implausible. If the primordial matter and antimatter had been differently proportioned, if the universe had expanded just a little more slowly, if the entropy of the universe were marginally greater, any of these adjustments and more would have prevented a life-permitting universe, yet all seem perfectly possible physically. The person who maintains that the universe must be life-permitting is taking a radical line, for which there is no evidence at all.

Sometimes physicists do speak of a yet-to-be discovered theory of everything (TOE), but such nomenclature is, like so many of the colorful names given to scientific theories, quite misleading. A TOE actually has the limited goal of providing a unified theory of the four fundamental forces of nature, but it will not even attempt to explain literally everything. For example, in the most promising candidate for a TOE to date, super-string theory or M-theory, the physical universe must be 11-dimensional, but why the universe should possess just that number of dimensions is not addressed by the theory. M-theory simply substitutes geometrical fine-tuning for fine-tuning of forces.

Furthermore, it seems likely that any attempt to reduce fine-tuning significantly will itself turn out to involve fine-tuning. This has certainly been the pattern in the past. In light of the specificity and number of instances of fine-tuning, it is unlikely to disappear with the further advance of physical theory.

What, then, of the alternative of chance? Teleologists seek to eliminate this hypothesis either by appealing to the specified complexity of cosmic fine-tuning (a statistical approach to design inference) or by arguing that the fine-tuning is significantly more probable on design (theism) than on the chance hypothesis (atheism) (a Bayesian approach). Common to both approaches is the claim that the universe's being life-permitting is highly improbable.

To save the hypothesis of chance, defenders of that alternative have increasingly recurred to the many worlds hypothesis (MWH), according to which a world ensemble of concrete universes exists, thereby multiplying one's probabilistic resources. To guarantee that by chance alone a universe such as ours will appear somewhere in the ensemble, an actually infinite number of such universes is usually postulated. But that is not enough; one must also stipulate that these worlds are randomly ordered with respect to the values of their constants and quantities, lest they be of insufficient variety to include a life-permitting universe.

Is MWH as good an explanation as the design hypothesis? It seems doubtful.

(i) *The design hypothesis is simpler*. According to Occam's razor, we should not multiply causes beyond what is necessary to explain the effect. But it is simpler to postulate one cosmic designer than to postulate the infinitely bloated and contrived ontology of MWH. Only if the MWH theorist could show that there exists a single, comparably simple mechanism for generating a world ensemble of randomly varied universes would he or she be able to elude this difficulty.

(ii) *There is no known way of generating a world ensemble*. Some proposals, such as Lee Smolin's cosmic evolutionary scenario, actually served to weed out life-permitting universes, while others, such as Andre Linde's chaotic inflationary scenario, turned out to require fine-tuning themselves.

(iii) *There is no evidence for the existence of a world ensemble apart from the fine-tuning itself*. But the fine-tuning is equally evidence for a cosmic designer. Indeed, the hypothesis of a cosmic designer is again the better explanation because we have independent evidence of the existence of such a being in the other theistic arguments.

(iv) *MWH faces a severe challenge from evolutionary biology.* According to the prevailing theory of biological evolution, intelligent life such as ourselves, if it evolves at all, will do so as late in the lifetime of its star as possible. Given the complexity of the human organism, it is overwhelmingly more probable that human beings will evolve late in the lifetime of the sun rather than early.[11] Hence, if our universe is but one member of a world ensemble, then it is overwhelmingly more probable that we should be observing a very old sun rather than a relatively young one. In fact, on MWH it is far more probable that all our astronomical, geological, and biological estimates of age are wrong and that the sun and the Earth's appearance of youth is a massive illusion.

It therefore seems that the fine-tuning of the universe is plausibly due neither to physical necessity nor to chance. Unless the design hypothesis can be shown to be even more implausible that its competitors, it follows that the fine-tuning is due to design.

Moral Argument

One such argument may be formulated as follows:

1. If God does not exist, objective moral values and duties do not exist.
2. Objective moral values and duties do exist.
3. Therefore, God exists.

Consider (1). To speak of objective moral values and duties is to say that moral distinctions between what is good or bad and right or wrong hold independently of whether any human being holds to such distinctions. Many theists and atheists alike agree that if God does not exist, then moral values and duties are not objective in this sense. For if God does not exist, what is the the basis for the value of human beings? In the absence of God it is difficult to see any reason to think that human beings are special. Moreover, why think that we have any moral obligations to do anything? As a result of socio-biological pressures, there has evolved among *Homo sapiens* a sort of "herd morality" that functions well in the perpetuation of our species in the struggle for survival. But there does not seem to be anything about *Homo sapiens* that makes this morality objectively binding. As the humanist philosopher Paul Kurtz puts it, "The central question about moral and ethical principles concerns this ontological foundation. If they are neither derived from God nor anchored in some transcendent ground, are they purely ephemeral?"[12]

Some philosophers, equally averse to transcendently existing moral values as to theism, try to maintain the existence of objective moral principles or supervenient moral properties in the context of a naturalistic world-view. But the advocates of such theories are typically at a loss to justify their starting point. Crudely put, on the atheistic view humans are just animals; and animals are not moral agents.

If our approach to meta-ethical theory is to be serious metaphysics rather than just a "shopping list" approach, whereby one simply helps oneself to the supervenient moral properties or principles needed to do the job, then some sort of explanation is required for why moral properties supervene on certain natural states or why such principles are true. Some philosophers seem to suppose that moral truths, being necessarily true, cannot have an explanation of their truth. But the crucial presupposition that necessary truths cannot stand in relations of explanatory priority to one another seems plainly false. For example, on a nonfictionalist account $2 + 3 = 5$ is necessarily true because the Peano axioms for standard arithmetic are necessarily true. Or again, *No event precedes itself* is necessarily true because *Temporal becoming is an essential and objective feature of time* is necessarily true. It would be utterly implausible to suggest that the relation of explanatory priority obtaining between the relevant propositions is symmetrical.

We therefore need to ask whether moral values and duties can be plausibly anchored in some transcendent, nontheistic ground. Let us call this view atheistic moral realism. Atheistic moral realists affirm that objective moral values and duties do exist but are not grounded in God. Indeed, moral values have no further foundation. They just exist.

It is difficult, however, even to comprehend this view. What does it mean to say, for example, that the moral value *justice* just exists? It is hard to know what to make of this. It is clear what is meant when it is said that a person is just; but it is bewildering when it is said that in the absence of any people, *justice* itself exists.

Second, the nature of moral obligation seems incompatible with atheistic moral realism. Suppose that values like *mercy, justice, forbearance,* and the like just exist. How does that result in any moral obligations for me? Why would I have a moral duty, say, to be merciful? Who or what lays such an obligation on me? On this view moral vices such as *greed, hatred,* and *selfishness* also presumably exist as abstract objects, too. Why am I obligated to align my life with one set of these abstractly existing objects rather than any other? In contrast with the atheist, the theist can make sense of moral obligation because God's commands can be viewed as constitutive of our moral duties.

Third, it is fantastically improbable that just those sorts of creatures would emerge from the blind evolutionary process who correspond to the abstractly existing realm of moral values. This seems to be an utterly incredible coincidence when one thinks about it. It is almost as though the moral realm *knew* that we were coming. It is far more plausible to regard both the natural realm and the moral realm as under the hegemony of a divine creator and lawgiver than to think that these two entirely independent orders of reality just happened to mesh.

Traditional arguments for God's existence such as the above, not to mention creative new arguments, are alive and well on the contemporary scene in Anglo-American philosophy. Together with the failure of antitheistic arguments, they help to explain the renaissance of interest in theism.

NOTES

1. "What Mathematical Truth Could Not Be," in Adam Morton and Stephen Stich (eds.), *Benacerraf and His Critics* (Oxford: Blackwell, 1996), p. 18.
2. The change has not gone unnoticed even in popular culture. In 1980 *Time* marveled, "In a quiet revolution in thought and argument that hardly anybody could have foreseen only two decades ago, God is making a comeback. Most intriguingly, this is happening not among theologians or ordinary believers, but in the crisp intellectual circles of academic philosophers, where the consensus had long banished the Almighty from fruitful discourse" ("Modernizing the Case for God," *Time*, April 7, 1980, pp. 65–66). The article cites the late Roderick Chisholm to the effect that the reason atheism was so influential a generation ago is that the brightest philosophers were atheists; but today, in his opinion, many of the brightest philosophers are theists, using a tough-minded intellectualism in defense of their belief.
3. "The Metaphilosophy of Naturalism," *Philo* 4, no. 2 (2001): 196–97. A sign of the times: *Philo* itself, unable to succeed as a secular organ, has now become a journal for general philosophy of religion.
4. One of the most significant developments in contemporary religious epistemology has been so-called reformed epistemology, spearheaded and developed by Alvin Plantinga, which directly assaults the evidentialist construal of rationality. With respect to the belief that God exists, Plantinga holds that God has so constituted us that we naturally form this belief under certain circumstances; since the belief is thus formed by properly functioning cognitive faculties in an appropriate environment, it is warranted for us, and, insofar as our faculties are not disrupted by the noetic effects of sin, we shall believe this proposition deeply and firmly, so that we can be said, in virtue of the great warrant accruing to this belief for us, to know that God exists.
5. On Jesus' resurrection, see N. T. Wright, *The Resurrection of the Son of God* (Minneapolis: Fortress Press, 2003).
6. "Introduction," in Daniel Howard-Snyder (ed.), *The Evidential Argument from Evil* (Bloomington: Indiana University Press, 1996), p. xi.
7. George Gamow, *One, Two, Three, Infinity* (London: Macmillan, 1946), p. 17.
8. See my "Naturalism and Cosmology," in A. Corradini et al. (eds.), *Analytic Philosophy without Naturalism* (London: Routledge, 2005).

9. See my "Time, Eternity, and Eschatology," in J. Walls (eds.), *Oxford Handbook on Eschatology* (Oxford: University Press, forthcoming).

10. *The Physics of Time Asymmetry* (London: Surrey University Press, 1974), p. 104.

11. In fact, Barrow and Tipler list ten steps in the evolution of *Homo sapiens each of which* is so improbable that before it would occur the sun would have ceased to be a main sequence star and incinerated the Earth! See John Barrow and Frank Tipler, *The Anthropic Cosmological Principle* (Oxford: Clarendon, 1986), pp. 561–65.

12. *Forbidden Fruit* (Buffalo: Prometheus Books, 1988), p. 65.

5   The Failure of Classical Theistic Arguments

The ontological, cosmological, and teleological arguments are generally taken to be the major classical theistic arguments; however, a case can be made for also including the argument from religious experience, since within each of the great extant theistic religions there is a mystical tradition for making claims about God's existence and nature on the basis of apparent direct nonsensory perceptions of God. Each of these four arguments is discussed in turn.

THE ONTOLOGICAL ARGUMENT

There are many different versions of this argument. What they have in common is an attempt to deduce God's existence from a mere analysis of the concept of God. Furthermore, they are a priori arguments, because all of their premises are supposed to be knowable independently of sense experience. They are the darlings of theists who are enamored of the mathematical style of reasoning. In response to critics, such as Hume and the logical positivists, who deny that existence can ever be deduced from an analysis of concepts, they could say that this is just what happens in mathematics when, for example, the existence of a number meeting certain conditions is deduced from axioms, definitions, and postulates, all of which are knowable a priori. And given that God resembles numbers in respect to not being in space or time, the possibility of deducing God's existence a priori must not be dismissed out of hand.

Seeds of the ontological argument are to be found in Plato and St. Augustine, but it was the medieval scholastics who first gave explicit formulations of it. The following version is found in Duns Scotus and in recent times in James Ross.

1. It is impossible that anything would prevent God from existing (a conceptual truth)
2. For any individual that either exists or fails to exist, it is possible that there is an explanation for its existing or failing to exist (a weak version of the principle of sufficient reason)

3. God does not exist (assumption for indirect proof)
4. It is possible that there is an explanation for God's not existing (from 2 and 3)
5. It is not possible that there is an explanation for God's not existing (from 1)
6. It is possible that there is an explanation for God's not existing, and it is not possible that there is an explanation for God's not existing (from 5 and 6 by conjunction)
7. It is not possible that God does not exist (from 3–6 by indirect proof)

From the proposition that God does not exist, an explicit contradiction is deduced, thereby showing that it is impossible that God does not exist.

An attractive feature of this argument is that it manages to make do in premise 2 with a very weak version of the principle of sufficient reason that requires that for every true existential proposition or its denial it is at least possible that there is an explanation, not that there actually is one. But in spite of this attractive feature, the argument comes up short. The fatal non sequitur occurs in the deduction of step 5 from premise 1. This deduction is valid only if the only possible explanation for the nonexistence of God is a causal one. To begin with, it should be noted that the explanation for God's existence is not a causal one, being based on an ontological argument, so why should the explanation of his existence have to be a causal one? The explanation for God's nonexistence could be based on some fact that logically, not causally, precludes his existence, such as that there are evils that are not justified and therefore cannot coexist with God.

Saint Anselm is the locus classicus for ontological arguments. He begins with a conception of God as a being that which a greater cannot be conceived. Such a being, which shall be called a *maximally excellent being*, essentially has every perfection, among which are omnipotence, omniscience, omnibenevolence, and sovereignty. The next step in his argument is to get his biblical fool opponent, the one who denied in his heart that God exists, to grant that it is at least possible that there exists some being that instantiates this concept. From this admission of possibility, he deduces that it is necessary that the concept is instantiated by the use of an indirect proof, in which a contradiction is deduced from the assumption that it is not instantiated – that the being than which none greater can be conceived does not objectively exist. On the assumption that existence is a great-making property – that, all things being equal, a being is greater in a circumstance in which it exists than it is in one in which it does not – it follows that if that than which none greater can be conceived does not in fact exist, then it could be conceived to be greater than it is. And that's a contradiction, thereby showing that the assumption is not just false but necessarily false, and thus it is necessarily true that God exists.

But is it really contradictory to say that that than which none greater can be conceived could be conceived to be greater than it is? Greater than it is in which world? As David Lewis cogently argued, this allegedly contradictory proposition suffers from incompleteness since there is an implicit free variable after the final "greater than it is." Only on some values for this variable does a contradiction result. To see why this is so, a perspicuous rendering must be given of the possibility premise. Lewis performs a great service to our understanding of Anselm's argument by giving a clear analysis of it in terms of the semantics of possible world. To say that it is possible that there exists a being than which a greater cannot be conceived, that is, a maximally excellent being, means that

1. There is some possible world, w, in which there exists a being, x, such that x has maximal excellence in w.

From 1 it cannot be deduced that w is the actual world. And if w is not, then it is true, *pace* Anselm, that this being, x, than which a greater cannot be conceived, could be greater than it is, provided that the free variable that follows "greater than it is" is replaced by "in the actual world," given that existence is a great-making property. Thus, from the possibility that the concept of that than which none greater can be conceived can be instantiated, which is perspicuously formulated by 1, it does not follow that the concept is instantiated by some existent being, a being that exists in the actual world.

Contemporary ontological arguers, such as Hartshorne, Malcolm, and Plantinga, have attempted to find a way around Lewis's objection. The underlying insight of their new version is that the greatness of a being in some possible world depends not just on how goes it with that being in that world but also on how goes it with that being in other possible worlds, the logical space that surrounds the individual. The requirement that a maximally excellent being must possess all of its omniperfections essentially takes note of this, since this assures that this being will be at its greatest greatness in every world in which it exists (which, unfortunately, does not entail that it exists in the actual world). The concept of God, accordingly, must get souped up so that a being than which none greater can be conceived be not just maximally excellent (essentially have all of the omniperfections) but also have necessary existence as well, in which a being has necessary existence if and only if it is necessary that it exists. Let us call a being that is both maximally excellent and necessarily existent an *unsurpassably great being.*

The problem is that whereas the fool rightly was willing to grant that it is possible that the concept of a maximally excellent being be instantiated, he would have to be not just a fool but a complete schmuck to grant that it is possible that the concept of an unsurpassably great being be instantiated. For in granting that it is possible that there is an unsurpassably great being, he is granting that it is possible that it is necessary that there is a maximally excellent being. But if his consent to the latter is to be an informed one, he must know that the nested modal operator, "It is possibly that it is necessary," is to be subject to the axiom of the S5 system of modal logic, according to which whatever is possibly necessary is necessary. This has the consequence that a proposition's modal status is world-invariant. Since it is possible that the proposition that it is necessary that there is a maximally excellent being is true, this proposition is true in some possible world. But given that a necessary proposition is true in every possible world, it follow that it is true in the actual world that there is a maximally excellent being. The fool is well within his rights to charge the S5-based ontological argument with begging the question in its possibility premise.

The intelligent S5 arguer, such as Plantinga, would grant that the argument does not succeed as a piece of natural theology, but then would point out that it nevertheless serves the purpose of showing that it is not irrational or epistemically impermissible to believe that God exists; for the argument is valid and has premises, including the possibility one, that are just as likely to be true as not.

If a stalemate of intuitions is to be overcome, the opponent of the argument must give some good argument for why its possibility premise is false. This could be done by finding some concept that intuitively seems to have more likelihood of being instantiatable than does the concept of being unsurpassably great and that is strongly incompatible with it in that if either concept is instantiated in any possible world, the other instantiated in none. The concept could be that of being an unjustified evil, meaning an evil that God does not have a morally exonerating excuse for permitting, that is, an evil that could not coexist with God. But since an unsurpassably great being, if it possibly exists, exists in every possible world, in no possible world is there an unjustified evil. But it certainly seems more likely that it is possible that there be an unjustified evil than that there be an unsurpassably great being. Even some theists seem to grant the possibility of an unjustified evil when they exercise themselves in constructing theodicies that attempt to show that the apparently unjustified evils of the world really have a justification. Thus, by souping up the concept of God in the way the S5 ontological arguer does, the foundation is laid for an ontological disproof of God, conceived of as an unsurpassably great being.

THE COSMOLOGICAL ARGUMENT

A cosmological argument typically has three components: a contingent, value-neutral existential fact, a suitably tailored version of the principle of sufficient reason (PSR) that requires that every fact of this kind have an explanation, and an explanatory argument to show that the only possible explanation for this fact is in terms of the causal efficacy of a necessarily existent God-like being. The first three ways of St. Thomas Aquinas are cosmological arguments but begin with different existential facts. The first way begins with the contingent fact that one object is moved by another, the second that one thing depends for its existence on the causal efficacy of a contemporaneous being, and the third that there exists a contingent being. These are commonplace observational facts that only a complete skeptic about our senses would want to challenge. The explanatory arguments in the first and second ways are based on the impossibility of there being, respectively, an infinite regress of objects simultaneously being moved by other objects or objects depending for their existence on the simultaneous causal efficacy of another being. These regresses, therefore, must terminate with a being that is capable, respectively, of moving another object without itself being moved by another or of causing the existence of something without itself being caused to exist. Thomas then identifies this first mover or cause with God on the basis of our common ways of speaking about God – "and this is what everyone understands by God" – thereby papering over a serious gap problem, since his arguments do not establish that these beings have all of the essential divine attributes.

The intuition underlying Aquinas' rejection of the possibility of an actual infinity of simultaneous movers or causers is far from obvious, especially since, according to most commentators, he did not think it impossible to have an actual past infinite regress of nonsimultaneous causes, as for example an actual infinite regress of past begetters. An attempt will be made to draw out his intuition in a way that gives some plausibility to it. The causal relation in a series of simultaneous causes or movers involves transitivity in that if X simultaneously moves (causes) Y and Y simultaneously moves (causes) Z, then X moves (causes) Z. Nonsimultaneous causation is not transitive, since, even though you were begotten by your parents and they in turn were begotten by their parents, you were not begotten by the latter.

One reason that might be given for the impossibility of an actual infinite regress of simultaneous causes or movers is that if there were such a regress, there would be no member of the regress that could be held to be morally responsible, a fit subject of either praise or blame, for the initial event or object in the regress. But this can't be the right reason, since not all causal explanations are forensic in the sense of giving an individual who is to be praised or blamed for the effect. Maybe Aquinas's underlying intuition can be fleshed out by considering these two examples. In one, a group of boys attempts to get into the movies free by having each boy point to the boy behind him as he enters the theater and when the ticket taker stops the last boy in the group for the tickets, he claims not to know who the other boys are. The last boy has to pay for himself but all the others get in free. Now suppose that the regress of boys pointing behind themselves to another boy is infinite. Plainly, the theater owner would not be happy with this arrangement, since he would never get paid, just as you would never succeed in cashing a check if it were covered by a bank account that in turn was covered by another and so on ad infinitum. A system of credit, like a succession of boys entering a theater, must terminate with some actual cash. A second example involves a train of cars that simultaneously push each other, such that the first car is simultaneously moved by a second, and the second by a third, and so on ad infinitum. If the regress of movers were infinite, there would be no explanation of where the oomph, the energy, the power to move, comes from.

There is an implicit appeal to a version of the PSR to the effect that something cannot come out of nothing. This can be made clearer by considering a circle of causes. Thomas ruled this to be impossible for the same intuitive reason that he proscribed an infinite regress of simultaneous movers or causes. Imagine that you meet someone who looks as you would look in ten years. She claims to be your future self and to have traveled ten years backward in time in order to give you instructions on how to build a time machine. Subsequently, you build one and then travel ten years backward in time so as to inform your past self about how to build a time machine. The intuitive grounds for Thomas's rejection of the possibility of this closed causal loop is that it violates the PSR, for there is no answer to the question of from whence came the knowledge of how to build a time machine. Similarly, there is no answer to the question of from whence came the power to move an object or causally sustain its existence in the case of an infinite regress of simultaneous movers or causers.

The Third Way begins with the unexceptionable contingent existential fact that there now exists at least one contingent being. Can some version of the PSR be employed so as to deduce that there exists a necessary being that causes the existence of this contingent being? A contingent being has the possibility of not being, and thus given an infinite number of times, either through an infinitely extended past or a past time interval that is comprised of an infinity of moments of time, this possibility will be realized at some past time. Each moment is like a roll of the dice, an opportunity for this possibility to be realized. The PSR tell us that something cannot come out of nothing, so there has to be a cause of this being's coming into existence at this past time. Therefore, something had to cause this being to come into being out of nothing. But why couldn't this cause be itself a contingent being and it, in turn, be caused to begin to exist by an even earlier contingent being, and so on ad infinitum? Thomas's answer as to why this regress of contingent beings is impossible seems to commit an egregious quantificational blunder. For he says that if there were to exist only contingent beings, then, since for each of them there is a past time at which it doesn't exist, there is a past time at which each one of them does not exist. And if there ever were nothing, then, given the PSR, nothing would subsequently exist, which contradicts the patent existential fact that there now exists at least one contingent being. This argument seems to commit the same howler as is committed by inferring from the fact that for every woman there is a man that there is a man who is for every woman (talk about polygamy!). In logical terms that fallacy is $(x)(\exists y)xRy \supset (\exists y)(x)xRy$.

The Kalam cosmological argument of the medieval Islamic philosophers, which has been defended in recent times by William Lane Craig (1979), also invokes the impossibility of infinite regress but in a different way than Aquinas did in his first two ways. It selects as its contingent existential fact that there now exists a universe – an aggregate comprised of all contingent beings. It then argues that the universe must have begun to exist, for otherwise there would be an actual infinite series of past events or time, which is conceptually absurd. Since something cannot come out of nothing, there had to be a cause for the universe coming into being at some time a finite number of years ago. And this cause is identified with God, which again occasions the gap problem. Notice that the version of the PSR that is appealed to is a restricted and thus less vulnerable version of the PSR; for whereas the unrestricted version requires explanation for every thing that exists or fails to exist, the unrestricted version requires an explanation only for a being's coming into existence.

Just why is it impossible for there to be an actual infinity of past events or times? The answer is not obvious. Thomas, for one, did not think it to be impossible. Two kinds of arguments have been given. First, there are descendants of Zeno's arguments. It is not possible actually to go through an infinite series of events, for before going through the last event of the series, one would already had to have gone through an infinite series, and before the second last event, one would already had to have traversed an infinite series, and so on: the task could never have begun. But if there were an actual infinity of past events, then our world has traversed an infinite set of events, which is impossible. This argument depends on an anthropocentric notion of "going through" a set. The universe does not go through a set of events in the sense of planning which to go through first, in order to get through the second, and so on.

The other kind of argument given by Kalam arguers is that the very concept of infinity is incoherent. Imagine Hilbert's Hotel, where there are infinitely many rooms, numbered 1, 2, 3, and so on, and where even if all rooms are occupied, space can always be found for a new visitor by shifting the occupant of room 1 to room 2, moving room 2's occupant to room 3 and so on. The slogan outside the hotel would say: "Always full, always room for more," and the Kalam arguer takes this to be incoherent. Or consider an infinite series of events, again numbered 1, 2, 3, and so on. Then, the subseries consisting of the even-numbered events should have fewer events in it. But in fact it does not, as can be seen by writing the two series one on top of the other:

1	2	3	4	5	6	7	. . .
2	4	6	8	10	12	14	. . .

and noting that each member of the top series corresponds precisely to each member of the bottom series. Hence, the series of even numbered events is both smaller and not smaller than the upper series. These arguments against an actual infinity, however, are all based on a confusion between two notions of "bigger than." One notion is numerical: a set is bigger than another if it has a greater number of members. The other notion is in terms of part-to-whole relations: a whole is bigger than any proper part. When dealing with finite quantities, anything that is bigger in the part-to-whole sense is also bigger in the numerical sense. But this is not so in the case of infinite quantities. Although in the part-to-whole sense there are more people in the hotel after a new guest arrives and there are more members of the original series of events, in the numerical sense there are not. Indeed, mathematicians take the failure of the part-to-whole sense of "bigger than" to imply the numerical sense to be the defining feature of infinity.

Probably the most powerful of the traditional cosmological arguments, since it involves the least amount of conceptual baggage and controversial assumptions, is the one given by Newton's follower Samuel Clarke at the beginning of the eighteenth century. Like the Kalam argument, it begins with the contingent existential fact that there now exists an aggregate of all the contingent beings there are, but unlike this argument it does not have to invoke any controversial claims about the impossibility of infinite aggregates. It demands an explanation for the existence of this universe on the basis of a more general version of the PSR than the one employed in the Kalam argument, namely, that there is an explanation for the existence of every contingent being, even if it always existed. For explanatory purposes the universe itself counts as a contingent being, since it is an aggregate of all the contingent beings there are. It therefore must have a causal explainer. This cause cannot be a contingent being. For if a contingent being were to be the cause, it would have to be a cause of every one of the aggregate's constituents. But since every contingent being is included in this aggregate, it would have to be a cause of itself, which is impossible. The cause, therefore, must be some individual outside the aggregate; and, since an impossible individual cannot cause anything, it must be a necessary being that serves as the causal explainer of the aggregate. This holds whether the aggregate contains a finite or infinite number of contingent beings. Even if there were to be, as is possible for Clarke, an infinite past succession of contingent beings, each causing the existence of its immediate successor, there still would need to be a cause of the entire infinite succession.

It is at this point that David Hume, writing about half a century after Clarke, raised what is considered by many to be a decisive objection to Clarke's argument. He claimed that for any aggregate, whether finite or infinite, if there is for each of its constituents an explanation, then there thereby is an explanation for the entire aggregate. Thus, if there were to be an infinite past succession of contingent beings, each of which causally explains the existence of its immediate successor, there would be an explanation for the entire infinite aggregate, and thus no need to go outside it and invoke a necessary being as its cause. Hume's claim that explanation is in general agglomerative can be shown to be false. For it is possible for there to be a separate explanation for the existence of each constituent in an aggregate, say, each part of an automobile, without there thereby being an explanation of the entire aggregate – the automobile. The explanation for the latter would be above and beyond these several separate explanations for the existence of its constituent parts, as for example one that invokes the assembling activity in a Detroit factory.

William Rowe has given a variant version of Clarke's argument. He chooses as his initial contingent existential fact that there exists at least one contingent being. This is the plaintive cry that one might hear in a coffeehouse, "Why is there something rather than nothing?" – to which, according to Sidney Morgenbesser, God's response is, "Look you guys, suppose I created nothing, you still wouldn't be happy." The point of Morgenbesser's witticism is that even if there were to be nothing, that is, no contingent beings, the PSR still would require that there be an explanation for this big negative fact. The PSR is an equal opportunity explainer, not giving a privileged status to positive reality. We ask, "Why is there something rather than nothing?" simply because there happens to be something rather than nothing. The PSR requires there be an explanation for the contingent fact that there exists at least one contingent being. It cannot be given in terms of the causal efficacy of another contingent being, since this would result in a vicious circularity. Thus, it must be in terms of the causal efficacy of a necessary being.

This completes our brief survey of traditional cosmological arguments. It is now time to evaluate them critically. It was seen that each faced an unresolved gap problem consisting in its failure to show that the first cause, unmoved mover, or necessary being has all of the essential divine attributes. The most serious form that the gap problem takes concerns the moral qualities of this being. Here the problem of evil has been appealed to by the likes of Hume to argue that probably it is not an all-good being but rather morally indifferent. This, no doubt, is the point of a bumper sticker that reads, "God does exist. He just doesn't want to get involved." To counter the challenge of evil, it is necessary to construct theodicies for the known evils and give convincing design arguments. (See the chapter by Andrea Weisberger on this.)

The most vulnerable premise in these arguments is its PSR, whether in its universal or restricted form. It is imposing on the nontheist opponent of these arguments to ask him or her to grant that every true contingent proposition (or some restricted set of them) actually has an explanation; for this, in effect, is to grant that the universe is rational through and through. And this occupies almost as high an echelon in one's wish book as does the existence of God. Hume argued that we can conceive of an uncaused event; and, since whatever is conceivable is possible in reality, PSR is false. Bruce Reichenbach charges that Hume confuses epistemic with ontological conditions. To be sure, there is a distinction between what is conceivable and what could exist, the former concerning the epistemic and the latter the ontological order. Nevertheless, Reichenbach's rebuttal is far too facile, for it fails to face the fact that our only access to the ontological order is through the epistemic order. The only way that we humans can go about determining what has the possibility of existing is by appeal to what we can conceive to be possible. Such modal intuitions concerning what is possible are fallible; they are only prima facie acceptable, since they are subject to defeat by subsequent ratiocination. They are discussion beginners, not discussion enders. In philosophy we must go with what we ultimately can make intelligible to ourselves at the end of the day, after we have made our best philosophical efforts. What can the defender of the PSR say to get us to give up our prima facie Humean modal intuition? Plainly, the onus is on him or her, since it is he or she who uses the PSR as a premise in the cosmological argument.

Some cosmological arguers claim that PSR is self-evident, in the way the law of excluded middle (that for every proposition p, p or not-p) might be, and accuse those who reject it with having a bias against theism. However, claims of self-evidence are of little use to those who are not party to them, just as that the law of excluded middle appears self-evident to us is of no help to those intuitionist mathematicians who do not see it this way. Claims of self-evidence simply end discussions, and accusations of bias are a two-edged sword.

Another way of supporting PSR is to show that it is pragmatically rational for an inquirer to believe it, since by believing that everything has an explanation the believer becomes a more ardent and dedicated inquirer and thus is more apt to find explanations than if he or she did not believe this. This pragmatic sense of rational concerns the benefits that accrue to the believer of the PSR proposition, as contrasted with the epistemic sense of rational that concerns reasons directed toward supporting the truth of the proposition believed. Since cosmological arguments attempt to establish the epistemic rationality of believing that God exists, they cannot employ a premise that concerns only the pragmatic rationality of believing some proposition, such as the PSR; for this would commit the fallacy of equivocation, since "rational" would be used in both the pragmatic and epistemic sense. In essence, it would be arguing that it is epistemically rational to believe a proposition p because it is pragmatically rational to believe some proposition q, from which p follows or which is needed for the deduction of p.

A more reasonable argument for the PSR is an inductive one based on our numerous and ever-increasing successes in explaining contingently true propositions. The problem with such an inductive argument is that there is a significant difference between the contingent events and objects within the universe that form its inductive sample and the universe as a whole. Thus, it is risky to infer that what holds for the former also holds for the latter.

THE TELEOLOGICAL ARGUMENT

This argument, like the cosmological arguments, begins with a contingent existential fact, only one that is normative in that it is good or desirable, such as that there are organisms and their organs that display design or purpose, natural beauty, widespread law-like regularity and simplicity, miracles. Whereas the cosmological argument contains an explanatory argument for a theistic-type explanation being the only possible one for its existential fact, the teleological argument appeals to some principle of inductive, analogical, or probabilistic reasoning to show that this is the best explanation for its existential fact, thereby avoiding the need to invoke the highly controversial PSR. Thus, the typical design argument has the following three components: a contingent valuable existential fact; some principle of inductive reasoning; and an explanatory argument to show that the probable explanation of this fact is in terms of the intentional actions of a supernatural, God-like being.

In one version of the classical teleological argument, which is given by Hume's Cleanthes, an analogy is drawn between a machine and the universe as a whole. And since a machine arises from the intentional efforts of an intelligent and powerful designer-creator, so does the universe, only one that is proportionately more intelligent and powerful. This argument is a nonstarter, because its analogical premise is destroyed by this striking disanalogy between a machine and the universe: Whereas a machine has a function, the universe as a whole cannot. This disanalogy is due to the fact that, whereas a machine must operate within an environment, the universe could not, given that it is the totality of what is.

A far more plausible version of the teleological argument is the one given by William Paley in which the analogy is drawn between an artifact, such as a watch, and an organism or one of its organs, the eye, for example. Were we to find a watch lying on a heath we would, after determining that its parts fit and work together in an intricate manner, infer that the watch was designed by an intelligent agent. We would infer this even if we had never seen a watch before. Similarly, when we look at biological mechanisms, we descry a similar complexity and we should likewise infer the biological mechanisms were designed, but by a proportionately more intelligent being.

There is a very serious gap problem in any teleological argument, for it fails to show that its very powerful and intelligent designer-creator is omnibenevolent, no less omnipotent and omniscient. It is here that the problem of evil comes to the fore (see the chapter by Andrea Weisberger). Since the goodness of the existential fact on which the argument is based is supposed to give some evidence for the goodness of the creator, the known evils of the world, especially the ones that seem to be gratuitous or unjustified, that is, ones for which we are unable to give a theodicy, should count as evidence for the badness of the creator. Maybe this good fact was a device by which this evil creator highlighted the evil!

What did in Paley's argument, however, was not the problem of evil, but Darwin's theory of evolution. The mechanisms that impressed Paley so much probably were generated by the natural process of organisms mutating and only the fitter ones surviving to reproduce. This theory provides a satisfactory explanation of the items in question by a nondesigned natural process, since that would challenge the claim that the theistic explanation is the only or the best one available. It might well be that *both* a theistic and a naturalistic explanation are true, but in the presence of a naturalistic one, the theistic one may not be needed or may not be the best one.

Post-Darwinian teleological arguers regrouped and made the evolutionary process the object of their explanatory demand. Again, the problem of evil arose, since the mechanism by which evolution proceeded involved nature red in tooth and claw, which seems hard to square with the alleged goodness of the designer-creator. Discussion of the evolution-based teleological argument is beyond the purview of this chapter, as are other more recent versions of the teleological argument, such as the one based on the fine-tuning of the natural constants (see the chapter by Keith Parsons).

THE ARGUMENT FROM MYSTICAL EXPERIENCE

This traditional argument is based on apparently direct, nonsensory perceptions of a very powerful, wise, and benevolent being who gives counsel, comfort, and the like. There are many highly sophisticated contemporary versions of it, most notably William Alston's, that are based on the claim that these experiences (hereafter to be called "M-experiences") are analogous to ordinary sense experiences in cognitively relevant respects. Since all but complete skeptics about the senses grant that sense experiences are cognitive – count as evidence for the objective existence of their apparent object – the same cognitive status should be accorded to M-experiences. For the analogy to support this inference, it is necessary that there are background checks and tests for the veridicality of M-experiences that are sufficiently analogous to those for the veridicality of sense experiences. Without this requirement, the test for the veridicality of M-experiences could be based on what a cult leader says.

The prominent tests for the veridicality of sense experiences are agreement in judgment among observers, predictive success, and being caused in the right way, which requires, among other things, that the perceiver be normal and in the right circumstances. Do these tests have suitable M-experience analogues?

The mystical analogue to this agreement test is woefully weak. In the first place, whereas there are objective, agreed-upon tests for determining when a person's sensory faculty is not functioning properly, there are no such tests for determining when a person's mystical faculty is not functioning properly. Furthermore, there is no mystical analogue to a sensory observer being properly positioned in space, since God does not stand in any spatial relations. That there is no mystical analogue to

normality of observer and circumstances results in a pernicious evidential asymmetry in that the occurrence of mystical experiences is taken
to be confirmatory, but the failure to have them, even when the mystical way of meditating, fasting, and the like is followed, is not taken
as disconfirmatory. Thus the mystical agreement test is one that can be
passed but not flunked, and thus is no test at all. It is like a "heads I win,
tails you lose" sort of con game.

There is no mystical analogue to the caused-in-the-right-way test,
because there are no supernatural causal chains or processes linking
God with worldly events. Furthermore, the defenders of the cognitivity
of mystical experiences cannot agree among themselves whether there
are any limitations on what is the right way for God to cause a mystical experience. For example, some are willing to count a drug-induced
mystical experience as veridical and others are not.

It is only the prediction test that seems to have any application to
mystical experiences. All of the great mystical traditions have taken
the subject's favorable spiritual and moral development and the beneficial consequences for his or her society to count as confirmatory of
the veridicality of the mystical experience. They reason that if one is in
direct experiential connect with God, no less realizing partial or complete unification with Him, then it should result in these favorable consequences. Thus, these good consequences are confirmatory of the experiences' veridicality in virtue of categoreal link between them and God's
omniperfections.

There are two difficulties with the mystical analogue to the prediction test. The less serious difficulty is that the predicted good consequences are just as likely to occur whether the mystical experience that
is being tested is veridical or not; that is, the probability that that there
will be these good consequences relative to background knowledge, k,
and that the experience is veridical is about the same as it is relative
to k alone, the reason being that k contains facts about the naturalistic
causes and consequences of mystical experiences. The more serious difficulty is posed by the existence of equally viable rival doxastic mystical
practices within the great extant religions, with their different conceptions of what constitutes desirable moral and spiritual development,
revealed truths that the experience must not contradict, and ecclesiastical authorities and past holy persons (for a further discussion of this,
see the chapter by Evan Fales).

Another way that the prediction test is appealed to is that it is more
probable that mystical experiences will occur if God exists than if He
doesn't, that is, the probability that mystical experience will occur relative to the existence of God and background knowledge k is greater than

the probability that mystical experiences will occur relative to k alone. But this is dubious, again, because k contains facts about the naturalistic causes of mystical experiences. This stands in stark contrast with sense experience, for which it unquestionably is the case that it is more probable that sense experiences will occur if there are physical objects than if there are not, assuming that k in this case contains neither that there are physical objects nor any evil demon–type hypothesis. What this shows is that a prediction test is confirmatory of the veridicality of an experience of an O-type object only if the existence of an O-type object has both explanatory value and prior probability with respect to O-type experiences. Mystical experiences of a God-type object have been seen to have neither.

The response of Alston to these alleged disanalogies is twofold. First, the disanalogies between how these tests apply to sense and mystical experience are not damaging because they result from a conceptual difference between the respective apparent objects of these experiences: physical objects and God. Because it is a conceptual truth that God is a completely free supernatural being whose behavior and linkage with the world is not nomically based, the analogical arguer should not be bothered by the fact that the tests work in radically different ways for the two types of experience. But to show the conceptual basis for a disanalogy between them does not explain away the disanalogy, just as explaining why one has a disease does not eliminate the disease. Furthermore, a conceptually based disanalogy is the most damaging sort there can be. Second, for each of the alleged disanalogies, it is granted that it somewhat lessens the force of the analogy but not so much as to render it incapable of supporting the analogical argument for the cognitivity of M-experiences. But this divide-and-conquer strategy fails to consider what results when all of the disanalogies are agglomerated, it being apparent that Alston has unwittingly given away the whole family farm acre by acre.

REFERENCES

Alston, William. *Perceiving God*. Ithaca: Cornell University Press, 1991.
Aquinas, Thomas. *Summa theologiae*, vol. 1: *The Existence of God: Part One: Questions 1–13*. Garden City, N.Y.: Image Books, 1969.
Craig, William L. *The Kalam Cosmological Argument*. London: Macmillan, 1979.
Gale, Richard M. *On the Nature and Existence of God*. London: Cambridge University Press, 1991.
Hume, David. *Dialogues Concerning Natural Religion*. Indianapolis: Hackett, 1980.
Lewis, David. "Anselm and Actuality." *Nous* 4 (1970): 175–88.
Paley, William. *Natural Theology, or, Evidences of the Existence and Attributes of the Deity*. London: Rivington.

Reichenbach, Bruce. *The Cosmological Argument*. Springfield, Ill.: Charles Thomas, 1972.

Rowe, William L. *The Cosmological Argument*. Princeton: Princeton University Press, 1975.

Ross, James. *Philosophical Theology*. New York: Bobbs-Merrill, 1969.

Saint Anselm's Proslogion, trans. M. J. Charlesworth. Notre Dame: Notre Dame University Press, 1979.

6 Some Contemporary Theistic Arguments

In this chapter, I examine some contemporary theistic arguments. By "theistic argument" I mean an argument for the truth of theism or the reasonableness of theistic belief. Obviously, this is a broad and unavoidably vague definition. Theistic arguments differ widely in what they claim, in the strength of the claim, in the kinds of premises they adduce, in the logical structure of the argument (whether deductive, inductive, or abductive), and in innumerable other details. Theistic philosophers differ widely in their epistemological, metaphysical, and theological convictions. Clearly, even the attempt to sketch a taxonomy of theistic arguments would require more space than I have here. The selection of the arguments examined here is therefore severely limited and unavoidably somewhat idiosyncratic, reflecting my own perception of the strengths, weaknesses, and significance of the arguments presently offered in defense of theism. A cursory glance at many arguments would be pointless, so I shall consider just a few. Fortunately, other chapters in this volume fill in the many lacunae inevitably left by the need to be so severely selective.

In my 1989 book *God and the Burden of Proof*, I chose Alvin Plantinga and Richard Swinburne as the two outstanding representatives of contemporary theistic philosophy. I see no reason to alter that judgment today, despite the noteworthy contributions of many other prominent theistic philosophers. Plantinga and Swinburne, in their polished, trenchant, voluminous, and very influential writings, have set the bar high. Also, they present an interesting and very distinct contrast in their approaches to the defense of theism. Swinburne takes a more traditional approach. His inductive versions of traditional arguments are a development of classical natural theology. Plantinga, coming from a very different epistemological and theological perspective, argues that theistic belief is rational because it is properly basic. This chapter therefore focuses on some of the key theistic arguments of Plantinga and Swinburne.

THE EVIDENTIALIST CHALLENGE

Plantinga and Swinburne both respond to what has been called the "evidentialist challenge." Critics of theism have often charged that centuries of diligent effort by theistic philosophers have produced a negligible yield of evidence. Plantinga thinks that the evidentialist challenge is expressed by these two claims:

1. It is irrational or unreasonable to accept theistic belief in the absence of sufficient evidence or reasons.
2. We have no evidence or at any rate not sufficient evidence for the proposition that God exists. (Plantinga 1983: 27)

He responds by arguing that it is reasonable to believe that God exists even if there are no arguments, reasons, or evidence for the claim that God exists. In short, Plantinga's response to the evidentialist challenge is to reject the challenge. Swinburne, on the other hand, accepts the challenge and offers a defense of theism as a well-confirmed hypothesis.

PLANTINGA ON EVIDENTIALISM AND CLASSICAL FOUNDATIONALISM

Plantinga claims that evidentialism is motivated by classical foundationalism, the epistemological framework underlying much of Western philosophy (Plantinga, 1983: 39–63). Foundationalist epistemologies distinguish between basic and nonbasic beliefs. A belief is basic if it is not inferred from any other belief or beliefs. A belief is nonbasic if it is inferred from some other belief or beliefs. For instance, my belief that you look pale might be a basic belief for me. I do not infer that you look pale; I just *see* that you do. I might then form the nonbasic belief that you are not feeling well by inferring this from my basic belief that you look pale and my further belief that people who look pale often are not feeling well.

Having made the distinction between basic and nonbasic beliefs, foundationalism offers a thesis about how our beliefs are justified. "Justification" (i.e., *epistemic* justification) is a slippery term that takes on different shades of meaning for different epistemologists. For foundationalists, and internalist epistemologies in general (see below), justification is, roughly, a matter of someone being aware of reasons that are sufficient to authorize acceptance of a given belief by that person at that time. Perhaps a more helpful way of understanding justification in this sense is in terms of epistemic rights and duties. Being rational means that we have certain duties with respect to our beliefs – such as the duty to strive to base our beliefs on adequate evidence and not to cling to them obstinately when they are discredited. If I violate an epistemic duty in holding a belief, then my belief is thereby irrational. However, if I violate no epistemic duties in holding a belief, then I am within my epistemic rights in believing it, and my belief is therefore rational. In short, rational beliefs are those that are *permissible*; that is, in holding them one flouts no epistemic duties.

For foundationalists, nonbasic beliefs are justified by being correctly inferred from other justified beliefs. If I am justified in thinking that you look pale, and my belief that people who look paler than usual are often not feeling well is also justified for me, then I am justified in inferring that you are not feeling well. If, however, one belief can be justified by inference from another, and that in turn by another, and so on, the question immediately arises: Where does the chain of justifying beliefs end?

Foundationalists think that the chain cannot extend ad infinitum or there would be no justification, so the sequence of justifying reasons cannot go on forever, but must terminate with *properly basic beliefs*. To say that a belief B is properly basic for a person S is to say that B is held by S, S did not infer B from any other belief, and B is justified for S. These properly basic beliefs therefore constitute the *foundation* of our entire body of knowledge inasmuch as all our justified beliefs are either properly basic or ultimately derived by deductive or inductive inference from properly basic beliefs.

No rational scheme of justification will allow just *any* sort of belief to count as properly basic. According to Plantinga, classical foundationalism (CF) is chiefly a thesis about what sorts of beliefs can count as properly basic (Plantinga 1983: 59). CF holds that a belief B is properly basic for a person S (i.e., basic and justified for S) if and only if B is (a) self-evident, (b) incorrigible, or (c) evident to the senses for S. It follows that, since for CF it is rational for a person S to hold a belief B only if B is justified for S, the only sorts of beliefs that it is *rational* for S to hold as basic beliefs are those that are self-evident, incorrigible, or evident to the senses. Further, it is rational to accept a nonbasic belief if and only if it is either inferred immediately from properly basic beliefs or is a link in a chain of correct inference stretching back to properly basic beliefs.

Evidentialists, working within the framework of CF, observe that the proposition "God exists" is not self-evident, incorrigible, or evident to the senses, and they conclude that the belief that God exists is not a properly basic belief. They also argue that God's existence cannot be inferred from beliefs that are self-evident, incorrigible, or evident to the senses. They conclude that theism cannot be justified and so cannot be rationally believed.

Since, in Plantinga's view, evidentialism is grounded in CF, he rejects CF and replaces it with an epistemological framework friendlier to theism. Plantinga's first version of such a "Reformed" or "Calvinist" epistemology was published in 1983. The most distinctive feature of this new epistemology was that it permitted the statement "God exists" to count as a properly basic belief. In 2000 Plantinga offered a revised view, based on an entirely different epistemological framework, which also argued for the proper basicality of theistic belief.

THEISM AS PROPERLY BASIC: 1983 VERSION

Plantinga says that the basic problem with CF is that it is self-defeating because it cannot meet its own standards (Plantinga 1983: 60). Consider the proposition P that asserts the conditions of proper basicality for CF: "A belief B is properly basic for a person S if and only if B is (a) self-evident, (b) incorrigible, or (c) evident to the senses for S." Does P express a belief that is self-evident, incorrigible, or evident to the senses? Clearly not, says Plantinga. Therefore, a classical foundationalist who accepted P as basic would therefore be guilty of irrationality on his own account. Can P be justified by inferences from properly basic beliefs, that is, can it be correctly inferred from beliefs that are self-evident, incorrigible, or evident to the senses? Plantinga asserts that it cannot (Plantinga 1983: 61). Plantinga therefore concludes that it is not reasonable to accept the conditions of proper basicality stipulated by CF. Of course, some philosophers have objected that this argument is facile and that foundationalism can easily be reformulated in a non-self-refuting way (see Kenny 1983), but we cannot linger over these points.

Though he repudiates CF, Plantinga agrees that some, and only some, kinds of beliefs should count as properly basic and that these will serve the same sort of justifying function that basic beliefs do for foundationalists. He also agrees with CF that there need to be *some* criteria for proper basicality; we cannot just say that "anything goes" as properly basic. Plantinga recommends that these criteria be determined by an *inductive* procedure (Plantinga 1983: 76). That is, we begin with instances of *obviously* properly basic beliefs, and after compiling many such examples, we try to generalize from these. We tentatively formulate criteria for proper basicality, and then test these against further beliefs that are candidates for properly basic status. Sometimes we repudiate those candidates on the basis of our criteria, and sometimes we modify our criteria when they conflict with our intuitions about what is and what is not properly basic. This procedure of hypothesis testing and revision should eventually lead to the formulation of a consistent, useful, and intuitively valid set of criteria for proper basicality.

But which beliefs are *obviously* properly basic? There is no reason to think that these will be the same for everybody. Why, Plantinga asks, cannot Christians make "God exists" one of their examples of properly basic beliefs (Plantinga 1983: 77)? Atheists might disagree, but so what? Christians have to be responsible to *their* examples, not some other group's (Plantinga 1983: 77). If "God exists" is a properly basic belief for some person S, then, by definition, it is a *rational* belief for S. Further, S is under no obligation to defend his or her belief that God exists by adducing reasons, arguments, or evidence for that belief.

Another way to express Plantinga's claim is to assert that Christians are within their epistemic rights in taking "God exists" as properly basic. In his 1983 work, Plantinga understands rationality in terms of epistemic duties and rights (Plantinga 1983: 30). Plantinga claims that Christians are within their epistemic rights in regarding theistic belief as basic, and so it is rational for them to believe in God even if they can offer no arguments, reasons, or evidence for that belief.

Further, Plantinga says that there are particular sorts of circumstances when it is entirely right and proper for Christians spontaneously to form the belief that God exists. God's existence will be obviously properly basic for Christians in such circumstances. For instance:

Upon reading the Bible one may be impressed with a deep sense that God is speaking to him. Upon having done what I know is cheap, or wrong, or wicked, I may feel guilty in God's sight and form the belief *God disapproves of what I have done*. Upon confession and repentance I may feel forgiven, forming the belief *God forgives me for what I have done*. (Plantinga 1983: 80; emphasis in original)

So Plantinga argues that there are many circumstances in which God's existence will be obviously properly basic for Christians. Such persons will therefore be within their epistemic rights in asserting God's existence, and that belief will be rational for them even if they can offer no reasons, arguments, or evidence for God's existence.

ASSESSING PLANTINGA'S 1983 ARGUMENT

The obvious objection is that Plantinga's argument makes the conditions of proper basicality so absurdly easy to meet that just about anything, however bizarre, could count as properly basic for someone. Plantinga recognizes this potential problem and refers to it as the "Great Pumpkin" objection (Plantinga 1983: 74–78). The other characters in the Peanuts comic strip ridicule Linus because he believes that every Halloween the Great Pumpkin returns to bestow gifts on good children. If Christians can declare that God's existence is obviously properly basic for them, what is to keep Linus from declaring that the existence of the Great Pumpkin is obviously properly basic for him?

Plantinga replies that just because the belief that God exists is properly basic for Christians does not mean that this belief is *groundless*. The same belief can be obviously properly basic in some circumstances but not in others. For me it would be obviously properly basic to believe that there is a tree right in front of me in certain circumstances – including the circumstance of being appeared to in certain tree-like ways – but not in many other circumstances. What are the circumstances that supposedly ground Christians' claim that God's existence is obviously properly basic for them? They are the sorts of circumstances that Plantinga mentioned: feeling guilty and then feeling forgiven upon repentance and confession, being inspired by Scripture, and so on. Plantinga says that such circumstances are frequently realized, whereas, outside of the comic strips, nobody encounters circumstances where it would be natural to form spontaneous beliefs about the Great Pumpkin. Belief in the Great Pumpkin would therefore be utterly gratuitous and groundless. Therefore, just because Christians rationally form the basic belief that God forgives them, or cares for them, or is inspiring them (and hence that God exists) in a variety of common circumstances, they are under no obligation to regard just *any* belief in *any* circumstances as properly basic (Plantinga 1983: 74).

Another response to the Great Pumpkin objection is that there exists a natural community, the community of Christians, who endorse and authorize certain beliefs as properly basic. James F. Sennett continues the argument:

Now, when applied to the Great Pumpkin objection, this community requirement is decisive. There *is* no Great Pumpkin community. There is no body of believers that will endorse Linus's belief or give him permission to hold it basically. But clearly there is such a community for the theist. This disanalogy shows the Great Pumpkin objection to be illegitimate and ineffective. (Sennett 2003: 227).

Now there might be no Great Pumpkin community, but there are unquestionably innumerable communities that endorse beliefs that, to outsiders, sound every bit as bizarre as the Great Pumpkin. Why cannot the core beliefs of members of such groups be properly basic *for them* just as the core beliefs of Christians are allegedly properly basic for Christians? For instance, if "God forgives me" is properly basic for Christians who feel a strong sense of atonement, why couldn't "Moloch demands that we sacrifice more of our children" have been properly basic for the Carthaginians when they were hard pressed by the Romans? If Christians are within their epistemic rights in basing their criteria of proper basicality on what seems obvious only to them, then innumerable other groups have that right too.

The critic of the 1983 version of reformed epistemology can therefore offer the following *reductio ad absurdum:*

(1) "God exists" is a properly basic belief for Christians. (assumption for *reductio*)
(2) If "God exists" is a properly basic belief for Christians, then innumerable patently irrational beliefs are properly basic for the groups that endorse them.
(3) Innumerable patently irrational beliefs are properly basic for the groups that endorse them. (from 1 and 2 by *modus ponens*)
(4) But this is absurd.
(5) Therefore: The assumption "God exists' is a properly basic belief for Christians" must be rejected.

Since (1) is the assumption for the *reductio*, and (3) follows from (1) and (2) by *modus ponens*, reformed epistemologists would need to reject (2) or (4). If they reject (2), then they have to explain why they are not thereby guilty of a blatant case of special pleading. What kind of argument could guarantee that core Christian claims are properly basic in certain circumstances, but that "Moloch wants us to sacrifice more of our children" was never properly basic for anyone in any circumstances?

Rejecting (4) looks like a much better bet. After all, surely anthropologists are right that many beliefs that sound absurd to Western, scientifically conditioned ears were in *some* sense perfectly rational for people of other times and places. Belief in the existence of Moloch, Odin, or Baal, or belief in the teachings of tribal Shamans, or belief in Zande witchcraft lore, and so on was surely rational for the members of some culture at some time. Perhaps tolerant and broad-minded people should not hasten to condemn even very strange-sounding beliefs, like voodoo. Voodoo-believers may be doing their epistemic best, that is, doing their best to form rational, responsible beliefs given their epistemic circumstances. In fact, in a reply to a Great Pumpkin–like argument made by Michael Martin (1990: 272–73), Plantinga admits that voodoo beliefs *are* justified for members of the community that practices voodoo; that is, members of that community are within their epistemic rights in accepting voodoo beliefs (Plantinga 2000: 346). Surely, though, reformed epistemologists need to make a stronger claim than that belief in God is equally rational to belief in Moloch or voodoo. If not, atheists should greet these arguments with a yawn and a shrug. The loudest objections are likely to come from other Christians who have traditionally wanted to make *much* stronger claims on behalf of their beliefs. In later writings Plantinga does argue that core Christian claims might not merely be justified for believers, but rational in a much stronger sense, so let's turn to those arguments.

THEISM AS PROPERLY BASIC: 2000 VERSION

Writing in the 1990s, Plantinga extended his critique of foundationalism to a rejection of all "internalist" epistemologies and adopted an "externalist" view (Plantinga 1993). Internalist epistemologies hold that a belief is rational for a person if and only if that belief is justified for that person. Further, a belief is justified for someone if and only if that person is aware of reasons, grounds, or evidence that adequately support that belief. Externalist epistemologies reject this whole account of rationality and the concomitant concepts of epistemic rights and duties. Plantinga now holds that a belief is rational if and only if it is "warranted." Warrant is an objective matter; it has nothing to do with anyone's subjective awareness of justifying reasons. The objective conditions of warrant are complex and cannot be spelled out in detail here. Briefly and roughly, Plantinga holds that a belief is warranted if and only if it is produced by the proper functioning of a cognitive faculty in the circumstances in which that faculty was designed (by God or evolution) to operate effectively. For instance, if it is broad daylight, my eyes are open, there is a tree right directly in front of me, there is nothing distracting me or blocking my view, and my optical and cognitive faculties are operating as designed, then my belief that there is a tree in front of me is warranted (in the remainder of this chapter, I mean "warrant" in this externalist sense).

The proper functioning of our faculties in appropriate circumstances sometimes produces beliefs that are "warrant basic," that is, beliefs that are both basic and warranted. Since warranted beliefs are, by definition, rational beliefs, a belief that is warrant basic will be properly basic. My belief that I called my wife a few minutes ago, given that my memory is functioning properly and as designed, is a warranted, and hence rational, proper, and basic belief.

Plantinga, following theologians such as John Calvin, believes that among our cognitive faculties is a *sensus divinitatis*, a faculty that, when operating properly and in an appropriate circumstance, will provide us with the warrant basic belief that God exists (Plantinga 2000: 167–86). In fact, Plantinga says that the awareness of God that the *sensus divinitatis* produces, if not strictly a case of *perceiving* God, is very like perception in the sense that the awareness of God it imparts is immediate and *palpable* for the one receiving it (Plantinga 2000: 181). Why doesn't *everyone* have such an immediate and perception-like awareness of God? Because, says Plantinga, *sin* has so corrupted the *sensus divinitatis* faculty of some persons that it no longer functions properly (Plantinga 2000: 184–85). Therefore, unbelief is a product of epistemic malfunction, just as blindness can result from damage to the eye. Since Plantinga's externalist epistemology defines "rational" in terms of proper function, and atheism is a result of malfunction, atheism cannot be rational.

But *is* there a *sensus divinitatis* that imparts warrant basic belief in the existence of God when functioning properly in the right circumstances? Very probably, if God exists, says Plantinga; very probably not, if there is no God (Plantinga 2000: 186–90). As Sennett puts it: "Regardless of whether or not theistic belief is properly basic, one thing seems clear: if the theistic God exists, it only seems obvious that He would form the world and human beings in such a way that they could rationally believe that He exists – indeed that they could *know* that He exists" (Sennett 2003: 230). On the other hand, if there is no God, there will be no *sensus divinitatis*, and it seems very unlikely that any other faculty would produce the warranted but false belief that God exists. The upshot, says Plantinga, is that the question of the *rationality* of the belief that God exists cannot be separated from the question of whether that belief is *true* (Plantinga 2000: 191). Plantinga contends that critics such as Marx and Freud who criticize the rationality of theistic belief will fail unless they also provide arguments that theism is *in fact* false. In other words, anyone who wants to argue that theistic belief is irrational will have to show that it is unwarranted, and, since it is highly probable that belief in God is warranted if God exists, the would-be critic must move beyond the realm of epistemology and offer substantial arguments against theism. Reformed epistemology therefore says that if God exists, there will be many persons whose belief in God is warrant basic and therefore rational in the strong sense that their belief is the product of a cognitive faculty operating properly in the circumstances in which it was designed to impart true beliefs. The belief that God exists, if true, will therefore constitute *knowledge* for such persons.

ASSESSING PLANTINGA'S 2000 ARGUMENT

As Sennett notes, Plantinga's reformed epistemology has a rather ironic conclusion (Sennett 2003: 230). Plantinga started off in 1983 arguing that theistic belief is rational, that is, justified in the internalist's sense, and indeed is properly basic, even if believers can offer no arguments, evidence, or reasons for the truth of theism. Now he argues that theistic belief is very likely warranted and properly basic, in the externalist sense, but only if theism is in fact true. This means that believers are in no position to argue that their belief in God is warrant basic unless they can adduce reasons, arguments, or evidence for the existence of God.

So we seem to have come full circle. Well, maybe not quite. Perhaps reformed epistemology has at least succeeded in shifting some of the burden of proof from theists to atheists. If theistic belief is defended in the context of an externalist epistemology, atheists cannot blithely invoke foundationalist criteria and defy theists to justify their belief in God on that basis. Plantinga might argue that the tables are now turned and that anyone wanting to convict theists of irrationality must *first* show that God does *not* exist, since if God exists, theistic beliefs very likely have warrant. In other words, it now looks like any objection to the rationality of theistic belief must *presuppose* that God does not exist.

Tyler Wunder notes the obvious fallacy of this reasoning:

[I]f God does exist, *then* very probably theism is warrant-basic; obviously by *modus tollens* the antecedent of this conditional can be negated if the consequent can. Therefore an epistemic argument (epistemic because it concerns the presence or absence of the epistemic concept warrant) could successfully *conclude with*, not *presuppose* a negative answer to the de facto question [i.e., the question of the *truth* of theism]. (Wunder 2002: 110; emphasis in original)

In other words, the atheist can stand Plantinga's argument on its head and argue that the fact that theistic belief is not warrant basic shows that there probably is no God! Further, when it comes to arguments questioning the rationality of theism, Marx and Freud are now the least of theists' worries. A number of recent works offer challenging naturalistic accounts of religious belief in terms of neuroscience, anthropology, and evolutionary theory (see, e.g., Guthrie 1993; Alper 2001; Boyer 2001; Wilson 2002; Broom 2003). If the arguments of these authors are cogent – and Plantinga gives no reason why they cannot be (unless we *presuppose* theism true) – then there is excellent reason to doubt that theistic belief is warrant basic, for such belief will have natural, nonrational causes – and not be caused by the proper functioning of a cognitive faculty designed to produce true beliefs. If the rationality question is contingent on the reality question (and vice versa), as Plantinga claims, these arguments will be doubly dangerous. Arguments against the *rationality* of theistic belief now become arguments also against the *truth* of theism. Reformed epistemology does indeed have an ironic conclusion: Its net effect is to multiply the arguments against the existence of God.

SWINBURNE ON THE CONFIRMATION OF THEISM

Since the scientific revolution, the natural sciences have enjoyed a reputation as the purest, surest, and most productive of human cognitive enterprises. Consequently, defenders of every sort of claim have sought to give their arguments a "scientific" basis. At one time, theistic apologetics and the sciences enjoyed a symbiosis. For instance, natural history revealed the "curious adapting of means to ends" (in Hume's phrase) throughout the organic world. For all but a few stalwart skeptics, the analogy between human artifice and divine design was therefore intellectually irresistible. However, the burgeoning success of naturalistic explanations left ever fewer gaps for God. Most notoriously, transcendent explanations of the adaptation of means to ends in nature became otiose after Darwin. It is now clear that theism is turned into pseudoscience only if it is made to compete with well-confirmed scientific theories, such as big bang cosmology or evolutionary theory (see the chapters by Dennett and Smith). It is also clear that no appeal to God-of-the-gaps arguments (i.e., arguments that locate lacunae in current scientific explanations and make those the loci of God's creative acts) will work. In short, a successful theistic argument cannot be a rival to science or an attempt to fill in the gaps in scientific explanations.

To his credit, Richard Swinburne commits neither blunder. He has no quarrel with evolution or cosmology, and he argues that even if science fills in all its gaps, much will be left unexplained. He says that there are some questions that need answers that, in principle, science cannot give. Questions such as these: Why is there a universe at all (why not nothing instead of something)? Why *this* universe, *this* kind of physical reality with *these* kinds of entities and laws, and not something entirely different?

Swinburne's explanation is the theistic hypothesis. He holds that theism can be confirmed as an explanatory hypothesis in much the same way that, broadly speaking, explanatory hypotheses are confirmed in science. His strategy is to offer a cumulative case for theism in which different pieces of confirming evidence contribute to the overall probability of the theistic hypothesis. For instance, suppose that e_1 is "there exists a complex physical universe." Swinburne claims that $p(h/e_1 \& k) > p(h/k)$, where h is the theistic hypothesis that God exists and k is background knowledge. Swinburne says that, with respect to the theistic hypothesis, k will be only "tautological" knowledge, that is, logically necessary truths (Swinburne 2004: 65–66). Showing that $p(h/e_1 \& k) > p(h/k)$, that is, showing that the existence of the God is more likely given that complex physical universe exists than it is given only tautological background knowledge, will give a successful C-inductive argument for the existence of God. A good C-inductive argument is one that adduces evidence that raises the probability of a hypothesis above its background probability. Further, Swinburne claims that when we consider *all* of the evidence $e_1, e_2, e_3, \ldots, e_n$ pertaining to God's existence, we will see that $p(h/e_1 \& e_2 \& e_3 \dots e_n \& k) > 1/2$, and so have a good P-inductive argument, that is, an argument that shows that the hypothesis is probably true.

It follows from Bayes' theorem that for any hypothesis h, evidence e, and background knowledge k, $p(h/e \& k) > p(h/k)$ if and only if $p(e/h \& k) > p(e/k)$. This is called the "relevance condition"; it specifies that for a piece of evidence e to confirm a hypothesis h, the truth of the hypothesis must be relevant to the occurrence of the evidence. That is, e must be more likely given h than it is given only background knowledge. A bit of algebraic manipulation shows further that the relevance condition is met if and only if the evidence is more likely to exist given that the hypothesis is true than if the hypothesis is false, that is, if and only if $p(e/h \& k) > p(e/^\wedge h \& k)$. This result is consistent with our intuitions about evidence: The fingerprints on the murder weapon are evidence against the butler if and only if they are more likely to be on the weapon if he committed the murder than if he did not.

For Swinburne, this means that to show that particular evidence e confirms God's existence, he must show that e is more likely given God's existence than if God does not exist. Because space here is limited, I shall restrict attention to Swinburne's cosmological argument, where e is the existence of a complex physical universe (Swinburne's other arguments, where e is the existence of certain kinds of order, or the existence of consciousness, are similar). If, therefore, e is the existence of a complex physical universe, Swinburne must show that such a universe is more likely to exist if God exists than if there is no God. There are two ways that a universe could exist if there is no God. A universe could be an uncaused, brute fact. A universe also could be caused – either intentionally created or unconsciously generated – by some being (or beings) or entity (or entities) other than the theistic God. For instance, as Hume speculated, perhaps our universe is the creation not of God but of a lesser demigod or a committee of demigods. Indefinitely many such scenarios are possible. Swinburne's argument with respect to the existence of a complex physical universe is that, though the existence of such a universe given God's existence, $p(e/h \& k)$, might not be very high, since there is no overriding reason to think that God would create a physical universe at all, it will still be much higher than the sum of the probabilities of all rival hypotheses. That is, $p(e/h \& k)$ will be much higher than $p(e/^\wedge h \& k)$, the probability that a complex physical universe exists uncaused plus the sum of the probabilities of all hypotheses postulating a cause other than God.

The reason, says Swinburne, that the theism has such an advantage over all its rivals, even far outweighing their cumulative probabilities, is that theism is a uniquely simple hypothesis:

> To start with, theism postulates a God with capacities as great as they logically can be. He is infinitely powerful, omnipotent. That there is an omnipotent God is a simpler hypothesis than that there is a God who has such-and-such limited power (e.g. the power to rearrange matter, but not the power to create it). (Swinburne 2004: 97)

So, theism is much simpler than any hypothesis postulating finite, limited causes, such as demigods. Swinburne also says that the thesis that a complex physical universe exists uncaused as brute fact is much less simple than theism. Consider our universe, for instance:

> A complex physical universe (existing over time or beginning to exist at some finite time) is indeed a rather complex thing... consider the vast diversity of galaxies, stars, planets, and pebbles on the seashore.... There is a complexity, particularity, and finitude about the universe which cries out for explanation. (Swinburne 2004: 150)

So, theism is also much simpler than the hypothesis that a complex physical universe exists as an ultimate, uncaused, brute fact. Because theism is so much simpler than its rivals, Swinburne concludes, it is far more likely that a complex physical universe exists given God's existence than that such a universe exists given that there is no God. Therefore, the existence of a complex physical universe is evidence for the existence of God. When combined with similar arguments with respect to other evidence, such as the existence of particular kinds of order in the physical world, or the existence of consciousness and morality, Swinburne contends that the cumulative evidence makes it probable that God exists (Swinburne 2004: 328–42).

ASSESSING SWINBURNE'S COSMOLOGICAL ARGUMENT

Swinburne's arguments are complex, drawing on many premises that might be subjected to skeptical probing. Here the critique focuses on a single sentence: "The intrinsic probability of theism is, relative to other hypotheses about what there is, very high, because of the great simplicity of theism" (Swinburne 2004: 109). Swinburne is talking mainly about ontological simplicity: A simple theory postulates few logically independent entities, a small number of kinds of entities with few properties, and so on (Swinburne 2004: 55). Three questions need to be asked: (1) Is theism ontologically simpler than any possible naturalistic rival? (2) If so, does theism achieve greater ontological simplicity at the price of greater conceptual complexity and explanatory obscurity? (3) Why should allegedly greater simplicity make theism intrinsically more probable than naturalism? In other words, why is God more likely to exist as an uncaused brute fact than the ultimate ontological posits of any possible, even if more complex, naturalistic cosmogony?

The present universe is enormously complex, but cosmologists say that it evolved from a very simple state. There are a number of conflicting theories about the beginning of the universe, and this is not the place to review each scenario and compare its simplicity point by point with Swinburne's. Nor is there any need to do so; Swinburne must say that theism is in principle simpler than any possible scientific cosmogony postulating an uncaused initial state of the universe. Swinburne supposes that God's unlimited attributes – omnipotence, omniscience, and so on – possess a simplicity that no finite, limited attributes could match (presuming that the postulated initial state possesses at least one finite attribute that is a brute fact and predicted by no deeper theory). However, the reasons why this should be so are elusive. Swinburne says that finite quantities have a definiteness or a particularity that infinite quantities lack: "A finite limitation cries out for explanation of why there is just that particular limit in a way that limitlessness does not" (Swinburne 2004: 97).

Now there may be contexts where scientists consider it simpler to assign an infinite value to some parameter instead of a finite number (e.g., medieval natural philosophers postulated that light had an infinite speed), but it is hard to see why this would be so here. Omnipotence, for instance, the maximum logically possible degree of power, seems to be as definite, particular, determinate, and distinct a degree of power as any other. Should future explorers discover an omnipotent being in deep space, why or how this being possesses such power would seem to cry out for an answer just as much as if that being could wield, say, only ten billion kilowatts of power.

Further, even if theism achieves a greater ontological economy than any possible naturalistic theory, it does so at the cost of introducing far greater conceptual complexity and explanatory obscurity into our total view of reality. Orthodox theism postulates an essentially mysterious being whose nature is largely incomprehensible and who possesses unique powers that he or she wields in unknowable ways for purposes that we can only dimly grasp. By contrast, the quest for a scientific theory of everything is the search for a theory that will, we hope, not only simplify our ontology but also, ideally, provide greater conceptual simplicity and explanatory clarity.

Finally, why suppose that, other things being equal, the ontologically simpler of two competing theories is more likely to be true? In his small book *Simplicity as Evidence of Truth* (1997) Swinburne offers this argument: Universally in scientific practice the hypothesis that, all other things being equal, provides the simplest explanation of the phenomena is the one accepted by scientists. All efforts to reduce, explain away, or eliminate the appeal to simplicity in theory-choice situations are failures.

Therefore, if science leads us toward truth, it must be true, a priori, that of the available hypotheses (and again making ceteris paribus stipulations) the hypothesis most likely to be true is the one that is simplest. Further, "In holding simpler theories to be more probable than complex theories, the inquirer is holding it to be more probable that the world as a whole is simple than that it is complex" (Swinburne 1997: 42).

But nothing justifies this last claim. Certainly, we should avoid introducing arbitrary complexity into our hypotheses. Why? Because we think it unlikely that nature will respect our arbitrary and groundless suppositions. Therefore, we regard hypotheses that make such suppositions as less probable than those that do not. However, we have no way of knowing ahead of time when nature will require us to complicate our theories, and, if the history of science is any guide, this happens pretty often. Much less do we have any grounds for saying, purely in the abstract and apart from any evidence, that what is likely to exist as an uncaused brute fact is more likely to be simple than complex.

The upshot is that the scientific practice of selecting the relatively simplest hypothesis vis-à-vis a given body of data does not underpin a metaphysical claim about theism versus naturalism. Scientific practice does not justify the claim that theism, in virtue of its allegedly greater simplicity, is intrinsically more probable than naturalism. So, Swinburne provides no reason to hold that $p(e/h\&k) > p(e/{\char`\~}h\&k)$, where e is the existence of a complex physical universe and h is the theistic hypothesis. The allegedly greater simplicity of theism over its rivals is not established, and, even if it were, there is no reason to think that it would thereby be more intrinsically probable. Swinburne therefore fails to meet the relevance condition; that is, he does not show that the existence of a complex physical universe is evidence for the existence of God.

CONCLUSION

The theistic arguments examined in this chapter clearly are the products of brilliant minds. This is to the credit of the authors of these arguments, but to the discredit of theism. Theistic belief obviously exerts great attraction; few doctrines in the history of ideas can boast such a stellar set of intellectual defenders, from Augustine and Aquinas to Plantinga and Swinburne. Yet the end product of all that brilliance is a set of arguments that, at least from the atheist's perspective, achieves very little. Is theistic belief warranted? Plantinga has given me no reason to think so. Is the theistic hypothesis confirmed by evidence? Swinburne's promise of a quasi-scientific theism fails to deliver. Is this the best that theism can offer in support of itself? I am forced to conclude that it is.

ACKNOWLEDGMENTS

I would like to thank Michael Martin and Tyler Wunder for reading a draft of this chapter and for their many helpful criticisms and suggestions.

REFERENCES

Alper, M. 2001. *The "God" Part of the Brain: A Scientific Interpretation of Human Spirituality and God.* Brooklyn, N.Y.: Rogue Press.

Boyer, P. 2001. *Religion Explained: The Evolutionary Origins of Religious Thought.* New York: Basic Books.

Broom, D. M. 2003. *The Evolution of Morality and Religion.* Cambridge: Cambridge University Press.

Bunge, Mario. *The Myth of Simplicity.* Englewood Cliffs, N.J.: Prentice-Hall.

Guthrie, S. 1993. *Faces in the Clouds: A New Theory of Religion.* Oxford: Oxford University Press.

Kenny, A. 1983. *Faith and Reason.* New York: Columbia University Press.

Martin, M. 1990. *Atheism: A Philosophical Justification.* Philadelphia: Temple University Press.

Parsons, K. M. 1989. *God and the Burden of Proof: Plantinga, Swinburne, and the Analytic Defense of Theism.* Buffalo, N.Y.: Prometheus Books.

Plantinga, A. 1983. "Reason and Belief in God." In A. Plantinga and N. Wolterstorff (eds.), *Faith and Rationality: Reason and Belief in God.* Notre Dame: University of Notre Dame Press, pp. 16–93.

Plantinga, A. 1993. *Warrant and Proper Function.* New York: Oxford University Press.

Plantinga, A. 2000. *Warranted Christian Belief.* Oxford: Oxford University Press.

Sennett, J. F. 2003. "Reformed Epistemology and the Rationality of Theistic Belief." In R. Martin and C. Bernard (eds.), *God Matters: Readings in the Philosophy of Religion.* New York: Longman, pp. 219–31.

Swinburne, R. 1997. *Simplicity as Evidence of Truth.* Milwaukee, Wis.: Marquette University Press.

Swinburne, R. 2004. *The Existence of God,* 2nd ed. Oxford: Oxford University Press.

Wilson, D. S. 2002. *Darwin's Cathedral: Evolution, Religion, and the Nature of Society.* Chicago: University of Chicago Press.

Wunder, T. 2002. "Review of Warranted Christian Belief." *Philo* 5, no. 1: 103–18.

7 Naturalism and Physicalism

Naturalism and physicalism are metaphysical positions commonly associated with atheism. Both are stronger than atheism: they entail atheism, conceived (minimally) as the denial that there is an all-powerful, omniscient, perfectly good disembodied personal being who has created the physical universe. Naturalism and physicalism are, therefore, natural allies of atheism, and offer a philosophical framework within which atheism finds a natural home.[1]

PHYSICALISM

Main Positions on the Mind/Body Problem

Physicalism may be understood, roughly, as the claim that minds are not distinct from matter and hence cannot exist apart from it. There are many varieties of physicalism. They may be graded, from most "extreme" to least, as follows.

ELIMINATIVE MATERIALISM. On this view, there simply are no mental events, and no "inner theater." Subjective experience is an illusion; all that is happening "in our heads" are neurochemical events in our brains.

REDUCTIVE MATERIALISM. This view allows that there are mental events, but holds that each mental event type is identical with a physical event type in the brain.

SUPERVENIENCE THEORIES. Supervenience is a relation that holds between a physical and a mental state just in case it is necessary that when that physical state obtains, so does the mental state. A supervenience theorist could hold, for example, that each instance (token) of a certain mental state type is identical to an instance of some physical state type, without holding that the two state types can be identified. For example, those who maintain that mental characteristics are functional properties often subscribe to such a view. There are those (such as Hilary Putnam) who define functional states in terms of their *logical* role in the execution of a computation (i.e., the formal states a computer is in when it executes a program) or those (such as David Lewis) who define them in terms of the *causal* role of the state.

PROPERTY DUALISM. Property dualists deny that mental properties are in any sense identical to physical properties. They may hold, however, that there are only material substances, some of which have mental properties. It is not clear in what principled way one ought to distinguish mental from physical properties. A property dualist may further hold that the instantiation of mental properties by a material thing is strongly dependent on which physical properties it has: that the relation between the instances is either one of nomological (lawlike) necessity or one of metaphysical necessity.

Mind/Body Positions and Atheism

All but the last two positions surveyed are physicalist positions, and entail atheism. Some versions of the last two are at least arguably physicalist, and also entail atheism. Since God has mental properties, and is neither a material substance nor dependent on any material substance, his existence is incompatible with any view that makes the instantiation of mental properties strongly dependent on the states of a physical substance. So even if mental properties or substances are not physical or explainable in terms of the physical, theism will still be ruled out so long as such a dependence relation exists between the mental and the physical. That leaves open the question of how the relation might be understood (given that it is not a matter of reduction); but one might have evidence that such a relation exists, even in the absence of an understanding of its nature.

Is Physicalism True?

Physicalism is a contested view in any of its versions. Two of the most difficult problems it faces are the problem of intentionality and the problem of *qualia*. To say that a mental state is intentional is to say that it is "about" something – that it is directed toward some object and that it can have this characteristic even if the object in question does not exist. Thus, I may think about the centaur Cheiron or the prophet Jonah, even if neither exists, and I may hallucinate a pink rat where there is none. The *qualia* that characterize an experience constitute "what it's like" to have that experience. Red *qualia* characterize the ordinary visual experience of red things.

Dualists will be quick to argue that physicalists have not solved these and various other problems concerning how a physical entity could think. Much depends, however, on whether it can be shown that these problems cannot *in principle* be solved, or whether it is merely claimed that they have not in fact been. The latter claim will strike most physicalists as mind-of-the-gaps psychology. Some philosophers have lately argued that the mind/body problem is too difficult for human minds to solve.[2] A more powerful strategy is to argue that thought is *in principle* not something a physical system could be capable of. Because such an argument must evidently invoke constraints on the causal powers of material objects, it is not easy to see how this could be done on purely conceptual or a priori grounds. Here we confront an issue (cosmology is another) that blurs the boundaries between philosophy and science, and both physicalists and dualists do well to attend to empirical developments in psychology and the neurosciences.

What reasons are there for accepting that mentality does not exist disembodied, even granting that the two difficulties just mentioned remain unsolved? The reasons can be divided into *empirical* and *conceptual* ones. Prominent are two empirical reasons. First, Darwinian evolution implies that human beings emerged through the blind operation of natural forces. It is mysterious how such forces could generate something nonphysical; all known causal laws that govern the physical relate physical states of affairs to other physical states of affairs. Since such processes evidently *have* produced consciousness, however construed, consciousness is evidently a natural phenomenon, and dependent on natural phenomena.

Second, as Hume points out, our *experience* tells us that consciousness results from, and is intimately dependent on, physical processes. It results from reproduction in animals possessed of conscious brains. It is depends on physical processes – most intimately, on the state of a brain.[3]

Are the two core phenomena of consciousness – *qualia* and intentionality – in fact not amenable to physicalist explanation? Take *qualia*. They seem to be nonphysical properties, exemplified only by or in minds. But there is another possibility. Our perception of the properties of "external" physical objects is mediated by causal processes: stimulation of sense organs and brain processes. What we directly experience, it may be argued, are only the *effects* produced by such stimuli in our minds. So our understanding of these properties is a matter of apprehending their effects. But what about our apprehension of the effects themselves – the *qualia*? That is not mediated perception but rather a kind of direct acquaintance: we are, arguably, in touch with the intrinsic nature of these subjective or mental properties. Might not *qualia* be just *physical* properties (of the brain) – only given in perception not mediately in terms of their associated causal powers, but immediately via direct acquaintance? That would explain why they are given to cognition in a distinctive way (e.g., as pain rather than neuron firings), a way that may lead us, mistakenly, to suppose they are not physical properties at all.[4]

If that solves the problem of explaining *qualia*, it directs us to the second hard problem, that of intentionality, for direct acquaintance is an intentional relation. Possibly, it is the most *fundamental* intentional relation, the basis for intentional relations to other sorts of properties and objects.[5]

Many physicalists, arguing along lines proposed by Fred Dretske and Ruth Millikan,[6] avoid direct acquaintance and hold that intentionality is a kind of goal-directedness. Goal-directedness in general is, according to the basic strategy, something ascribable to an organism or to subsystems in an organism when the organism possesses those systems as a result of natural selection. Thus, an animal that has heat receptors is sensitive to heat. It has heat indicators. But a minimally necessary condition for our saying that the animal *perceives* heat is that it has inherited from its ancestors mechanisms that enable the animal to detect temperatures in ways that promote survival.

One could, of course, be a physicalist concerning human (and animal) minds, but hold that there are disembodied mental substances: that God is one such, and that there are perhaps others (e.g., angels). Such a view would be inelegant. Holding that God is an immaterial substance but that human minds are physical substances invites, at least, questions about how consciousness can be realized in such different substances. Most theists are dualists, because they hold both that God doesn't have a body and that there is a part of human persons – a soul or mind – that survives the destruction of the body.[7] Conversely, one could be a dualist but hold that minds are not – cannot be – disembodied. Property dualism is one way to articulate this. But a substance dualist could also hold that a mind must be intimately connected to, or dependent on, a body, in such a way that disembodied minds cannot exist.[8] This possibility, we shall see, adds a complication to the task of determining what naturalism is.

NATURALISM

An initial difficulty that faces any discussion of naturalism is that there is surprisingly little agreement over just what naturalism *is*. Many different positions have been characterized as naturalistic, and it would be tendentious to bestow special status to any one of these. Nevertheless, we may investigate what they may have in common. It will be helpful to distinguish ontological and epistemological theses that have been central to various naturalistic programs. We shall also have to consider a recent claim that naturalism is not an ontological or epistemological position at all, but rather is best construed as a "research program." Naturalism is best understood in terms of its ontological commitments, but there is considerable disagreement over just what ontology a naturalist should accept – or, alternatively, over just what calling a view "naturalistic" amounts to. There is a range of possibilities; these can be roughly organized along a spectrum from the ontologically sparse or stringent to the most liberal.

Varieties of Naturalism

Some philosophers distinguish among ontological, epistemological, and methodological naturalism. The distinctions can be somewhat misleading, inasmuch as ontology often motivates epistemology, and epistemology often motivates methodology (and sometimes vice versa). Nevertheless, it is useful to examine the varieties of naturalism under these three headings, discussing their interconnections and their bearing on the claim that God does not exist. However, it will be helpful to consider first the view that naturalism is not an ontological, epistemological, or methodological thesis at all, but rather a "research program."

NATURALISM AS A RESEARCH PROGRAM. The claim that naturalism is most properly understood as a research program has recently been advanced by Michael Rea.[9] Rea defines a research program, rather idiosyncratically, as a set of methodological dispositions. Research programs can be rejected on the basis of evidence, but cannot be adopted on the basis of evidence, for what counts as evidence is determined by the program.

On historical grounds, Rea argues that the defining methodological disposition of naturalism is a commitment to follow the methods and results of science wherever they lead. Naturalism cannot be formulated as a set of theses, because both the methods and the results of science can change. Indeed, there is no way to rule out a priori the possibility that science will come to accept theism. Rea argues that the naturalist's commitment to science precludes formulation of naturalism as an ontological, epistemological, or methodological thesis. For example, naturalism cannot be an ontological thesis that is incompatible with the existence of God, for the reason, just noted, that science could come to accept theism as a well-supported hypothesis. Such an outcome can indeed not be excluded a priori; but that fact should provide grounds to doubt that naturalism is, fundamentally, just a commitment to a scientific world-view.

METHODOLOGICAL NATURALISM. Scientists are sometimes accused of (or themselves stoutly advocate) restricting scientific investigation to natural phenomena – that is, roughly, to those phenomena that only involve or can be explained by configurations of matter in space and time. Steven Jay Gould, for example, regularly proclaimed that this was the proper purview of science; he went on to claim that the proper domain of religion was values and normative judgments – that is, ethics.[10] (This position, when combined with a noncognitivist or antirealist view of norms, entails that the domain of science covers all the objective facts. It is, however, implausible to divest all religious belief of factual claims.)

On the other side of the ideological spectrum, "scientific creationists" and their fellow anti-Darwinians, the advocates of "intelligent design," often accuse scientists of *assuming* naturalism as a metaphysical commitment (concerning which see below), and therefore being committed methodologically to excluding a priori the possibility that supernatural entities play any role in explaining natural phenomena.[11] But scientists don't simply adopt methodological naturalism a priori.

There are at least three considerations that have motivated methodological naturalism. First, the methodological naturalist can appeal to the claim – tentative, but well supported – that there are no supernatural causes to be investigated. (He or she can, for example, point to the long and rather sordid history of paranormal claims that have, on careful investigation, proved to be either without merit or fraudulent.) On this approach, methodological naturalism is not so much fundamentally a *methodological* commitment as it is a (well-confirmed) *finding* of science, one that enjoins the rule: always look for natural causes (or explanations) of phenomena; supernatural hypotheses are to be entertained only as a last resort. One who employs such a rule does not exclude the supernatural on principle, but rather is taught by experience that supernatural hypotheses are unlikely to bear fruit.

A second – and much more problematic – ground for adopting methodological naturalism is that the supernatural (or nonnatural; see below) is *in principle* beyond scientific investigation. Why might one suppose that? One reason often given is this: to say that something is nonnatural or supernatural is to say that it exists outside time or space, or both. But there is no way to detect such a thing; it escapes objective measurement. (It is often added that the source of religious beliefs is "merely" subjective experience.)

It is important, however, not to beg the question here. We should not incautiously presume to know enough about causation to rule out dogmatically the possibility that an agent existing somehow outside space or time (or both) could causally interact with physical matter. There are indeed serious difficulties with such a supposition (see the section on miracles, below). But suppose we grant, for the sake of argument, that God does act in the world. Could such actions be identified and scientifically investigated?

One can stipulate that science should investigate only the space-time world and natural causes. But a more sensible proposal is that the mission of science is to explain whichever phenomena we discover; and in particular, to discover the causes of things. Whatever has causal influence on the material world can, in principle, be detected and measured. So, if supernatural beings exercise such influence, why should science refrain from characterizing the causes of phenomena so produced? There would be no guarantee of success (there never is); supernatural causes might be elusive. But that is not the same thing as saying that they cannot in principle be discovered. What *can* fairly be said on this score is that supernaturalistic explanations have, to date, been decidedly arid in articulating causal mechanisms or proposing experimental procedures.

A third argument sometimes encountered is that scientific investigation of the world – including, in particular, any historical study of the past – would be rendered impossible by the admission of supernatural interventions in the world.[12] The argument is that inferences about the past (and future), indeed, inferences of any kind from known effects to unobserved causes, or known causes to unobserved effects, require that nature behave in orderly ways. So the very possibility of history – and of science generally – assumes that natural events are governed by laws without supernatural interference. We may, then, with reason adopt as a methodological principle the proposition that nature, at least so far as it can properly be brought within the purview of scientific investigation, is free of supernatural causes.

A plausible objection to this argument grants that if nature were to become too erratic – say, because of the persistent intervention of erratic supernatural agents – then science would indeed be unable to provide knowledge of the world. But why suppose that? Why could not God intervene on rare and significant occasions in ways that do not massively disrupt the order of nature, without thereby incapacitating our scientific methods?[13] Why, further, must we suppose that the actions of agents (whether divine or finite) must be erratic or inexplicable?

This objection does not perhaps fully appreciate the force of the difficulty. The odd miracle might indeed not so disrupt the order of nature as to vitiate scientific efforts to understand the world. But if miracles are possible, how can we know that they occur only sparsely, and with limited effects on the course of nature? Must not the evidence for such a claim itself presuppose the validity of scientific methods – and hence presuppose that the world is not chaotically miracle-infested?

The admission that miracles occur seems, on this showing, to raise a ground for deep skepticism about inductive inference, over and above the grounds that philosophers have otherwise discovered. But precisely because on this point the issue becomes a version of the problem of radical skepticism, we shall set it aside. We shall, however, have to return to the subject of miracles: how they are to be conceived, and what evidence for the supernatural they could provide.

EPISTEMOLOGICAL NATURALISM. This term can easily mislead. The program of naturalizing epistemology has important conceptual connections to naturalism (concerning which see below); but it is easy to confuse this approach in epistemology with a thesis more strictly and properly denoted epistemological naturalism – namely, the thesis that the supernatural lies beyond the scope of what we can know. Theism has traditionally sought an understanding of God from two sources: natural theology (relying on human reason working with sensory inputs) and revelation (the authenticity of which was, traditionally, taken to be certified by associated miracles). Epistemological naturalism rejects both of these as possible sources of knowledge concerning the supernatural.

Naturalized epistemology. Naturalizing epistemology is a matter of looking to science to enlighten us about what can be known, especially about our cognitive faculties. On one main formulation, naturalized epistemology is a subdiscipline of cognitive psychology.[14] Here we trace, with extremely broad brush strokes, the philosophical ancestry of this idea. In classical foundationalism, knowledge begins with propositions about subjective experience. Only these propositions, and propositions they support, are justifiably believed; only to these do we have cognitive *access*.

Skeptical difficulties led to two sorts of responses. One – Quine's – was to abandon foundationalism. The second, taken up by Goldman and many others, was to abandon the access requirement.

The first option moves to a coherence theory of justification, and allows, without obvious circularity, the doctrine that science can settle epistemological questions. The second option, more common among contemporary epistemologists, is to reject the access requirement in favor of externalism. This option has the advantage, for the naturalist, of permitting a natural alliance with epistemic and scientific realism. A reliabilist epistemology will naturally look to scientific theory, realistically understood, to furnish reasons to believe that our sensory and cognitive mechanisms do furnish us with a largely accurate picture of the world.[15]

Now both types of naturalized epistemology are entirely compatible with theism, provided – in the first type – that the existence of God can be made to cohere with current science or – in the second – that there are reliable processes by means of which human beings can come to experience or know about God. But if to naturalized epistemology is added the proposition that there can be no causal interaction between the supernatural and the natural world (hence, no way of integrating the supernatural into a scientific understanding of the world, and no reliable belief-producing processes that bring us into contact with the divine), then naturalized epistemology yields epistemological naturalism more narrowly conceived.

Epistemological naturalism. The term "epistemological naturalism" should more properly be used to denote the position that human beings have epistemic access only to items that inhabit the spatiotemporal domain. These include material objects, human persons, and their causally accessible properties. Arguably, they include states of affairs[16] and events that involve those things. They exclude abstracta, such as Platonic universals and propositions, and any particulars not locatable in space and time, such as disembodied minds. Epistemological naturalism does not assert that these things do not exist, but it denies that we can have knowledge of or even evidence for them.[17]

The best argument for epistemological naturalism has three premises:

(1) We are not directly acquainted with things not locatable in space or time.
(2) If something is not an object of direct (perceptual) acquaintance, knowledge of it requires that there be a causal connection between it and the knower.
(3) Things not located in space or time cannot enter into causal relations.

Epistemological naturalism follows from these premises. Each premise is controversial. Premise (1), for example, will be denied by those who claim that we are directly acquainted with (Platonic) universals by virtue of being directly acquainted with instances of them. Premise (2) will be denied by those who claim that the intellect is capable of directly "grasping," nonperceptually, certain items (such as numbers) and truths about them. Premise (3), as noted before, presumes perhaps more than we can properly claim to understand about causal relations.[18] Nevertheless, each of these premises has considerable plausibility.[19]

ONTOLOGICAL NATURALISM. Naturalism is often understood as an ontological doctrine. But which ontological doctrine? Several views might with justice lay claim to the title. There is little point in assigning proprietary rights to one of these. Rather we shall survey the possibilities.

View 1. In perhaps its most restrictive version, ontological naturalism denies the existence of anything other than space, time, and matter. What about their properties? This view is compatible with nominalism, trope theory, and Aristotelian or immanent realism. The admissible properties will be the properties posited by physics: those that can be detected or measured and that figure in the laws of physics. A trope theorist may, further, take material objects to be just bundles or structured collections of tropes.[20]

View 2. A naturalist might liberalize his or her ontology by admitting certain abstract objects. Quine, famously, conceded the existence of sets. The more ontologically ambitious (or, by some lights, promiscuous) will find reason to allow propositions, possible worlds, Platonic universals, numbers, mathematical spaces, and other such abstracta. Economy can be achieved by showing that some abstracta are reducible to others. View 2 is a genus that splinters into species, according to which abstracta are admitted and which are taken to be ontologically fundamental.

Why should any such view qualify as a variety of naturalism? Typically, the reasons are dialectical. Admission of abstracta, while unparsimonious, improves explanatory power; for example, causation – so some think – involves a relation between universals, and hence requires universals. A naturalist will not want to forgo causation.

View 3. A naturalist who is not sanguine about the reducibility of the mental to the physical has several options. These include token-token identity theories such as functionalism, property dualism, and – more daringly – substance dualism. How true is each of these to the spirit of naturalism? Opinions vary. Property dualism and token-token identity theories posit properties, or state-kinds, that do not as such figure in the laws of physics.[21] Mental states understood, for example, as computational states are not the sorts of state kinds that carve up the world along the lines recognized by physical law. Nevertheless, that there are mental states is indisputable,[22] and if they are not reducible to physical states, the naturalist can maintain that they are part of the ordinary furniture of our world, no more problematic than material objects, and moreover not outside the ambit of scientific investigation. Indeed, they are states of physical objects – human and other animal bodies. The world remains a world of physical objects located in space and time. But what about substance dualism? Is *that* a position that cannot be accepted by a naturalist?

View 4. It is useful to consider whether there is some minimal conception of metaphysical or ontological naturalism that captures, in a principled way, the minimal core beliefs bearing on the issue of atheism. A plausible proposal is that the naturalist is committed to the claim that there are no disembodied minds. This view is not incompatible with substance dualism, but requires that, if there are immaterial mental substances, they cannot be things that exist apart from embodiment in a physical substance. Thus, it is a view that denies the existence of disembodied gods, angels, demons, souls, and the like; in short, most of the denizens of the supernatural, as ordinarily conceived.[23]

Evidence for and against Metaphysical Naturalism

As noted earlier, some theists – most notably, those advocating scientific creationism or intelligent design theory, such as Phillip Johnson – insist that metaphysical naturalism is a world-view accepted on *faith* by the established scientific community (and by many philosophers). The implication is that metaphysical naturalism is epistemically on equal footing with religious belief; that neither is accepted on the basis of empirical evidence, though both may place constraints on how evidence is to be interpreted.[24] This charge reflects apparent ignorance of the grounds on which a naturalistic view is characteristically adopted. Here we have space to consider only the evidence for and against view 4 above; and that only in brief and summary fashion.

The primary evidence for holding that there are no disembodied minds is not at all esoteric. In our experience minds are invariably created by the physical process of procreation, and reside in bodies. Moreover, there is massive correlation between our mental states and physical states of our bodies. This ordinary evidence is supplemented by a growing body of evidence from the neurosciences, and strongly suggests that mental states depend, by nomological necessity, on appropriate states in bodies.

But might there be also evidence of *disembodied* minds? There are four primary sources of such evidence. First, a posteriori arguments from natural theology – primarily, the various cosmological and teleological arguments. Second, some claim directly to have experienced supernatural entities, via, for example, mystical experiences. Third, there are paranormal phenomena – psychokinesis, "astral projection," and near-death experiences – that are taken to show that there are disembodied minds and that minds can exert influence through nonphysical means. Fourth, we have miracle claims and prophecy.[25] The first of these is outside our purview. But some brief remarks are in order respecting the others.

MYSTICAL EXPERIENCES. Theists have argued at length for the position that some religious experiences afford their subjects with first-hand knowledge of God and of other supernatural beings.[26] Certain mystical experiences are allegedly a variety of *perceptual* experience, whose object appears to be God. Such experiences are properly taken to be veridical experiences of God, if certain other conditions are met, just as ordinary perceptual experiences are properly taken, barring disqualifying conditions, to be veridical experiences of ordinary objects. It is generally conceded that mystical experiences provide *weaker* grounds for religious beliefs than ordinary cases of sense perception provide for beliefs about our physical environment, in part because mystical experiences are rare, usually fleeting, and have a content not accessible to others in the way a public object such as a tree would have. Nevertheless, mystical experiences provide prima facie grounds for religious belief and, in the absence of counterevidence, are claimed to make such beliefs rational, at least for members of a religious community within which the relevant mystical practices are established.

It may be granted that mystical experiences provide some prima facie grounds for belief. It does not follow that, taken by themselves or together with the legitimating conditions imposed by a religious tradition, they provide sufficient grounds for rational belief – especially as tradition-based criteria (e.g., consonance with some canonical revelation) are typically question-begging.

It is true of any experience whose putative object is not a subjective item that it is not an experience *of* that item unless, had that item not been in some suitable way present to or in contact with the subject, the subject would not have had that experience. In inquiring whether a supernatural object is veridically perceived by a subject, therefore, we must ask whether such an object stands in a suitable causal relation to the mystical experience of the subject. That may appear initially to be the most natural explanation; but it may be far from the best all-things-considered explanation.

A naturalist will naturally seek a natural explanation for mystical experiences. Two worthy of mention are a sociological one and a neurophysiological one.[27] The sociological research appears to indicate that mystical experiences, and the revelations that are purportedly conveyed to the mystic, play an essential role in certain contexts in providing the mystic, or a group whose interests he or she represents, with social authority.[28] At the neurophysiological level, several studies, including brain scans of experiencing subjects and artificial induction of mystical experiences by electrical stimulation of brain loci, have elucidated some of the neural mechanisms that underlie such experiences. Furthermore, the known functions (often, malfunctioning) of the implicated brain centers appear well suited to explain the affective and cognitive features of mystical experiences. This research already shows promise of resolving some long-standing disputes about the nature of mystical experiences, for example, their cross-cultural commonalities and differences.[29]

We noted above that a mystical experience can provide some prima facie warrant for the existence of its object; if that object is God, then it provides some evidence for God's existence. But how much? A major obstacle is that mystical experiences cannot be independently verified.[30]

A second difficulty is generated by the striking variety in the content of mystical experiences, at least as interpreted by mystics. Nor are these interpretations compatible: one religion's gods are another religion's demons or delusions. That is difficult to explain on the supposition that there is a single God who infinitely loves all of his creatures. The privacy, phenomenology, and clashing contents of mystical experiences all militate against the supposition that they have a theistic rather than a natural source.

PARANORMAL PHENOMENA. A variety of paranormal effects, were they genuine, would provide evidence for supernatural beings, disembodied human minds, or nonnatural forces. They include alleged cases of reincarnation, clairvoyance, psychokinesis, and out-of-body experiences, especially those associated with near-death episodes (NDEs). Because such phenomena suggest the possibility of extra-bodily existence, of nonphysical channels of communication between minds, and of minds influencing distant physical objects directly, they have attracted the attention not only of laypeople but of philosophers. Philosophical interest was, however, much stronger in the 1920s and 1930s. Exposure of a series of fraudulent spirit mediums and hoaxes and, subsequently, of both incompetent and manipulated scientific investigations has justifiably made the philosophical community much more cautious. We should nevertheless take brief note of a few ongoing research efforts that retain some credibility. We confine ourselves to work on NDEs.

Near-death experiences. Near-death experiences of a kind that include phenomenology of travel out of the body, often through a tunnel to a bright realm in which, sometimes, deceased relatives or familiar supernatural figures are met give color to the conventional (Christian) view of the afterlife (for the saved). There has been extensive reporting of such experiences, beginning with the studies of Elizabeth Kubler-Ross. It seems that subjects are sincere in their reports. How significant are these phenomena? A number of efforts have been made to corroborate alleged out-of-body observations of real-world conditions; the results suggest hallucination or are at best inconclusive.[31] Sometimes a dying subject is met "on the other side" by friends who are in fact alive. Susan Blackmore and others have proposed biochemical and neurological hypotheses that appear to account for many of the phenomenological data and that suggest some similarity to mechanisms that can produce mystical experiences.[32]

MIRACLES. Our discussion of miracles will have to be unconscionably brief. We may identify three problems that attend appeal to miracles. The first of these is *conceptual*: what is a miracle? It is common to understand miracles as violations of laws of nature. But if laws entail perfect regularities, that cannot be accepted.[33] Instead, we may see miracles as involving an *added supernatural influence* – an added force that has a supernatural source. But that would nevertheless involve violation of the laws of conservation of momentum and energy. So appeal to miracles requires rejecting these laws, which are among the most highly confirmed in physics.

A second problem is *metaphysical*. Can a being that is not in space (and, arguably, not in time) causally affect the physical world? Perhaps, at best, it can be said that we do not understand the nature of causation well enough to determine whether this is possible or not.

Third, there are *epistemological* difficulties. By what means can it be determined that a miraculous event has occurred – both that the event did occur and, if it did, that it is a miracle? And further, by what criteria can it be ascertained whether a given miracle (supposing one to be identified) was caused by the God of Abraham, by Satan, or by some other deity?

CONCLUSION

May we conclude, then, that there is strong support for at least the most "liberal" versions of physicalism and naturalism? I believe we may. Yet – surprisingly – there are entities of a kind that might with some reason be called "supernatural" that such ontologies can allow. These are worth mention because they may hold the key to an explanation of the origins of religious belief. In his classic *The Elementary Forms of the Religious Life*, Emil Durkheim proposed that primitive beliefs in gods and spirits are just unconscious "projections" of early human recognition of the existence and power of *social* realities: tribes, nations, and social institutions. The claim that these projections were unconscious is (I think) unwarranted; it is more parsimonious to suppose that the gods and spirits just *were* (understood to be) social realities, reified and personified. As Durkheim realized, nations, and so on, and their actions are most naturally understood to be (corporate) *persons* that are not spatially locatable (though variously embodied in natural persons and certain of their actions). The parallels between gods and corporate persons are much more extensive than this, as are those between souls and social roles.[34]

Such a hypothesis, of course, requires it to be explained how thought about social/political realities came to be transformed into something different – thought about "spooky" things. Nevertheless, at least if social facts are not – as is debatable – reducible to facts about natural persons, there is some reason to allow into a naturalistic picture of the world entities (e.g., persons) that are "supernatural" – "super" because they supervene upon features of the natural world, and not natural because they are products of human artifice, not nature.

NOTES

1. Two minor qualifications. One could be a theist of sorts – panentheists and Mormons might qualify – and still accept some forms of physicalism and naturalism. Second, one could hold that finite minds must be embodied, while an infinite mind need not or cannot be. Such limited-scope physicalism would not entail atheism.

2. See Bernard Williams, "Can We Solve the Mind-Body Problem?" *Mind* 98 (1989): 349–66.

3. A common competing theistic view is that God is the *Ur*-substance; both matter and finite minds derive their being from Him. On the usual view, human bodies are endowed with finite (human) minds by God at some stage in human development. That explains our observations. But the relation between this view and a biblical understanding is problematic at best (see note 7).

4. Grover Maxwell has suggested this possibility; see Maxwell, "Rigid Designators and Mind-Brain Identity," in C. W. Savage (ed.), *Perception and Cognition* (Minneapolis: University of Minnesota Press, 1978), pp. 365–404.

5. See Evan Fales, *Causation and Universals* (New York: Routledge, 1990), esp. chaps. 8 and 12.

6. See, e.g., Fred Dretske, *Naturalizing the Mind* (Cambridge, Mass.: MIT Press, 1995), and Ruth Garrett Millikan, *White Queen Psychology and Other Essays for Alice* (Cambridge, Mass.: MIT Press, 1993).

7. There are vexed questions that arise concerning the best way to understand traditional – especially biblical – views of the ontology of persons. It is possible to read the New Testament as holding that the dead simply remain in their graves as corpses until they are bodily raised, though a few passages suggest a kind of "holding pattern" in heaven for the souls of the dead between death and resurrection. The most explicit remarks are perhaps those of Paul, but Paul's anthropology is obscure. We know that Paul mentions "*nous*," roughly, mind or intelligence; "*psyche*," translated as "soul"; *pneuma*, usually translated as "spirit"; and *soma*, body. In the resurrection, the saved acquire a "spiritual body" – a *soma pneumatikon* (in express contradistinction to a *soma psychikon*). Unfortunately, Paul does not do much to clarify this notion, beyond supplying metaphors or analogies in I Cor. 15.

8. What is the modal strength of the "cannot" here? Clearly enough, the impossibility is not logical or conceptual; it could however be nomological or metaphysical.

9. Michael C. Rea, *World without Design: The Ontological Consequences of Naturalism* (Oxford: Oxford University Press, 2002).

10. Steven Jay Gould, "Nonoverlapping Magisteria," *Natural History* 106 (March 1997). See Grover Maxwell, "Rigid Designators and Mind-Brain

Identity," in C. W. Savage (ed.), *Perception and Cognition* (Minneapolis: University of Minnesota Press, 1978), pp. 365–404.

11. Phillip E. Johnson regularly levels this charge against Darwinians; see, e.g., Johnson, *Darwin on Trial*, 2nd ed. (Downers Grove, Ill.: Intervarsity Press, 1993), chaps. 13 and 14.

12. See, e.g., Anthony Flew, "Miracles," in Paul Edwards (ed.), *The Encyclopedia of Philosophy* (New York: Macmillan, 1967), pp. 346–53.

13. Thus William Alston, "Divine Action: Shadow or Substance?" in Thomas F. Tracy (ed.), *The God Who Acts: Philosophical and Theological Explorations* (University Park: Pennsylvania State University Press, 1994), pp. 49–50, and Alvin Plantinga, *Warranted Christian Belief* (Oxford: Oxford University Press, 2000), pp. 405–6.

14. W. V. O. Quine, *Theories and Things* (Cambridge, Mass.: Belknap/Harvard University Press, 1981), p. 72; Alvin Goldman, "A Priori Warrant and Naturalistic Epistemology," *Philosophical Perspectives* 13 (1999): 1–28, esp. p. 2.

15. Alvin Plantinga has challenged this sort of appeal, on the grounds that the evolution of our cognitive faculties, if proceeded by purely Darwinian mechanisms, cannot be supposed to have conferred reliability with high likelihood. See Plantinga, *Warrant and Proper Function* (Oxford: Oxford University Press, 1993), chaps. 11 and 12, and responses to Plantinga's argument in James Beilby, ed., *Naturalism Defeated?* (Ithaca, N.Y.: Cornell University Press, 2002).

16. E.g., for David Armstrong, for whom states of affairs are a fundamental ontological category. See Armstrong, *A World of States of Affairs* (New York: Cambridge University Press, 1997).

17. When epistemological naturalism is combined with verificationism, it does yield a kind of ontological naturalism, which may be described as semantic naturalism: talk of nonnatural entities is meaningless.

18. Combined with a causal theory of reference, this premise entails that direct reference to such entities is not possible. There remains, however, the possibility of reference via a definite description.

19. Another argument, specifically directed against knowledge of God, claims that there are no criteria for identifying particulars that exist outside space and time; see Richard Gale, *On the Nature and Existence of God* (New York: Cambridge University Press, 1991), chap. 8.

20. Keith Campbell, *Abstract Particulars* (Oxford: Oxford University Press, 1990). Tropes are instances of properties.

21. See Donald Davidson's argument for anomalous monism in "Mental Events," reprinted in Davidson, *Essays on Actions and Events* (Oxford: Clarendon, 2001), essay 11.

22. Or not sensibly disputable: I am dismissing eliminative materialism.

23. An even narrower – albeit vague – conception of metaphysical naturalism has been proposed by Alvin Plantinga: naturalism is the view that there are no gods, or anything very much like a god.

24. Quite incongruously, creationists always proceed nevertheless to provide what they take to be evidential grounds for theism.

25. There is a fifth source, not of evidence but purportedly of *knowledge* of truths about God that has been championed by Alvin Plantinga. According

to Plantinga, certain such truths are vouchsafed to (at least some) Christians by the internal action of the *sensus divinitatis* and the Holy Spirit. See his *Warranted Christian Belief* (Oxford: Oxford University Press, 2000). For a critical survey of the arguments, see Evan Fales, "Critical Discussion of Alvin Plantinga's *Warranted Christian Belief*," *Nous* 37 (2003): 353–70.

26. Some main contributions to this discussion are William Wainwright, *Mysticism: A Study of Its Nature, Cognitive Value, and Moral Implications* (Madison: University of Wisconsin Press, 1981); William P. Alston, *Perceiving God: The Epistemology of Religious Experience* (Ithaca, N.Y.: Cornell University Press, 1991); Keith E. Yandell, *The Epistemology of Religious Experience* (New York: Cambridge University Press, 1993); and Jerome I. Gellman, *Experience of God and the Rationality of Theistic Belief* (Ithaca, N.Y.: Cornell University Press, 1997).

27. For psychological explanations, see the chapter by Beit-Hallahmi in this volume.

28. See I. M. Lewis, *Ecstatic Religion: A Study of Shamanism and Spirit Possession*, 2nd ed. (1971; London: Routledge, 1989).

29. See Robert K. C. Foreman, *Mysticism, Mind, Consciousness* (Albany: SUNY Press, 1999), versus Steven Katz (ed.), *Mysticism and Philosophical Analysis* (New York: Oxford University Press, 1978). Katz argues from within a kind of culturally relativized neo-Kantian framework. If we jettison the problematic philosophical matrix, we are nevertheless left with the observation that mystical experiences – or at any rate the descriptions of them provided by mystics – display enormous, and clearly culture-influenced, variety.

30. See Evan Fales, "Mystical Experience as Evidence," *International Journal for Philosophy of Religion* 40 (1996); 19–46, esp. 30–32.

31. Perhaps the most convincing case, that of Pam Reynolds, is at best inconclusive: see Mark Fox, *Religion, Spirituality, and Near-Death Experience* (New York: Routledge, 2003), p. 210.

32. Susan Blackmore, *Dying to Live: Near-Death Experiences* (Buffalo, N.Y.: Prometheus Books, 1993).

33. Probabilistic laws introduce a complication. And there are conceptions of laws that allow for the possibility of violation; see, e.g., John Foster, *The Divine Lawmaker* (Oxford: Oxford University Press, 2004). I shall not discuss these issues here.

34. See Evan Fales, "The Ontology of Social Roles," *Philosophy of the Social Sciences* 7 (1977): 139–61.

8   Atheism and Evolution

Descartes, in the Meditations (1641), notes that "there are only two ways of proving the existence of God, one by means of his effects, and the other by means of his nature or essence" (AT VII, 120). The latter, a priori path, represented paradigmatically by the ontological argument of St. Anselm (and its offspring, including Descartes' own version), has perennial appeal to a certain sort of philosopher, but leaves most people cold. The former, represented paradigmatically by the argument from design, is surely the most compelling of all arguments against atheism, and it apparently arises spontaneously whenever people anywhere are challenged to justify their belief in God. William Paley's example of finding a watch while strolling on the heath epitomizes the theme and leads, he says, to "the inference we think is inevitable, that the watch must have had a maker – that there must have existed, at some time and at some place or other, an artificer or artificers who formed it for the purpose which we find it actually to answer, who comprehended its construction and designed its use" (Paley 1800). Until Darwin came along, this was a respectable argument, worthy of Hume's corrosive but indecisive broadside in his *Dialogues Concerning Natural Religion* (1779). Descartes himself subscribed to a version of the argument from design, in his notorious Third Meditation argument that his idea of God was too wonderful to have been created by him. Though Descartes surely considered himself intelligent, and moreover an accomplished designer of ideas, he could not imagine that he could be the intelligent designer of his own idea of God.

The familiar idea that the marvels of the universe prove the existence of God as its creator is perhaps as old as our species, or even older. Did *Homo habilis*, the "handy" man who made the first crude tools, have some dim and inarticulate sense that it always takes a big fancy smart thing to make a less fancy thing? We never saw a pot making a potter, or a horseshoe making a blacksmith, after all. This trickle-down, mind-first vision of design seems self-evident at first. A creationist propaganda

Passages in this chapter are drawn, with revisions, from Dennett 1995 and 2005.

pamphlet I was once given by a student exploits this intuition with a mock questionnaire:

TEST TWO
Do you know of any building that didn't have a builder? [YES] [NO]
Do you know of any painting that didn't have a painter? [YES] [NO]
Do you know of any car that didn't have a maker? [YES] [NO]
If you answered YES for any of the above, give details: _____
_____

The presumed embarrassment of the test taker when faced with this tall order evokes the incredulity that many – probably most – people feel when they confront Darwin's great idea. It does seem just obvious, doesn't it, that there couldn't be any such designs without designers, any such creations without a creator! The vertigo and revulsion this prospect provokes in many was perfectly expressed in an early attack on Darwin, published anonymously in 1868:

In the theory with which we have to deal, Absolute Ignorance is the artificer; so that we may enunciate as the fundamental principle of the whole system, that, IN ORDER TO MAKE A PERFECT AND BEAUTIFUL MACHINE, IT IS NOT REQUISITE TO KNOW HOW TO MAKE IT. This proposition will be found, on careful examination, to express, in condensed form, the essential purport of the Theory, and to express in a few words all Mr. Darwin's meaning; who, by a strange inversion of reasoning, seems to think Absolute Ignorance fully qualified to take the place of Absolute Wisdom in all the achievements of creative skill. (MacKenzie 1868)

Exactly! Darwin's "strange inversion of reasoning" was in fact a new and wonderful way of thinking, completely overturning the mind-first way that even David Hume had been unable to cast aside, and replacing it with a bubble-up vision in which intelligence – the concentrated, forward-looking intelligence of an anthropomorphic agent – eventually emerges as just one of the products of mindless, mechanistic processes. These processes are fueled by untold billions of pointless, undesigned collisions, some vanishing small fraction of which fortuitously lead to tiny improvements in the lineages in which they occur. Thanks to Darwin's principle of "descent with modification," these ruthlessly tested design innovations accumulate over the eons, yielding breathtakingly brilliant designs that never had a designer – other than the purposeless, distributed process of natural selection itself.

The signatures of these unplanned innovations are everywhere to be found in a close examination of the marvels of nature, in the inside-out retina of the vertebrate eye, the half-discarded leftovers in the genes and organs of every species, the prodigious wastefulness and apparent cruelty of so many of nature's processes. These departures from wisdom, "frozen accidents," in the apt phrase of Francis Crick, confront the theist with a dilemma: if God is responsible for these designs, then his intelligence looks disturbingly like human obtuseness and callousness. Moreover, as our understanding of the mechanisms of evolution grows, we can sketch out ever more detailed accounts of the historical sequence of events by which the design innovations appeared and were incorporated into the branching tree of genomes. A voluminously predictive account of the creative process is now emerging, replete with thousands of mutually supporting details, and no contradictions at all. As the pieces of this mega–jigsaw puzzle fall into place with increasing rapidity, there can be no reasonable doubt that it is, in all its broad outlines if not yet in all its unsettled details, the true story of how all living things came to have the designs we observe.

Unreasonable doubt flourishes, however, thanks to the incessant propaganda efforts of creationists and intelligent design (ID) spokespeople, such as William Dembski and Michael Behe, who have managed to persuade a distressingly large proportion of the lay population that there are genuine scientific controversies brewing in biology about its backbone theory, evolution by natural selection. There are not. Genuine scientific controversies abound in every corner of biology, but none of them challenges evolution. The legitimate way to stir up a storm in any scientific discipline is to come up with an alternative theory that

1. makes a prediction that is crisply denied by the reigning theory but turns out to be true or
2. explains something that has been baffling defenders of the status quo or
3. unifies two distant theories, at the cost of some element of the currently accepted view

To date, the proponents of ID have not produced a single instance of anything like that. There are no experiments with results that challenge any standard neo-Darwinian understanding, no observations from the fossil record or genomics or biogeography or comparative anatomy that undermine standard evolutionary thinking, no theoretical unifications or simplifications, and no surprising predictions that have turned out to be true. In short, no science – just advertising. No ID hypothesis has even been ventured as a rival explanation of any biological phenomenon. To formulate a competing hypothesis, you have to get down in the trenches and offer some details that have testable implications, but the ID proponents conveniently sidestep that requirement, claiming that they have no specifics in mind about who or what the intelligent designer might be.

To see this shortcoming in relief, consider an imaginary hypothesis of intelligent design that could explain the emergence of human beings on this planet:

About six million years ago, intelligent genetic engineers from another galaxy visited Earth and decided that it would be a more interesting planet if there was a language-using, religion-forming species on it, so they sequestered some primates (from among the ancestors of both humans and chimpanzees and bonobos), and genetically re-engineered them to give them the language instinct, and enlarged frontal lobes for planning and reflection. It worked.

If some version of this hypothesis were true, it could actually explain how and why human beings differ from their nearest relatives, and it would disconfirm all the competing neo-Darwinian hypotheses that are currently being pursued on this fascinating question. We'd still have the problem of how these intelligent genetic engineers came to exist on their home planet, but we could safely ignore that complication for the time being, since there is not the slightest shred of evidence in favor of this hypothesis. And – here is something the ID community is reluctant to discuss – no other intelligent-design hypothesis has anything more going for it. In fact, my farfetched – but possible – hypothesis has the distinct advantage of being testable in principle: we could look in the human and chimpanzee genome for unmistakable signs of tampering by these genetic engineers (maybe they left a "Kilroy was here" message in human DNA for us to decode!). Finding some sort of user's manual neatly embedded in the apparently functionless "junk DNA" that makes up most of the human genome would be a Nobel Prize–winning knock-out coup for the ID gang, but if they are even looking, they are not telling anyone. They know better. Ironically, William Dembski's "design infer-ence" argument is supposed to set up a sure-fire test for finding just such telltale signs of intelligent tinkering in the causal ancestry of phenom-ena, but instead of trying to demonstrate the test in action, Dembski (2005) settles for the observation that the ID perspective "encourages biologists to investigate whether systems that first appear functionless might in fact have a function" – and no neo-Darwinian would disagree with that strategy.

Between the richly detailed and ever-ramifying evolutionary story and the featureless mystery of God the creator of all creatures great and small, there is no contest. This is a momentous reversal for the ancient conviction that God's existence can be read off the wonders of nature. Anyone who has ever been struck by the magnificent intricacy of design and prodigious variety of the living world and wondered what – if not God – could possibly account for its existence must now confront not just a plausible alternative, but an alternative of breathtaking explanatory power supported by literally thousands of confirmed predictions and solved puzzles. Richard Dawkins has put the point crisply: "Although atheism might have been logically tenable before Darwin, Darwin made it possible to be an intellectually fulfilled atheist" (1986: 6).

Undermining the best argument anybody ever thought of for the existence of God is not, of course, proving the nonexistence of God, and many careful thinkers who have accepted evolution by natural selection as the explanation of the wonders of the living world have cast about for other supports for their continuing belief in God. The idea of treating mind as an effect rather than as a first cause is too revolutionary for some. Alfred Russel Wallace, the codiscoverer with Darwin of natural selection, could never accept the full inversion, proclaiming that "the marvelous complexity of forces which appear to control matter, if not actually to constitute it, are and must be mind-products" (quoted by Gould 1985: 397). More recently, the physicist Paul Davies, in his book, *The Mind of God* (1992: 232), opines that the reflective power of human minds can be "no trivial detail, no minor by-product of mindless purposeless forces." This is a most revealing way of expressing a familiar denial, for it betrays an ill-examined prejudice. Why, we might ask Davies, would its being a by-product of mindless, purposeless forces make it trivial? Why couldn't the most important thing of all be something that arose from unimportant things? Why should the importance or excellence of anything have to rain down on it from on high, from something more important, a gift from God? Darwin's inversion suggests that we abandon that presumption and look for sorts of excellence, of worth and purpose, that can emerge, bubbling up out of "mindless, purposeless forces."

But before we settle into the bubble-up perspective on ultimate importance, with whatever comfort we can muster, we need to deal with the residual skepticism of the traditional trickle-down perspective: once mindless, purposeless evolution gets under way, it generates magnificent design over time, but how did it get started? Don't we need God to kindle the process by miraculously and improbably assembling the first self-replicating thing? This hope – and the contrary conviction that the origin of life can be accounted for somehow by a natural series of events of low but not negligible probability – grounds the intense interest, not to say passion, surrounding contemporary research on the origin of life. The details of the process are not yet settled, but the presence of fairly complex building blocks – not just amino acids and basic "organic" molecules – in the prebiotic world is now established, and the problem confronting scientists today is less a matter of imponderable mystery than an embarrassment of riches: so many possibilities are not yet excluded. The conviction that it must have taken a miracle – a temporary violation of the standing laws of physics and chemistry – for life to get initiated has lost whatever plausibility it ever had.

But, then, those standing laws themselves require an explanation, do they not? If God the Artificer and God the Kindler have lost their jobs, what of God the Lawgiver? This suggestion has been popular since the earliest days of Darwinian thinking, and Darwin himself toyed with this attractive retreat. In a letter in 1860 to the American naturalist, Asa Gray, an early supporter, Darwin wrote, "I am inclined to look at everything as resulting from *designed* [emphasis added] laws, with the details whether good or bad, left to the working out of what we may call chance" (Darwin 1911: 105).

Automatic processes are themselves often creations of great brilliance. From today's vantage point, we can see that the inventors of the automatic transmission and the automatic door-opener were no idiots, and their genius lay in seeing how to create something that could do something "clever" without having to think about it. Indulging in some anachronism, we could say that to some observers in Darwin's day, it seemed that he had left open the possibility that God did his handiwork by designing an automatic design maker. And to some of these, the idea was not just a desperate stop-gap but a positive improvement on tradition. The first chapter of Genesis describes the successive waves of Creation and ends each with the refrain "and God saw that it was good." Darwin had discovered a way to eliminate this retail application of intelligent quality control; natural selection would take care of that without further intervention from God. (The seventeenth-century philosopher Gottfried Wilhelm Leibniz had defended a similar hands-off vision of God the Creator.) As Henry Ward Beecher put it, "Design by wholesale is grander than design by retail" (Rachels 1991: 99). Asa Gray, captivated by Darwin's new idea but trying to reconcile it with as much of his traditional religious creed as possible, came up with this marriage of convenience: God intended the "stream of variations" and foresaw just how the laws of nature he had laid down would prune this stream over the eons. As John Dewey later aptly remarked (1910: 12), invoking yet another mercantile metaphor, "Gray held to what may be called design on the installment plan."

What is the difference between order and design? As a first stab, we might say that order is mere regularity, mere pattern; design is Aristotle's "telos," an exploitation of order for a purpose, such as we see in a cleverly designed artifact. The solar system exhibits stupendous order, but does not (apparently) have a purpose – it isn't for anything. An eye, in contrast is for seeing. Before Darwin, this distinction was not always clearly marked. Indeed, it was positively blurred:

In the thirteenth century, Aquinas offered the view that natural bodies [such as planets, raindrops, or volcanos] act as if guided toward a definite goal or end "so as to obtain the best result." This fitting of means to ends implies, argued Aquinas, an intention. But, seeing as natural bodies lack consciousness, they cannot supply that intention themselves. "Therefore some intelligent being exists by whom all natural things are directed to their end, and this being we call God." (Davies 1992: 200)

Hume's Cleanthes, following in this tradition, lumps the adapted marvels of the living world with the regularities of the heavens – it's all like a wonderful clockwork to him. But Darwin suggests a division: give me order, he says, and time, and I will give you design. Let me start with regularity – the mere purposeless, mindless, pointless regularity of physics – and I will show you a process that eventually will yield products that exhibit not just regularity but purposive design. (This was just what Karl Marx thought he saw when he declared that Darwin had dealt a deathblow to teleology: Darwin had reduced teleology to nonteleology, design to order.)

A more recent idea about the difference – and tight relation – between design and order will help to clarify the picture. This is the proposal, first popularized by the physicist Erwin Schrödinger (1967), that life can be defined in terms of the second law of thermodynamics. In physics, order or organization can be measured in terms of heat differences between regions of space-time; entropy is simply disorder, the opposite of order, and according to the second law, the entropy of any isolated system increases with time. In other words, things run down, inevitably. According to the second law, the universe is unwinding out of a more ordered state into the ultimately disordered state known as the heat death of the universe. What then are living things? They are things that defy this crumbling into dust, at least for awhile, by not being isolated – by taking in from their environment the wherewithal to keep life and limb together. The psychologist Richard Gregory summarizes the idea:

Time's arrow given by Entropy – the loss of organization, or loss of temperature differences – is statistical and it is subject to local small-scale reversals. Most striking: life is a systematic reversal of Entropy, and intelligence creates structures and energy differences against the supposed gradual "death" through Entropy of the physical Universe. (1981: 136)

Gregory goes on to credit Darwin with the fundamental enabling idea: "It is the measure of the concept of Natural Selection that increases in the complexity and order of organisms in biological time can now be understood." Not just individual organisms, then, but the whole process of evolution that creates them, can thus be seen as fundamental physical phenomena running contrary to the larger trend of cosmic time.

A designed thing, then, is either a living thing or a part of a living thing, or the artifact of a living thing, organized in any case in aid of this battle against disorder. It is not impossible to oppose the trend of the Second Law, but it is costly. Gregory dramatizes this with an unforgettable example. A standard textbook expression of the directionality imposed by the second law of thermodynamics is the claim that you can't unscramble an egg. Well, not that you absolutely can't, but that it would be an extremely costly, sophisticated task, uphill all the way against the second law. Now consider: how expensive would it be to make a device that would take scrambled eggs as input and deliver unscrambled eggs as output? There is one ready solution: put a live hen in the box! Feed it scrambled eggs, and it will be able to make eggs for you – for a while. Hens don't normally strike us as near-miraculously sophisticated entities, but here is one thing a hen can do, thanks to the design that has organized it, that is still way beyond the reach of the devices created by human engineers.

The more design a thing exhibits, the more R&D work had to have occurred to produce it. Minds are among the most designed of entities (in part because they are the self-redesigning things). But this means that they are among the most advanced effects (to date) of the creative process, not – as in the old version – its cause or source. Their products in turn – the human artifacts that were our initial model – must count as more designed still. This may seem counterintuitive at first. A Keats ode may seem to have some claim to having a grander R&D pedigree than a nightingale – at least it might seem so to a poet ignorant of biology – but what about a paper clip? Surely, a paper clip is a trivial product of design compared with any living thing, however rudimentary. In one obvious sense, this is true, but reflect for a moment. Put yourself in Paley's shoes, but walking along the apparently deserted beach on an alien planet. Which discovery would excite you the most: a clam or a clam rake? Before the planet could make a clam rake, it would have to make a clam rake maker, and that is a more designed thing by far than a clam.

Only a theory with the logical shape of Darwin's could explain how designed things came to exist, because any other sort of explanation would be either viciously circular or an infinite regress (Dennett 1975). The old way, the mind-first way, endorsed the principle that it takes an intelligence to make an intelligence. Children chant, "It takes one to know one," but an even more persuasive slogan would seem to be

"It takes a greater one to make a lesser one." Any view inspired by this slogan immediately faces an embarrassing question, however, as Hume had noted: If God created and designed all these wonderful things, who created God? Supergod? And who created Supergod? Superduper-god? Or did God create himself? Was it hard work? Did it take time? Don't ask! Well then, we may ask instead whether this bland embrace is any improvement over just denying the principle that intelligence (or design) must spring from intelligence. Darwin offered an explanatory path that actually honored Paley's insight: real work went into designing this watch, and work isn't free. Richard Dawkins summarizes the point:

Organized complexity is the thing we are having difficulty explaining. Once we are allowed simply to postulate organized complexity, if only the organized complexity of the DNA/protein replicating engine, it is relatively easy to invoke it as a generator of yet more organized complexity.... But of course any God capable of intelligently designing something as complex as the DNA/protein replicating machine must have been at least as complex and organized as the machine itself.... To explain the origin of the DNA/protein machine by invoking a supernatural Designer is to explain precisely nothing, for it leaves unexplained the origin of the Designer. (1986: 141)

As Dawkins goes on to say, "The one thing that makes evolution such a neat theory is that it explains how organized complexity can arise out of primeval simplicity" (p. 316). But still, that primeval simplicity exhibits order, and what of the laws of nature themselves? Don't they manifest the existence of a lawgiver? The physicist and cosmologist Freeman Dyson puts the point cautiously: "I do not claim that the architecture of the universe proves the existence of God. I claim only that the architecture of the universe is consistent with the hypothesis that mind plays an essential role in its functioning" (Dyson 1979: 251). Since, as Dawkins notes, the hypothesis that (organized, complex) mind plays such a role could not possibly be explanatory, we should ask: With what other hypotheses is the architecture of the universe consistent? There are several.

As more and more has been learned about the development of the universe since the big bang, about the conditions that permitted the formation of galaxies and stars and the heavy elements from which planets can be formed, physicists and cosmologists have been more and more struck by the exquisite sensitivity of the laws of nature. The speed of light is approximately 186,000 miles per second. What if it were only 185,000 miles per second, or 187,000 miles per second? Would that change much of anything? What if the force of gravity were 1 percent more or less than it is? The fundamental constants of physics – the speed of light, the constant of gravitational attraction, the weak and strong forces of sub-atomic interaction, Planck's constant – have values that of course permit the actual development of the universe as we know it to have happened. But it turns out that if in imagination we change any of these values by just the tiniest amount, we thereby posit a universe in which none of this could have happened, and indeed in which apparently nothing life-like could ever have emerged: no planets, no atmospheres, no solids at all, no elements except hydrogen and helium, or maybe not even that – just some boring plasma of hot, undifferentiated stuff, or an equally boring nothingness. So isn't it a wonderful fact that the laws are just right for us to exist? Indeed, one might want to add, we almost didn't make it!

Is this wonderful fact something that needs an explanation, and if so, what kind of explanation might it receive? According to the anthropic principle, we are entitled to infer facts about the universe and its laws from the undisputed fact that we (we anthropoi, we human beings) are here to do the inferring and observing. The anthropic principle comes in several flavors. In the "weak form" it is a sound, harmless, and on occasion useful application of elementary logic: if x is a necessary condition for the existence of y, and y exists, then x exists. Believers in any of the proposed strong versions of the anthropic principle think they can deduce something wonderful and surprising from the fact that we conscious observers are here – for instance, that in some sense the universe exists for us, or perhaps that we exist so that the universe as a whole can exist, or even that God created the universe the way he did so that we would be possible. Construed in this way, these proposals are attempts to restore Paley's argument from design, readdressing it to the design of the universe's most general laws of physics, not the particular constructions those laws make possible. Here, once again, Darwinian countermoves are available.

The boldest is that somehow there might have been some sort of differential reproduction of whole universes, with some varieties having more "offspring" than others, due to their more fecund laws of nature. Hume's mouthpiece Philo toyed with this idea, in the *Dialogues Concerning Natural Religion*, when he imagined a designer-god who was far from intelligent:

And what surprise must we entertain, when we find him a stupid mechanic, who imitated others, and copied an art, which, through a long succession of ages, after multiplied trials, mistakes, corrections, deliberations, and controversies, had been gradually improving? Many worlds might have been botched and bungled, throughout an eternity, ere this system was struck out: Much labour lost: Many fruitless trials made: And a slow, but continued improvement carried on during infinite ages of world-making. (part V)

Hume imputes the "continued improvement" to the minimal selective bias of a "stupid mechanic," but we can replace the stupid mechanic with something even stupider without dissipating the lifting power: a purely algorithmic Darwinian process of world-trying. Hume obviously didn't think this was anything but an amusing philosophical fantasy, but the idea has recently been developed in some detail by the physicist Lee Smolin (1992). The basic idea is that the singularities known as black holes are in effect the birthplaces of offspring universes, in which the fundamental physical constants would differ slightly, in random ways, from the physical constants in the parent universe. So, according to Smolin's hypothesis, we have differential reproduction and mutation, the two essential features of any Darwinian selection algorithm. Those universes that just happened to have physical constants that encouraged the development of black holes would ipso facto have more offspring, which would have more offspring, and so forth – that's the selection step. Note that there is no grim reaper of universes in this scenario; they all live and "die" in due course, but some merely have more offspring. According to this idea, then, it is no mere interesting coincidence that we live in a universe in which there are black holes. But neither is it an absolute logical necessity; it is rather the sort of conditional near-necessity you find in any evolutionary account. The link, Smolin claims, is carbon, which plays a role both in the collapse of gaseous clouds (or in other words, the birth of stars, a precursor to the birth of black holes) and, of course, in our molecular engineering.

Is the theory testable? Smolin offers some predictions that would, if disconfirmed, pretty well eliminate his idea: it should be the case that all the "near" variations in physical constants from the values we enjoy should yield universes in which black holes are less probable or less frequent than in our own. In short, he thinks our universe should manifest at least a local, if not global, optimum in the black hole–making competition. The trouble is that there are too few constraints, so far as I can see, on what should count as a "near" variation and why, but perhaps further elaboration on the theory will clarify this. Needless to say, it is hard to know what to make of this idea yet, but whatever the eventual verdict of scientists, the idea already serves to secure a philosophical point. Freeman Dyson, and others who think they see a wonderful pattern in the laws of physics, might be tempted to make the tactical mistake of asking the rhetorical question, "What else but God could possibly explain it?" Smolin offers a nicely deflating reply. If we follow the Darwinian down this path, God the Artificer turns first into God the Lawgiver, who then can be seen to merge with God the Lawfinder, who does not invent the laws of nature, but just eventually stumbles across them in the course of blind trial and error of universes.

God's hypothesized contribution is becoming less personal – and hence more readily performable by something dogged and mindless!

But suppose, for the sake of argument, that Smolin's speculations are all flawed; suppose selection of universes doesn't work after all. There is a weaker, semi-Darwinian speculation that also answers the rhetorical question handily. Hume also toyed with this weaker idea, in part VIII of his *Dialogues*:

Instead of supposing matter infinite, as Epicurus did, let us suppose it finite. A finite number of particles is only susceptible of finite transpositions: And it must happen, in an eternal duration, that every possible order or position must be tried an infinite number of times.....

Suppose ... that matter were thrown into any position, by a blind, unguided force; it is evident that this first position must in all probability be the most confused and most disorderly imaginable, without any resemblance to those works of human contrivance, which, along with a symmetry of parts, discover an adjustment of means to ends and a tendency to self-preservation.... [S]uppose, that the actuating force, whatever it be, still continues in matter....Thus the universe goes on for many ages in a continued succession of chaos and disorder. But is it not possible that it may settle at last...? May we not hope for such a position, or rather be assured of it, from the eternal revolutions of unguided matter, and may not this account for all the appearing wisdom and contrivance, which is in the universe?

This idea exploits no version of selection at all, but simply draws attention to the fact that we have eternity to play with. There is no five-billion-year deadline in this instance, the way there is for the evolution of life on Earth. Several versions of this speculation have been seriously considered by physicists and cosmologists in recent years. John Archibald Wheeler (1974), for instance, has proposed that the universe oscillates back and forth for eternity: a big bang is followed by expansion, which is followed by contraction into a big crunch, which is followed by another big bang, and so forth forever, with random variations in the constants and other crucial parameters occurring in each oscillation. Each possible setting is tried an infinity of times, and so every variation on every theme, both those that "make sense" and those that are absurd, spins itself out, not once but an infinity of times.

It is hard to believe that this idea is empirically testable in any meaningful way, but we should reserve judgment. Variations or elaborations on the theme just might have implications that could be confirmed or disconfirmed. In the meantime it is worth noting that this family of hypotheses does have the virtue of extending the principles of explanation that work so well in testable domains all the way out. Consistency and simplicity are in its favor. And that, once again, is certainly enough to blunt the appeal of the traditional alternative. Here's why: if the universe were structured in such a way that an infinity of different "laws of physics" get tried out in the fullness of time, we would be mistaken to think that there is anything special about our finding ourselves with such exquisitely well-tuned laws. It had to happen eventually, with or without help from a benign God. This is not an argument for the conclusion that the universe is, or must be, so structured, but just an argument for the more modest conclusion that no feature of the observable "laws of nature" could be invulnerable to this alternative, deflationary interpretation.

Once these ever more speculative, ever more attenuated Darwinian hypotheses are formulated, they serve – in classic Darwinian fashion – to diminish by small steps the explanatory task facing us. All that is left over in need of explanation at this point is a certain perceived elegance or wonderfulness in the observed laws of physics. If you doubt that the hypothesis of an infinity of variant universes could actually explain this elegance, you should reflect that this has at least as much claim to being a non-question-begging explanation as any traditional alternative; by the time God has been depersonalized to the point of being some abstract and timeless principle of beauty or goodness, not an artificer or a lawgiver or even a lawfinder but at best a sort of master of ceremonies, it is hard to see how the existence of God could explain anything. What would be asserted by the "explanation" that was not already given in the description of the wonderful phenomenon to be explained? The Darwinian perspective doesn't prove that God – in any of these guises – couldn't exist, but only that we have no good reason to think God does exist. Not a classical reductio ad absurdum argument, then, but nevertheless a rational challenge that reduces the believer's options to an absurdly minimalist base. As the Reverend Mackerel says, in Peter De Vries's comic novel, *The Mackerel Plaza* (1958), "It is the final proof of God's omnipotence that he need not exist in order to save us."

Evolutionary biology also supports atheism indirectly by providing an explanatory framework for what we might call the genealogy of theology. Since belief in God cannot be justified by any scientific or logical argument, but is nevertheless a nearly ubiquitous ingredient in human civilization, what explains the maintenance of this belief? This is an oft-neglected part of the atheist's burden of proof: not merely showing the fallacies and dubieties in the various arguments that have been offered for the existence of God, but explaining why such a dubious proposition would be favored by anybody in the first place. There has been no shortage of dismissive hypotheses offered over the centuries: neuroses that are the inevitable by-products of civilization, a conspiracy of ultimately selfish priests, and sheer stupidity, for instance, are perennially popular hunches. Recent works in evolutionary social science (Boyer 2001; Atran 2002; Dennett 2006) demonstrate that there are both more interesting and more plausible – and scientifically confirmable – hypotheses to pursue.

REFERENCES

Atran, Scott. 2002. *In Gods We Trust*: *The Evolutionary Landscape of Religion*. New York: Oxford University Press.

Boyer, Pascal. 2001. *Religion Explained*: *The Evolutionary Origins of Religious Thought*. New York: Basic Books.

Darwin, Francis. 1911. *The Life and Letters of Charles Darwin*. 2 vols. New York: Appleton (original edition, 1887).

Davies, Paul. 1992. *The Mind of God*. London: Simon and Schuster.

Dawkins, Richard. 1986. *The Blind Watchmaker*. London: Longmans.

De Vries, Peter. 1958. *The Mackerel Plaza*. Boston: Little, Brown.

Dembski, William. 2005. "In Defense of Intelligent Design." Http://www.designinference.com. Forthcoming in Philip Clayton (ed)., *Oxford Handbook of Religion and Science*.

Dennett, Daniel. 1975. "Why the Law of Effect Will Not Go Away." *Journal of the Theory of Social Behaviour* 5: 179–87.

Dennett, Daniel. 1995. *Darwin's Dangerous Idea*. New York: Simon & Schuster.

Dennett, Daniel. 2005. "Show Me the Science." *New York Times* op/ed page, August 28, 2005.

Dennett, Daniel C. 2006. *Breaking the Spell: Religion as a Natural Phenomenon*. New York: Viking Penguin.

Descartes, Rene. 1641. *Meditations on First Philosophy*. Paris: Michel Soly.

Dewey, John. 1910. *The Influence of Darwin on Philosophy*. New York: Henry Holt; Bloomington: Indiana University Press, 1965.

Dyson, Freeman. 1979. *Disturbing the Universe*. New York: Harper and Row.

Gould, Stephen Jay. 1985. *The Flamingo's Smile*. New York: Norton.

Gregory, Richard L. 1981. *Mind in Science: A History of Explanations in Psychology and Physics*. Cambridge: Cambridge University Press.

Hume, David. 1779. *Dialogues Concerning Natural Religion*. London.

MacKenzie, Robert Beverley. 1868. *The Darwinian Theory of the Transmutation of Species Examined*. London: Nisbet & Co. Quoted in a review, *Athenaeum*, no. 2102 (February 8): 217.

Paley, William. 1800. *Natural Theology*. Oxford: J. Vincent.

Rachels, James. 1991. *Created from Animals: The Moral Implications of Darwinism*. Oxford: Oxford University Press.

Schrödinger, Erwin. 1967. *What Is Life?* Cambridge: Cambridge University Press.

Smolin, Lee. 1992. "Did the Universe Evolve?" *Classical and Quantum Gravity* 9:173–91.

Wheeler, John Archibald. 1974. "Beyond the End of Time." In Martin Rees, Remo Ruffini, and John Archibald Wheeler (eds.), *Black Holes, Gravitational Waves and Cosmology: An Introduction to Current Research*. New York: Gordon and Breach.

9   The Autonomy of Ethics

Our commitment to the *objectivity of ethics* is a deep one. Ethics is objective just in case there are facts or truths about what is good or bad and right or wrong that obtain independently of the moral beliefs or attitudes of appraisers. A commitment to objectivity is part of a commitment to the *normativity* of ethics. Moral judgments express normative claims about what we *should* do and care about. As such, they presuppose standards of behavior and concern that purport to be correct, that could and should guide conduct and concern, and that we might fail to accept or live up to. Normativity, therefore, presupposes *fallibility*, and fallibility implies objectivity.[1] Of course, this presupposition could be mistaken. There might be no objective moral standards. Our moral thinking and discourse might be systematically mistaken.[2] But this would be a revisionary conclusion, to be accepted only as the result of extended and compelling argument that the commitments of ethical objectivity are unsustainable.[3] In the meantime, we should treat the objectivity of ethics as a kind of default assumption or working hypothesis.

Many people believe that the only way to make sense of objective moral standards is in terms of *divine commands*. They assume that moral laws require a lawgiver, such as God, and that a world without God – a purely natural world – would contain nō moral standards or distinctions. This assumption explains the frequent appeal to religious scholars and members of the clergy as authorities on issues of moral significance. It also explains why, despite the tradition of the separation of church and state, many people could suppose that constitutional rights depend on divine commandments in the Judeo-Christian tradition.[4]

In writing this chapter, I am conscious of debts to Terence Irwin, Michael Moore, and Sam Rickless. I have also benefited from Michael Moore's "Good without God," in R. George (ed.), *Natural Law, Liberalism, and Morality* (New York: Oxford University Press, 1996), pp. 221–70. Earlier versions of this material were presented at the Westminster Theological Seminary (Escondido, California) and at a symposium on ethical and religious commitment at the University of San Diego.

This view assumes that morality requires a religious foundation. As such, it denies the *autonomy* of morality. If an objective ethics presupposes divine command, then an objective ethics stands or falls with religious belief. On the one hand, ethics will be objective if God exists and issues divine commands, and we can acquire moral knowledge insofar as we can know what God has commanded. On the other hand, if theism is false, then the presupposition of an objective ethics fails, and we must embrace moral nihilism (the thesis that there are no facts or truths about ethics) or relativism (the thesis that moral facts and truths are relative to the moral attitudes or beliefs of appraisers). Either way, the assumption that morality requires a religious foundation requires us to reject the possibility of an objective secular morality.

This assumption deserves scrutiny and should be rejected. We should, instead, embrace the autonomy of ethics. The autonomy of ethics implies that the objectivity of ethics is not hostage to the truth of theism. This is a welcome conclusion to the extent that theism is itself a problematic commitment.[5] Our discussion assumes not that theism is false, only that it is not obviously true. The autonomy of ethics allows the atheist to recognize objective moral standards. But the autonomy of ethics should not be of interest only to atheists. Whatever its ultimate merits, theism itself is more attractive if we accept the autonomy of ethics. Indeed, a good case can be made that the objectivity of ethics itself requires the autonomy of ethics.

DIFFERENT MORAL ROLES FOR RELIGION

To determine whether morality requires a religious foundation, we need to distinguish three different roles God might play in morality. God plays a *metaphysical* role in morality if the existence and nature of moral requirements depend on his existence and will. On one such view, it is God's attitudes toward various courses of action that make them good or bad and right or wrong. Second, even if God does not play this metaphysical role, he might play an *epistemological* role if he provides us with an essential source of evidence about what is morally valuable. Even if God's will does not make something good or bad, it may be a reliable indicator of what is. Third, God plays a *motivational* role in ethics if he provides us with a necessary incentive or reason to be moral. It is a common view that if we reckon only the earthly costs and benefits of virtue, we cannot show that one is always better off being moral. But if God rewards virtue and punishes vice in an afterlife, then he can provide a prudential motivation for morality.

These three potential moral roles for God all deserve discussion. But our focus should be on whether God plays a metaphysical role in

morality. It is this role that has the most direct bearing on the autonomy of ethics.

VOLUNTARISM, NATURALISM, AND THE EUTHYPHRO PROBLEM

We might formulate this metaphysical claim as the doctrine that things
are morally good or right just in case God approves of them. In assessing
this claim, we would do well to consider Socrates' discussion of a related
issue. In Plato's *Euthyphro* Socrates considers Euthyphro's definition of
piety as what (all) the gods love (10a–11b).[6] He does not dispute the
truth of this claim; instead, he distinguishes two different ways it might
be true.

(a) Something is pious, because the gods love it.
(b) Something is loved by the gods, because it is pious.

Socrates does not label these two claims. We might call the first claim
voluntarism, because it makes something's piety depend on God's will.
We might call the second claim *naturalism*, because it makes something's piety depend on its nature. Voluntarism claims that the attitudes
of the gods make things pious, whereas naturalism claims that something's piety is part of its nature, which the gods' attitudes recognize
and track. Socrates thinks that reflection will show us that we tacitly
accept naturalism. What it is for something to be god-beloved is simply
for it to be loved by the gods. But what makes the gods take this attitude
toward anything must be some *other* feature of the thing. The gods love
pious things, because they are pious. This seems especially plausible if
we bear in mind that Socrates and Euthyphro think that piety is part of
justice. One loves just things, because they are just, and one recognizes
them to be just. If so, the god-beloved character of pious things depends
on their being pious, not vice versa. Euthyphro accepts naturalism, and
Socrates concludes that Euthyphro's claim fails as a definition, because it
states a symptom or correlate, rather than the cause or essence, of piety.

Despite superficial differences, Socrates' concern is closely related to
ours. We can adapt the Euthyphro Problem to our discussion of whether
morality requires a religious foundation by considering the following
conditional formulation of the doctrine of divine command.

Divine Command: If God exists, x is good or right if and only if God approves
of x.

Divine command, like Euthyphro's definition of piety, admits of both
voluntarist and naturalist interpretations, and the debate between them
has a distinguished history.

Voluntarism captures the metaphysical dependence of morality on religion. Voluntarists, such as William of Occam (ca. 1287–1347), make something's moral value consist in God's attitudes; there would be no moral attributes but for God's will. Notice that voluntarism and atheism together imply moral nihilism.

By contrast, naturalism accepts the autonomy of ethics. Ethical naturalists, such as Thomas Aquinas (1225–74), claim that the moral properties of persons and situations depend on their nature. If so, moral qualities do not presuppose a God, though a perfectly wise and good God would approve of all and only good and right things. Naturalism does not itself preclude God from playing an epistemic role in morality (telling us reliably what is morally good and bad) or a motivational role (providing divine incentives for moral behavior). But naturalism does deny theism a metaphysical role.

Notice the conditional nature of divine command: *If* God exists and enjoys the attributes usually ascribed to him – omniscience, omnipotence, and perfect goodness – then he will approve of all and only good and right things. Because naturalism does not make moral qualities depend on God's existence or will, it implies that these qualities would exist even if God does not. Thus, naturalism implies that atheism does not entail nihilism or relativism.

How do we decide between voluntarist and naturalist interpretations of divine command? Socrates' reasoning about piety applies here as well. What it is for something to be God-approved is simply for it to be loved by God. What makes God take this attitude toward anything must be some *other* feature of the thing. But, it seems, God would love good things because they are good. His attitudes would be *principled*. If so, the God-approved character of good things would depend on their being good, not vice versa.

We might also notice a counterintuitive implication of voluntarism. Voluntarism implies that all moral truths are contingent on what God happens to approve. If God's attitudes had been different and he had approved of very different things, then very different things would have been good and bad, right and wrong; and if God were to come to approve of things very different from those he now approves of, then the moral status of these things would change. Thus, for example, had God not condemned genocide and rape, these things would not have been wrong, or, if God were to come to approve these things, they would become morally acceptable. But these are awkward commitments, inasmuch as this sort of conduct seems necessarily wrong.[7]

Theists may reply that God would not approve of such things, because he is himself perfectly good. But this reply is not available to the voluntarist. For this reply understands his approval as resting on a *sensitivity* to what is good or bad, right or wrong, in itself, independently of his attitudes. But then appeal to God's goodness undermines, rather than supports, voluntarism. Indeed, it looks as if the voluntarist would have to understand God's goodness as consisting in his approving of himself. But that approval would be equally arbitrary and contingent. If, as most theists presumably believe, his self-approval reflects a perception of his own worth, then his attitudes presuppose, rather than constitute, what is of value. The consistent voluntarist account of God's own goodness is problematic.

The way in which the voluntarist must represent moral facts as contingent on God's will is counterintuitive in another way. It is common to believe that the moral properties of actions, persons, institutions, and situations depend in a systematic way on the natural properties – for instance, the biological, psychological, legal, and social properties – of those things. Philosophers refer to this relation of systematic dependence as one of *supervenience*. The moral properties of a situation supervene on its natural properties just in case a full specification of the natural properties of the situation fix or determine its moral properties. This implies that two situations cannot differ in their moral properties without differing in their natural properties. So, for example, the racial injustice of the system of apartheid supervened on a complex set of legal, political, social, and economic restrictions on the opportunities of black South Africans and a culture of discriminatory attitudes toward them. Any social system qualitatively identical in all natural respects to this system of apartheid would also be unjust, and any social system containing both blacks and whites that was not unjust would have to differ in some of its natural (legal, political, social, economic, and psychological) properties from the system of apartheid. But if the natural properties of a situation determine its moral properties, then its moral properties cannot depend on God's will. For if voluntarism were true, then two situations could have different moral properties even if there were no natural differences between them whatsoever. One system of apartheid could be unjust, but a complete clone of that system need not be unjust – if God's attitudes to the two tokens of the same type were different.[8] In this conflict between supervenience and voluntarism, it is easier to accept supervenience than voluntarism.

These are reasons to reject voluntarism and accept naturalism. However, an obvious worry about naturalism is that it compromises God's omnipotence. If moral requirements are independent of and inform God's will, then they are outside his control. But if moral laws are outside God's control, they appear to challenge his omnipotence.

Of course, this is a worry only for traditional monotheists who believe in a personal God who is omnipotent. Atheists and theists of other stripes need not be concerned by this objection to naturalism. Whether traditional monotheists should regard it as a good objection to naturalism depends on how we conceive of omnipotence. If we conceive of omnipotence as the capacity to do anything, then naturalism does compromise God's omnipotence. Theists would then have to choose whether to accept voluntarism (to maintain omnipotence) or sacrifice omnipotence (to avoid voluntarism). But traditional theists face a comparable dilemma anyway. It is difficult to believe that God could change the laws of logic (e.g., the principle of noncontradiction) or the truths of arithmetic (e.g., that $2 + 2 = 4$). These are necessary truths, true in all possible worlds, and we can't conceive of what a world would be like in which they weren't true. If so, then we already recognize some necessary truths that are beyond God's control. Do they compromise his omnipotence? That depends on how we understand omnipotence. If we understand omnipotence as the power to do anything, then we have independent reason for questioning God's omnipotence. But perhaps omnipotence is not the power to do anything, but rather the power to do anything possible, not inconsistent with necessary truths and laws. If so, God's inability to change laws of logic and mathematics need not compromise his omnipotence. But equally, God's inability to make intrinsic goods bad or intrinsic evils good need not compromise his omnipotence. But then naturalism need not compromise God's omnipotence.

This survey suggests a strong case for rejecting voluntarism and accepting naturalism. Naturalism not only explains how the atheist can recognize moral requirements but also allows theists to explain God's goodness and to represent his commands as principled, rather than arbitrary. In this way, naturalism appears to be the best bet for atheists, agnostics, and theists alike.[9] But, unlike voluntarism, which challenges the autonomy of ethics, naturalism vindicates the autonomy of ethics. If we accept the autonomy of ethics, then the objectivity of ethics is not hostage to the truth of theism.

Indeed, we are now in a position to see how the objectivity of ethics actually requires the autonomy of ethics. Ethical objectivity, we said, claims that there are moral facts or truths that obtain independently of the moral beliefs or attitudes of appraisers. Ethical *subjectivism* is one way to deny ethical objectivity. It claims that what is good or bad and right or wrong depends on the moral beliefs or attitudes of appraisers. But voluntarism is just *subjectivism at the highest level*. If God exists and is both omniscient and perfectly good, then his approval – if only we could ascertain it – would be a perfectly reliable – indeed, infallible – indicator of what was good or right. This is what naturalism claims. But voluntarism implies that God's attitudes play a metaphysical, not just an epistemic, role in morality; his attitudes make things good or right.

This is a form of subjectivism about ethics. But then the supposition that morality requires a religious foundation, as voluntarism insists, threatens, rather than vindicates, the objectivity of morality.

VARIETIES OF NATURALISM

Naturalism says that moral requirements are not constituted by God's attitudes or will. Put positively, the moral properties of situations depend on the nature of those situations, independently of God's (or anyone else's) attitudes. Indeed, understanding these independent moral properties would help us to understand why God wills what he does (if he exists). But what do moral requirements or qualities consist in if they do not consist in God's attitude or will?

This raises a different inquiry, one within secular moral theory. It is relevant to our inquiry about whether morality requires a religious foundation only insofar as the plausibility of the autonomy of ethics depends on there being some promising accounts of what moral requirements and distinctions do consist in. In developing and assessing such accounts, we necessarily rely on our views about the nature of morality, its demands, and its relation to other concerns.

It might be useful to distinguish moral claims at different levels of abstraction or generality. Some moral claims and judgments are *particular*. They concern the moral properties of particular actions or action tokens, as in the claim that it would be wrong for Ben to break his promise to Sam. Some moral claims are more general and concern classes or types of action. They identify morally relevant factors and take the form of moral *rules*, as in the claim that one ought to keep one's promises. Some moral claims are more general still, concerning many or perhaps all types of actions, and saying why these various factors are all morally relevant. These are moral *principles*. There may be a plurality of moral principles, or, in the limit, there might be only one master principle, such as the principle of utility – which demands that one ought to perform actions that promote human happiness – or Kant's categorical imperative – which demands that one always treat rational agents as ends in themselves and never merely as means.

There is a kind of asymmetrical dependence among the moral claims at these three levels. Particular moral truths (e.g., that it would be wrong to break this particular promise) obtain in virtue of the truth of moral rules (e.g., that promise keeping is a right-making factor). If there are moral truths more general than moral rules – moral principles – then the moral rules express truths in virtue of some more general principle being true that explains why that particular factor is a morally relevant factor.

Some have inferred from this asymmetrical metaphysical dependence that the justification of our moral beliefs must exhibit a parallel structure. They claim that we can justify particular judgments in terms of moral rules and that moral rules can be justified in terms of fundamental moral principles, but that at some point justification must come to stop with either a plurality of principles or a single master principle that states an ultimate moral factor. Because these first principles state ultimate moral factors, there is nothing further in terms of which they can be justified. First principles must be self-evident.

But this leads to an awkward conclusion. We may be uncertain about some particular moral judgments and rules, but surely there are some particular judgments and rules of which we are very certain, much more certain than we are about any recondite first principle. For instance, I am much more certain that the Holocaust was wicked or that genocide is wrong than I am about the truth of utilitarianism or Kant's categorical imperative. Moreover, we need to be able to provide reasons for accepting or rejecting putative first principles.

Fortunately, asymmetrical metaphysical dependence does not imply asymmetrical epistemic dependence. A first principle states a or the ultimate moral factor (e.g., F). It makes no sense to ask of a first principle that we take to be true, "In virtue of what further property is F an ultimate factor?" If there were some more ultimate factor, F would not be an ultimate factor after all. But we can sensibly ask about some putative first principle, "Is that first principle true?" or "Is F really an ultimate factor?" The answer to these questions may appeal to the principle's ability to sustain and explain moral judgments that we find independently plausible. So the metaphysical priority of first principles does not show that our evidence for which first principle is true cannot include our defeasible particular moral convictions.

This conclusion suggests a methodology for secular moral theory. We can try to resolve uncertainty or disagreement at more particular levels of moral thought by trying to find plausible or common ground at a more general level. But we can also try to resolve uncertainty or disagreement at a more general level by testing the implications of a potential moral principle for particular cases against our own independent assessment of those cases. Thus, we introduce a moral principle in order to systematize our considered moral convictions, especially about particular cases and moral rules. We examine candidate principles, in part, by drawing out their implications for real or imagined cases and comparing their implications with our own existing or reflective assessments of those cases. If a principle has counterintuitive implications, this counts against it. But if this counterintuitive implication is fairly isolated, and the principle explains our views better than alternative principles, then this is

reason to revise the particular moral judgment or moral rule that con-
flicted with the principle. Ideally, we modify our principles, considered
moral convictions, and other views in response to conflicts, as coherence
seems to require, until our ethical views are in dialectical equilibrium.[10]
On the one hand, dialectical equilibrium begins from and assigns proba-
tive value to our considered moral convictions. As such, we have some
reasonable expectation that any acceptable theory should accommodate
many of our considered moral convictions. On the other hand, dialectical equilibrium is an ideal that none of us now meets and that we
can at most approximate. Therefore, we should expect dialectical equilibrium to force some revisions in our moral beliefs, and it is hard to
say in advance just how revisionary the moral principles with the best
dialectical fit would be.

   Secular moral theory should begin with considered moral convictions.
For many purposes, appeal to these convictions will be adequate. We
have already relied on such convictions – for instance, the prohibitions
on genocide and rape – in assessing voluntarism. But if we take the
demands of dialectical equilibrium seriously, we must try to identify
moral principles that provide a suitable dialectical fit with these convictions. Let me sketch three different theoretical approaches to secular
morality.

   Much of commonsense morality requires compliance with norms
prohibiting aggression (at least, unprovoked aggression), enjoining cooperation, fidelity, and aid, and condemning individuals who free-ride on
the compliance of others. We each benefit from the compliance of others
with such norms, but others won't be compliant toward those who are
known to be noncompliant, and fairness requires that we enjoy the benefits of others' compliance only if we comply ourselves. On this view,
we might identify the demands of morality with norms of social behavior the general observance of which is mutually beneficial. This appeal
to *mutual advantage* and *reciprocity* promises an account of the origin
and content of morality that explains our interest in being moral and
the interest of the community in instilling a moral sense or conscience
in its members.

   But this approach appears to limit moral concern to those with whom
one regularly interacts. This is in tension with Christian and Enlightenment views that stress the wide scope of moral concern.[11] We might
understand morality's wide scope as reflecting a perspective that seeks to
transcend the agent's personal interests and loyalties. On this view, the
moral point of view demands an *impartial* concern for all. Impartiality
can itself be understood in different ways. On one conception, it requires
that agents take into account the interests of affected parties equally, balancing benefits to some against harm to others, as necessary, so as to

determine the outcome that is best overall. This *aggregative* conception of impartiality involves a utilitarian or consequentialist approach to morality that identifies one's duty with promoting human happiness or other good consequences.[12] However, the aggregative conception lets the interests of many outweigh the interests of a few. An alternative conception of impartiality rejects this sort of interpersonal balancing and insists that a concern with each affected party requires that we act only on principles that no one could reasonably reject. This distributed concern for each yields a *contractualist* conception of impartiality.[13]

Still another approach is the *Kantian* one that attempts to account for the content of moral requirements on the basis of what it is to be a moral agent subject to moral requirements. To be a moral agent is to be responsible. Nonresponsible actors, such as brutes and small children, act on their strongest desires; or, if they deliberate, they deliberate only about the instrumental means to the satisfaction of their desires. By contrast, a responsible agent must be able to distinguish between the intensity and authority of his or her desires, deliberate about the appropriateness of his or her desires, and regulate his or her actions in accordance with his or her deliberations. If so, moral agency requires capacities for practical reasoning. If moral requirements depend on features of moral agents as such, then they depend on what agents would care about insofar as they are rational agents. This arguably requires a concern for rational agents as such, which is roughly how Kant derives his famous demand that we treat all rational agents as ends in themselves and never merely as means.[14]

These are mere sketches of a few familiar secular conceptions of moral theory. Our commitment to the autonomy of ethics requires only that some of them look intellectually promising.

MORAL EVIDENCE AND DIVINE WILL

Even if God's will does not make something morally good or bad, it could still be a reliable indicator of what is and provide us with evidence about what our moral duties are. Indeed, if God exists and is morally perfect and omniscient, then his will must be a perfect indicator of what is (independently) valuable. Wouldn't this give religion a significant epistemological role for morality?

Even if God's will provided one source of evidence about morality's demands, it needn't be the only or the most important source. After all, if naturalism is true, then morality's demands have a metaphysical source other than God's will. Moral demands will presumably be a matter of what promotes justice, rights, and happiness. It is open to us to reason directly about these moral matters, by engaging in secular moral reasoning, rather than obliquely by consulting a divine barometer of these matters.

Does divine will provide even one source of moral guidance? Of course, God must exist to provide a moral barometer, and theism is open to serious question. Atheists will think that this direct, secular evidence is all the evidence there is. But even theists should recognize this direct evidence and prefer it if indirect evidence about God's will is sufficiently hard to obtain.

How, after all, are we to ascertain God's will? Appeal to religious tradition and scripture is problematic for several reasons. First, there are multiple traditions and scriptures. Insofar as they say competing things about God's will, they cannot all be true. But it is hard to know how to determine which traditions and scriptures are more reliable. Even within a single religious tradition, questions remain. On some possible moral topics, tradition and scripture may be silent. On other topics, tradition and scripture may speak but in conflicting ways.[15] Even when tradition and scripture speak unequivocally, we may wonder whether what is said should be interpreted literally. For example, a literal reading of the Old Testament yields a date for the age of the Earth and claims about the history of plant and animal species that are contradicted by the fossil and geological records.[16] It also yields problematic moral claims, such as Deuteronomy's claims that parents can and should stone to death rebellious children (21:18–21) and that the community can and should stone to death any wife whose husband discovers that she was not a virgin when he married her (22:13–21).[17] We have more reason to accept secular scientific and moral claims than we do to accept a literal reading of these particular religious texts.

A common theistic response to these interpretive puzzles is to endorse the interpretation of tradition and scripture that yields the morally more defensible conception of divine will. This moralized approach to interpretation makes good sense for the theist if, as the naturalist claims, God's omniscience and perfect goodness ensure that his will perfectly tracks all morally relevant facts. But, on this conception of interpretation, so far from our knowledge of God's will supplying evidence about the nature of morality, it is our beliefs about the nature of morality that are supplying evidence about God's will. The moralized interpretation of religious scripture and tradition shows religion to be dependent on morality, rather then morality to be dependent on religion.

MORAL MOTIVATION AND THE AUTHORITY OF MORALITY

God plays a motivational role in ethics if he provides a needed incentive to be moral. If we reckon only the earthly costs and benefits of virtue, it appears we cannot always show that one is better off being moral. But if justice requires punishing vice and rewarding virtue, then God's perfect justice seems to imply that he would use heaven and hell to reward virtue and punish vice. Because the afterlife is eternal, its sanctions and rewards would dwarf the earthly costs and benefits of virtue and vice. It follows that the prospect of divine sanctions and rewards could provide a prudential motivation for morality that appears unavailable if we restrict our attention to secular sanctions and rewards.

The question "Why be moral?" is a normative question about why one should care about moral demands. But this normative question cannot be seeking a moral reason to be moral. That question is too easy to answer. Instead, it is asking whether behaving morally is a requirement of practical reason. In this sense, the question really asks about the *rational authority of morality*. That question arises for most of us because of a perceived tension between the other-regarding demands of morality and a broadly prudential conception of practical reason, according to which what one has reason to do is to promote one's own aims or interests. For meeting the demands of nonaggression, cooperation, fidelity, fair play, and charity often appears to constrain one's pursuit of one's own aims or interests.

When one asks whether virtue pays, one is looking for a prudential defense of the authority of morality. A traditional secular defense of morality is to argue that the demands of morality and enlightened self-interest coincide. As we have seen, much of other-regarding morality involves norms of cooperation (e.g., fidelity and fair play), forbearance, and aid. Each individual has an interest in the fruits of interaction conducted according to these norms. Though it might be desirable to reap the benefits of other people's compliance with norms of forbearance and cooperation without incurring the burdens of one's own, the opportunities to do this are infrequent. Noncompliance is generally detectable, and others won't be forbearing and cooperative toward those who are known to be noncompliant. For this reason, compliance is typically necessary to enjoy the benefits of others' continued compliance. Moreover, because each has an interest in others' cooperation and restraint, communities will tend to reinforce compliant behavior and discourage noncompliant behavior. If so, compliance is often necessary to avoid social sanctions. Whereas noncompliance secures short-term benefits that compliance does not, compliance typically secures greater long-term benefits than noncompliance. In this way, we can provide a secular prudential justification of morality.

However, as long as we understand the prudential justification of morality in terms of instrumental advantage, the secular coincidence between other-regarding morality and enlightened self-interest must remain imperfect. Sometimes noncompliance would go undetected; and even where noncompliance is detected, the benefits of noncompliance sometimes outweigh the costs of being excluded from future cooperative interaction. Moreover, even if the coincidence between morality and self-interest were extensionally adequate, it would be counterfactually fragile. For compliance involves costs, as well as benefits. It must remain a second-best option, behind undetected noncompliance, in which one enjoys the benefits of others' compliance without the costs of one's own. But then, as Glaucon and Adeimantus observe in Plato's *Republic* (357a–367e, esp. 359c–361d), if one had some way of ensuring that one's own noncompliance would go undetected, one could enjoy the benefits of others' compliance without the burdens of one's own, and one would have no reason to be compliant. The imperfect coincidence of morality and self-interest implies that immorality need not always be irrational.

It is clear that an omniscient, omnipotent, and perfectly good God could arrange eternal sanctions and rewards so as to make the coincidence of morality and self-interest perfect. In this way, appeal to divine sanctions and rewards could strengthen the secular prudential justification of morality. But we might wonder whether morality requires a perfect prudential justification. Perhaps doing the morally correct thing is not always prudent too.

We might also wonder whether this sort of prudential justification of the authority of morality is desirable. For, on this conception of moral motivation, each person has an *instrumental* justification for being moral, namely, that being moral is both necessary and sufficient for a blissful afterlife. On this conception, moral behavior is good, not in itself, but for its extrinsic consequences. But it is common to think that *virtue should be its own reward*. Indeed, it is sometimes supposed that when one behaves morally for purely instrumental reasons this diminishes the moral value of one's action.[18] God can choose to reward selfless altruism, but the prospect of this reward cannot be what motivates such agents without robbing those actions of the very features he would like to reward.

If virtue should be undertaken for its rewards, this implies a prudential justification of morality's authority. However, if virtue should be undertaken for its *own* rewards, this justification should eschew appeal to the extrinsic benefits of virtue, which are separable conceptually from the fact of virtue, and appeal instead to benefits that are inseparable from virtue itself. Both the Greek eudaimonist tradition – especially Socrates, Plato, Aristotle, and the Stoics – and the British idealist tradition – especially T. H. Green – defend the intrinsic benefits of virtue, arguing that other-regarding virtues make a constitutive contribution to the agent's own happiness (eudaimonia). Whether these conceptions of the intrinsic rewards of virtue are defensible is a complex matter.[19] What is important for present purposes is that if virtue is its own reward, then there will be an important sense in which appeal to divine sanctions and rewards provides a prudential justification of morality that is both unnecessary and unwelcome.

Alternatively, the justification of altruism might eschew prudential mediation, whether extrinsic or intrinsic. This conception of the authority of morality must insist that the fact that I meet some legitimate moral demand of another person is itself a reason for me to act, whether or not I benefit thereby. This would be an *impartial* conception of practical reason that recognizes nonderivative reason to benefit others. This conception has been most fully developed within the Kantian tradition.[20] Whether this conception is defensible is also a complex matter.[21] What is significant for present purposes is that this conception of the authority of morality rejects the prudential justification of morality embodied in many religious traditions.

The idea that virtue should be its own reward exposes problems with the adequacy of appeal to divine sanctions and rewards to provide a prudential justification of morality. Whether we decide that virtue is its own reward or that no reward is necessary, it looks as if we can justify moral conduct and concern in ways that assign no role whatsoever to God.

CONCLUDING REMARKS

Despite widespread belief that morality requires a religious foundation, that doctrine is hard to support. Voluntarism is the heart of that doctrine and denies the autonomy of ethics. But voluntarism leaves moral requirements unacceptably contingent and arbitrary. It is better to embrace the autonomy of ethics. Indeed, voluntarism is itself best understood as a form of subjectivism. But then it follows that the autonomy of ethics is not only compatible with the objectivity of ethics, but necessary for it. If we accept the autonomy of ethics, then atheism does not force us to moral nihilism or relativism. If we are theists, the autonomy of ethics allows us to explain how God's attitudes and behavior reflect the operation of moral principles. Indeed, it is this moralized conception of the gods that set Socrates apart from the sort of unprincipled polytheism of his ancestors and contemporaries.[22] Though the autonomy of ethics denies that moral distinctions rest on God's will, it does not preclude religion from playing other roles in morality. But it is hard to articulate plausible epistemological and motivational roles for God to play in morality. We can see how morality helps religion. It is harder to see how religion helps morality.

NOTES

1. Different grades of objectivity correspond to different degrees of fallibility. Just how much fallibility and objectivity it is reasonable to expect from ethics is an interesting question, which I won't pursue here.

2. This sort of "error theory" is defended by J. L. Mackie, *Ethics: Inventing Right and Wrong* (New York: Penguin Books, 1977), chap. 1. Also see Gilbert Harman, *The Nature of Morality* (New York: Oxford University Press, 1977), esp. chaps. 1 and 2.

3. For systematic defense of ethical objectivity, see David O. Brink, *Moral Realism and the Foundations of Ethics* (New York: Cambridge University Press, 1989).

4. For example, Chief Justice Roy Moore of the Alabama Supreme Court erected a giant granite monument of the Ten Commandments at his courthouse, claiming that the authority of the Constitution derives from God's commandments. When the monument was ruled to violate the constitutional separation of church and state and was ordered to be removed, Moore refused. He was eventually removed from office for his refusal. See, e.g., "Alabama Panel Ousts Judge over Ten Commandments" *New York Times*, November 14, 2003, p. A16. More recently, the United States Supreme Court has given mixed signals about whether public displays of the Ten Commandments violate the anti-establishment clause of the First Amendment. In *McCreary County v. ACLU*, 125 S. Ct. 2722 (2005), in a 5–4 decision the Court ruled that the display of the Ten Commandments by themselves in two county courthouses reflected manifest religious purposes and violated the anti-establishment clause. However, in *Van Orden v. Perry*, 125 S. Ct. 2854 (2005), in a 5–4 decision the Court ruled that the display of the Ten Commandments as one of many sculptures in a park in the Texas State Capitol did not violate the anti-establishment clause.

5. My own view is that there is no credible evidence for the existence of God, that atheism is the best response to the problem of evil, and that there are perfectly good functional explanations for why people should persist in religious belief despite its falsity.

6. Plato's *Euthyphro* and other dialogues are collected in *Plato: Complete Works*, ed. J. Cooper (Indianapolis, Ind.: Hackett, 1997).

7. The issue is sometimes raised in the Judeo-Christian tradition by the Old Testament story in which God asks Abraham to sacrifice his only son Isaac (Genesis 22:1–14). Because Abraham resolves to sacrifice his son, God retracts his command to do so. But this doesn't alter the question of whether God's demanding the sacrifice would have made it right.

8. Voluntarism, like any dispositional theory, which identifies the moral valence of something with its disposition to elicit approval in a suitable appraiser, is committed to a form of moral particularism. I believe, but cannot argue here, that this commitment is further reason for rejecting voluntarism.

9. In "Abraham, Isaac, and Euthyphro: God and the Basis of Morality," in D. Stump (ed.), *Hamartia: The Concept of Error in the Western Tradition* (New York: Edwin Mellen Press, 1983), Norman Kretzmann endorses many of the doubts expressed here about the viability of voluntarism. But he argues that

we can still see God's will as constituting moral requirements if we appeal to doctrines associated with perfect being theology. In particular, Kretzmann appeals to the idea that God's relation to goodness is one of identity, rather than (as usually conceived) predication. I don't fully understand this proposal, but I would note some concerns about it. If God is to be identified with goodness, we might regard this as a reductive identification such that our notion of God is now exhausted by our conception of morality. This would be a revisionary conception of God insofar as it treats God as a moral attribute, rather than a person who might possess moral attributes. Also, it is not clear whether such a view is a rival to naturalism. Someone who was otherwise an atheist and accepts naturalism could accept theism if it amounts to nothing more than recognizing moral goodness.

10. Cf. the method of "reflective equilibrium" in John Rawls, *A Theory of Justice* (Cambridge: Harvard University Press, 1971), pp. 19–21, 46–51, and 577–79.

11. The wide scope of moral concern is recognized, for example, in the parable of the Good Samaritan (Luke 10:29–37), who recognizes a duty to rescue someone in need with whom he has no prior association.

12. The best introduction to utilitarianism and consequentialism is still John Stuart Mill, *Utilitarianism* (originally published 1861), ed. R. Crisp (Oxford: Clarendon, 1998). Some influential contemporary work in this tradition is collected in S. Darwall (ed.), *Consequentialism* (Oxford: Blackwell, 2003).

13. Important work within the contractualist tradition includes Rawls, *A Theory of Justice*; David Gauthier, *Morals by Agreement* (Oxford: Clarendon, 1986); and T. M. Scanlon, *What We Owe to Each Other* (Cambridge: Harvard University Press, 1998).

14. See Immanuel Kant, *Groundwork for the Metaphysics of Morals* (originally published 1785), in *Kant's Practical Philosophy*, trans. M. Gregor (New York: Cambridge University Press, 1996).

15. Inconsistency is at stake, for example, when we juxtapose the Old Testament doctrine of an "eye for an eye" (Exodus 21:23, 24; Leviticus 24:19, 20; and Deuteronomy 19:21) and the New Testament doctrine of "turning the other cheek" (Matthew 5:38–42; Luke 6:27–31).

16. A literal reading of Genesis implies that Earth was created in six (24-hour) days approximately 6,000–10,000 years ago and that all plants and animals were created at the same time. Geological and fossil records indicate that Earth is approximately 4.6 billion years old, that life first appeared on Earth approximately 3.5 billion years ago, and that many species of plants and animals evolved and, hence, did not exist at the same time.

17. These claims are the tip of a rather large and awkward iceberg of Old Testament passages whose literal interpretation is morally problematic. Cf. (1) Whoever strikes his parents shall be put to death (Exodus 21:15). (2) One cannot kill a slave outright, but one can beat him to death provided that he survives the beating a day or two (Exodus 21:20; but see Exodus 21:26). (3) "[E]veryone who curses his father or mother shall be put to death..." (Leviticus 20:9). (4) The death penalty is appropriate punishment for various sexual offenses, including adultery and homosexuality (Leviticus 20:10–16). (5) Blasphemy is punishable by death (Leviticus 24:13–16, 23). (6) God instructs the Israelites to stone to death a man found collecting sticks on the Sabbath (Numbers 15:32–36).

18. Cf. Kant's contrast between prudential motivation and a sense of duty in his discussion the good will (*Groundwork* 390, 393–99).

19. For further discussion, see David O. Brink, "Self-love and Altruism," *Social Philosophy and Policy* 14 (1997): 122–57.

20. See, esp., Kant, *Groundwork*, and Thomas Nagel, *The Possibility of Altruism* (Princeton: Princeton University Press, 1970).

21. For further discussion, see David O. Brink, "Kantian Rationalism: Inescapability, Authority, and Supremacy," in G. Cullity and B. Gaut (eds.), *Ethics and Practical Reason* (Oxford: Clarendon, 1997).

22. This moralized conception of the gods may also be responsible for Socrates being brought to trial on the charge of impiety, though we may find his moralized conception more pious than its unprincipled rival.

10 The Argument from Evil

Where was God? Where was the intelligent designer of the universe when 1.5 million children were turned into smoke by zealous Nazis? Where was the all powerful, all knowing, wholly good being whose very essence is radically opposed to evil, while millions of children were starved to death by Stalin, had their limbs chopped off with machetes in Rwanda, were turned into amputees by the diamond trade in Sierra Leone, and worked to death, even now, by the child slave trade that, by conservative estimates, enslaves 250 million children worldwide? Without divine justice, all of this suffering is gratuitous. How, then, can a wholly good, all-powerful God be believed to exist?

The existence of evil is *the* most fundamental threat to the traditional Western concept of an all-good, all-powerful God. Both natural evil, the suffering that occurs as a result of physical phenomena, and moral evil, the suffering resulting from human action, comprise the *problem of evil*. If evil cannot be accounted for, then belief in the traditional Western concept of God is absurd.

THE ARGUMENTS

To address the problem of evil, arguments have been formulated to highlight the apparent contradiction generated by the existence of an omnipotent, omnibenevolent being and the abundance of evil, or gratuitous suffering, in the world. These *arguments from evil* do not argue against the existence of God per se, but do argue that a particular concept of God fails; namely, one that possesses the attributes of omnipotence, omniscience and omnibenevolence. Arguments from evil rest on the claim that there is an inconsistency of one sort or another – either a blatant contradiction or evidence to the contrary – between the claims about God and the facts of the world. The basic intuition of the inconsistency involved in the problem of evil is captured by the following formulation, from Michael Martin:

1. God is all-powerful.
2. God is all good.
3. Evil exists in great abundance.[1]

166

There are two main arguments from evil that can be characterized at the outset: the *logical* and the *evidential*. The *logical*, a priori, or *deductive* argument, as it is also known, asserts that theism is incoherent due to a logical inconsistency, which results from both the adoption of specific claims about the nature of God and the affirmation of the existence of evil. The *evidential*, a posteriori, or the *inductive* argument, in contrast, refers to actual instances, types and degrees of suffering to show how the scale and scope of evil functions as evidence against the existence of the traditional Western God.

THE LOGICAL ARGUMENT

The deductive argument from evil claims that there is a contradiction inherent in affirming both the existence of an omnipotent, omniscient, and wholly good God and the existence of evil. Most philosophers today agree that an inconsistency is not readily apparent, and surely no direct contradiction is generated by the three premises, without the addition of qualifying statements.

A clear example of a qualifying statement needed to generate the contradiction for the logical argument from evil has been offered by the late J. L. Mackie: "[G]ood is opposed to evil, in such a way that a good thing always eliminates evil as far as it can, and that there are no limits to what an omnipotent thing can do...."[2] The surest way for the logical argument to succeed is the addition of such a premise, one that is acceptable to the theist and shows theistic belief to be self-contradictory.

Alvin Plantinga, a champion of the free-will defense, stipulates those conditions that, he believes, must be met for any additional premise to succeed: it must be "either necessarily true, or essential to theism, or a logical consequence of such propositions."[3] Plantinga claims that the nontheist must show that the claim "there is unjustified evil in the world" is *necessarily* true since, he believes, such a statement is not essential to theism or a logical consequence of theistic belief. On the flip side, the theist need only argue, according to Plantinga, that it is logically possible that God has a morally sufficient reason for permitting evil, and need not argue, as the nontheist might contend, that every evil is, in fact, justified.

In response to Plantinga's challenge, Richard La Croix[4] has offered a way to show that the logical argument succeeds. La Croix grants Plantinga's conditions for the additional proposition (i.e., that it must be necessarily true, or essential to theism, or the logical consequence of such proposition). Plantinga claims that the proposition the nontheist needs is:

(f4) An omnipotent, omniscient person is wholly good only if he eliminates every evil, which is such that for every good that entails
it, there is a greater good that does not entail it.[5]

This statement does not create a direct contradiction when conjoined with the initial triad, but it does result in the claim that: "(g) Every evil E is entailed by some good G such that every good greater than G also entails E."[6] Plantinga contends that the nontheist must then show the denial of (g) or that: "*There is at least one evil state of affairs such that for every good that entails it, there is a greater good that does not.*"[7] In other words, Plantinga claims that the nontheist must show that there is at least one good state of affairs that is not necessarily connected with an evil state of affairs, and this must be deduced from the conjunction of (f4), the initial triad, and the proposition(s) that satisfy Plantinga's conditions.

To meet this challenge, La Croix constructs a number of propositions, all of which are consistent with traditional Western theism and lead to the very statement Plantinga contends the nontheist needs to produce. What follows is a summarized reconstruction of La Croix's argument beginning with those propositions that Plantinga should allow as essential to theism.

(i) There is a God who created everything that exists.
(ii) Before God created there was nothing but God.
(iii) After God created, everything is causally dependent on God.

Now, according to traditional Western theism:

(iv) God had the choice of whether or not to create this world.
(v) In one possible scenario, God could have chosen not to create anything at all.
(vi) If this choice were actualized, God would not have created a world in which evil existed.
(vii) Since God is perfectly good, if God had not created anything, all that would exist would be perfect goodness.

This results in: "*The existence of perfect goodness does not entail that any evil exist,*" which is essentially a denial of (g). Plantinga's challenge is met since the addition of the above propositions coupled with the initial triad, (f4), and (g) result in the following: "*There is at least one evil state of affairs such that for every good that entails it, there is a greater good that does not.*" And this is precisely the statement that Plantinga contends the theist needs to produce: the claim that there is at least one good state of affairs, which is not necessarily connected with an evil state of affairs.[8]

Another version of the logical argument from evil, also via Plantinga, is offered by Quentin Smith.[9] Smith utilizes Plantinga's views on free will to distinguish various types of freedom that rational beings might enjoy. The pivotal distinction is that of logical freedom, namely, the ability to choose freely to do wrong but to be logically determined to do only what is right. This is the type of freedom God has, since the deity is incapable of wrongdoing by its very nature, yet has the ability to make choices, which are not necessarily actualized. In other words, God does not have the freedom to commit morally wrong actions.

In addition, it is routinely acknowledged that God is the greatest good, and, according to Plantinga, one of the reasons God is considered to be "maximally valuable" is that God is incapable of nothing less than omnibenevolence in any possible world. Now clearly this is one major difference between human beings and God, since human beings not only can choose to commit wrong but, in fact, commit wrong.

The relevant issue then is the possibility of necessarily good creatures, or even necessarily good human beings. Smith offers this as a qualifying proposition: "It is possible that: free humans who always do what is right exist without there being any natural evil, and if God creates these humans, he will not create natural evil." Now Plantinga allows that the following statement is a necessary truth: "An omniscient and omnipotent [and wholly good] being eliminates every evil that it can properly eliminate."[10] "Properly eliminate" is Plantinga's way of indicating that an evil is a candidate for elimination insofar as its destruction does not entail eliminating a greater good or creating greater evil. A rough reconstruction of Smith's proposed argument from evil is as follows:

(1) God exists and is omnipotent, omniscient, and wholly good.
(2) There is evil.
(3) An omniscient and omnipotent [and wholly good] being eliminates every evil that it can properly eliminate.
(4) It is possible for God to create free humans who always do what is right without there being any natural evil, and if God creates these humans, it will not create natural evil.
(5) There is no evil. [entailed by (1), (3), and (4)]

But, of course, there is evil in the world – generating the needed contradiction. This is the gist of Smith's argument, which, he maintains, shows that the logical argument from evil succeeds.

The weakest premise of this type of argument is (4), which Plantinga might object to on the grounds that necessarily good creatures such as these would rival God's greatness and are therefore disallowed.

In response to this move it might be pointed out that, according to Christian, Judaic, and Islamic doctrine, angels exist. Angels are creatures who perform only morally correct choices (else they are classified as demons). If God could populate the world with only these creatures rather than morally fallible humans – and it would not seem logically impossible for God to do so – then the argument succeeds. A world full of angels, instead of the current one, would eliminate evil. This would bring about the contradiction needed for the logical argument from evil to prevail.

THE EVIDENTIAL ARGUMENT

In December 2004 an earthquake registering a 9.0 magnitude on the Richter scale created a tsunami, or massive tidal wave, which devastated portions of Southeast Asia. Entire villages in Indonesia, Thailand, and Sri Lanka were annihilated, and estimates are that more than 180,000 people were killed. Experts predict possibly twice as many more will die of resulting disease. What is at issue in the a posteriori approach to the problem of evil is the plausibility of the God hypothesis in the face of such catastrophes. Horrendous suffering functions as *evidence* against the claim for an omnipotent, omniscient, and wholly good God.

Premise (3) of the initial formulation of the argument from evil (evil exists in great abundance) could be taken as prima facie evidence against the existence of the traditional Western concept of God if there is no sufficient reason for God allowing it. Yet the skeptical theist might argue that there could be sufficient reason for God allowing evil, though we simply do not know what it is. In other words, the skeptical theist grants that seemingly gratuitous evil exists, but disagrees that "actual gratuitous evil" can be inferred from "seemingly gratuitous evil." The claim here is that it is logically possible that God could have reasons for allowing evil, and therefore, there are warrants for theistic faith. In other words, it is not irrational to believe in God despite the abundance of unexplained evil. This move rapidly refocuses the argument from evil away from the plausibility of the existence of God to the warrantability of belief in God.[11]

In response, the nontheist might point out that this line of reasoning leads to skepticism about any epistemic claim regarding the natural world. It might be, for example, that God gave us evidence of dinosaurs to make the world appear eons old, yet the world is only as old as biblical dating allows, namely, thousands of years. If God is believed to have unknown reasons for apparent gratuitous evil (making it no longer gratuitous), even though these reasons remain inscrutable to us, then one might as well believe that God deceives in other areas. All knowledge claims would be suspect at best, outright mysteries at worst.

Morally speaking, how the concept of inscrutable evil comforts those suffering monumental loss is an added mystery. And we might ask whether it is reasonable to believe that a greater good is so connected with this suffering such that God could not have obtained it without causing creatures to suffer. These types of proposals, along with the claim that an answer to the argument from evil just may not be available to date,[12] are highly unsatisfactory.

There are a number of proposed solutions to the evidential argument from evil that attempt to reconcile the existence of various types of evil, as well as the scale and scope of evils, with the God hypothesis. These explanations, known as *theodicies,* can be grouped into roughly two major categories, representative of the types of evil addressed: *natural* and *moral.* The natural type of theodicy aims at providing reasons for the vast array of natural phenomena that produce suffering in sentient creatures, while the moral type focuses on the evil resulting from free-willed agents.

NATURAL EVIL THEODICIES

If it is possible to show that the suffering that exists could exist in less abundance, then some suffering is unnecessary, or gratuitous, and is unaccounted for by the God hypothesis. Therefore, the existence of natural evil must be somehow justified if the God hypothesis is to maintain plausibility. Some typical theodicies offered to justify the existence of natural evil are:

(1) Evil is necessary as a counterpart to good
(2) Evil is necessary as a means to good
   (i) Evil is necessary for short- or long-term good
   (ii) Evil is necessary as punishment for sin
   (iii) Evil is necessary as a warning system in nature/for human-kind
(3) Evil is a necessary by-product of causal laws

Evil Is Necessary as a Counterpart to Good

If good and evil are related in such a way that it is impossible to create one without the other, then a limitation is placed on God's omnipotence. If "omnipotence" means doing what is only within the bounds of logical possibility, then the theist must show that the creation of one of the counterparts alone is a logical impossibility. Thus, good and evil must be taken as logically necessary counterparts for the required notion of omnipotence to function. Now what could this mean? Is it impossible to experience pleasure without experiencing pain, for example? On its face, this seems patently false.

Interpreted as an epistemic distinction (i.e., to know what is good, we would need to know what is bad), it fares no better. Nonhuman creatures, for example, derive no epistemic benefit from protracted and agonizing bouts with cancer.

Evil Is Necessary as a Means to Good

On this view, evil is not viewed as a logical counterpart of good but as the vehicle, which is necessary, to bring about good; without evil in the world good could not materialize. The following variations are most often appealed to as justifiers of natural evil.

1) EVIL IS NECESSARY FOR SHORT- OR LONG-TERM GOOD. Generally, the example of a surgeon or dentist is used to justify suffering for short-term good: it hurts to have a rotten tooth pulled, but the overall benefit of oral health outweighs this. Similarly, recovery from open-heart surgery may be painful, but such surgery saves lives. A number of problems surface here that make this explanation absurd. First, the types of evil found in the world are simply not analogous to this model, but are more akin to a surgeon performing elective surgery willy-nilly without anesthesia – no short-term good is apparent in the mutilation and death resulting from Cambodian children stepping on land mines. Second, this explanation does not account for the animal suffering that exists. What overriding good comes from wild raccoons dying on our roadways?

But what about long-term good? For example, if there is a God, we should not expect 150,000 people to die for no good reason. Thus, the Southeast Asian tsunami must be necessary for the occurrence of some long-term good. The theist, if asked to produce evidence to support this claim, might argue that this long-term good may be known only to God and we may never be privy to this information. Yet the problem with the long-term good is not merely limited to its inscrutability. For one, it is unclear why there are short-term evils. It would seem that God could have created a world in which the evils were not as terrible as they are now, a world in which pain was not quite as excruciating, and less evil was needed for the attainment of future goods.

It can also be argued that the short-term evils, such as they are, are too pricey for the end result. Watching a young child suffer and die of Tay-Sachs disease seems unjustified by the measly comfort of imagining that child sitting at the right hand of God. And since the theist believes that God is capable of contravening the laws of nature and performing miracle cures, such suffering appears all the more gratuitous. With regard to animal suffering, unless we are to imagine all the creatures that died agonizingly from forest fires, monsoons, exposure, and predation frolicking happily in heaven, this proposal offers no justice. (Similarly, we can always wonder why we were instilled with the desire to relish eating the flesh of living creatures.)

It seems an all-powerful, all-good being could bring about good without evil, or with at least a lesser amount than the terrible suffering the world currently contains.

II) EVIL IS NECESSARY AS PUNISHMENT FOR SIN. To argue that all sufferers were given their just deserts is as absurd as supposing that the millions Hitler annihilated, the millions who died as a result of Stalin's purges, or the millions who were slaughtered by the Khmer Rouge were punished by God because of some sin they committed. And of course this explanation does not apply to animals, quite large numbers of which are affected by natural disasters and disease. A multitude of evil is left unaccounted for on this view: for to be punished for sin requires the ability to choose otherwise, as well as knowledge of one's actions. And it is simply implausible to suppose that trout are epistemically responsible moral agents deserving of punishment.

III) EVIL IS NECESSARY AS A WARNING SYSTEM IN NATURE/FOR HUMANKIND. This explanation proposes that suffering is needed as a warning system in the natural world, such as pain warning of life-threatening danger. Yet it is not the case that *all* pain and suffering function as a warning. Further, pains due to physical degeneration, illness, or emotional suffering, such as a dog grieving over a lost master, do not seem to warn animals of anything. A system involving a particular sound, temperature change, or vibration would seem more efficient than the suffering abundant in the world today.

Another claim involved here is that the great power of God, evidenced by natural catastrophes, shocks those who are on the road to error into behaving appropriately. Yet sufferers are more prone to ask, "why me?" or to question the existence of an all-good, all-powerful God than they are to revere such a destructive power. A mass miracle now and then such as ending the slaughter in the Sudan, or turning the land mines of Cambodia into flowers, would better inspire awe and reverence than the devastation wreaked by earthquakes, hurricanes, floods, volcanic eruptions, and pandemics.

Evil is a Necessary By-Product of Causal Laws

This theodicy, recently proposed in detail by Clem Dore,[13] contends that all evil is nothing more than a polluting by-product of the proper functioning of the laws of nature in their industrious manufacture of the *summum bonum*. The unimpeded functioning of the laws of nature is seen as necessary for the production and creation of a justifying (indiscernible) end. Evil or suffering is merely a foreseen but unfortunate by-product of this natural machinery.

On this view, every molecule that now exists in the world is somehow required to bring about this indiscernible, justifying end (E), else God could step in to intervene. Moreover, any other instantiation of the known world, with different causal laws, would also somehow dissipate E.

There are a number of difficulties with this view, and perhaps the most needed clarification regards the nature of this indiscernible, justifying end, that is, is it a temporal or atemporal realm, is it a nonmaterial/spiritual realm or a physical entity, and so on.

On the other hand, even if we were to allow that the laws of nature are necessary for bringing about E, we can still note that there would be a great deal less evil in the world if we could know these laws in advance. If a cure for AIDS or cancer were to be discovered tomorrow rather than years from now, or never, a great deal of suffering could be avoided, not only in human lives but in those animals utilized for such experimental research.

MORAL EVIL THEODICIES

The type of suffering that results from the actions of moral agents perhaps dwarfs the vast amount of suffering caused by natural disasters. An estimated 20–30 million were starved to death in Stalin's purges, approximately 9 million were killed by Hitler's Third Reich, and at least 3 million were murdered by Pol Pot's Khmer Rouge. In the United States alone it is estimated that 60 million animals a year are sacrificed on the altar of fast food. Millions of others are tortured to provide profits for pharmaceutical mega-corporations. All of this is planned and executed by "moral" agents. Some of the justifications for such unspeakable suffering in the face of a good and all-powerful God are:

(1) Evil is necessary for building character
(2) Evil is necessary for free will

Evil is Necessary for Building Character

This proposed explanation for moral evil typically argues that if there were no dangers or pains or suffering in the world, there would also be no courage, charity, sympathy, and the like. Difficulties such as these produce better characters and make the world a better, more civilized place.

The purpose of God's creation, therefore, is to allow humans to develop freely into mature moral creatures. Though others have defended this view, the strongest version is presented as the "soul-making" solution by John Hick.[14] There are three, conjointly necessary pillars to this solution: epistemic distance, eschatology, and mystery.

EPISTEMIC DISTANCE. For rational agents to develop moral character in a free and autonomous way, there must be what Hick calls "epistemic distance" from God. This amounts to existing in a world in which it seems as if there is no God. Therefore, our environment must include hardship, danger, and suffering to generate the higher order goods of strong moral character. It is not enough for people to *have* higher order character traits, such as charity, compassion, and sympathy for those less fortunate, but it is the *development* of these traits that is so valuable, all of which require that we make wrong choices and inflict harm. The moral perfection of humanity, or soul making, requires epistemic distance, which, in turn, requires evil.

In response, we can note that there are many human endeavors that can fulfill these criteria that do not have the extremely debilitating effects of much of the evil in the world. It is hard to imagine how the Holocaust did more to build character than occurrences with a greatly lessened threat of injury or death. It seems that a moderate probability of disaster would suffice for this schema to work, and there is unnecessary or gratuitous suffering for this purpose. Moreover, one might ask: "Why does epistemic distance logically require the existence of evil?" In other words, couldn't God have made a world in which it *appeared* as if there was no God without introducing evil? The existence of evil is not the only basis for a case against theism, since one might find the concept of God incoherent, or show that arguments that attempt to prove God's existence fail, without ever referring to the existence of evil. For epistemic distance to function as a justifier for evil, some logical connection between the two is needed, else it is not at all obvious that evil is required for individuals to believe God is absent.

ESCHATOLOGY. The stubborn fact that not all people develop into morally superior beings during their lifetime poses a serious problem for the soul-making thesis. Many people, in fact, become so embittered by the hardships of their lives that they turn away from God, while others never seem to acknowledge God at all. If the existence of suffering is to serve God's purpose of creating morally superior creatures, then it has failed. The process of soul making, which requires obstacles for its completion, must then continue in another realm. And this reveals a serious flaw with the entire soul-making explanation for evil, namely, the alteration of epistemic distance. If the current amount of epistemic distance is necessary for genuine freedom, then a lessening of epistemic distance implies either (1) that a lesser degree of freedom is allowed for soul making or (2) that some epistemic distance is not required for soul making, and, thus, some evil remains unjustified by the soul-making thesis.

MYSTERY. The amount of evil in the world seems to go beyond that which is instrumental for the purpose of soul making. This extra amount of evil Hick labels "dysteleogical surplus."[15] It is the concept of mystery that explains this inequity, that is, the mysteriousness of the amounts and distributions of suffering encourage soul making. If we were to exist in a world containing no unjust, undeserved, or excessive suffering, then suffering would not evoke in us the response of sympathy or spur us on to heroic acts. We would recognize that individuals suffer because they deserve it in some way and we would have no motive to alleviate their pain. Suffering, then, must be haphazard and apparently unmerited in order for it to elicit a sympathetic response.

Yet it is difficult to see how the mass slaughter now occurring in the Sudan, for example, is necessary. It certainly seems that, with all else being equal, the nonoccurrence of the genocide in Darfur would not diminish the effect of other haphazard suffering. And if one event, such as the Sudanese genocide, could be avoided without affecting the role played by other suffering, then this event is unnecessary even for the establishment of mystery. In other words, there is a surplus of suffering needed to establish even the concept of mystery.

Perhaps more damaging is the type of God portrayed. A just God would not allow millions to suffer excruciating deaths merely to promote spiritual growth in others. Moreover, it is morally reprehensible to torture millions of creatures simply to create an environment in which evil appears haphazard.

Evil Is Necessary for Free Will

Perhaps the most popular mode of diffusing the argument from evil lies in the appeal to free will. The free-will defense runs as follows:

(1) Humans have free will, and moral evil is a result of the exercise of free will.
(2) A world in which there is free will, even though it contains evil, is better than a world in which humans have no free will and are mere automata who always do good because they are determined to do so.

(3) Free will is seen to be of such value that it justifies the existence of moral evil.

Two major elements are needed for the free-will defense to succeed. First, it must be agreed that free will is this highly valuable asset without which humanity would suffer a great loss. Second, it must be shown that having free will is necessarily connected to evil in the world such that there could not be free willed creatures without evil.

Regarding the value of free will, we again might ask, "Given the choice between this world and a world in which there is no evil and merely the appearance of free will, which is more valuable?" The answer would strongly depend on the respondent's perspective. Suffice it to say it is an open question for many people. Nevertheless, the free-will defender maintains that all would agree that free will is intrinsically valuable and that it is sufficient to justify the resulting evil, even though no reasons have been forthcoming in support of this claim.

We are then left with the issue of whether this intrinsically valuable commodity could obtain in humans without the existence of evil in the world, or at the very least, as much evil in the world as now abounds. For even if it be granted to the theist that, yes, the exercise of free will requires that there be evil, we might still wonder why so much of it is needed.

Even though it is not obvious that there is an impossibility, logical or otherwise, in the existence of humans with free will who have the inability to deliberately sin (or at the very least, the inability to commit the heinous crimes we have been witness to), Alvin Plantinga argues against this possibility. He claims that: "it was not within God's power to create a world containing moral good but no moral evil."[16] Plantinga is credited with arriving at the notion of "transworld depravity," or that in any world where a person is significantly free, that person would, on some occasion, act morally wrongly. As Plantinga phrases it: "If S' were actual, P would go wrong with respect to A" (where S' is a possible world, P is a person, and A is an action).[17] Not only, Plantinga claims, is it possible that there are persons who suffer from transworld depravity, but he argues that it is possible that all of us suffer from it. And if we all suffer from transworld depravity, then there is no world that God could create in which any of us would both be free and always do what is right. If persons are instantiated essences and if all essences are transworld-depraved, then "no matter which essences God instantiates, the resulting persons, if free with respect to morally significant actions, would always perform at least some wrong actions."[18] Moral good, according to Plantinga, is created only by the instantiation of significantly free persons.

A word is needed about the concept of freedom that Plantinga is utilizing. By "free choice," Plantinga is referring to actions that are not determined by forces external to an individual, such as duress, coercion, or God stepping in and causing us to act in a certain way. Significantly free individuals are also not determined to act in a certain way because of forces internal to an individual, such as a psychological obsession, compulsion, or prior physical limitations. And Plantinga also wants significantly free individuals to possess another kind of freedom, one in which for every action that a person freely performs, there is another possible world in which that person freely chooses not to perform that action. It should be noted that this latter type of freedom, logical freedom, is not shared by God since God cannot do what is evil, by definition.[19]

Now Plantinga is not committed to the position that every possible person essence in every possible world must suffer from transworld depravity. Rather, Plantinga argues, it is the case that in any possible world, which God could actualize, every possible person would in fact go astray. On this view, God could not instantiate perfect-person essences that would not ever sin. Although Plantinga argues that these instantiated beings are significantly free in that they could have done otherwise (i.e., not sinned), it does seem that his claim about transworld depravity amounts to a claim about the existence of a necessary connection obtaining between freedom and evil.

One response to Plantinga's scenario is to offer the idea of person essences, which have the ability to do wrong but, in fact, never commit wrong. Clem Dore suggests this option by offering the concept of Q-essences that possess property X: "the property of being such that there are *some* occasions on which one has a capacity for wrongdoing and no occasions on which one in fact does wrong."[20] The freedom to choose would be preserved, and there would be no evil due to the fact that sinful actions were not chosen. The question of why God did not instantiate Q-essences, rather than the person essences currently in existence, is left unanswered.

There are other modes of diffusing the free-will defense. We can easily draw a distinction between the ability to choose to act freely and the commission of those acts. This highlights a distinction between an epistemic and an ontological rendering of the concept of free will. We all have the experience of choosing to pursue goals that never came to pass, but this does not mean that our choices were not free simply because we were unaware of the inability, perhaps even the impossibility, of our choices being actualized. It seems perfectly reasonable to claim that one can choose freely without being able to actualize that choice, and it is this that seems sufficient for the attribution of free will. To claim that free will depends on facts that pertain to action is to beg the question: precisely what is at issue is whether "free will" should refer to "being able to do otherwise" or "being able to choose other wise." If we allow that free choice not need to include "being able to do otherwise" but rather exists if the condition of "being able to choose otherwise" is met, then we can question why God does not render choices to commit heinous evil unattainable.

This would not necessarily require God's direct intervention. We can imagine a world identical to the present except that human beings are endowed with a special power not currently possessed. This power would enable anyone witnessing a commission of an evil act to prevent the resulting harm. Anyone witnessing a murder, anyone in a concentration camp, anyone witnessing a situation wherein harm will come to another, can stop the harm from occurring by rendering the attacker's actions ineffective. Evil could be prevented only if a witness freely chose to use this power, and this power could not, by its nature, be used for harm (it would be ineffective). People could still continue to commit evil deeds; they would just have to do so in private on unsuspecting victims. Large-scale evils, however, such as mass slaughter, would be rendered obsolete. Moreover, since using this power would be a matter of choice, no one's free will would be infringed on, at least not in a way that the free-will defender should object to.

If some evil can be avoided, while preserving the traditional idea of free will, then clearly there is gratuitous suffering in the world. Ultimately, it has not been successfully argued that free will is incompatible with the continued avoidance of wrongdoing or that free will is incompatible with less evil in the world than currently exists.

CONCLUSION

There is an abundance of evil in our world. If we can prevent it, then we are morally obligated to do so. How much more obligated a perfectly powerful and perfectly good God must be to do the same? The theist, who maintains that such a God exists, must explain why this abundance of evil persists and why the number of rapes, murders, child torturers, serial killers, bombings, animal cruelties, and the like proliferate at a rate that threatens to exhaust and suffocate us. Could all of this be necessary for some great end? Could all of this be necessary to build the character of those survivors of this catastrophic century of misery? Could this all be a warning of some kind? A punishment, perhaps, intended to force us to change our ways?

But all of these responses have been found deficient in one respect or another: none can account for the tremendous amount of suffering in a world in which an allegedly omnipotent, omniscient, and wholly good

God reigns. The conclusion to which we are drawn, therefore, is that the existence of such a God is implausible. The evidence that suffering, both human and animal, moral and natural, presents leaves only one ground on which to base claims about such a God: that of faith. And this faith has no rational basis in light of the 1.5 million children burned in the ovens of the Third Reich, or the 150,000 drowned by the Southeast Asian tsunami, or the slaughter in the Sudan, or the millions of sentient creatures agonizingly snuffed out each year, or the myriad other instances of preventable evil which no one, not even God, steps in to alleviate.

NOTES

1. Michael Martin, "Is Evil Evidence against the Existence of God?" *Mind* 87 (1978): 429–32.
2. J. L. Mackie, "Evil and Omnipotence," *Mind* 64 (1955): 201. Reprinted in Marilyn McCord Adams and Robert Adams (eds.), *The Problem of Evil* (New York: Oxford University Press, 1991).
3. Alvin Plantinga, *God and Other Minds: A Study of the Rational Justification of Belief in God* (Ithaca, N.Y.: Cornell University Press, 1967), p. 117.
4. Richard R. La Croix, "Unjustified Evil and God's Choice," *Sophia* 13 (1974): 20–28.
5. Ibid., p. 21.
6. Ibid.
7. Ibid.
8. La Croix notes that Plantinga might reject his argument on the grounds that free will is a good that would not exist if God had not created it, but offers an analogous argument to the above to counter Plantinga's objection on those grounds. See La Croix's article in full for his complete rebuttal of Plantinga.
9. Quentin Smith, "A Sound Logical Argument from Evil," in Quentin Smith, *Ethical and Religious Thought in Analytic Philosophy of Religion* (New Haven and London: Yale University Press, 1997), pp. 148–56.
10. Quotations taken from ibid.
11. As William Rowe has argued, if we cannot conceive of sufficient reasons for the apparently gratuitous and horrendous suffering in the world, then belief in the God hypothesis is not justified. See "The Evidential Argument from Evil: A Second Look," in Daniel Howard Synder (ed.), *The Evidential Argument from Evil* (Indianapolis: Indiana University Press, 1996), in which probabilistic arguments are utilized to determine the warrantibility of belief.
12. Peter Van Inwagen suggests it is reasonable to conclude that we may never find a reason for God allowing apparently gratuitous evil ("The Problem of Evil, the Problem of Air, and the Problem of Silence," in Synder (ed.), *The Evidential Argument from Evil*), and Fitzpatrick advocates that theists adopt the "uncertainty position" with regard to this question and animal suffering (F. J. Fitzpatrick, "The Onus of Proof in Arguments about the Problem of Evil," *Religious Studies* 17(1981): 25).
13. Clement Dore, *Theism* (Dordrecht: D. Reidel, 1984). For a complete refutation of Dore's position, see Andrea M. Weisberger, "The Pollution Solution:

A Critique of Dore's Reponses to the Argument from Evil." *Sophia* 36 (1997): 53–74.

14. Swinburne has argued this position as well in "Some Major Strands of Theodicy," in Synder (ed.), *The Evidential Argument from Evil*, but Hick's soul-making theodicy, as expressed in *Evil and the God of Love*, revised ed. (New York: Harper & Row, 1977), remains the most thorough exploration of the position.

15. Hick explains, "Moreover, I do not now have an alternative theory to offer that would explain in any rational or ethical way why men suffer as they do. The only appeal left is to mystery" (*Evil and the God of Love*, pp. 333–34).

16. Alvin Plantinga, *God, Freedom and Evil* (Grand Rapids, Mich.: William B. Eerdmans, 1974), p. 54.

17. Ibid., p. 48.

18. Ibid., p. 53.

19. See Smith's discussion of freedom in "A Sound Logical Argument from Evil," pp. 150–51.

20. Clement Dore, *Moral Scepticism* (New York: St. Martin's Press, 1991), p. 57.

SUGGESTED READING

Drange, Ted. *Nonbelief and Evil: Two Atheological Arguments*. Amherst, N.Y.: Prometheus Books, 1998.

Draper, Paul. "Pain and Pleasure: An Evidential Problem for Theists." *Nous* 23 (1989): 331–50.

Hume, David. *Dialogues Concerning Natural Religion*. New York: Penguin Classics, 1990.

Mackie, J. L. *The Miracle of Theism*. Oxford: Claredon; and New York: Oxford University Press, 1982.

Madden, E. H., and P. H. Hare. *Evil and the Concept of God*. Springfield, Ill.: Charles C. Thomas, 1968.

Martin, Michael. *Atheism: A Philosophical Justification*. Philadelphia: Temple University Press, 1991.

O'Connor, David. *God and Inscrutable Evil: In Defense of Theism and Atheism*. Lanham, Md.: Rowman & Littlefield, 1998.

Russell, Bruce. "Defenseless." In Daniel Howard Synder (ed.), *The Evidential Argument from Evil*. Indianapolis: Indiana University Press, 1996.

Smith, George H. *Atheism: The Case against God*. Buffalo, N.Y.: Prometheus Books, 1979.

Tattersall, Nicholas. "The Evidential Argument from Evil." Http://www.infidels.org/library/modern/nicholas_tattersall/evil.html, accessed April 8, 2006.

Weisberger, A. M. *Suffering Belief: Evil and the Anglo-American Defense of Theism*. New York: Peter Lang, 1999.

11 Kalam Cosmological Arguments for Atheism

1. INTRODUCTION

Cosmological arguments for God's existence have two parts. The first part aims to establish that there is a cause of the universe. The second part aims to establish that this cause is God or God's act of creation. My goal is to show that this second "theistic" part is unsound and that there is a sound "atheistic" second part that shows that the universe is self-caused.

The cosmological and teleological arguments are two types of arguments for the existence of God. They are different from other types in that they are about the entire universe; the cosmological argument seeks to find a causal explanation of why some universe exists, and the teleological argument seeks to find an explanation of the designed or apparently designed nature of the universe. In this way they differ from the ontological and conceptual arguments, which are a priori, and from the arguments from mystical experience, moral conscience, and human consciousness. The cosmological and teleological arguments are about the empirical facts of the universe, the mystical, moral, and consciousness arguments are about empirical facts concerning humans, and the ontological and conceptualist arguments endeavor to deduce God's existence from a priori concepts alone, without needing any observational evidence about the universe.

The traditional cosmological arguments are of three types. One is the *Kalam* argument, which aims to establish that there is a cause of the beginning of the universe and that this cause is God. The Thomistic arguments aim to establish that there is a sustaining cause of the universe at each present time. The Leibniz cosmological argument is that the whole series of contingent beings (that make up the universe) requires an external cause that is not contingent, but necessary.

The Kalam cosmological argument is often stated in this manner:

1. Whatever begins to exist has a cause.
2. The universe began to exist.
3. Therefore, the universe has a cause.

Since the key element that seems to introduce the requirement of causality is something's *beginning to exist*, the argument aims to establish that the universe's beginning to exist is not uncaused. Discussions of the argument typically focus on a cause of the universe's beginning to exist. Since this is left implicit in the more or less vague way of stating the conclusion, we can make it more precise by making its meaning explicit, namely, that the universe's beginning to exist has a cause. Whether or not the universe needs a cause of its remaining in existence is not obvious one way or the other from the vague way the conclusion 3 is stated, so I concentrate on what the argument obviously implies, namely, that there is a cause of the universe's beginning to exist. This is what William Lane Craig (2002: 69) meant when he recently named the argument as "the Kalam cosmological for a First Cause of the beginning of the Universe."

The Kalam cosmological argument was first formulated in medieval Islamic scholasticism, and it was revived and has been a topic of widespread discussion since 1979, when Craig published *The Kalam Cosmological Argument*. This argument has attracted much more interest than agreement, even among theist philosophers of religion. The reason seems to be that many theists do not accept Craig's argument that the *past is necessarily finite* and therefore that the universe must begin to exist, and many theists are not as confident as Craig that the first premise is "obviously true," the first premise being "whatever begins to exist has a cause." Nonetheless, a count of the articles in the philosophy journals shows that more articles have been published about Craig's defense of the Kalam argument than have been published about any other philosopher's contemporary formulation of an argument for God's existence. Surprisingly, this even holds for Plantinga's argument for the rational acceptability of the ontological argument and Plantinga's argument that theism is a rationally acceptable basic belief. The fact that theists and atheists alike "cannot leave Craig's Kalam argument alone" suggests that it may be an argument of unusual philosophical interest or else has an attractive core of plausibility that keeps philosophers turning back to it and examining it once again.

I shall not take one of the usual routes that critics take, namely, arguing that the past can be infinite or that it is not obvious that whatever begins to exist has a cause. I have done this elsewhere (Craig and Smith 1993). Rather, I am going to accept the first half of the Kalam argument, parts (1)–(3), and disagree with the second half of it, the argument that the first cause is God. But I differ from Craig in that I accept (1)–(3) on empirical grounds rather than on a priori grounds. One version of Einstein's general theory of relativity is formulated as "big bang cosmology," which is used to explain the observations that the universe began to exist about 15 billion years ago in an extremely small explosion of densely packed matter and energy. This matter and energy was compacted so densely that it was smaller than an electron. Due to the explosive force of the big bang explosion, the universe began to expand, and it has been expanding ever since. The pieces of matter grouped together into clumps and became stars and galaxies. The theory of this big bang explosion implies that the universe is causally determinist, that is, that each state of the universe is sufficiently caused by an earlier state. On this basis I can accept premise (1), that whatever begins to exist has a cause, on the basis of the empirical evidence for the empirical laws of nature of the so-called big bang cosmology. (Bohm's interpretation of quantum mechanics is causally determinist; since I hold this interpretation (Smith 2003), I need not worry about "uncaused quantum events.") I can also accept that the universe began to exist, because observations tell us that it did; but I do not accept Craig's a priori arguments that an actually infinite past is impossible. My goal is to show that the *cause* of the universe's beginning, which both Craig and I agree *exists*, has a *nature* different from what Craig believes it has. I argue that the cause of the universe's beginning is not God but the universe itself. More precisely, I argue that the universe's beginning to exist is *self-caused*.

It is often said that "nothing can cause itself to exist." I agree with this sentence in the sense in which it is usually used. But I disagree with this sentence if it expresses a different sense, in particular, a different sense of "cause itself to exist." In this second sense, "itself" refers to a whole of parts, not to a simple being. The elucidation of this second sense of "causes itself to exist" or "self-caused" takes up most of this chapter.

My conclusion will be that the Kalam cosmological argument, when formulated in a manner consistent with contemporary science, is not an argument for God's existence but an argument for God's nonexistence and an argument for a complete atheistic explanation of the beginning of the universe's existence. Let us call the beginning of the universe B. My Kalam cosmological argument has for its conclusion that the beginning of the universe's existence is self-caused. "B is self-caused" does not mean the same as "B causes B" but means the same as "each part of B is caused by earlier parts of B, B's existence is logically entailed by its parts' existence, and the basic laws instantiated by these parts are caused to be instantiated by earlier parts that also instantiate these laws."

2. THE BEGINNING OF THE UNIVERSE'S EXISTENCE

The physical sciences indicate that the universe began to exist with a big bang, an explosion of matter and energy that occurred about 15 billion years ago. The question that the theist and atheist are faced with is: What is the cause of this explosion? An atheist may hold that it is uncaused, as I used to believe (Smith 1988, 1994; Smith and Craig 1993), but if the theist can formulate a compelling causal explanation of the big bang explosion, then the atheist should believe the big bang does have a cause.

According to contemporary physical science, in particular, big bang cosmology, there is no first instant $t = 0$. If there were such a first instant, the universe would exist in an impossible state at this time; the whole spatially three-dimensional universe would occupy or exist in a point that had no spatial dimensions. Such a state of affairs would be described by nonsensical mathematical statements.

For example, at $t = 0$, the density of the universe's matter would be (to give a simplified example) of the form 25 grams per zero unit of space, that is, 25/0. But this is a mathematically nonsensical sentence, since there exists no mathematical operation of dividing by zero. The alleged fraction 25/0 is not a number but merely marks on a page, since there is no fraction with zero for a denominator and a positive number for its numerator. The universe began to exist later than the hypothetical time $t = 0$.

An instant is a temporal point, that is, a time with no duration. An instantaneous state of the universe is a state that exists for an instant. An interval of time is a set of instants, in fact, infinitely many instants.

According to big bang cosmology, time is continuous, which means each real number (each decimal number) corresponds to a distinct instant in the interval. Intervals are demarcated into times of various lengths or durations, for example, years, hours, minutes, and seconds. A temporally extended state of the universe occupies some interval of time; for example, we can talk of the first hour-long state of the universe's existence.

An interval is closed if it has two boundary points, an instant that is the earliest instant of the interval and an instant that is latest instant of the interval. If the hour-long interval from noon to 1 P.M. is closed, its earliest instant is the instant denoted by "noon" and its latest instant is the instant denoted by "1 P.M."

An interval is half-open in the early direction if it has no earliest instant. If we delete the instant denoted "noon" from the mentioned hour, it would be an hour that is half-open in the early direction. The first hour would be closed if the hypothetical first instant $t = 0$ actually existed. But since it does not exist, the first hour is half-open in the early direction.

I use the idea in big bang cosmology that the first hour (minute, second, etc.) of the universe's existence is half-open in the earlier direction. This means there is no instant corresponding to the number zero in the real line interval that contains an infinitely many (continuum-many) numbers greater than zero and either less than one or one. $0 > x <$ or $= 1$. If time is continuous, then there is no first instant x that immediately follows the hypothetical "first instant" $t = 0$. This is because between any two instants, there are an infinite number of other instants. If we "cut out" the instant $t = 0$ that corresponds to 0 in the interval $0 > x <$ or $= 1$, we will not find a certain instant that immediately comes after the "cut out" instant $t = 0$. For example, the instant y corresponding to the number 0.5 cannot be the first instant, since between the number 0 and the number 0.5 there is the number 0.25 and some instant z corresponding to 0.25. The same holds for any other number in the interval $0 > x <$ or $= 1$.

3. CRAIG'S KALAM COSMOLOGICAL ARGUMENT FOR THEISM

This account of instants, intervals, and the beginning of the universe provides us with enough information to see why Craig's Kalam cosmological argument for theism is unsound.

Let us consider how Craig attempts to justify the first half of the Kalam cosmological argument for theism (or atheism). I mean the three sentences stated at the beginning of this chapter, namely, (1) whatever begins to exist has a cause; (2) the universe began to exist; and the inference to the conclusion, (3) the universe has a cause (implying that the universe's beginning to exist has a cause).

I am going to make two points in this section. First, Craig's theory is inconsistent with big bang cosmology, which is the theory Craig uses in his empirical argument for the thesis that the universe began to exist. Second, Craig's theory of mathematics is false a priori, which makes his interpretation of the Kalam argument false of logical necessity, regardless of what the empirical facts are.

I am first going to explain how set theory is an essential part of big bang cosmology and how this entails that Craig's empirical argument for the beginning of the universe is falsified.

Consider the first second-long state of the universe's existence. This is an interval that has continuum-many instantaneous states as its parts. This interval is a set. Since this set has an actually infinite number of members, it is inconsistent with Craig's theory, for Craig believes it is "metaphysically impossible" for there to be an actual infinite.

Below I mention several technical words, such as "higher order predicate logic," "manifold," and "topology." It is not necessary to understand these words or phrases to understand my argument. It suffices to know that Craig's theory is inconsistent with the concepts expressed by these words or phrases.

According to big bang cosmology and Einstein's general theory of relativity, the universe has a topology, which is a set of actually infinite subsets that have certain relations to each other. These theories also state that the universe is a continuous manifold, which is a set of an actual infinite, specifically, actual continuum-many points. The universe also has a metric, which demarcates time into intervals of various lengths, hours, days, years, and so on. The intervals demarcated by the metric are sets of actually infinite, continuum-many instants. Furthermore, the metric requires an actually infinite and continuous manifold and topology. In general relativity and big bang cosmology a metric is defined on (in terms of) a point in an actually infinite continuum.

Craig denies that there is an actual infinite. His theory implies there cannot be an actually infinite topological structure of the universe, there cannot be an actually infinite manifold, there cannot be a metric defined on a point in an actually infinite continuum of points, and so on. Big bang cosmology implies that there is an actually infinite manifold, topology, and metrication. It logically follows that the sentences of his version of the *Kalam* argument (e.g., "The universe began to exist"), under Craig's interpretation of their semantic content, expressed highly disconfirmed propositions. Craig's theory that there is a "potential infinite" alone also makes his theory inconsistent with contemporary physical science, specifically, big bang cosmology.

Further, Craig's a priori argument for a merely potential infinity is self-contradictory. Craig is committed to the contradiction that "x has a potentiality to be infinite" and "x does not have to have a potentiality to be infinite." This is because x's possibility or potentiality for becoming realized cannot be realized, because if it were, there would be an actual infinite. Craig mentions this contradiction and seems to think a mere question-begging denial made in a few sentences by Aristotle solves it. Aristotle writes [*Physics*, 3.6.206]:

the infinite has a potential existence. But the phrase "potential existence" is ambiguous. When we speak of the potential existence of the statue, we mean that there will be an actual statue. It is not so with the infinite. There will not be an actual infinite.

If by saying that the infinite has a potential existence, and we do not mean it can actually exist, what could "potential" mean? This trades a self-contradictory theory for an unintelligible theory. If "potential" has a special meaning for the case of infinity, we may ask what is said by "the infinite has a potential existence.... There will not be an actual infinite."

No sense can be made of his claim that the infinite has a "potential" existence. But we do learn that "there will not be an actual infinite." This implies that in every case there is actual only *finite* series or things.

But Craig claims that "finite" means something different than "potential infinite." Again, this is either self-contradictory or unintelligible.

If Craig's theory is both empirically disconfirmed and logically self-contradictory, this does not pose any obstacle for the construction of a Kalam cosmological argument for atheism.

4. THE KALAM COSMOLOGICAL ARGUMENT FOR ATHEISM

Every instantaneous state of the universe corresponding to a number in the interval $0 > x <$ or $= 1$ preceded and is caused by earlier instantaneous states. There is no instantaneous state in the first half-open second, or the first half-open one-billionth of a second, that is uncaused. Since the beginning of the universe's existence is the instantaneous states that are members of a half-open interval, it follows from what I have said that the universe's beginning to exist is internally caused. This needs some elaboration.

Some theists might ask: What causes *the whole sequence* of instantaneous states? Regarding the universe's beginning to exist, it may be asked, what causes the first half-open *hour* or the first half-open interval of *one-billionth of a second*, of the universe's existence? Each instantaneous member of the interval-long state is causally related to earlier and later instantaneous members, but *none* of these is causally related to the whole interval-long state. Nor do *all* of the instantaneous members jointly cause the interval-long state. Does the interval-long state, the set of the instantaneous states, need an external cause, such as a divine cause?

Swinburne says that the interval or set of states does need an external cause: "[I]f the only causes of its past states are prior past states, *the set* of past states as a whole will have no cause and so no explanation" (1991: 124, emphasis added). Swinburne argues that there will be an explanation if God causes the set of past states. But this argument is unsound since a *set*, by definition, is an abstract object and an *abstract object* (by definition) cannot enter into causal relations with other objects, including a concrete object such as God. Thus, the argument that there is something above and beyond the states, namely, *the set* of states, cannot lead to an external cause since the "something" that is posited is not the sort of thing that can be caused.

A problem about sets is also present in William Rowe's discussion of whether or not the universe can be causally explained. Rowe's (1975, 1989) argument is in one respect advantaged over Swinburne's, since Rowe admits at the outset that the set of all the states is not a candidate for causal explanation. He emphasizes that the question "Why does the infinite series exist?" should not be construed as asking for a causal reason for the set's existence (since an abstract object cannot have a cause of its existence); rather, it should be construed as asking for a causal reason for the fact that the set has these members rather than some other members or no members at all. Suppose "A is the set of dependent beings. In asking why A exists we are not asking for an explanation of the existence of an abstract entity; we are asking why A has the members it has rather than some other members or none at all" (1989: 150). According to Rowe, this question may be coherently answered by saying that A has the members it actually possesses because some being apart from the members is causally responsible for A having these members.

However, it seems to me that Rowe's discussion exhibits a set-theoretic fallacy, even though it is different from Swinburne's. A set necessarily contains its members. This is an axiom of set theory and one of the axioms of second-order predicate logic with identity. Accordingly, the question "why does the set A contain the members it actually contains?" – if it makes sense at all – has the answer "every set necessarily contains all and only the members it actually contains, and A is a set." Rowe's question therefore cannot admit of the answer "the set A of dependent beings contains all and only the beings it actually contains because God caused A to contain these beings rather than some other beings." God cannot make choices about logically impossible states of affairs, such as choosing whether or not the set [Jack, Jill] should contain Jack and Jill or some other members instead.

Why does the first half-open second-long state of the universe exist? It exists because (1) the existence of each instantaneous state that is a member of this second-long state is caused by earlier instantaneous states, and (2) the state is the set of these instantaneous states and is logically entailed by these states (where "logically" means higher order predicate logic with identity). If one wishes "logical entailment" to be a relation between propositions or interpreted sentences, then we can say that the proposition expressed by "these instantaneous states exist" logically entails the proposition expressed by "the set of these instantaneous states exists."

The first half-open interval is not caused by any or all of its instantaneous states and is not caused by any external cause. If Jack and Jill are each caused to exist, then the set [Jack, Jill] does not need an extra cause of its existence. This is because the existence of Jack and Jill *logically entail* the existence of the set [Jack, Jill]. In each possible world in which Jack and Jill exist, the set [Jack, Jill] exists. In each possible world in which the set [Jack, Jill] exists, Jack and Jill exist. If we call this set S, we may say that "S exists" and "Jack and Jill exist" express logically equivalent propositions.

The same holds for the earliest minute-long or one-second-long half-open interval of the universe's existence. This interval is a set S_I of continuum-many instantaneous states C, where "C" denotes the continuum-many states that are members of the set. By parallel reasoning, we can conclude that "C exists" and "S_I exists" express logically equivalent propositions. One cannot nontrivially ask, "C exists, but why does S_I exists?" for the answer to the question is logically implied by the question itself, namely, that C exists. Accordingly, questions such as those of Swinburne, Rowe, and many others both entail and even contain the answers to their questions, "C exists, but why does S_I exist?" or "S_I exists, but why does C exist?"[1]

What does the "the beginning of the universe's existence" refer to? It seems that it cannot refer to any half-open interval-long state, since for any half-open interval-long state there is a briefer state that would seem to constitute a better candidate for being the state with which the universe's beginning should be identified. Since there is no first instant and there are an infinite number of briefer and briefer first intervals of a given length, "the beginning of the universe" does not refer to one instant or one interval. It must refer to many instants or intervals.

Nor can the beginning be a closed interval of any length. If we ask about an earliest closed hour, we will receive the answer that there is no one earliest closed hour. Each instant but the last instant of time (if the universe is closed in the future direction) is the early boundary of the earliest closed intervals of many lengths; the same instant is the early boundary of a closed hour, a closed second, and so on. But there is no first closed hour because that would require an instant that is the earliest boundary of the closed hour, and this would be the first instant at which the universe exists. Each instant later than the hypothetical $t = 0$ is an early boundary of a closed hour in some sequence of closed hours. There are infinitely many such sequences, since there are infinitely many instants later than the hypothetical $t = 0$. Thus, every first, closed hour h_2 in some sequence T_2 of nonoverlapping hours begins later than some earlier closed hour h_1 that is the first hour of some other sequence T_I of nonoverlapping hours, such that the earlier closed hour h_I partly overlaps h_2.

We are dealing with an empirical theory, big bang cosmology, and this provides a way of defining the beginning of the universe. There are different kinds of states of the universe; for example, one kind of state is the electro-weak era, the era when the electromagnetic force was not differentiated from the weak force. Earlier than that there may be a strong-electro-weak state, which would be a state in which the electromagnetic force was unified with the weak force and strong force, leaving only the gravitational force as the other force. Some have speculated that at an even earlier time the gravitational force was unified with the other three forces, and that this kind of state had a temporal length of 10^{-43} seconds. This is usually called "the Planck era." This would be the first kind of state of the universe. Physicists speculate that there is no subinterval of this interval wherein the universe is in a different kind of state that any later subinterval of this interval. On empirical grounds, this justifies the use of "the beginning the universe" to refer to the earliest Planck state.

The argument I have given may be called an atheistic version of the Kalam cosmological argument for an explanation of the universe's beginning to exist. My explanation mentions only beings that exist contingently; the universe might not have existed and the states of the universe might not have existed. Since the existence of each state is caused by earlier states, and since the existence of all these states entails the universe's existence, there is an explanation for everything that contingently exists. This falsifies a belief that is held by virtually everyone. For example, Jordan Howard Sobel writes that "if anything is contingent, then it is not possible that, for every fact or entity, x, there is a reason of some sort or other for x" (Sobel 2004: 222).

It also invalidates Sobel's and others' belief that a complete explanation of the universe's existence requires that the premises all be necessary truths and that the conclusion thereby be a necessary truth. My atheistic cosmological argument is a complete explanation of the universe's existence, and its premises are the contingent truths: There is an earliest interval I of each length that is half-open in the early direction. The existence of each instantaneous state S that belongs to the interval I is sufficiently causally explained by earlier states. Each half-open interval I of states is explained by virtue of being logically equivalent to the states (or, if you prefer, "I exists" is logically equivalent to "C exists," where C is the continuum-many instantaneous states that are members of the set I). Note, furthermore, that the conclusion logically derived from these premises is the contingent truth, "the universe begins to exist."

Is this a complete explanation? Does it leave any explanatory factors unexplained? There remains an apparent problem about why our basic laws of nature obtain and not others. But there is an explanation of why these basic laws obtain rather than other basic laws.

5. BASIC LAWS OF NATURE

Why do the basic the law of nature, L, obtain? Examples of basic laws are the law of conservation of mass-energy and the law of increasing entropy or disorder. Since we are working with big bang cosmology, and this cosmology is a solution to Einstein's equation in the general theory of relativity, we may include in our basic laws Einstein's equation (which says, very roughly, that the curvature of space-time is dependent on the mass-energy in space-time and vice versa). The Friedman universe of big bang cosmology is not specified by a basic law of nature, since this law (i.e., equation) is derived from the Einstein equation in conjunction with initial conditions.

Why do the basic laws of conservation, entropy, and general relativity obtain? In brief, the basic laws are instantiated for the reason that these laws instantiated themselves. But what could this mean?

Basic laws of nature, such as L, are defined in terms of the states of the universe. Each of these states is a particular that has among its properties a certain dispositional property L; L is a disposition each state possesses to cause a later state to exist with certain kinds of properties and relations. A state S_2's disposition L is occurrently realized by the state S_2 if S_2 is caused to realize this disposition by an earlier state S_1 that possesses the kinds of properties and relations (e.g., a certain degree of entropy) that are required to make S_2 occurrently realize this disposition.

Since a basic law L is a property of each state, the explanation of why the basic law L obtains, rather than some other possible laws, is that each state that exemplifies L is caused to exemplify L by an earlier state that exemplifies L (and other relevant properties). The obtaining of the basic law of nature L is nothing over and above each state's exemplification of the dispositional property L. Since each state's exemplification of L is caused by an earlier state, the obtaining of L is explained. What other explanation could there be? God cannot cause the laws to be instantiated by the states, since the earlier states have already performed this task, so to speak.

State S_1's disposition to conserve matter and energy is occurrently realized. This realization consists in the fact that the instantaneous end point of a series of states C coincides at the instant t with the beginning point of a later series E. The last instantaneous state of C causally affects the beginning point of E. The last state of C causally acts on the first state of E by bringing it into existence with the same amount of mass and energy possessed by the last state of C and by every earlier state of C.

6. GALE'S ARGUMENT THAT WHOLES CANNOT BE EXPLAINED IN TERMS OF CAUSES OF THEIR PARTS

The reader may feel that there is some issue not yet addressed. What is this issue? Is it the problem that it might have been the case that there was a different whole, composed of different parts, and nothing explains why the actual whole of parts exists? Indeed, why is there a whole of parts rather than nothing at all? These questions have already been answered. The reason why this whole of parts exists, rather than some other possible whole, is that this whole's existence is logically required by the existence of its parts, and its parts exist. The parts of the merely possible whole do not exist, and therefore the actual existence of this merely possible whole is not logically required.

But why these parts? These parts exist because all of them have been caused to exist by earlier parts. Other possible parts do not exist because nothing causes them to exist.

But why is there something rather than nothing? The whole of parts is something. The reason it exists is that every one of its parts has been caused to exist by earlier parts and the whole's existence is logically required by the existence of the parts. The reason there is not nothing is that a universe caused itself to begin to exist and the basic laws governing this universe instantiated themselves.

But why is there such a thing as a universe that causes itself to begin to exist? The reason is that this universe's existence is logically required by the existence of its parts and its parts exist because each of them is caused to exist by an earlier part.

But haven't some philosophers, such as Richard (Gale 1991) shown that a whole cannot be explained by the fact that each of its parts is explained? Isn't this a "truism" or at least a platitude now accepted by both atheists and theists? I agree that this is a platitude, but not all platitudes are true. Gale (1991: 252–84) has argued against the Hume-Edwards thesis that a causal explanation of each part of whole suffices to explain the existence of the whole. But Gale's argument, although sound, is logically irrelevant to the Kalam cosmological argument for atheism I have presented.

Gale states that the existence of each part of an automobile has a causal explanation (e.g., the carburetor is made by Delco-Remy in Chicago, the starter motor by United Motors in Kansas City, and so on for each other part of the car). But this does not explain the existence of the automobile. The explanation of its existence is that its various parts are assembled by certain workers in a Detroit assembly plant. The notion of *assembling* particulars into a whole is crucial to Gale's criticism of the Hume-Edwards thesis.

Gale does not categorize wholes or define assemblies (or even use this word as a name of a kind of whole), but the examples he offers imply that he is talking about assemblies. If a whole is not a set, it may be an assembly, and this is a kind of whole that can have an external causal explanation in terms of an assembler or assemblers, in addition to the causal explanations of each of its parts. Furthermore, the causes of these parts would also be external to this whole; for example, a tire is a part of a car, but the people and tools (or their causal activities) that made the rubber, steel, and so on that belong to the tire are not parts of the car.

The difficulty arises in trying to show that the universe is relevantly analogous to a car or some other sort of assembled whole (e.g., a computer or bridge).

There is a difference in the senses of "part" that applies to automobiles and the universe or a succession of causes and effects. Each state of the universe is caused by earlier parts and causes later parts. But the door of a car is not a cause or effect of the steering wheel or some other such part, and there is no series of causes and effects consisting of a door, wheel, roof, transmission, and so on, by means of which the car can be conceived as a finite series of causally interrelated particulars, such that each particular part is caused to exist by another particular part.

Gale did not argue that the causal succession that is the topic of the Kalam or other cosmological arguments is an assembly. The point that is often overlooked is that Gale's argument refutes only Hume's general claim that the existence of *every kind of whole* is explained if each of its parts is causally explained. The fact that the half-open causal process that consists of the universe causing itself to begin to exist cannot be an assembly is consistent with Gale's argument being sound, but it also makes Gale's argument logically irrelevant to my Kalam argument for an atheistic explanation of the universe's beginning to exist.

7. CAUSATION OF INSTANTANEOUS STATES

It might be objected that the existence of the beginning of the universe, a half-open temporally extended state of a very brief length, cannot be explained by my Kalam atheistic explanation. There might be a feeling that my explanation is circular, or question-begging, or that the explananda (the explained parts, their whole, and the self-instantiated laws) are already defined in terms of the explanans (what explains the parts, whole, and basic laws). But there is nothing circular or question-begging in the explanations; what is being explained is *the existence of the parts, the existence of the whole,* and *the instantiation of the basic laws* L. What explains these facts is that each part is *caused to exist by an earlier part* of the whole, the whole is *logically required to exist by the existence of the parts,* and each instantiation of L is *caused by an earlier part that also instantiates* L, and so on ad infinitum, so there never is a brute fact that "L just is instantiated, without any causal explanation of why it is instantiated."

The skeptic appears to have no arguments left. The skeptic seems reduced to imaginative appeals to alleged counterexamples to my claim that the universe's beginning to exist is self-caused by virtue of the fact that the earliest intervals of any length are half-open in the earlier direction. We can find theists such as Burke, Vallicella, Deltete, Pruss, and many others that have been reduced to this state of imagining bizarre counterexamples.

They appeal to some half-open state and note that it is intuitively implausible that this state's existence is explained by the fact that each of its parts is caused by an earlier part. They do not change the subject, as Gale did (he changed the subject to cars and other assemblies), but imagine alleged counterexamples to a set of instantaneous states whose explanation is internal to it.

For example, Burke (1984) and others wish to refute what I have called the complete atheist explanation of the beginning to exist of the universe. Burke formulates a principle he believes this explanation is committed to:

(P) For any set S of times and any physical object x: If for every time belonging to S there is an explanation of why x exists at that time, these explanations, taken collectively, explain why it is that x exists at every time belonging to S.

Burke asks us to suppose that a fully grown duck sprang into existence on our table. The duck exists throughout a finite interval of time I that is half-open in the earlier direction; there is no first instant at which the duck exists. For every instant t at which the duck exists, there is a causal explanation of why the duck exists at t; the explanation is that the duck existed at some instant t' earlier than t, and it is a natural law that a healthy duck would endure throughout the brief period from t' to t.

Burke asserts that this does not explain why the duck exists at every time in the interval I rather than at no time during I. He maintains that in this case we would say the duck spontaneously came into existence, with no cause or explanation of its existence, and that we have here a clear violation of the principle of causality.

The problems with such alleged counterexamples are easy to see: the counterexample includes its own refutation in the last clause, "we have here a clear violation of the principle of causality." Of course we do, and that is why this cannot be a counterexample to the principle of causality in big bang cosmology or to its application to the beginning of the universe's existence. The causal law that is a part of big bang cosmology is that, for each temporally extended effect E, such as a duck resting on a table for five minutes, there is an earlier temporally extended cause C, such that the end point of the causal series C coincides at the same instant t with E's beginning point. At this instant t, the end point of the causal process C has a causal relation R_1 to the beginning point of the affected process E, such that C's endpoint causes E's beginning point to exist at t. The causal relation R_{I} is C's endpoint exercising its causal power on the beginning point of the affected series E. This is a case of simultaneous causation.

The causal law of big bang cosmology is that, apart from cases where there is a singularity, each temporally extended effect E has a first instantaneous state that both closes E in the earlier direction and coincides with (is simultaneous with) the last instantaneous state of the earlier temporally extended cause C, a state that closes C in the later direction. The causal power is transferred from earlier to later instants in C until it reaches the last instant of C, at which time the end point of C exercises this power on the beginning point of E by instantaneously bringing this beginning point into existence. The end point of C causally acts on the beginning point of E and thereby "expends" the causal power on the beginning point of E. This beginning point is affected by the end point of C, and the nature of this beginning point is determined by this causal impact.

The beginning point then causes to exist other points in E; each of these points is also causally influenced by earlier points in E, points that are later than the beginning point but earlier than the causally influenced point.

It is nomically impossible for the duck's state of resting on the table to exist in a half-open temporally extended interval, with no beginning point on which the cause of this state of rest can act. It is nomically necessary that there be an earlier causal process, such as someone laying the duck down on the table, whose last instant coincides with the beginning point of the duck's state of rest, such that the last instant of this causal process causally acts on the beginning point of the duck's state of rest by bringing it into existence.

An interval is half-open in the earlier direction only if its beginning point is a singularity, that is, its alleged beginning point is in fact physically impossible and does not exist. This interval, at the big bang, is a case where the causal law does not apply, by virtue of there being a singularity. For the second and later intervals of any given length, the intervals are closed and the causal law applies. The first interval of any given length is half-open in the earlier direction because it is physically impossible for it to be closed in the earlier direction. Accordingly, there is no first instant of the universe's beginning to exist that is uncaused and that requires an external cause, such as God, to bring it into existence.

For any set S of times that is free from singularities, the explanation of why x exists at the first instant of the set S is that the end point of an earlier causal process S_{I} coincides with x at t, causally acts upon x at t, and causes x to exist at t. For each later time in the set S, x exists at that time because earlier instants in S cause x to exist at that time, such that the nature of this causation is determined in part by the way in which the end point of the earlier causal process S_1 affected the beginning point of the set S.

But if the beginning point of the set S is a singularity, this beginning point does not exist, and the set S is half-open in the earlier direction. In this case, each instantaneous state in S is caused by earlier instantaneous states in S, but there is no instantaneous state in S that instantaneously coincides with the end point of an earlier causal process that is external to S. S is internally caused. The beginning of the universe's existence, since it is half-open, is internally caused.

Once we distinguished singularities from normal points, it violates the causal laws of big bang cosmology to hypothesize bizarre examples, such as ducks springing into existence on desks or the motion of a ball occurring without any force being exerted on the ball.

My atheistic explanation of the universe's beginning to exist is a complete explanation. It is a complete explanation in that what is explained, the explanandum, cannot possibly (logically possibly) be given an additional or further genuine and nonredundant explanation. For example, God cannot cause the whole, the parts, or the instantiation of the laws, since these have an internal explanation; God's attempt to cause something to exist would be ineffectual since the item in question is already sufficiently caused to exist by earlier parts of the whole. A partial explanation of the explanandum is such that it is logically possible to provide an additional genuine explanation, so as to make up a complete explanation of the explanandum.

My atheist argument is a contingently true explanation of why other contingently true statements are, in fact, true. In fact, my "atheistic second half of the Kalam argument" implies that there is no contingent truth whose truth is left unexplained. This shows that atheists and theists are mistaken in believing that it is logically impossible for every contingently true statement to have an explanation. In fact, as we have seen, this is not only logically possible but empirically actual (to the extent that big bang cosmology is empirically confirmed).[2]

NOTES

1. I should emphasis that Rowe has acknowledged the difficulties that set-theoretic concepts introduce into the cosmological argument and wishes to take a different approach (Rowe 1997, 1998). This answers my criticisms of the aspect of Rowe's theory that consists in its set-theoretic ways of being formulated, but does not answer the other, more fundamental, criticisms presented in this chapter.

2. I would like to thank Michael Martin for his helpful and constructive remarks on earlier versions of this essay.

REFERENCES

Burke, Michael. 1984. "Hume and Edwards on Explaining All Contingent Beings." *Australasian Journal of Philosophy* 62: 355–62.

Craig, William Lane. 1979. *The Kalam Cosmological Argument*. New York: Harper and Row.

Craig, William Lane, ed. 2002. "Natural Theology: Introduction." In *Philosophy of Religion*. New Brunswick, N.J.: Rutgers University Press.

Craig, William Lane, and Quentin Smith. 1993. *Theism, Atheism and Big Bang Cosmology*. Oxford: Oxford University Press.

Gale, Richard. 1991. *The Existence and Nature of God*. Cambridge: Cambridge University Press.

Rowe, William. 1975. *The Cosmological Argument*. Princeton: Princeton University Press.

Rowe, William. 1989. "Two Criticisms of the Cosmological Arguments." In W. Rowe and W. Wainwright (eds.), *Philosophy of Religion*. San Diego: Harcourt Brace Jovanovich.

Rowe, William. 1997. "Circular Explanations, Cosmological Arguments, and Sufficient Reasons." *Midwest Studies in Philosophy* 21: 188–1201.

Rowe, William. 1998. *The Cosmological Argument*, 2nd ed. Bronx, N.Y.: Fordham University Press.

Smith, Quentin. 1988. "The Uncaused Beginning of the Universe." *Philosophy of Science* 55: 39–57.

Smith, Quentin. 1994. "Did the Big Bang Have a Cause?" *British Journal of the Philosophy of Science* 45: 649–68.

Smith, Quentin. 2002. "Time Was Caused by a Timeless Point: An Atheist Explanation of Spacetime." In Gregory E. Ganssle and David Woodruff (eds.), *God and Time*. New York: Oxford University Press. (This presents an atheist explanation given the assumption that the singularity is an existent point.)

Smith, Quentin. 2003. "Why Cognitive Scientists Cannot Ignore Quantum Mechanics." In *Consciousness: New Perspectives*. Oxford: Oxford University Press.

Smith, Quentin, and William Lane Craig. 1993. *Theism, Atheism and Big Bang Cosmology*. Oxford: Oxford University Press. (See Smith's chapters, in particular.)

Sobel, Howard. 2004. *Logic and Theism*. Cambridge: Cambridge University Press.

Swinburne, Richard. 1978. *The Existence of God*. Oxford: Oxford University Press.

12 Impossibility Arguments

Among the most telling atheistic arguments are those to the effect that the existence of any being that meets standard divine specifications is impossible – that there not only is not but could not be any such being.

All such arguments depend crucially on sets of divine specifications. A core traditional notion of God is one that specifies him as necessarily existent, omniscient, omnipotent, and morally perfect. God is also standardly conceived of as being a free creator, and is often spoken of as immutable or transcendent. Some impossibility arguments attack a single attribute – attempting to show that the notion of omniscience is logically incoherent on its own, for example. Others attack combinations of attributes – arguing that it is not logically possible for a being to be omniscient *and* a free creator, for example. If either form of argument succeeds, we will be able to show that there can be no God as traditionally conceived.

Because the arguments at issue operate in terms of a set of more or less clear specifications, of course, it is always possible for a defender of theism to deflect the argument by claiming that the God shown impossible is not *his* God. If he ends up defending a God that is perhaps knowledgeable but not omniscient he may escape some arguments, but at the cost of a peculiarly ignorant God. The same would hold for a God that is perhaps powerful but is conceded to be less than omnipotent, or historically important but not literally a creator. If the term "God" is treated as infinitely redefinable, of course, no set of impossibility arguments will force the theist to give up a claim that "God" in some sense exists. The impossibility arguments may nonetheless succeed in their main thrust in that the "God" so saved may look increasingly less worthy of the honorific title.

A more frequent reaction, perhaps, is not redefinition but refuge in vagueness: continued use of a term "God" that is allowed to wander without clear specification. Here as elsewhere – in cases of pseudoscience, for example – resort to vagueness succeeds in deflecting criticism only at the cost of diluting content. If a believer's notion of God entails anything like traditional attributes of omniscience, omnipotence, and moral perfection, the force of impossibility arguments is that there can be no such being. If a believer's notion of God remains so vague as to escape *all* impossibility arguments, it can be argued, it cannot be clear to even him what he believes – or whether what he takes for pious belief has any content at all.

In what follows I concentrate on central impossibility arguments turning on (1) omnipotence and (2) omniscience. Problems for the notion of a morally perfect being and against the co-possibility of some standard attributes are given a briefer treatment in a final section.

I. THE IMPOSSIBILITY OF OMNIPOTENCE

Is it logically possible for any being to be omnipotent?

The traditional problem for omnipotence is the paradox of the stone: Could God create a stone too heavy for him to lift? If so, there is something God could not do – he could not lift such a stone. If not, there is again something God could not do – he could not create such a stone. In either case, there is something God could not do. It follows that there are things no God could do; neither he nor any other being (for we could substitute any other name for "God") could be omnipotent.

The history of the problem is a competition between (1) refinements of a notion of omnipotence meant to capture the core of a traditional conception while avoiding such arguments, and (2) more sophisticated versions of the paradox of the stone intended to show that logical problems for omniscience remain.

If omnipotence means – as it certainly appears to mean – an ability to do anything, then there is an even simpler argument that there can be no omnipotent being. No being could create a square circle, or an even integer greater than two and smaller than four. Because there logically could not be such things, there could be no being that could create them. Here Aquinas' response has been influential: that what omnipotence requires is the ability to perform any task, and "create a square circle" does not specify a genuine task.[1] Quite generally, it can be held, contradictory specifications fail to specify anything – precisely because they are contradictory – rather than specifying something of a peculiarly contradictory type. If so, contradictory task specifications fail to designate genuine tasks, and thus fail to designate tasks required of any omnipotent being. With regard to contradictory specifications, at least, God and omnipotence are off the hook.

The paradox of the stone, however, is not escaped so easily. Here we can use a task specification that is clearly not contradictory. I could certainly create a mass of concrete too heavy for me to lift. Could God? If so, there would be something he could not do: lift that mass of concrete.

If not, there is again something he could not do, though even I could do it: create such a mass of concrete.

Here again one reaction has been to object to the task specification, on the grounds not that it is contradictory but that it contains token reflexives or indexicals: terms that shift in their designation with the person we suppose to be performing the task. The task at issue is specified as creating a mass of concrete too heavy for one to lift. But, it is objected, this is not a uniform task description: in my case it demands only that I create a mass of concrete that I cannot lift. In God's case it demands that God create a mass of concrete not that I cannot lift, but that God cannot.[2]

Are there tasks that are essentially indexical? There certainly seem to be. J. L. Cowan gives the example of tasks assigned in a wilderness survival course, such as building, alone and without aid, a boat that both will support its builder and that its builder can easily portage. Smith and Brown succeed. Jones fails. Have Smith and Brown not succeeded at a task that Jones has not? If there are any reflexive tasks of such a sort involving two inversely coordinated powers – such as creating and lifting a heavy stone – omnipotence as an ability to perform any task is simply impossible.[3]

In coordination with work in contemporary metaphysics, and perhaps in an attempt to escape from the problem of indexically specified tasks, more recent work on omnipotence has been formulated in terms of bringing about states of affairs. The core notion of an omnipotent being, on such an approach, would be one able to bring about any state of affairs. Without restrictions on "states of affairs," however, it is unclear that such a move would avoid the difficulties of indexically specified tasks, since there appear to be indexically specified states of affairs as well. You and I may face the same state of affairs, for example, when neither of us has paid our taxes.

More recent work has also taken on a different character. The task of defending a full notion of omnipotence – as an ability either to perform any (consistently specifiable) task or to bring about any consistently specifiable state of affairs – seems to have been abandoned. In that sense a traditionally omnipotent God seems to have been given up as indefensible. As Peter Geach has put it, "When people have tried to read into 'God can do everything' a signification not of Pious Intention but of Philosophical truth, they have only landed themselves in intractable problems and hopeless confusions...."[4] What has taken its place has been an attempt to formulate some lesser notion that does not fall victim to impossibility arguments and yet has enough connection with notions of exaggerated power to be able to claim *some* theological legitimacy.

There are a number of ways in which omnipotence has been limited, often tied to other attributes someone might wish to build into a notion of God. A number of philosophers have taken it to be impossible to change the past, and have on that basis constructed definitions of omnipotence that do not require an omnipotent being to bring about a past state of affairs.[5] Such a move seems to concede that God is temporally bound as well as less than fully omnipotent. Individual freedom has also appeared as a crucial issue. Can some other agent bring it about that an agent *freely* chooses a particular course of action? Are there counterfactuals of freedom, of the form "If agent A were in circumstances C, A would freely do X"? Some philosophers have assumed a negative answer to the first question and a positive answer to the second, and have as a result sought to define omnipotence so that it does not require bringing about states of affairs in which other agents make certain free decisions.[6] If God must be morally perfect, provision might be made so as to define omnipotence in a way that doesn't require an ability to do evil. If God's existence entails that this is a best possible world, on the other hand, some have argued that evil becomes impossible and thus that evil acts need not be written out of the definition of omnipotence.[7]

These offer various routes for definition. All, however, seem to concede the basic point of impossibility arguments: that omnipotence in any full and traditional sense cannot be maintained, and thus that any omnipotent God in that sense cannot exist. The rest is merely fiddling as to what less to settle for. It is interesting, nonetheless, to follow some of the recent attempts to define a crippled notion of omnipotence.

T. Flint and A. Freddoso present an account of omniscience that is limited in a number of the ways specified:

S is omnipotent at t in W if and only if for any state of affairs p and world-type-for-S Ls such that p is not a member of Ls, if there is a world W^* such that:

    (i) Ls is true in both W and W^*, and
    (ii) W^* shares the same history with W at t, and
    (iii) at t in W^* someone actualizes p,
then S has the power at t in W to actualize p.[8]

The core idea of the account is that those states of affairs required of an omnipotent being are only those states of affairs that *some* being could produce at that time: hence the two worlds W and W^*, the specification of p as a state that someone actualizes in W^*, and the limitation of omnipotence to S having the power to actualize p in W. Omnipotence is defined as omnipotence at a time t; the specification that W and W^* share the same history prior to t, which introduces significant definitional dangers of its own, is an attempt to allow a being to qualify as omnipotent even though he cannot change the past. Finally, those p's required for omnipotence are restricted to those that are not included in the "world-type-for-S," a set of counterfactuals of freedom regarding other agents "over whose truth-value [S] has no control."[9]

As a counterexample to this account, Hoffman and Rosenkrantz offer a state of affairs in which: "A snowflake falls and no omnipotent agent ever exists." A nonomnipotent agent might well actualize such a state of affairs in a world W^* at t, they argue, by making a snowflake fall in a case in which it is true that no omnipotent being ever exists. Suppose a companion world W at which an individual, Oscar, becomes omnipotent for the first time at t. On the grounds that Oscar's instantaneous omnipotence is possible, Hoffman and Rosenkrantz argue that Flint and Freddoso's account must be inadequate, since on their account Oscar could not be omnipotent: there is another individual at a companion world W^* that can bring about a state of affairs that Oscar cannot.[10]

Edward Wierenga offers another limited account of omnipotence:

> A being x is omnipotent in a world W at a time $t =_{df}$. In W it is true both that (i) for every state of affairs A, if it is possible that both $S(W, t)$ obtains and that x strongly actualizes A at t, then at t x can strongly actualize A, and (ii) there is some state of affairs which x can strongly actualize at t.[11]

Here the basic idea is to require for omnipotence only that a being be able to actualize those states of affairs that that being is essentially such that it can actualize. If God is essentially such that he cannot do evil, for example, that will not be required for him to qualify as omnipotent. If he is essentially such that he cannot create a rock too heavy for him to lift, that too will not be required in order for him to qualify as omnipotent.

Were it not for clause (ii), a powerless stone would qualify as omnipotent on such an account. Since it is essentially incapable of doing anything, there is nothing it is possible for it to do that it cannot strongly actualize. Addition of clause (ii), however, does not seem able to avoid the basic difficulty. A classic objection is that of McEar, a being that is essentially such that he is capable of doing only one thing: scratching his ear. Since he is capable of doing something, he satisfies clause (ii), and yet surely should not qualify as omnipotent.[12]

A third attempt at a satisfactorily restricted definition for omnipotence is offered by Hoffman and Rosenkrantz:

> X is omnipotent at $t =_{df}$ for all s (if it is possible for some agent to bring about s then at t x has it within his power to bring about s).

Hoffman and Rosenkrantz explicitly limit this to cases of s that include only temporally repeatable events. To qualify as omnipotent, a being must merely be able to bring about any repeatable event that it is possible for some agent to bring about. This definition escapes the counterexample they present against Flint and Freddoso, they argue – a snowflake falls and no omnipotent agent ever exists – because "no omnipotent agent *ever* exists" fails to qualify as a repeatable event.

It is clear that there are other easy counterexamples, however. Consider, for example: "A snowflake falls through no effort of an omnipotent being." This is a state of affairs that a nonomnipotent can bring about, and is moreover a state of affairs such a being could bring about repeatedly. But no omnipotent being could bring it about. On Hoffman and Rosenkrantz's account, therefore, there could still be no omnipotent being.

A genuinely traditional and unlimited notion of omnipotence, we have seen, is simply impossible: there impossibility arguments are victorious. Here I have tried to detail some of the sorrows of recent attempts at even crippled notions of "omnipotence." New accounts of this sort, subject to new counterexamples, can be expected to continue.

It may be possible, however, to draw some general philosophical lessons from the examples above. In one way or another, essential indexicals continue as a major problem for even restricted notions of omnipotence. As long as indexically specified tasks or states of affairs are included, no "omnipotent" being, however defined, seems capable of doing even all the things that I can. The paradox of the stone is phrased in terms of indexicals, and several of the counterexamples above turn on indexicals or something similar, notably, states of affairs specified in terms of the nonexistence of or nonproduction by omnipotent beings. The one approach that seems to avoid these sorts of counterexamples is Wierenga's, which demands for omnipotence only that a being be able to do all that it is logically possible for *that being* to do. Such an approach immediately faces the sorrow, demonstrable in terms of examples such as McEar, of demanding far too little of omnipotence. It might also be argued that even that account manages only to disguise rather than to escape the problems of indexicals: that a Wierenga-like definition, phrased in terms of what it is logically possible for *that being* to do, suffers as it does precisely because it builds an indexical into the definition itself. The role of indexicals in impossibility arguments regarding omnipotence is of particular interest because – as detailed in the following section – essential indexicals plague omniscience as well.

2. THE IMPOSSIBILITY OF OMNISCIENCE

Is it logically possible for any being to be omniscient?

Until relatively recently, impossibility arguments regarding omniscience have not been so clearly developed as those regarding omnipotence. There is no single argument against omniscience with the ancient history and logical impact of the paradox of the stone, for example. There are, however, (1) a handful of major difficulties turning on different types of knowledge and (2) a set of severe difficulties turning on some of the more sophisticated findings of contemporary logic and set theory.

What would it be for a being to be omniscient? The core notion is undoubtedly that of a being that knows all that is knowable, or all that can be known. But it is clear that we speak of a variety of things as knowledge: knowing *that* something is the case (propositional knowledge), knowing *how* to do something, and knowing both things and feelings by acquaintance. I know that Albany is the capital of New York, for example, but I also know how to fix the lawnmower, I know the beauty of your smile and the sting of disappointment.

Knowing how raises clear impossibilities for any traditional and omniscient God. If God is a being without a body, he cannot know how to juggle, how to balance on the parallel bars, or how to compensate for a strained muscle in the right calf. If omniscience demands knowing everything that can be known, therefore, no disembodied being can be omniscient.[13] This form of difficulty can also be developed without appeal to other attributes. One of the things that I know is how to find out things that I do not know; I know how to find out what I do not know about the planet Jupiter, for example. Were an omniscient being to have all propositional knowledge, there would be nothing it did not know in the propositional sense. There must then be a form of knowledge *how* that I have but that any such being would lack: knowing how to find the propositional knowledge it lacks. Any being that possessed all propositional knowledge would for that very reason lack a form of knowledge how.

Knowledge by acquaintance also raises clear impossibilities for any traditional and omniscient God. Among those feelings that nonomniscient beings know all too well are lust and envy, fear, frustration, and despair. If a God is without moral fault, he cannot know lust or envy, and thus cannot qualify as omniscient. If a God is without limitation, he cannot know fear, frustration, or despair.[14] Here too the argument can be pressed without appeal to other attributes. One of the feelings I know all too well is the recognition of my own ignorance. An omniscient being would have no ignorance, and thus this is a feeling no omniscient being could know. There can then be no omniscient being.

Here as in the case of omnipotence, the theistic options appear to be limited to cutting omniscience down to some logically coherent size. A first move is to limit omniscience to propositional knowledge. Omniscience has often been defined, for example, as follows:

A being x is omniscient $=_{df}$ for all p, p is true IFF x knows that p.[15]

This clearly will not do, since it allows an omniscient being to hold any number of false beliefs. An improvement that avoids that difficulty is the following:

A being x is omniscient $=_{df}$ for all p, $((p$ is true IFF x believes that $p)$ and $(x$ believes that p IFF x knows that $p)$).[16]

Limitation to merely propositional knowledge, however, is by no means enough to save a notion of omniscience. There appear, first of all, to be forms of knowledge that one being can have and that no other being can have. In comparison with the paradox of the stone as a perennial problem regarding omnipotence, it is of interest that these forms of knowledge involve essential indexicals.

Consider a case borrowed from John Perry.[17] I follow a trail of spilled sugar around and around a tall aisle in the supermarket, in search of the shopper who is making a mess. Suddenly I realize that the trail of sugar that I have been following is spilling from a torn sack in *my* cart, and that *I* am the culprit – *I* am making a mess.

What it is that I realize at that point is that

1. I am making a mess.

The interesting point is that this proposition is *not* the same as

2. Patrick Grim is making a mess,

nor can it be the same proposition as

3. *He* is making a mess.

where I am the "he" that is indicated.

We can easily construct stories in which I know (2) or (3) without knowing (1). In an amnesia case I may know that Patrick Grim is making a mess without realizing that I am Patrick Grim, for example. I may see that *he* is making a mess – that oaf in the fish-eye mirror – without yet realizing that oaf is *me*. What I express by (1) is not therefore simply what is expressed by (2) or (3).

One clear indication that (2) and (3) cannot express the same proposition as (1) is that (1) offers a complete explanation for things that (2) and (3) cannot. When I stop myself short in the supermarket, gather up my broken sack, and start to tidy up, my doing so may be quite fully explained by saying that I have realized what I express by (1). But it could not be fully explained by saying that I realize (2) or (3). For either of these to offer a *full* explanation for my behavior, we would have to add at least that I also know that I am Patrick Grim, or that I know that *he* is me.

What I know when I know (1) thus includes some aspect of knowledge to which expression using an indexical "I" or "me" is essential. Neither (2) nor (3), nor any other indication of me that is either merely descriptive or de re (of the thing), can capture what I know when I know (1). To capture *that* we need to add some additional knowledge that is itself indexical in character: the knowledge that *I* am Patrick Grim, for example, or that I am *he*.

Because of the role of the essential indexical, what I know when I know that I am making a mess is something that no other being can know. An omniscient being, it appears, would clearly have to know all that I know. Since I am not omniscient, and no other being can know what I know when I know that I am making a mess, there can be no omniscient being.[18] Here the essential indexical used is "I," but a similar argument can be phrased to show that no timeless being can know all that someone can know *now*, nor can a being that has no spatial location know what someone can know *here*.[19]

What routes remain open for the defender of omniscience in the face of the essential indexical? One route is to restrict omniscience to the propositional and to insist that indexical knowledge does not qualify as propositional. There are precedents for such a move in other work on indexicals. Consider, for example, the case in which I see the mess-maker in the fish-eye mirror at the end of the aisle and come to the conclusion that *he* is making the mess. My further realization a moment later that it is *I* who am making a mess, it has been proposed, involves no new proposition but merely a change of perspective.[20] But this is drastically counterintuitive. At the point at which I see the man in the mirror there is clearly something that I *haven't* yet realized and that I *don't* yet know: that it is *me* in the mirror and that *I* am making a mess. That is something I realize only a moment later, and it is clear that there is then something new I have learned, some new piece of information I didn't have before. That is precisely the role for which the term "proposition" is designed.

Another move, recently pursued by Yujin Nagasawa, is to follow some of the attempts outlined above at limited notions of omnipotence: to grant that it is impossible that anyone else know what I know when I know I am making a mess, but to cut omniscience down to size by redefinition. Though it is not made fully clear in Nagasawa, the basic idea is to define omniscience as having all propositional knowledge that it is possible for a particular being to have.[21] The account of omnipotence this immediately brings to mind is Wierenga's, which is hardly a promising start. A stone is essentially incapable of knowing anything. Were omniscience to require of a being knowing merely all that a being of that type could essentially know, any stone would qualify as omniscient. There would be literally as many omniscient beings as grains of sand on a beach. Were we to require that an omniscient being know *something* and know all that such a being could essentially know (once again following Wierenga) we would be faced with the prospect of McIgnorant, who is essentially such that his knowledge is extremely limited and yet who would have to be declared omniscient on the basis of such a definition.

There are also a range of impossibility arguments regarding omniscience that use central results in set theory and central concepts from the limitative theorems of twentieth-century logic. For reasons of space I set aside the more complex of these, which parallel Gödel's theorems and related results.[22] There is, however, an elegant set-theoretical argument against the possibility of omniscience that can be presented fairly simply.

Omniscience, even if limited to the propositional and even if propositions were taken to exclude knowledge involving essential indexicals, would require a being to know all (objective) truths. It can clearly be established, however, that there can be no plurality of all truths. There is no "all" of the sort omniscience would require.

The result is most simply expressed in terms of sets: that there can be no set of all truths. For suppose any set of truths $\mathbf{T}$:

$$\mathbf{T} = \{t_1, t_2, t_3 \ldots\}^{23}$$

And consider the elements of its power set $\mathbf{PT}$, containing all subsets of $\mathbf{T}$:

$\{\varnothing\}$
$\{t_1\}$
$\{t_2\}$
$\{t_3\}$

.

.

.

$\{t_1, t_2\}$
$\{t_1, t_3\}$

.

.

.

$\{t_1, t_2, t_3\}$

.

.

.

To each element of the power set there will be a unique truth – at least the truth that that element contains a particular truth t_1 as a member, for example, or that it does not contain t_1 as a member:

$$t_1 \in \{t_1, t_2, t_3\}$$
$$t_1 \notin \{t_2, t_3\}$$

By Cantor's theorem, we know that the power set of any set is larger – contains more members – than the set itself. There will then be more truths than are contained in **T**. But **T** can be taken as *any* set of truths. For any set of truths, we can show that there are more truths than it contains. There can therefore be no set of *all* truths.

This argument seems to strike at a crucial assumption essential to any notion of omniscience – that truth and knowledge themselves have an intrinsic maximum. With regard to both truth and knowledge, that assumption is provably false. If neither truth or knowledge can have a maximum degree, there can be no degree of knowledge that counts as maximal – and thus there can be no omniscience.

Is there any escape from the Cantorian argument? One reply, which appears in pieces by Richard Cartwright, D. A. Martin, Keith Simmons, and John Abbruzzese, concentrates on the term "set."[24] If we speak of "all" the truths but refuse to collect them as a "one," it is supposed, the argument can be avoided. It can be shown, however, that this move is futile; the argument does not depend in any essential way on reference to a single class, set, or collection of all truths. It has precisely the same force against omniscience if phrased directly in terms of formal relations and "many" truths, treated entirely in the plural.[25]

Another reply appears informally in work by Keith Simmons and Alvin Plantinga, developed formally in different ways by Gary Mar and Howard Sobel.[26] All of these attempt to disable the Cantorian argument by denying the diagonal. A crucial step in the full argument is that for any proposed mapping between (1) a supposed set of all truths and (2) the elements of its power set, there will be those truths that are not members of the set of truths to which they are assigned. This is the "diagonal." None of these authors denies that there are precisely these truths. What they all attempt to deny is the step that follows: that there will then be some truth about them. Although such a move would work as a formal stop-gap, the *philosophical* demands it would entail seem to be flatly unacceptable, compromising the notion of truth itself. For the philosophical instantiation of such a move it would have to be maintained that there is a specific group of things – that there really are these things – but that there is *no* truth about them, not even that there are these things or that they are the things they are. Indeed the claim that there is no truth about precisely these things would, if true, be *itself* a truth about them of precisely the sort that is being denied. This does not appear to be a way out.

Here we have concentrated on impossibility arguments regarding omniscience considered alone, just as we concentrated on impossibility arguments regarding omnipotence alone in the preceding section. Both of these attributes, however, also fall victim to mixed arguments. Can a being be both omniscient and morally perfect? Omnipotent and morally perfect? Omniscient and free?

3. THE IMPOSSIBILITY OF COMBINED ATTRIBUTES

Of the three major properties attributed to God in Western theism – omnipotence, omniscience, and moral perfection – impossibility arguments against the third are the least developed. One reason for this may be that conflicts between major ethical theories remain unresolved – should one approach the idea of moral perfection in terms of utilitarianism, deontology, or virtue theory? Far from seeming invulnerable to impossibility arguments, however, the notion of divine moral perfection seems ripe for them. This is an area worthy of further work.

There are also a range of impossibility arguments that turn on other attributes in combination with omnipotence, omniscience, or moral perfection. God is certainly conceived as a free agent, for example – indeed as a free creator. But is that conception consistent with other standard attributes?

It is far from clear that free choice is compatible with omniscience. One cannot make a free choice between options A and B, it can be argued, if one knows with complete certainty in advance that one will take course A. If so, since an omniscient God would know in advance (and from all eternity) all actions it would take, there can be no point at which such a God could make a genuine choice. Omniscience and freedom appear to be incompatible.[27]

Impossibility arguments regarding divine freedom and moral perfection are the subject of the classical Leibniz-Clarke correspondence.[28] Leibniz's problem was that God's moral perfection would entail that he must of necessity create the best of all possible worlds, and thus it could not be maintained that he was free to create any inferior world. Clarke insists on God's freedom, and therefore insists that he *could* create an inferior world, therefore contradicting a notion that God is of necessity morally perfect. Despite attempts on both sides to finesse a distinction in which God's choice is necessitated in one sense and not in another, the central difficulty remains.

Peter Geach and Nelson Pike have a similar exchange regarding omnipotence and moral perfection.[29] Both admit an inconsistency in the idea that any being is both omnipotent and impeccable, or unable to do wrong. Because of that inconsistency, Pike denies impeccability. Geach, on the other hand, denies omnipotence. Either course results in the denial of a traditional God.

A simpler impossibility may lie in the notion of necessary moral perfection itself. Mark Twain contrasts his moral status with that of George Washington: "I am different from Washington; I have a higher, grander standard of principle. Washington could not lie. I can lie, but I won't." If God *cannot* act wrongly, it is impossible for him to face any real moral choices.[30] If so, he cannot be praised for making the correct choices, and if he is not morally praiseworthy, he can hardly qualify as morally perfect. *Necessary* moral perfection seems to exclude the possibility of precisely those choices that genuine moral perfection would demand.

Other impossibility arguments using multiple attributes abound. God's timelessness and immutability appear to be inconsistent with omniscience regarding tensed facts, knowable only at a particular time,[31] and immutability may similarly be inconsistent with the notion of a creator God.[32]

We have seen reason to believe that both omnipotence and omniscience are intrinsically impossible, and to suggest that the same may hold for necessary moral perfection as well. Further impossibilities follow from the assumption of such attributes in combination.

There is a related atheological argument of major importance that we have not considered here because it relies not on divine specifications alone but on an obvious but contingent fact as well. As such it fails to qualify as a pure impossibility argument in our sense. What that argument demands is the obvious but contingent fact that our world abounds with unnecessary suffering. This is the problem of evil, discussed in chapter 10 in this volume.

NOTES

1. Thomas Aquinas, *Summa theologiae*, part I, Q. 25, art. 3. See also J. L. Cowan, "The Paradox of Omnipotence," *Analysis* 25 (1965/supplement): 102–8, reprinted in Michael Martin and Ricki Monnier (eds.), *The Impossibility of God* (Amherst, N.Y.: Prometheus Books, 2003).

2. George Mavrodes takes such a tack in "Some Puzzles Concerning Omnipotence," *Philosophical Review* 72 (1963): 221–23.

3. J. L. Cowan, "The Paradox of Omnipotence Revisited," *Canadian Journal of Philosophy* 3 (1974): 435–45. Reprinted in Martin and Monnier, *The Impossibility of God*.

4. Peter Geach, *Providence and Evil* (Cambridge: Cambridge University Press, 1977), p. 4.

5. See, e.g., Thomas P. Flint and Alfred J. Freddoso, "Maximal Power," in A. Freddoso (ed.), *The Existence and Nature of God* (Notre Dame: University

of Notre Dame Press, 1983), 81–113; Edward Wierenga, *The Nature of God: An Inquiry into Divine Attributes* (Ithaca, N.Y.: Cornell University Press, 1989); and Joshua Hoffman and Gary S. Rosenkrantz, *The Divine Attributes* (Oxford: Blackwell, 2002).

6. Here Flint and Freddoso, "Maximal Power," is a prime example.

7. Hoffman and Rosenkrantz, *The Divine Attributes* and "Omnipotence," entry in the *Stanford Encyclopedia of Philosophy*, http://plato.stanford.edu, accessed April 30, 2006.

8. Flint and Freddoso, "Maximal Power," p. 99.

9. Ibid., p. 97.

10. Joshua Hoffman and Gary S. Rosenkrantz, "Omnipotence Redux," *Philosophy and Phenomenological Research* 49 (1988): 283–301, and "Omnipotence."

11. Edward Wierenga, "Omnipotence Defined," *Philosophy and Phenomenological Research* 43 (1983): 363–75, and *The Nature of God*, p. 25.

12. McEar seems to appear for the first time in Alvin Plantinga's *God and Other Minds* (Ithaca, N.Y.: Cornell University Press, 1967), pp. 168–73. Flint and Freddoso claim to find a medieval anticipation of the basic argument, however, in an anonymous note added to one of the manuscripts of Ockham's *Ordinatio*. See Flint and Freddoso, "Maximal Power," pp. 109–10, n. 4.

13. See Michael Martin, "A Disproof of the God of the Common Man," *Question* 7 (1974): 114–24. Martin develops the idea further in a chapter in *Atheism: A Philosophical Justification* (Philadelphia: Temple University Press, 1990), reprinted as "Conflicts between the Divine Attributes," in Martin and Monnier, *The Impossibility of God*. Similar issues are raised in Henry Simoni, "Omniscience and the Problem of Radical Particularity: Does God Know How to Ride a Bike?" *International Journal for Philosophy of Religion* 42 (1997): 1–22.

14. The latter point is developed particularly nicely in David Blumenfeld, "On the Compossibility of the Divine Attributes," *Philosophical Studies* 34 (1978): 91–103, reprinted in Martin and Monnier, *The Impossibility of God*. See also Marcel Sarot, "Omniscience and Experience," *International Journal for Philosophy of Religion* 30 (1991): 89–102, and Henri Simoni, "Divine Passability and the Problem of Radical Particularity: Does God Feel Your Pain?" *Religious Studies* 33 (1997): 327–47.

15. This is Peter Geach's definition in *Providence and Evil*, and is equivalent to definitions offered by A. N. Prior in "The Formalities of Omniscience," *Philosophy* 37 (1962): 114–29; Richard Swinburne in *The Coherence of Theism* (Oxford: Clarendon, 1977); James F. Ross in *Philosophical Theology* (New York: Bobbs-Merrill, 1969); and William E. Mann in "The Divine Attributes," *American Philosophical Quarterly* 12 (1975): 151–59.

16. In "Conflicts between the Divine Attributes," Michael Martin recognizes this definitional difficulty but unfortunately fails to correct it. The definitions he considers are of the general form "Person P is omniscient = For any true proposition p, P believes that p, and P believes that p IFF P knows that p...." Since the quantification here is limited to true propositions, it still allows an omniscient being to believe any number of falsehoods.

17. Perry, "The Problem of the Essential Indexical," *Nous* 13 (1979): 3–21. Perry's central argument here and in "Frege on Demonstratives," *Philosophical Review* 86 (1977): 474–97, is anticipated in Hector-Neri Castañeda, "'He': A Study of the Logic of Self-Consciousness," *Ratio* 8 (1966): 130–57. See also David Lewis, "Attitudes *de dicto* and *de se*," *Philosophical Review* 88 (1979): 513–43.

18. This argument is radically misunderstood as if it were an argument that turned essentially on feelings in John Abbruzzese, "The Coherence of Omniscience: A Defense," *International Journal for Philosophy of Religion* 41 (1997): 25–34. For a corrective, see Grim, "The Being That Knew Too Much," *International Journal for Philosophy of Religion* 47 (2000): 141–54, reprinted in Martin and Monnier, *The Impossibility of God*.

19. Related indexical problems for omniscience are developed by A. N. Prior in "Thank Goodness That's Over," *Philosophy* 34 (1959): 12–17, and "The Formalities of Omniscience," *Philosophy* 37 (1962): 114–29, both reprinted in *Papers on Time and Tense* (Oxford: Clarendon, 1968).

20. See Perry, "Frege on Demonstratives," and Steven Boër and William Lycan, "Who, Me?", *Philosophical Review* 88 (1980): 427–66.

21. Yujin Nagasawa, "Divine Omniscience and Knowledge *de se*," *International Journal for Philosophy of Religion* 53 (2003): 73–82.

22. These appear in Grim, "Logic and Limits of Knowledge and Truth," *Nous* 22 (1988): 341–67, and are fully developed in Grim, *The Incomplete Universe* (Cambridge: MIT Press, 1991).

23. Despite the linear presentation, there is no suggestion here that any such set need be denumerable. The argument is generalizable to a set of any infinite size.

24. Richard Cartwright, "Speaking of Everything," *Nous* 28 (1994): 1–20; D. A. Martin, "Sets versus Classes," quoted in Keith Simmons, "On an Argument Against Omniscience," *Nous* 27 (1993): 22–33; John Abbruzzese, "The Coherence of Omniscience."

25. See Grim, *The Incomplete Universe*, and "The Being That Knew Too Much."

26. Keith Simmons, "On an Argument against Omniscience," paper presented at APA Central Division, New Orleans, April 1990. The importance of this particular objection is significantly reduced in Simmons's published paper, *Nous* 27 (1993): 22–33. Also see Alvin Plantinga and Patrick Grim, "Truth, Omniscience, and Cantorain Arguments: An Exchange," *Philosophical Studies* 71 (1993): 267–306; Gary Mar, "Why 'Cantorian' Arguments against the Existence of God Do Not Work," *International Philosophical Quarterly* 33 (1993): 429–42; and J. Howard Sobel, *Logic and Theism* (Cambridge: Cambridge University Press, 2004).

27. See, e.g., Tomis Kapitan, "Agency and Omniscience," *Religious Studies* 27 (1991): 105–20, and later discussion. A form of the argument also appears in Theodore M. Drange, "Incompatible-Properties Arguments: A Survey," *Philo* 1 (1998): 49–60, reprinted in Martin and Monnier, *The Impossibility of God*.

28. Samuel Clarke and Gottfried Leibniz [1717], *The Leibniz-Clarke Correspondence*, ed. H. G. Alexander (Manchester: Manchester University Press, 1956). William Rowe offers a thorough discussion in "Divine Freedom," in the *Stanford Encyclopedia of Philosophy*, http://plato.stanford.edu.

29. Peter Geach, "Omnipotence," *Philosophy* 48 (1973): 7–20, and *Providence and Evil*; Nelson Pike, "Omnipotence and God's Ability to Sin," *American Philosophical Quarterly* 6 (1969): 208–16.

30. It is indeed a tenet of Christian theology dating back at least to Augustine that the saints and angels have been perfected to the degree that they not only do not sin but are no longer *able* to sin, a perfection applied to God as well. See Pike, "Omnipotence."

31. See, e.g., Wiliam Lane Craig, "Omniscience, Tensed Facts, and Divine Eternity," *Faith and Philosophy* 17 (2000): 225–41.

32. For a range of often novel incompatibility arguments, see Drange, "Incompatible-Properties Arguments."

III. Implications

13   Atheism and Religion

What is the relationship between religion and atheism? Is atheism itself a religion? Can there be atheistic religions? Is atheism necessarily an antireligious position?

In this chapter I argue that atheism itself is not a religion. However, I maintain that three world religions – Jainism, Buddhism, and Confucianism – are atheistic in one of the primary senses of that term as defined in the general introduction to this volume: the denial that a theistic God exists. I also show that in an important sense atheism does not even stand in opposition to theistic religions.

THE CONCEPT OF A RELIGION

The concept of religion was developed historically in the Judeo-Christian context and still has its clearest application in this context. Just as the concept of atheism applied outside its original historical context can be misleading, so too can the concept of religion applied outside its original context. Nevertheless, it will be assumed here that cautious application outside its clearest historical context can be also illuminating at least to Western readers. To answer the separate questions of whether atheism is a religion, and whether there are atheistic religions a prior question must be considered: What does it mean to say that something is a religion? It is impossible here to discuss the many attempts to define religion in philosophy, religious studies, and social science. Since my training and background is philosophical, I consider two of the best recent analyses of the concept of religion to be found in the philosophical literature.

William Alston approaches the concept of religion by specifying what he calls "religious making" characteristics.[1] These are the following.

(1) Belief in supernatural beings.
(2) A distinction between sacred and profane objects.
(3) Ritual acts focused on sacred objects.
(4) A moral code believed to be sanctioned by the gods.

217

(5) Characteristically religious feelings (awe, sense of mystery, sense of guilt, adoration) that tend to be aroused in the presence of sacred objects and during the practice of ritual and that are connected in idea with the gods.

(6) Prayers and other forms of communication with gods.

(7) A world-view or a general picture of the world as a whole and the place of the individual therein. This picture contains some specification of an overall purpose or point of the world and an indication of how the individual fits into it.

(8) A more or less total organization of one's life based on the world-view.

(9) A social group bound together by the above.

According to Alston these characteristics "neither singly nor in combination constitute tight necessary and sufficient conditions for something being a religion."[2] Yet, he says, "each of them contributes to making something a religion." He continues: "When enough of these characteristics are present to a sufficient degree, we have a religion."[3] Alston argues that there is no more precise way than this of saying what a religion is.

For Alston, Roman Catholicism and Orthodox Judaism are paradigm cases of religions; they are the sorts of cases in which the term "religion" most certainly and unmistakenly applies. However, he argues "there can be a variety of cases that differ from the paradigm in different ways and to different degrees, by one or another of the religion-making characteristics dropping out more or less." Ritual drops out entirely in Quakerism and is de-emphasized in Protestantism; belief in supernatural beings is "whittled away to nothing, as in certain forms of Unitarianism, or may never be present, as in certain forms of Buddhism."[4]

As more and more of the religious characteristics drop out either partly or completely, Alston maintains, "we feel less secure about applying the term 'religion.'" Indeed, "we encounter less and less obvious cases of religion as we move from, for example, Roman Catholicism through Unitarianism, humanism, and Hinayana Buddhism to communism."[5] The best one can do, according to Alston, is to specify the features of the paradigm cases and then specify the respects in which less clear-cut cases differ from the paradigms.

This approach to analyzing the concept of religion is salutary in that the attempt to specify the essence of a complex and manifold phenomena such as religion in terms of a set of necessary and sufficient conditions is very difficult. Alston's religion making characteristic approach allows us to include under the rubric of religion all we want to include and enables us to compare less clear cut cases with the paradigm ones.

Nevertheless, there is a problem with Alston's approach. It is important to notice that four of the nine characteristics explicitly mention a god or gods. Reference to god also enters Alston's explanation of some of his other characteristics. For example, sacred objects are explained in part by Alston as objects that are "the habitation or manifestation of a god." Thus, given the fact that atheism rejects gods, there could not be clear-cut or paradigmatic cases of an atheistic religion. Since, however, Buddhism is considered a paradigm case of a religion and Buddhism is atheistic, one may well wonder about the neutrality of Alston's criteria.

Monroe Beardsley and Elizabeth Beardsley have also attempted to define the concept of religion.[6] In contrast to Alston, they hold that the sets of beliefs, emotions, and actions that are called "religions" include not only well-known ones, such as Christianity, Judaism, Islam, Hinduism, Buddhism, Taoism, and Shintoism, but also ancient religions and the religions of nonliterate societies. Arguing that one cannot define "religion" in terms of a belief in god or in a soul because such beliefs are not found among all religions, they propose that "religion" be defined in terms of the attempt to answer basic religious questions. These are the following.

(1) What are the fundamental characteristics of human beings and the chief problems they face?
(2) What are the characteristics of nonhuman reality that are of greatest significance for human life?
(3) Given the nature of man and the universe, how should men try to live?
(4) Given the answers to the first three questions, what practices will best develop and sustain in men an understanding of the nature of human and nonhuman reality and a dedication to the ideal of human life?
(5) In seeking true answers to the first four questions, what method or methods should be used?

According to Beardsley and Beardsley, the first two questions are primarily metaphysical, the third and fourth are primarily ethical, and the fifth is epistemological. They take all five questions to be closely related and maintain that the interconnections among them give each religion a unified outlook on life and the world. Having isolated these basic questions, they define religion as any set of interrelated religious beliefs providing answers to all the basic religious questions, together with the attitudes and practices determined by those beliefs.

Their definition avoids the faults of Alston's. Indeed, they anticipate and answer the major questions that critics might raise. To the anticipated objection that their definition is circular, Beardsley and Beardsley reply that they introduce the five basic religious questions without using the term "religion."[7] For them, a religious belief is simply an answer to one of the five basic questions. Consequently, the meaning of "religious belief" and "religious question" is specified independently of a "religion."

In response to the objection that their definition is too intellectual, they point out that the five basic questions have a practical and emotional urgency that "removes them from the sphere of purely theoretical inquiries."[8] Further, they argue that the definition includes reference not only to beliefs but also to attitudes and practices.

Beardsley and Beardsley reject the objection that their definition is too broad in that there are sets of interrelated beliefs, attitudes, and practices that meet their specifications and are not recognized as world religions. On the one hand, they say that a restriction on the meaning of religion in terms of the content of beliefs, attitudes, or actions cannot be given. On the other hand, they point out that increased cultural and historical knowledge has tended to broaden what is counted as a religion and that their usage is in harmony with this trend. They also maintain that a term is needed to refer to all serious attempts to answer the basic religious questions and that "religion" is the appropriate one to use. And finally, they say that their definition is in harmony with common usage, in it includes all those sets of beliefs, emotions, and actions that have been commonly called a "religion."

Beardsley and Beardsley admit that there are controversial cases of religion, and they put both humanism and Marxism in this category. Although their definition includes the disputed case of humanism, they leave open the question of whether Marxist communism is a religion.

In conclusion, both Alston's and Beardsley and Beardsley's definitions allow for the possibility of atheistic religions. However, Alston's excludes atheistic religions from being clear paradigm cases of religion, while Beardsley and Beardsley's allows this possibility. The question remains whether any actual religions are atheistic.

Is Atheism a Religion?

In 1971 the prominent atheist Madelyn Murray O'Hair[9] argued that atheism was not the religion of the future since atheists, although numerous, were unorganized and complacent and were unwilling to fight the legal and political encroachments of christianity in the United States. Christianity is gaining more and more political power, she said, and atheists are doing nothing to stop it.

A naive reading of O'Hair's speech might well lead one to suppose that she believed that if atheists were to do what she advised, atheism would be the religion of the future, but it is not clear how seriously O'Hair's speech is to be taken. Whatever her intentions may have been, it can be safely said that atheism is not the religion of the past, present, or future because it is not a religion at all.

Using either one of the definitions of religion introduced above, atheism fails to meet the conditions of being a religion. Negative atheism – that is, not having a belief in God or gods – lacks all of the religion-making characteristics specified by Alston, and it does not provide answers to any of the basic religious questions specified by Beardsley and Beardsley; not even to question (2): What characteristics of nonhuman reality are significant for human life? Positive atheism – the belief that there is no God or gods – is not a religion either, according to our two definitions of religion. It has none of the religion-making characteristics specified by Alston; indeed, it entails the negation of those that mention a god or gods. And the only basic religious question of Beardsley and Beardsley it can even remotely be thought to answer is question 2.

Are There Atheistic Religions?

Now it does not follow from the fact that atheism is not itself a religion that there are no atheistic religions. Some scholars of religions have argued that Jainism, Buddhism (in some of its forms), and Confucianism fall in this category.[10] There can be no doubt that they are religions. Acknowledged as such by scholars, they meet the requirements of Beardsley and Beardsley's definition since they do provide answers to the five basic religious questions. Moreover, although they are not paradigm cases of religions on Alston's account, they certainly possess enough religious-making characteristics to be numbered among his less clear cases. Exactly how many religious-making characteristics they possess depends on whether belief in a god or gods is a part of them. So the question is not whether Jainism, Buddhism, and Confucianism are religions but whether they are atheistic religions. In what follows I explore this issue for Jainism, Buddhism, and Confucianism in turn.

Jainism

Jainism, a religion with about 5 million members who are found mostly in India,[11] is considered by religious scholars to have arisen in India in the sixth century B.C. along with Buddhism as a reaction to certain excesses of orthodox Vedic (early Hindu) practices and beliefs.[12] Its founder was Natapitta Vardhmana, known to followers as Mahavira (the Hero or Great Man). Mahavira opposed several aspects of the Hinduism of his time: in particular, the ritualistic killing of animals, the caste system, and the idea that the individuality of the soul is absorbed into Brahman. He believed in the equality of all souls, advocated the principle of noninjury to all creatures, even the lowest insects, held that the soul is individual, and argued that eternal salvation – the separation of the soul from matter – did not result in the loss of individuality.

Jainists themselves believe that their religion is of a very ancient origin and that Mahavira is simply the last of the twenty-four Jinas or Tirthankaras (literally, the builders or makers of a crossing). Persons who have reached the ultimate state of spiritual purity are souls who have "crossed over" the stream of existence and obtained salvation and are released from the cycle of birth and rebirth. Most scholars believe that only Mahavira, the twenty-fourth Tirthankara who lived in the sixth century B.C., and Parsvanatha, the twenty-third Tirthankara who lived in the eighth century B.C.were actual historical figures.

On the question of whether Jainism is an atheistic religion, scholars flatly disagree. E. Royston Pike asserts: "Jain theology does not exist, since Jainism is completely atheistic. God, spirits, demons – all are equally rejected; the only supernatural beings are the Tirthankaras, who are good men made perfect."[13] Similarly, Herbert Stroup argues, "Original Jainism had no teachings regarding the existence of God, whether the deity be conceived as personal, transpersonal or impersonal. Mahavira rejected the polytheistic beliefs of Vedic and Brahmanic Hinduism, a rejection apparently based on the conviction that the gods are superfluous."[14]

On the other hand, J. Jaini maintains that Jainism "is accused of being atheistic. This is not so, because Jainism believes in Godhood and in innumerable gods; but certainly Jainism is atheistic in not believing its gods to have created the Universe."[15] S. Gopalan, in turn, says that "to categorically dub Jainism as atheistic is both unwarranted and unphilosophical, for we find in Jainism only the rejection of a 'supremely personal god' and not godhead itself."[16]

Gopalan goes on to say that in Jainism "there is a deep analysis of the concept of God as the Supreme Cause of the Universe and a systematic refutation of the arguments of the philosophers who have sought to prove the existence of God."[17] Gopalan argues that the term "god" in Jainism is "used to denote a higher state of existence of the jiva or the conscious principle. The system believes that this state of godly existence is only a shade better than that of ordinary human beings, for, it is not free from the cycle of birth and death."[18] Thus a god can ascend to the highest spiritual plane and become a Tirthankara who is free from the cycle of birth and death or descend to earth if he exhausts his good karma. Gopalan points out that even the Tirthankaras, the perfected beings of Jainism, "have cut themselves away from the world of life and death (samsara) and so, by hypothesis, cannot exert any influence over it. Hence, the function of a Supreme Ruler, Creator and Regulator cannot be attributed to them."[19] Thus, one could say that the gods of Jainism, unlike the gods of Western religions, operate within the uncreated universe and are no help in our spiritual salvation, for they too must escape from the cycle of rebirth through their own efforts.

In the general introduction to this volume I introduced a distinction between a broad sense of atheism that rejects all gods and a narrow sense of atheism that only rejects the theistic creator God. Using this distinction one can say that Jainism is an atheistic religion in the narrow sense in that it rejects the theistic creator God but not in the broad sense since it accepts lesser gods who have no spiritual significance.

Moreover, Jainism would seem to be a positive atheistic religion in that Jainists actually disbelieve that an all-good, all-knowing, and all-powerful being who created the universe exists. They do not just fail to believe in such a God. Furthermore, reasons and arguments for this disbelief are available in Jainist intellectual circles.

Jainist philosophers were vigorous in attacking the arguments used by some Nyaya philosophers, a school of Hindu philosophers who attempted to prove various theological propositions by logical reasoning. Indeed, Jainists philosophers use many of the same arguments that Western philosophers do against the existence of God. In some instances they have even anticipated them. Some of these Jainists's counterarguments are reminiscent of Hume's famous rebuttal of the argument from design. Jainist philosophers also ask: "If every existent object must have a maker, that maker himself would be explained by another – his maker etc. To escape from this vicious circle we have to assume that there is one uncaused, self-explaining cause, god. But then, if it is maintained that one being can be self-subsistent, why not say that there are many others also who are uncreated and eternal similarly?" Hence, "it is not necessary to assume the existence of any first cause of the universe."[20]

In conclusion, despite the frequent claim that Jainism is an atheistic religion, without qualification this is not true. Jainism is atheistic only in the narrow sense. However, since the gods Jainism does assume have little power and play no role in the Jainist goal of salvation, they could be eliminated from Jainism without serious loss to the essentials of the religion. Thus, although Jainism is not in fact an atheistic religion in the broad sense, it could easily become one.

Buddhism

The founder of Buddhism, Siddhartha Gautama (probably 563–483 B.C.) – called the Buddha or the Enlightened One by his followers – is believed to have abandoned a life of princely luxury at age twenty-nine and to have set out to discover the cause of human suffering and misery and its spiritual remedy.[21] He tried various spiritual paths, including extreme asceticism and mortification of the flesh, but he did not find these conducive to spiritual insight. Eventually obtaining Enlightenment while seated in meditation beneath a bodhi tree, he shortly after preached his first sermon just outside the city of Sarnath. The rest of his life was spent in meditation, preaching, and guiding his followers.

Buddhism, unlike Jainism, spread to Burma, Cambodia, China, Japan, Korea, Laos, Nepal, and Thailand, although it declined in India and by the thirteenth century was virtually extinct there. Today there are about 350 million followers of Buddhism.[22]

At present there are two main schools of Buddhism: Mahayana and Hinayana (or Theravada). The doctrine of Theravada Buddhism (the doctrine of the elders) is generally believed to represent the original Buddhist teachings, but from another of the early sects a school developed that gave itself the name of Mahayana Buddhism (the greater vehicle) and referred to Theravada Buddhism and related schools as Hinayana Buddhism (the lesser vehicle).

The religious ideal of Hinayana Buddhism is the arahat, the person who has achieved nirvana and escaped the cycle of rebirth. In contrast, the religious ideal of the Mahayana school is the bodhisattva, the person who vows to postpone entrance into nirvana, although deserving it, until all others become enlightened and liberated. The term "bodhisattva" is also used to refer to a class of celestial beings who were worshipped.

In addition to advocating a spiritual ideal different from that of the original Buddhism, Mahayana Buddhism in its later development became more metaphysical. In this later development the historical Buddha, Gautama, is simply one among many historical incarnations of the cosmic Buddha nature, the metaphysical absolute. This cosmic Buddha nature is portrayed as working in all ages and in innumerable worlds for the liberation of all sentient beings.

No one disputes that Buddhism in all its forms is a religion, but, as in the case of Jainism, there is disagreement among religious scholars over whether Buddhism is atheistic. To be sure, it is not disputed that belief in a god or god is a part of Mahayana Buddhism. The numerous bodhisattvas, the Buddha Amitabha, and the cosmic Buddha nature seem to be like the gods or god of Western religion. What is disputed is whether original Buddhism was atheistic; or, what amounts to the same thing, whether Theravada Buddhism, which is generally recognized to be close to the original Buddhism, is atheistic.

The standard orthodox interpretation is that Theravada Buddhism is atheistic. Thus, Herbert Stroup tells us that Buddhism "is more accurately described as atheist than as theist";[23] E. Royston Pike asserts that Buddhism in its original form maintained no belief in God;[24] and Ninian Smart holds that in Theravada Buddhism, which he considers most likely to represent the basic teaching of the Buddha, "there is no belief in God, nor even a divine Absolute."[25]

This standard interpretation has been challenged, however, by Helmuth von Glasenapp, who argues that old Buddhist texts "confirm unmistakenly and authoritatively that since the oldest times Buddhists believed in the existence of gods (devas)"[26]; that is, the finite and impermanent gods of the Hindu religion. However, the power of these gods or devas is limited, von Glasenapp says, to the fulfillment of worldly petitions: "to create the world, to change its order, to bestow a good rebirth on a suppliant, or to grant him liberation, is not within their power."[27] Furthermore, these gods are subject to birth and death. According to Glasenapp, besides granting worldly petitions, devas proclaim the Buddha glory. Essentially, he suggests that devas serve the same function as angels and saints in Christian and Islamic theological thought. He also draws parallels between them and, for example, Roman, Viking and ancient Indian gods.

Von Glasenapp claims that Buddhism has no permanent gods of the sort associated with the Hebrew-Christian tradition. In particular, he argues that Buddhism rejects any idea of God as a creator. He points out that Buddhist philosophers, like Jainist philosophers, have developed arguments that attempt to refute the idea of a creator God. Thus, for example, the earliest Buddhist literature is said to emphasize the incompatibility of the idea of a good and almighty god with both evil in the world and the doctrine of freedom of will. Some modern Buddhists argue that if the world is traced back to God as the single cause, one must ask the further question: From what cause has God arisen? Other Buddhist thinkers have pointed out that different schools of religious thought regard different gods as the creator of the world. But, these philosophers ask, whose opinion is correct? Still other Buddhist philosophers maintain that if God's decision is the sole cause of the world, then the world was created at one time. But, they argue, things often arise in succession. These and other arguments, at least some of which are also put forward by Western skeptics, have been used by Buddhist philosophers to refute the idea that a theistic creator God exists.

Jamshed K. Fozdar has launched an even more radical challenge to the orthodox atheistic interpretation of original Buddhism.[28] He argues that it is vitally important to understand Buddhism within the context of the Hindu tradition. So understood, Buddha was a reformer of the

Hindu religion and not a creator of a new religion. Using textual analysis of Buddhist and Hindu documents, he argues that Buddha believed not only in devas but in the uncreated, the unborn, the unoriginated – in short, the absolute of the Hindu religion.

Fozdar maintains that the absolute or God is the ultimate reality that lies behind nirvana and the laws of karma. What Buddha was opposed to, he says, was not belief in God but belief in an anthropomorphic personal God whom one can understand in human terms and speak about using commonsense notions. In contrast, the absolute or God for Buddha was beyond all comprehension and could be understood only in an ineffable mystic state. Thus Fozdar not only opposes the orthodox atheistic interpretation of Buddhism. He also maintains that the interpretations by the Buddhist philosophers referred to above who argue against the absolute or God are based on a misunderstanding of Buddha's original teaching.

Now even if Fozdar and von Glasenapp are correct in their interpretations of original Buddhism, it must not be supposed that Buddhists today all understand Buddhism in this way. Some Buddhists reject the old "myths" and "superstitions" of the traditional teaching on the grounds that they are incompatible with contemporary experience and science.[29] But given this contemporary and scientific view, the gods (devas) of original Buddhism have to be rejected too. In addition, some Buddhists today even reject a literal interpretation of rebirth. But then it seems quite possible for Buddhism to be interpreted in an atheistic way even when atheism is understood broadly.

In conclusion, if von Glasenapp is correct that belief in devas, the impermanent gods borrowed from Hinduism, was originally part of Buddhism, then Buddhism is not an atheistic religion in the broad sense. Although these gods play no role in the Buddhist path to salvation manifested in the Four Noble Truths and the Noble Eightfold Path, on von Glasenapp's interpretation they were a part of the Buddhist's world-view from the very beginning. Further, although devas have no role in the creation of the universe and function only within it, they are divine beings with powers to grant certain prayers. Because it posits the existence of devas, original Buddhism cannot be considered an atheistic religion in the broad sense.[30] However, on von Glasenapp's interpretation, Buddhism is an atheistic religion in the narrow sense. Indeed, in this sense it, like Jainism, is a positive atheistic religion based on rational arguments. As we have seen, the Buddhist intellectual tradition provides reasons not only for not believing in a theistic God, but for disbelieving in one.

But what about the thesis that original Buddhism posits a belief in the Absolute? If this interpretation is correct, then whether or not early

Buddhism is atheistic in the narrow sense depends on whether the notion of an all-good, all-powerful, and all-knowing personal God who is the creator of the universe is considered anthropomorphic. If it is, then even on Fozdar's interpretation, Buddhism is atheistic in the narrow sense.

Confucianism

Confucianism was founded by Confucius (551–479 B.C.) and has been a way of life followed by countless millions of Chinese for over two thousand years.[31] Over the centuries it spread to all parts of China and to neighboring countries, especially Japan and Korea. Emperor Wu of the Han Dynasty established appointments for textual specialists of the Confucian Classics and thereby reputedly initiated Confucianism's ascendancy to the imperial ideology and state cult of China. Until 1905 Chinese civil service exams were focused on Confucian doctrine. Although the influence of Confucianism has decreased markedly in mainland China since the victory of Communism in 1947, it still has many followers in neighboring countries – especially Korea[32] – and in the West, thanks to overseas Chinese and their fans.[33]

As in the case of Jainism and Buddhism, there is disagreement among scholars over whether Confucianism is an atheistic religion. Part of the problem of correctly interpreting Confucianism is that early Christian missionary scholars tried to make the ancient Chinese teachings more easily translatable into Christian theological doctrines, and later secular scholars and reformers had their own agendas.[34] For example, Jesuit scholars in the seventeenth and eighteenth centuries argued that since Confucianism was basically an ethical system, its followers could be converted to Christianity without giving up their own views. Later Protestant missionary scholars, such as James Legge (1815–97), argued that although Confucius himself was a religious skeptic, the traditional view of heaven held by the common people was the true God of the Christian religion.[35]

In the first half of the twentieth century, interpretations of Confucian doctrines tended to be motivated not by religious goals but by the wish to discover a rational mode of thinking in China's past that justified its entrance into the modern world. Thus, the scholar and modernist reformer Hu Shi (1891–1962) maintained from a Chinese point of view that although Confucius was an agnostic humanist, his views were submerged in a cultural context of superstition. On the other hand, the scholar Herrlee Creel in 1935 cited passages from Confucius' writing to refute the view that Confucius was an agnostic. By 1949, however, Creel was no longer convinced of his earlier religious interpretation and returned to the agnostic ethical interpretation of Confucius of earlier centuries.[36]

Given this interpretative history it is small wonder that it is difficult to determine whether Confucius believed in God. Consider the contrasting readings in a sample of reference books. Pike maintains that there is no God or pantheon in Confucianism.[37] However, he does not explain what is meant by God. According to Wing-tsit Chan, although Confucius did not believe in an anthropomorphic god, he held that heaven (t'ien) was a cosmic spiritual-moral power.[38] Chan also points out that Confucius prayed, attended sacrifices, and even swore by heaven.[39] Although Chan does not draw this inference, these actions may mean that Confucius held a personal view of God and did not merely believe in a spiritual-moral power.

Rejecting the usual translation of t'ien as heaven, Herbert Giles understands the term to refer to a personal deity in Confucian literature.[40] He argues that Confucius not only believed in the existence of the deity of his fathers "more vaguely perhaps than did the anthropomorphic worshippers of early times; but he was conscious, and expressed his consciousness openly, that in his teaching he was working under divine guidance."[41] Giles also shows that Confucius very probably believed in various spiritual beings as well. When asked what constituted wisdom, Confucius replied: "To cultivate earnestly our duty towards our neighbors and to reverence spiritual beings, while maintaining always a due reserve may be called 'wisdom.'" He also said: "How abundantly do spiritual beings make their presence manifest among us!"[42]

Although Giles's evidence does not show that Confucius believed in a personal God, it does suggest that he believed in some supernatural beings and that a belief in a personal God would therefore not have been completely foreign to him. In addition, Giles shows that Mencius (372?–289 B.C.), a sage second only in importance to Confucius himself in Confucian literature, believed in God – and a rather anthropomorphic God at that.[43] Again, although this does not demonstrate that Confucius himself believed in a personal God, it does indicate that a personal God is to be found in some Confucian thought and suggests that it is not implausible that Confucius held a belief in a personal God. However, some Confucian scholars who came after Mencius, most notably Hsün-tzu (298–238 B.C.) and Wang Chong (A.D.27–100), gave Confucius' thought a naturalistic interpretation. For example, Hsün-tzu was very concerned to combat what he considered superstitious practices such as praying for rain, and Wang Chong gave a materialistic explanation of the origin of the universe.[44]

In sum, there is some evidence that suggests that Confucius did believe in some form of a supreme being or God, although just how personal his view of God was is a matter of controversy. Since in any case it seems very likely that he believed in various spiritual beings, we can conclude that Confucius was probably not an atheist in the broad sense of rejecting belief in all gods. Whether he was an atheist in the narrow sense of rejecting belief in the theistic God is not completely certain. It should be emphasized, however, that even if he did believe in some supreme being, there is no evidence that he believed in a being that is all-good, all-knowing, all-powerful, and a creator of the universe; indeed, it seems unlikely that he held such a view. Thus, it is not implausible to suppose that Confucius was a negative atheist in the narrow sense; that is, that he did not hold the view that an all-good, all-knowing, and all-powerful God exists. There is not enough evidence, however, to speculate intelligently about whether he was a positive atheist in the narrow sense – that is, whether he disbelieved that such a God exists or whether he gave rational arguments for his atheism.

Now it might be maintained that the essential aspects of Confucian thought, namely, its moral philosophy, can be divorced from belief in God and spiritual beings, and it might further be urged that Confucius' views are humanistic in that they emphasize the value of human beings and the cultivation of human learning and virtues. But although these claims may well be true, it is important to stress that humanism in several of its senses is compatible with belief in God[45] and that although Confucianism can be interpreted in purely secular terms, Confucius did not do so. Virtue and right conduct were tied in his view to following the way of heaven and, at least on some interpretations, they were tied to following the way of a personal God.

This is not to deny that one may eliminate belief in a God and spiritual beings from Confucianism and follow Confucius' teachings concerning virtue and right conduct. Indeed, some later Confucian scholars did seem to interpret Confucius' views in naturalistic way. For these people at least, Confucianism, in this modified form, is an atheistic religion in the broad sense.

Is Atheism Antireligious?

Now that we have seen that there are in fact atheistic living religions, the question "Is atheism anti-religious?" has a quick answer: since some religions are atheistic in the narrow sense, atheism is not necessarily opposed to religion. Further, although Jainism, Buddhism, and Confucianism are not atheistic in the broad sense, it would seem to be possible to eliminate any God or gods from these religions without practical import, for the way to spiritual salvation and the way of life specified by these religions would not seem to be affected to any major extent by eliminating all gods.

A more interesting question is whether an atheist in the narrow sense must in all consistency oppose any religion that requires of its members belief in an all-good, all-powerful, and all-knowing God. Yes, an atheist must be opposed to the theological beliefs of the religion, but this is compatible with an admiration for other aspects of the religion.

Recall that according to Alston, ritual acts that focus on sacred objects and a moral code believed to be sanctioned by the gods are religious-making characteristics. Now an atheist could admire the rituals of a theistic religion on aesthetic grounds without believing that the objects in the ritual were sacred.[46] An atheist could maintain that the ethical code of a theistic religion is correct while rejecting the idea that God sanctioned it.

Recall too that according to Beardsley and Beardsley, a religion consists not only in a set of interrelated religious beliefs providing answers to all the basic religious questions, but in attitudes and practices determined by those beliefs. An atheist could argue that the attitudes and practices determined by the beliefs of a religion are worthwhile and yet maintain that the beliefs that determine these attitudes and practices are unjustified or even false.

In conclusion, although I have argued that atheism itself is not a religion, I have maintained that certainly Jainism, probably Buddhism, and perhaps Confucianism are atheistic in the narrow sense. After noting the belief in some sort of God or gods in all three of these religions, I have also suggested that they could get along without any belief in any gods. Consequently, it seems that these religions could be construed as atheistic in the broad sense without significant loss. Finally, since there are atheistic religions, it follows that atheism and religion do not necessarily stand in opposition to one another. Atheists can even support aspects of theistic religions on, for instance, aesthetic and moral grounds.

NOTES

1. William P. Alston, "Religion," in Paul Edwards (ed.), *Encyclopedia of Philosophy* (New York: Macmillan and Free Press, 1967), vol. 7, pp. 140–45.
2. Ibid., p. 142.
3. Ibid.
4. Ibid.
5. Ibid.
6. Monroe C. Beardsley and Elizabeth Lane Beardsley, *Philosophical Thinking: An Introduction* (New York: Harcourt, Brace and World, 1965), chap. 1.
7. Ibid., pp. 38–43.
8. Ibid., p. 38.

9. Madelyn Murray O'Hair, "Is Atheism the Religion of the Future?" Pacifica Tape Library, BC0044, 1971.

10. These religions may not exhaust the living religions that have been considered atheistic. See, e.g., Rik Pinxten, "Atheism and Its Cultural Anthropological Context," in L. Apostel, R. Pinxten, R. Thibau, and F. Vandamme (eds.), *Religious Atheism?* (Gent, Belgium: E. Story-Scientia, 1982), pp. 103–24 for an atheistic interpretation of the Navajo religion. See also Shlomo Biderman, "Religion without God in Indian Philosophy," in ibid., pp. 125–31, for an atheistic interpretation of the Mimamsa school in Hindu religious thought.

11. *The 2002 New York Times Almanac*, p. 489.

12. Umakant Premanand Shah, "Jainism," in *Encyclopaedia Britannica*, 15th ed. (1984), vol. 10, pp. 8–14; Ninian Smart, "Jainism," in Paul Edwards (ed.), *Encyclopedia of Philosophy* (New York: Macmillan and Free Press, 1967), vol. 4, pp. 238–39; E. Royston Pike, *Encyclopaedia of Religion and Religions* (New York: Meridian Books, 1958), pp. 203–5; and Herbert Stroup, *Four Religions of Asia* (New York: Harper and Row, 1968), pp. 81–114.

13. Pike, *Encyclopaedia of Religion and Religions*, p. 204.

14. Stroup, *Four Religions of Asia*, p. 100.

15. Jagomandar Lal Jaini, *Outlines of Jainism* (Westport, Conn.: Hyperion Press, 1982), pp. 4–5.

16. Subramania Gopalan, *Outlines of Jainism* (New York: Halsted Press, 1973), p. 38.

17. Ibid.

18. Ibid., pp. 38–39

19. Smart, "Jainism," p. 238.

20. Gopalan, *Outlines of Jainism*, p. 41.

21. Sources for this section include Stroup, *Four Religions of Asia*, pp. 115–67; Ninian Smart, "Buddhism," in Edwards (ed.), *Encyclopedia of Philosophy*, vol. 1, pp. 416–20; Karen Christiana Lang, "Unbelief within Buddhism," in *The Encyclopedia of Unbelief* (Buffalo, N.Y.: Prometheus, 1985), vol. 1, pp. 74–77; and Helmuth von Glasenapp, *Buddhism: A Non-Theistic Religion* (New York: George Braziller, 1966).

22. *The 2002 New York Times Almanac*, p. 489.

23. Stroup, *Four Religions of Asia*, p. 158.

24. Pike, *Encyclopaedia of Religion and Religions*, p. 71.

25. Smart, "Buddhism," p. 417.

26. Von Glasenapp, *Buddhism*, p. 19.

27. Ibid., p. 21.

28. Jamshed K. Fozdar, *The God of Buddha* (New York: Asia Publishing, 1973), chap. 4.

29. Lang, "Unbelief within Buddhism," p. 76.

30. Cf. Arvind Sharma, "Buddhism and Atheism," *Sophia* 16 (1977): 27–30. Sharma argues that Buddhism cannot be classified as atheistic under several definitions of "atheism." However, according to Sharma, Buddhism *is* atheistic in the sense that it denies the significance of *god* or gods for salvation. I do not dispute this but wish to maintain that Buddhism is also atheistic in the narrow sense defined in the first chapter.

31. Wing-tsit Chan, "Confucianism," in *Encyclopaedia Britannica*, vol. 4, pp. 1091–108; Pike, *Encyclopaedia of Religion and Religions*, pp. 107–9.
32. *The 2002 New York Times Almanac*, p. 489, estimates that there are 5 million Confucians in the world.
33. See Robert Neville, *Boston Confucianism* (Albany: SUNY Press, 2000).
34. Paul A. Rule, *K'ung-tzu or Confucius? The Jesuit Interpretation of Confucianism* (London: Allen and Unwin, 1986), and Lionel M. Jensen, *Manufacturing Confucianism* (Durham: Duke University Press, 1997).
35. Thomas A. Wilson, *On Sacred Ground* (Cambridge: Harvard University Press, 2002), pp. 3–6.
36. Ibid., pp. 7–9.
37. Pike, *Encyclopaedia of Religion and Religions*, p. 107.
38. Chan, "Confucianism," p. 1092.
39. Ibid., p. 1093.
40. Herbert A. Giles, *Confusianism and Its Rivals* (London: William and Norgate, 1915), pp. 9 and 71.
41. Ibid., p. 67.
42. Ibid., p. 74.
43. Ibid., pp. 89–95.
44. See Donald MacInnis, "Unbelief in China," in *The Encyclopedia of Unbelief*, vol. 1, pp. 95–96.
45. See Michael Martin, *Atheism: A Philosophical Justification* (Philadelphia: Temple University Press, 1990), pp. 472–73.
46. This seemed, in fact, to be the position of Santayana. See George Santayana, *The Life of Reason* (New York: Scribner's, 1905–6), vol. 3, p. 30.

14   Feminism and Atheism

In this chapter I explore the question of whether or not feminism is compatible with theism, or whether being a feminist also requires that one be an atheist. By "atheism" I shall mean what Michael Martin calls "positive atheism," the belief that there is no God (Martin 1990: 463–64). And by "God" I shall mean "a personal being who is omniscient, omnipotent, and completely good and who created heaven and earth" (Martin 1990: 463).

The investigation of the relationship between feminism and atheism requires looking at feminist critiques of religion and of theism. I draw not only on the works of feminist philosophers but also on the works of feminist theologians. Throughout this discussion I am primarily concerned with monotheistic religions in the Jewish/Christian/Islamic tradition in the twentieth and twenty-first centuries, and with feminism as manifested since its "rebirth" during the 1960s within the Western world. This is not to say that other forms and periods of religion are of no interest in the study of atheism, or that either pre-twentieth-century feminism or non-Western feminism of any age is irrelevant to the issue. However, although some feminist discussions of religion acknowledge the role of native religions, Buddhism, and Hinduism, most focus primarily on the Jewish/Christian/Islamic tradition. And most of the systematic examination of religion and theism has been undertaken by feminists within the last thirty years.

The first point to be made about the topic of feminism and atheism is that there is not a lot written about it.[1] There is plenty of published material on feminism and religion, on feminism and theology, on women and religion, and even on feminism and God.[2] But on feminism and atheism there is, relatively speaking, very little indeed.

Second, when feminist philosophers and theologians write about religion, they are not usually interested in the ontological question of whether or not a God or gods, or even a Goddess or goddesses, exist, and what the arguments for their existence might be. Nor, for that matter, have feminist philosophers been interested in rational disproofs of the existence of a God or gods, a Goddess or goddesses, or in supporting atheism on rational grounds. It appears, on the one hand, that almost all feminists who are self-identified atheists have simply walked away from religious belief and practice, and therefore do not discuss the relationship between atheism and feminism. And on the other hand, those feminists who have not walked away from religious belief and practice have attempted to significantly reconceptualize God, the divine, and the spiritual, thereby retaining their feminism without (or so they think) being compelled to declare themselves atheists.

Moreover, feminists have shown little interest in the tools of conceptual analysis and rational argument to evaluate the truth of and evidence for religious claims. In the words of Pamela Anderson, they are suspicious of the "formally rational arguments concerning the existence of God of traditional theism" (Anderson 1998: 15), which merely serve to "confirm the status quo of patriarchy in the history of western philosophy" (Anderson 1998: 16). Anderson says that more important questions concern to whom theistic beliefs belong, and for whom they were constructed (Anderson 1998: 16). Similarly, Grace Jantzen writes, "[F]eminists are, I expect, much more likely to ground our philosophies of religion in women's experiences as the source of religious knowledge than in the traditional categories of revelation and reason: I cannot quite imagine what a feminist rendering of the ontological argument might look like" (Jantzen 1994: 204).[3]

I agree that a "feminist rendering of the ontological argument" is implausible. It may in fact be impossible: It would probably be a category mistake to attempt to rework the ontological argument from a feminist perspective – other than, perhaps, to deconstruct it as a social product of its time. Nonetheless, I see no reason why feminist philosophers of religion should not use the tools of conceptual analysis and rational argument; indeed, I think it is essential to use them. And these are the tools that I bring to the question of whether there might be one or more distinctively feminist arguments in favor of atheism.

What characteristics would make such arguments distinctively feminist? I suggest that there are four. First, the use of the concept of gender and/or sex as an analytic category in the interpretation and evaluation of religious claims (Frankenberry 1994: 1). Second, an awareness of the diverse experiences of women. Third, knowledge of the oppression of women *qua* women, oppression that can take many different forms and that is linked to and manifested in various guises through other forms of oppression, such as ageism, racism, ableism, heterosexism, and classism. And fourth, the hope for and moral goal of ending all oppression based on sex/gender and on other irrelevant categories of identification.

Because there is not a lot of material on feminist arguments for atheism, what is present in the literature must be reinterpreted in order to serve the investigation of feminism and atheism, a scholarly task that most feminist theologians do not recognize and that most feminist philosophers of religion apparently have chosen not to pursue. In the sections that follow I present and evaluate five main feminist approaches to religions and ideas about God and their relevance for the defense of atheism.

I. RELIGION HARMS WOMEN: A FEMINIST VERSION OF THE ARGUMENT FROM EVIL

The most obvious feminist argument in support of atheism is a version of the argument from evil, derived from the observation that monotheistic religions harm women.

Most feminists who study religion have engaged in what Amy Newman calls "uncovering the gender subtext within both religious and antireligious rhetoric [and]...unraveling the interconnections between this gender subtext and other oppressive practices with which it may be linked" (Newman 1994: 30). Feminists are sharply critical of the concept of women and the status and roles attributed to them in monotheistic religions. Historically, women have been excluded from education, including religious and theological education; hence they have not been involved in shaping religions or theologies. Women have also been denied leadership positions as priests, ministers, rabbis, and imams and have had only a subordinate participation in the life of many religions. The result is that women have been expected to be silent and almost invisible within religious contexts, as in other aspects of social life. Moreover, traditional monotheistic religions stereotype women, either putting them on a pedestal as mothers and saints or demonizing them as temptresses and whores, the source of evil that contaminates men and society.[4] Religions have restricted women's sexuality and required procreative conformity. Birth control, abortion, and divorce were traditionally banned and still are in some religions; sexual behavior outside heterosexual marriage has been condemned; and women have been expected to create and sustain a family as their major or even exclusive role in life, serving primarily as devoted wives and caring mothers of children raised within the faith. Elderly women are regarded as of little or no importance once they are no longer considered to have sexual or procreative value (Christ 1979: 280–81).

Such stereotyping and repression of women are regarded by many feminists as the epiphenomena of a more fundamental characteristic of

monotheistic religions: the view of God as a cosmic and divine patriarch.
Marjorie Hewitt Suchocki writes,

Characteristics traditionally attributed to God, such as strength, wisdom,
immutability, dependability, and righteousness, are similar to values stereotypically attributed to men, whereas the corollary values applied to humanity, such
as weakness, ignorance, vacillation, and sinfulness, are stereotypically applied to
women. Thus the concept of God as male serves to define men and male roles,
and to reinforce the inferior definition and roles of women. (Hewitt Suchocki
1994: 58)

In striving to improve themselves spiritually, men, as religious believers,
must strive to rid themselves of what are regarded as exclusively female
and debased characteristics. The second-class status traditionally allot-
ted to women has been taken to justify sexual and procreative abuse of
women and violence toward girls and women who defy religious stric-
tures or even just fail to conform adequately. As a result, domination by
men and the subordination of women are "not marginal, but an integral
part of what has been received as mainstream, normative traditions"
(Ruether [1981] 1992: 246). As Mary Daly memorably expresses it, "if
God is male, then the male is God" (Daly 1985: 19).

The shameful and dispiriting litany of harms inflicted on women by
proponents of monotheistic religions suggests that such religions are not
compatible with feminism and that freeing women from involvement in
or allegiance to monotheistic religions would increase women's liberty,
autonomy, well-being, and freedom from discrimination and stereotyping. One might, however, take the argument further, by suggesting that
this empirical evidence offers a specifically feminist version of the more
general argument from evil against the existence of God. The existence
of oppression of and injustice to women and children and members of
many other groups, both human and nonhuman, on this planet is evidence not just of the harmfulness of monotheistic religions, but also that
there is no God in the traditional monotheistic sense. At the very least,
the postulated divine entity is neither omnipotent, nor omniscient, nor
not wholly moral (Noddings 2003: 215–16).

However, the indisputable fact that monotheistic religions have a history of being harmful to women may not, in itself, be sufficient evidence
that positive atheism is correct and that there is no God in the traditional
monotheistic sense. Why not? There are two possible counterarguments
purporting to show that the facts adduced are not enough to constitute a
successful feminist argument for atheism. First, some feminists – those
who are sympathetic to the claims of theism – have raised epistemological and ontological questions about the standard concept of God,
the interpretation of scriptures, the historical record of God's supposed

interventions within human history, and the relationship of traditional religions to God's will, questions that, if answered in certain ways, are intended to preserve the plausibility of belief in the divine and its consistency with feminist principles. Second, other believers – and here I think of fundamentalists from any of Christianity, Judaism, and Islam, who have no sympathy for the metaphysical, moral, and political claims of feminism – defend belief in the existence of God against the charge that it is vitiated by the subordinate position typically forced on women by arguing that the concept, status, and roles assigned to women in traditional monotheistic religions are just the way they should be: consistent with God's will and his divine plan for "man"kind. Moreover, the abuse women have suffered is in accord with their second-class status or is the righteous result of their failure to be obedient to God's commands or is in some cases a consequence of the fallibility of men who interpret their God-given status as a license to mistreat.

I examine each of these counterarguments in turn.

2. RECONSTRUCTING THE CONCEPT OF GOD

Many progressive philosophers and theologians, for whom the equal personhood of women is indisputable, have reacted to the powerful feminist critique of the oppressive role of religion, with its patriarchal God, by attempting to reconstruct God. They agree that, as Catherine Keller puts it, "[T]he matter of God-language and thus of its gender is no trivial or supernatural pursuit, but a way of encoding the gender of ultimate values" (Keller 1998: 226) and that, in the words of Rachel Adler, "An exclusively masculine God-language is ethically objectionable because it fosters injustice, but it is also theologically inadequate" (Adler 1998: 250). Their thought is that this patriarchal concept of God is mistaken, that established religions have failed to understand what and who God is, and that the injustice and oppression inflicted on women by monotheistic religions can be obviated by means of a nonoppressive concept of the divine. Monotheistic religion must be reinvented, either by reforming existing religions or going outside them to create new ones (Ruether [1981] 1992: 246). Feminists have therefore suggested reexamining religious history, to discover the liberating roles some women played (Ruether [1981] 1992: 247); reinterpreting scriptures, trying to show how their original meaning was overlaid with masculinist assumptions (Keller 1998: 226); working to ensure equal access by women to religious institutions and structures; transforming "structures, knowledge, and praxis" (Adler 1998: 247–48); and introducing new religious rituals and practices. As Nel Noddings puts it, "Some writers try to show that a religion has departed from its origins when it discriminates against women. The basic argument here is that the existing great religions started out as emancipatory movements. A return to original commitments would, then, restore the equality of women" (Noddings 2003: 223).

There is, however, divergence among feminist theologians and philosophers of religion as to how to respond to the endemic masculinity of God. Attempting to reconstruct God but still within the confines of the monotheistic Judeo-Christian tradition, some feminist theologians hope to recover or reinterpret God in "feminine" or "maternal" terms (see Daly 1985: 19 and Ruether 1993). This means that in addition to the traditional masculine properties of God – power, knowledge, control, justice – characteristics that are stereotypically associated with women, such as love, gentleness, and connectedness, must also be attributed to him. In effect, God is seen as an androgynous being, one who possesses characteristics (stereotypically) associated with *both* males exclusively and females exclusively (Ruether 1983: 56–61). Taking the idea further, some have criticized the gendered patriarchal God by arguing that God is "beyond maleness and femaleness," a being who can therefore restore both women and men to "full humanity" (Ruether 1993: 492, 493). Such an approach rejects the idea that the categories of sex and gender are applicable to God; instead, thinking of God as male or masculine is seen as a type of category mistake.

Other feminist theologians, however, have boldly declared their allegiance to the centrality of gender by creating, recovering from ancient historic or prehistoric times, or reinventing God as the Goddess.[5] Carol Christ argues that "women need the Goddess" and describes the Goddess as the affirmation of female power, the female body, the female will, and women's bonds and heritage (Christ 1979: 276). However, the ontological status of the Goddess is ambiguous. Christ suggests three possibilities:

(1) The Goddess is divine female, a personification who can be invoked in prayer and ritual; (2) the Goddess is symbol of the life, death, and rebirth energy in nature and culture, in personal and communal life; and (3) the Goddess is symbol of the affirmation of the legitimacy and beauty of female power. (Christ 1979: 278)

I suggest that Christ's second and third possible answers are really very similar. Each one sees the Goddess as having only a symbolic existence, albeit a potentially powerful one, and not an existence independent of human beings. In this respect, as Christ explains it, "the Goddess symbol reflects the sacred power within women and nature, suggesting the connectedness between women's cycles of menstruation, birth, and menopause, and the life and death cycles of the universe" (Christ 1979: 278). Only the first answer, which defines the Goddess as a divine female, is an assertion of the independent existence of the Goddess.

Christ, however, appears to want to have it both ways. She notes that some feminists do regard the Goddess "as a divine female protector and creator and would find their experience of Goddess limited by the assertion that she is not *also* out there as well as within themselves and in all natural processes" (Christ 1979: 278, emphasis in original). And she writes,

> When asked what the symbol of Goddess means, feminist priestess Starhawk replied, "It all depends on how I feel. When I feel weak, she is someone who can help and protect me. When I feel strong, she is the symbol of my own power. At other times I feel her as the natural energy in my body and the world." How are we to evaluate such a statement? Theologians might call these the words of a sloppy thinker. But my deepest intuition tells me they contain a wisdom that Western theological thought has lost. (Christ 1979: 278–79)[6]

Not only might theologians call these ideas sloppy thinking; many philosophers are also likely to be unimpressed and to regard Starhawk's belief system as unhelpfully relativist. It is easy enough to understand the Goddess as a powerful idea that can not only symbolize strong women and nature, but also provide psychological help for those in need (Gross 1996: 226–27). But the statement that there is an autonomous, transhuman entity called the Goddess is a much stronger claim, an onto-logical claim that requires epistemic justification. The two are not con-sistent with each other.

Moreover, the postulation by feminists of a replacement for the tra-ditional God – whether it be a feminine God, an androgynous God, a God beyond sex or gender, or a Goddess – is still vulnerable to four main sorts of objections from a feminist perspective.

The first objection to the feminist reinterpretations of God derives from the exegetical question as to whether the reinterpretation of monotheistic religions in ways that are less sexist and apparently more woman-friendly are valid and warranted on the basis of scriptures and other types of archeological evidence that are standardly taken by believ-ers as justification for belief in a divine being. For example, Helene P. Foley, who is herself sympathetic to feminist perspectives on religion, argues that archeological evidence does not support the feminist reap-propriations of the Goddess and that feminists have treated texts incon-sistently: "[T]hose aspects of ancient tradition that reflect the feminist reading of prehistory are read literally, while the rest is treated metaphor-ically" (Foley 2001: 219). However, since this question is an in-house issue for theologians, feminist and nonfeminist, a problem about the literary, anthropological, and historical foundations for these claims

(Ruether 1993: 491), I shall not attempt to explore it. Moreover, the philosophical assessment of the truth value and epistemic strength of feminist claims about the divine is not dependent on it.

The second objection to the feminist reinterpretations of God rests on concerns about where the burden of evidence lies. (The idea of "the burden of evidence" seems fairer than "the burden of proof" because it may be as unfair to expect proof in philosophy of religion as anywhere else in philosophy.) And I suggest the burden of evidence rests on anyone who claims that there is a reconfigured God or Goddess. The mere convenience and greater moral acceptability of a nonsexist divinity are not enough to show that such a divinity exists. Following Antony Flew, I suggest that it is up to the believer in a nonsexist God or Goddess to show, first, that the concept of the nonsexist God or Goddess makes sense (i.e., the words "God" or "Goddess" must have a "meaning such that it is theoretically possible for an actual being to be so described") and, second, that there are good reasons for believing that the concept has "an application" (Flew 1984: 15–16), that is, that a nonsexist God or Goddess exists. This burden of evidence does not mean starting with the positive atheist assumption that there is no nonsexist God or Goddess; it does, however, mean starting with the absence of any belief at all in a nonsexist God or Goddess (a version of what Martin calls "negative atheism" (Martin 1990: 463–64)), and then seeking from believers sufficient reasons to believe. She who asserts the existence of something new in reality must be required to show why that assertion should be accepted.

Now, Martin argues, within the context of traditional ideas about God, regardless of where the burden of proof lies in the debate between theism and atheism, the epistemic and rhetorical role of the nonbeliever is not affected. For the nonbeliever is still compelled to make a case: he or she must, at least, reply to the arguments put forward by the believer (Martin 1990: 30). However, as I've already observed, feminist philosophers and theologians have not been concerned to build a case in support of their beliefs in the divine. In particular, they have not provided arguments in support of the claim that the Goddess exists. But the epistemic responsibility rests on the Goddess-acceptor to provide evidence in support of the claim that there is a Goddess.

The third objection to feminist reinterpretations of God is that, even if one or more of these reinterpretations are justified in exegetical terms, nonetheless, insofar as they are claiming objective existence for the divine, they are open to most of the same attacks on monotheistic arguments and vulnerability to atheist arguments that are brought forward against traditional theism. As Noddings states, "I see no more evidence for the actual existence of a benevolent 'Creatress' than I do for an all-good male God" (Noddings 2003: 216). The pragmatic fact – *if* it is a fact, and no empirical evidence has been assembled to demonstrate it – that belief in a nonsexist God or Goddess (if these concepts truly make sense) is less likely than belief in the traditional God to support the oppression of women is not sufficient to show that there is such a being. At most what such a fact, if it is a fact, would show is that religions based on a nonsexist God or Goddess are potentially less destructive than traditional God-based religions.

Fourth, some feminists have wondered whether the reconfigured feminist God reinforces, despite feminist intentions, antifeminist beliefs. Foley, for example, questions whether the celebration of the Goddess "runs the risk of representing a naively unitary view of the female and of reflecting and reproducing dominant cultural assumptions about women" (Foley 2001: 221). That is, the cult of the Goddess is implicitly essentialist in ways that ignore the true diversity of women across time and space. Other feminist objections to feminist reinterpretations of God are concerned with the role of hierarchy and power within any religious system that is monotheistic. Hence, Jantzen writes, "substitution of 'Mother God' for 'Father God,' while leaving the concept of God otherwise the same ('God in a skirt'), in itself does not change very much" (Jantzen 1998: 269). As Carol Christ herself acknowledges, "Some [feminists] would assert that the Goddess definitely is *not* 'out there,' that the symbol of a divinity 'out there' is part of the legacy of patriarchal oppression, which brings with it the authoritarianism, hierarchicalism, and dogmatic rigidity associated with biblical monotheistic religions" (Christ 1979: 278, emphasis in original). Feminist reinterpretations of God rely on the same suspect dualisms that infect traditional theism: dualisms between the immanent and the transcendent, the human and the divine, the feminine or female and the masculine or male, the supremely good and the inherently morally flawed. Such dualisms have long been the focus of feminist criticism. If feminist theologians and philosophers of religion postulate a nonsexist God or Goddess with objective existence, independent of human beings, this postulate in no way obviates the central feminist hermeneutic suspicion that it is the notion of a supreme being, as ruler, designer, and creator, that provides both the cultural opportunity and the moral justification for belief in and adherence to a hierarchical view of human beings that regards certain types of human – the male, the heterosexual, the white, the wealthy, the strong, the young, and the Christian (or Jewish or Muslim) – as superior to other types of human beings. Moreover, proposing a feminine God, an androgynous God, or a Goddess retains an overgeneralized gender dualism, with all of its dubious implications for human interactions. So feminist reconstructions of God fail to avoid the kinds of moral, metaphysical, and epistemological objections that atheists have so successfully leveled at the traditional God.

3. A FEMINIST MORAL ARGUMENT FOR ATHEISM

The other way in which a theist might defend belief in the existence of God against the charge that it is vitiated by the evil done to women in the name of religion is by arguing that the status and roles assigned to women in traditional monotheistic religions are just the way they should be: in agreement with God's will and his divine plan for "man"kind. Whatever women have experienced is in accord with their second-class status or is the righteous result of their failure to be obedient to God's commands or is in some cases a consequence of the fallibility of men who interpret their God-given status as a license to mistreat. Obviously, this counterargument is not one that feminist believers would advance, but rather a recognizable part of contemporary right-wing fundamentalist belief.

I choose to give some attention to this counterargument to the feminist argument from evil because doing so helps to suggest another feminist argument for atheism, based on what Noddings calls "ethical objections" (Noddings 2003: 214). For whether such a counterargument can be successful depends on a background assumption about what one takes to be more fundamental: a conviction about the equal personhood of women or a conviction about the patriarchal nature of God.

Through the mouth of Socrates, Plato famously posed the question, "Is what is holy holy because the Gods approve it, or do they approve it because it is holy?" (Plato 1961: 178). If God commands us to do X because it is right, then there is a standard for right action that is independent of God's will. Hence, God is unnecessary as a moral touchstone. On the other hand, if X is right because God commands it, then morality is, apparently, dependent on nothing but God's will, and therefore, potentially, any apparently heinous-seeming actions (including those that are sexist and misogynist) might turn out to be right if God were to command them.

Faced with that dilemma, feminist atheists argue that women are indeed persons, and that we know this to be true regardless of what God is supposed to have said. So feminist atheists adopt the first fork of the Euthyphro dilemma: ethical standards are independent of God's will. If believing in the traditional God requires abandoning women's equal personhood, then feminist atheists argue that the moral choice is to reject God, not women's personhood.

A related moral objection to theism is that focusing on God, in whatever form, is, in the words of Carol Christ, "an escape from difficult but necessary political work" (1979: 274).[7] Religious indoctrination can easily draw human beings away from difficult moral goals of social justice, gender and racial equality, peace, and environmental sustainment. There is a real danger that religious service can promote acquiescence in the status quo, either seeing it as a part of God's created world or hoping for redemption in an afterlife. Belief in God is a moral encumbrance, a distraction from feminist goals.

Now, feminist theists might argue that in fact many religious believers are active in social justice causes and that progressive theology supports liberationist agendas. Holding a belief in God can be highly motivating, inspiring believers to become the moral beings that God is said to want them to be. But this objection can be challenged by means of the Euthyphro question: Do feminist theists know that it is right to work for freedom from oppression because God told them? Or do feminist theists antecedently know that it is right to work for freedom from oppression and then conclude that this goal must also be part of God's agenda? Feminist atheists argue that we don't need God to endorse activism or even to inspire it; it is justified on nontheistic grounds. In terms of political effectiveness as well as moral consistency, therefore, it makes sense not to believe in the monotheistic God.

4. OTHER FEMINIST APPROACHES TO RELIGIOUS BELIEF

Downplaying the Role of Belief

Some feminist theists attempt to dodge feminist objections to theism by reconceptualizing and de-emphasizing the role of belief within religion.

As was stated near the beginning of this chapter, feminist theologians and philosophers of religion have not been much interested in the idea of rational proofs for God's existence. These feminists give a number of reasons both to explain and to justify what they take to be the lack of importance of philosophical arguments with respect to God. Feminist theists such as Amy Hollywood and Grace Jantzen are critical of perspectives on God that treat religion as if it primarily or even exclusively consists of a set of beliefs, as if belief were the foundation of all religious practice, and that ignore other aspects of religious life (Jantzen 1998; Hollywood 2004). Those other aspects include religious experience, rituals, and practices, the embodied celebration of and homage to the divine (Thie 1994: 231; Gross 1996: 228). Thus, for example, the feminist Jacqueline Scott, who is a convert to Judaism, writes that in Judaism, "One's faith is measured primarily by one's acts as opposed to beliefs. The understanding is that carrying out the ritual of certain actions will aid in developing the attendant beliefs. One works from the outside to the inside" (Scott 2003: 135). As a person of faith, Scott says, she is not expected to be rational, and does not try (and is not expected to try) to explain her beliefs and practices rationally:

While I entered into the process of conversion as a theoretical, academic exercise, I have emerged from it focusing on the practical and spiritual. Unlike with the philosophical and even feminist aspects of my art of living, I do not feel constrained to be able to understand fully varying points of view and to come to a conclusion as to which ones are best. I do not feel constrained to be rationally consistent in terms of the rituals I adopt or the way in which I practice them. (Scott 2003: 137)

Alternatively, some feminists suggest that a feminist belief in God, perhaps a reconstructed God as Goddess, may be justified on pragmatic grounds. Although she describes herself as an atheist, Noddings, for example, writes, "If a change in the image of the deity can move us toward a greater appreciation for creation and kindness over destruction and cruelty, it is a change to be encouraged.... The value of feminist theologies has to be located in their consequences for human life" (Noddings 2003: 217). Noddings seems to think it is possible to have and to use this concept without making "ontological claims" about anything corresponding to the concept. Feminist theists also argue that religion and religious belief are paramount for people's capacity to endure, to keep on keeping on. Christ claims, "Symbol systems cannot simply be rejected, they must be replaced. Where there is not any replacement, the mind will revert to familiar structures at times of crisis, bafflement, or defeat" (Christ 1979: 275).

It is, however, implausible to suppose there could be a monotheistic religion that encompasses no beliefs. Whatever else a monotheistic religion is – and of course it is likely to contain many diverse practices, activities, and rituals – at the very least it includes beliefs. Noddings recognizes that "a symbol system with no ontological base is somehow spiritually unsatisfying" (Noddings 2003: 217), but more than that, a symbol system with no ontological base cannot be a monotheistic religion.

Moreover, abandoning reason, as Scott says she has, seems like a counsel of despair. While it may be liberating in certain respects to feel that one need not understand or explain or justify, it is also dangerous. Surrendering epistemic responsibility in this fashion may lead to irrationality or foolishness in other areas of one's life. In addition, feminist promoters of nondoxastic theism must acknowledge that a religion that is comprised primarily of experience, practices, rituals, celebration, and homage is as vulnerable to being implicated in the oppression of women as is a doxastic theism. These experiences and practices can involve feelings of humility and insignificance and activities of self-abasement and self-surrender that invoke the patriarchal master-slave relationship just as much as traditional monotheistic beliefs do.

Is there a pragmatic loss for feminists if they do not believe in the monotheistic God? I would say not, since the liberatory effects of the independence and self-confidence that feminism offers are more powerful than the anomie that may be created by losing the belief. Moreover, it cannot be good for members of a subordinated group to hold onto a view of reality that the evidence strongly indicates is false.

An Immanent Divine

Some feminists are atheists in the negative sense, that is, they do not hold a belief in God as a personal creator (Martin 1990: 463–64), yet they feel a need for a way of understanding what Noddings calls our "spiritual longing" (Noddings 2003: 222). One way to do this is what Hewitt Suchocki calls "rejection of the transcendence of God in favor of a totally immanent God" (Hewitt Suchocki 1994: 58), that is, the adoption of pantheism. In adopting a pantheistic perspective on the universe, feminists such as Jantzen reject both traditional monotheistic religions and positive atheism, while maintaining an accepting attitude toward spirituality. Frankenberry explains: "[Some] contemporary women's articulation of a relation between God and the world depicts the divine as continuous with the world rather than as radically transcendent ontologically or metaphysically. Divine transcendence is seen to consist in total immanence" (Frankenberry 2004: 11). Yet this form of pantheism is not mere reductionism. As Jantzen explains it, "the world is to God somewhat as my body is to me: it is my body-self, yet I am not reducible to its physiological processes" (Jantzen 1998: 265).

Like mystical perspectives on the idea of the divine (Stace 1960), pantheism is antithetical to the self/other, creator/created, sacred/secular dualism that is presupposed by traditional theism. As Jantzen says,

To suggest that in some sense the divine is inseparable from the physical universe, as pantheism does, would not merely be to suggest a change of theological doctrine.... If pantheism were seriously to be entertained, the whole western symbolic, constituted as it is by the binary polarities which run through it like a fault-line, would thereby be brought into question.... Instead of the mastery over the earth which is rapidly bringing about its destruction there would be reverence and sensitivity; instead of seeing domination as Godlike we would recognize it as utterly contrary to divinity. (Jantzen 1998: 267–68)

Thus, "what is divine, what is of ultimate value and worth, cannot be defined as separable from the material universe and its diversity but rather must be constitutive of it and constituted by it" (Jantzen 1998: 269).[8]

Feminist pantheism is very different from belief in the transcendent monotheistic God in the sense used at the beginning of this chapter – "a personal being who is omniscient, omnipotent, and completely good and who created heaven and earth" (Martin 1990: 463), and it raises its own set of ontological and epistemological issues.[9] Although I regard pantheism as being of great interest, the assessment of pantheism is beyond the scope of this chapter because its concept of the divine is so different from that of monotheism.

5. CONCLUSION

According to Keller, "atheist or agnostic feminists ignore the God-word at their own peril" (Keller 1998: 228). She means that atheist and agnostic feminists should not lightly reject the concept of God and its power within Western culture. And she is correct: feminists must investigate and understand the social, cultural, and economic influence of monotheistic religions and ideas about God. Nonetheless, there are good reasons for feminists not to believe in such a God.

Can there be distinctively feminist arguments against the existence of the Judeo-Christian God? My answer is that there are several reasons for feminists to be atheists in the positive sense. Feminist atheists can use a version of the argument from evil, citing the suffering and abuse that women and children have suffered as a result of monotheistic religions. Moreover, the attempts by some feminists to reconstruct God as feminine, as androgynous, as genderless, or as a Goddess are inadequate because they raise unanswered questions about the justification of belief in such a being. In response to antifeminists who may claim that the oppression of women is an expression of God's will, feminist atheists can put forward a moral argument that the knowledge of women's personhood requires rejecting a God who preaches women's inferiority.

Theism cannot be preserved by asserting the importance of religious practices while denying the significance of beliefs, concepts, and arguments. Finally, although some feminists are pantheists, their pantheism is consistent with negative atheism with respect to the traditional, personal God.

NOTES

1.   For example, there is no entry for "atheism" in what are arguably some of the key texts in the new field of feminist philosophy of religion: *A Feminist*

Philosophy of Religion (Anderson 1998), *Becoming Divine: Towards a Feminist Philosophy of Religion* (Jantzen 1998), and *Feminist Philosophy of Religion: Critical Readings* (Anderson and Clack 2004). Nor is there any entry for "atheism" in *A Companion to Feminist Philosophy* (Jaggar and Young 1998).

2. See, e.g., *Feminism and World Religions* (Sharma and Young 1999) and *Feminism in the Study of Religion: A Reader* (Juschka 2001).

3. But see also Jantzen's discussion of the epistemic hazards of grounding philosophy of religion in too simplistic a notion of women's experience in Jantzen 1998: 100–127.

4. See, e.g., Daly 1968; 1985 for an extensive discussion of misogyny in Christianity.

5. It is instructive to note that while "God" is readily used as a proper name, "Goddess" is not, and indeed discussions of the latter usually use the term "Goddess" as a category name – "*the* Goddess" – rather than as a proper name.

6. Starhawk herself says, "People often ask me if I *believe* in the Goddess. I reply, 'Do you believe in rocks?' It is extremely difficult for Westerners to grasp the concept of a manifest deity. The phrase 'believe in' implies that we cannot *know* the Goddess, that she is somehow intangible, incomprehensible. But we do not *believe* in rocks ... we know them. ... In the Craft, we do not believe in the Goddess – we connect with Her through Nature and ourselves" (Starhawk, quoted in Foley 2001: 218, Starhawk's emphasis).

7. Jantzen also suggests that those believers who think that the traditional argument from evil has been satisfactorily answered by theists may be less likely to struggle against evil, believing that it is permitted by God for good reasons (Jantzen 1998, 261).

8. Some of what Starhawk says about the Goddess also sounds pantheistic. For example, "The Goddess does not rule the world. ... She is the world. She can be known internally by every individual, in all her magnificent diversity" (Starhawk, quoted in Foley 2001: 218).

9. And some feminist theists reject pantheism at least partly on the supposed grounds that human beings need the monotheistic God, or at least need to believe in that God, for moral reasons. Thus, Frankenberry asks, "Should we be skeptical of attempts to steal from the Gods in order to raise the self to the level of divinity? Can we trust the self, alone, unchecked by an alterity so radical as only to be called 'divine'?" (Frankenberry 1994: 8).

BIBLIOGRAPHY

Adler, Rachel. 1998. "Judaism." In Alison M. Jaggar and Iris Marion Young (eds.), *A Companion to Feminist Philosophy*. Malden, Mass.: Blackwell, pp. 245–52.

Anderson, Pamela Sue. 1998. *A Feminist Philosophy of Religion*. Oxford: Blackwell.

Anderson, Pamela Sue, and Beverley Clack, eds. 2004. *Feminist Philosophy of Religion: Critical Readings*. London: Routledge.

Christ, Carol P. 1979. "Why Women Need the Goddess." In Carol P. Christ and Judith Plaskow (eds.), *Womanspirit Rising: A Feminist Reader in Religion*. New York: Harper & Row, pp. 273–87.

Daly, Mary. 1968. *The Church and the Second Sex*. New York: Harper and Row.

Daly, Mary. 1985. *Beyond God the Father: Toward a Philosophy of Women's Liberation*. Boston: Beacon Press.

Flew, Antony. 1984. *God, Freedom, and Immortality: A Critical Analysis*. Buffalo, N.Y.: Prometheus Books.

Foley, Helene P. 2001. "A Question of Origins: Goddess Cults Greek and Modern." In Elizabeth A. Castelli (ed.), with the assistance of Rosamond C. Rodman, *Women, Gender, Religion: A Reader*. New York: Palgrave, pp. 216–36.

Frankenberry, Nancy. 1994. "Introduction: Prolegomenon to Future Feminist Philosophies of Religion." *Hypatia: A Journal of Feminist Philosophy* 9 (4): 1–14.

Frankenberry, Nancy. 2004. "Feminist Approaches." In Pamela Sue Anderson and Beverley Clack (eds.), *Feminist Philosophy of Religion: Critical Readings*. London: Routledge, pp. 3–27.

Gross, Rita M. 1996. *Feminism and Religion: An Introduction*. Boston: Beacon Press.

Hewitt Suchocki, Marjorie. 1994. "The Idea of God in Feminist Philosophy." *Hypatia: A Journal of Feminist Philosophy* 9 (4): 57–68.

Hollywood, Amy. 2004. "Practice, Belief and Feminist Philosophy of Religion." In Pamela Sue Anderson and Beverley Clack (eds.), *Feminist Philosophy of Religion: Critical Readings*. London: Routledge, pp. 225–40.

Jaggar, Alison M., and Iris Marion Young, eds. 1998. *A Companion to Feminist Philosophy*. Malden, Mass.: Blackwell.

Jantzen, Grace M. 1994. "Feminists, Philosophers, and Mystics." *Hypatia: A Journal of Feminist Philosophy* 9 (4): 186–206.

Jantzen, Grace M. 1998. *Becoming Divine: Towards a Feminist Philosophy of Religion*. Manchester: Manchester University Press.

Juschka, Darlene M. 2001. *Feminism in the Study of Religion: A Reader*. London: Continuum.

Keller, Catherine. 1998. "Christianity." In Alison M. Jaggar and Iris Marion Young (eds.), *A Companion to Feminist Philosophy*. Malden, Mass.: Blackwell, pp. 225–35.

Martin, Michael. 1990. *Atheism: A Philosophical Justification*. Philadelphia: Temple University Press.

Newman, Amy. 1994. "Feminist Social Criticism and Marx's Theory of Religion." *Hypatia: A Journal of Feminist Philosophy* 9 (4): 15–37.

Noddings, Nel. 2003. "A Skeptical Spirituality." In Ruth E. Groenhout and Marya Bower (eds.), *Philosophy, Feminism, and Faith*. Bloomington: Indiana University Press, pp. 213–26.

Plato. 1961. "Euthyphro," trans. Lane Cooper. In Edith Hamilton and Hunting Cairns (eds.), *The Collected Dialogues of Plato*. New York: Pantheon Books, pp. 169–85.

Ruether, Rosemary Radford. [1981] 1992. "The Feminist Critique in Religious Studies." In Janet A. Kourany, James P. Sterba, and Rosemarie Tong (eds.), *Feminist Philosophies*. Englewood Cliffs, N.J.: Prentice Hall, pp. 244–53.

Ruether, Rosemary Radford. 1983. *Sexism and God-Talk: Toward a Feminist Theology*. Boston: Beacon Press.

Ruether, Rosemary Radford. 1993. "The Female Nature of God." In Burton F. Porter (ed.), *Religion and Reason: An Anthology*. New York: St. Martin's Press, pp. 487–93.

Scott, Jacqueline. 2003. "Into the Crucible." In Ruth E. Groenhout and Marya Bower (eds.), *Philosophy, Feminism, and Faith*. Bloomington: Indiana University Press, pp. 120–39.

Sharma, Arvind, and Katherine K. Young, eds. 1999. *Feminism and World Religions.* Albany: SUNY Press.

Stace, W. T. 1960. *Mysticism and Philosophy.* London: Macmillan.

Thie, Marilyn. 1994. "Epilogue: Prolegomenon to Future Feminist* Philosophies of Religions." *Hypatia: A Journal of Feminist Philosophy* 9 (4): 229–39.

15 Atheism and the Freedom of Religion

The legal protection of religious liberty has become an increasingly common phenomenon during the last century. The growth of religious liberty can be linked to the development of modern political theories organized around the concept of constitutional democracy. These theories combine the traditional democratic emphasis on popular control of government with an elaborate constitutional framework. This framework is characterized by structural limits on the exercise of governmental power, the development and protection of civil society, guarantees of personal privacy, and the legal protection of a broad range of individual civil liberties. A comprehensive version of this theory has been articulated and applied by the U.S. Supreme Court since World War II. More recently, variations on this theory have become primary features of the domestic constitutional systems of countries comprising the European Union and in the development of the constitutional structure governing the union as a whole.

A central theme of modern theories of constitutional democracy is that certain aspects of private belief, expression, and behavior are placed beyond the government's control. Religious belief and practice are quintessential examples of activities that are protected by this presumption that citizens are intellectually and spiritually autonomous. Democratic governments are therefore required to leave matters of faith and religious observance to private individuals and their voluntary associations. Likewise, modern theories of constitutional democracy prohibit governments from overtly or subtly coercing religious belief by granting benefits or imposing sanctions or punishments based on the nature of an individual's religious faith.

For more than two hundred years the U.S. Constitution has included religious exercise among several individual rights specifically protected by a Bill of Rights. Likewise, the governments of many Western countries – along with the European Union itself – have begun to incorporate into their own written constitutions the explicit protection of private thought, expression, and behavior. Like the U.S. Constitution, the European constitutional provisions also specifically include the protection of religious activity, and European countries have begun rigorously enforcing these protections through some type of judicial review of governmental action. Asian countries such as the People's Republic of China and Thailand also have constitutional provisions guaranteeing religious liberty, although judicial enforcement of these provisions is more sporadic and inconsistent than in the West.

The framework of limited democratic government within a regime of constitutionally protected private action provides a structure for protecting atheists and agnostics, as well as religious dissenters and other followers of nontraditional faiths. The democratic notion that religious liberty is a private affair that is immune from governmental control renders religion irrelevant to the exercise of government power. Thus, the logic of modern democratic theory would seem to require that atheists enjoy the same protections traditionally offered to a diverse range of mainstream religious believers.

The religious liberty jurisprudence in most constitutional democracies recognizes the need to protect atheists and agnostics. Most countries that extend legal protection to diverse forms of religious belief also protect nonbelievers from the imposition of direct government sanctions. But even in countries that have strong legal protections of religious liberty, governments are often permitted to profess the nation's collective allegiance to religious belief in a manner that subtly marginalizes atheists. Although most European countries no longer maintain officially established churches, many of those countries continue to provide government funds for religious schools and other church expenses.

In addition to formal legal recognition or endorsement of religious belief, many cultural factors also serve to limit the extent to which atheists can fully exercise their political rights. This is especially true in countries such as the United States, where religious belief and public devotion play a prominent role in the political culture. In the United States, atheists are culturally and politically isolated because of the common assumption that political actors must demonstrate religious devotion as part of their public duties. This assumption persists despite the fact that the U.S. Constitution has one provision protecting religious exercise, another provision separating church and state, and a vibrant history of judicial enforcement of religious liberty. Thus, in the United States and other countries with similar traditions of religious liberty, atheism often suffers from a quasi-legal cultural ostracism that is inconsistent with the principles that provide the justification for the formal legal protection of individual rights of conscience.

The scope of legal protection afforded atheists and agnostics within most existing democratic systems can best be understood by identifying two different but related aspects of religious liberty. The first involves protection from the imposition of direct governmental sanctions on the refusal to embrace religious faith. The second involves the prohibition of official government favoritism toward religion in general or toward a select group of religions in particular. Most modern constitutional democracies effectively enforce the first aspect of religious liberty; it is the second aspect of religious liberty that often receives inadequate protection. The details of both aspects of religious liberty are discussed below after a brief review of how atheists were treated during the period in which modern conceptions of religious liberty developed.

I. ATHEISM AND THE EARLY DEVELOPMENT OF RELIGIOUS LIBERTY

Prior to the development of modern conceptions of religious liberty, atheists had no effective legal protection. The legitimacy of premodern governments rested on claims of divine right, which were directly threatened by atheistic beliefs that denied the existence of the divinity. Because of the political threat posed by atheists, premodern governments denied any protection to atheists, and indeed targeted atheists for the most serious kinds of legal persecution. Philosophical support for this persecution is abundant in early Western philosophy. Western philosophers as diverse as Plato and Thomas Aquinas argued that atheism is inherently dangerous to the social and political culture and therefore should be punished as a crime against society. They argued that atheists should be excluded from the political culture, forcibly reeducated, and in some cases put to death.[1] The notion that the disbelief in God disqualifies the atheist from political participation or legal protection was common even among early humanists. Thomas More, for example, described a utopia in which religious tolerance would extend to all residents except those who did not believe in God or the immortality of the soul.[2]

The modern tradition of religious liberty in the West can be traced to the efforts of classical liberals, such as John Locke, who, like Thomas More, attempted to describe a legal regime in which the state would tolerate individual adherents of diverse religious creeds. Unlike his more illiberal predecessors, Locke did not advocate the execution of atheists. However, his tolerance was not complete. Although Locke's efforts to protect religious dissenters advanced the cause of liberty for religious believers who belonged to unpopular sects, Locke resembled his preliberal humanist predecessors in that he refused to grant atheists and agnostics the same political and legal rights and privileges enjoyed by their more devout fellow citizens. Locke would not kill atheists, but neither would he trust them with the full benefits of citizenship.

There is an ongoing debate about the reasons for Locke's reluctance to grant tolerance to atheists. Although modern theorists such as David A. J. Richards have attempted to salvage from Locke a form of tolerance that encompasses atheists as well as believers,[3] it is difficult to avoid the sectarian exclusionism of early liberal theory. Locke's stated reasons for refusing to tolerate certain groups were directly related to his conception of democracy. Locke denied protection to members of the Muslim and Catholic faiths, for example, because he believed that the members of those religious groups were inherently disloyal.[4] Locke believed that the members of those faiths instinctively owed allegiance to other sovereigns, and therefore could not be tolerated in a liberal democratic state. Like John Milton, Locke viewed Catholicism as "'a priestly despotism under the cloak of religion,' which 'extirpates all religious and civil supremacies.'"[5]

In contrast to his attitude toward Catholics and Muslims, Locke denied toleration to atheists not because atheists were traitors, but rather because atheists could not be trusted to uphold oaths and promises. "Promises, covenants, and oaths, which are the bonds of human society, can have no hold upon an atheist. The taking away of God, though but even in thought, dissolves all."[6] Locke focused on the perceived untrustworthiness of atheists in part because he believed that this characteristic is relevant to two areas of legitimate governmental concern: first, the government's ability to ensure that an atheist is capable of providing truthful testimony under oath in a court of law, and, second, the government's ability to enforce contractual promises. As to the latter interest, untrustworthy atheists threatened to undermine the ability of the new liberal governments to protect the economic marketplace that was developing in conjunction with the political structure of classical liberalism.[7]

Locke also argued that the tolerance of atheists would lead to other politically problematic consequences. In addition to undermining promises and oaths, Locke believed that permitting atheists to speak freely potentially could weaken the religious faith that is necessary for the general population to exercise sound moral judgment. Thus, atheism poses a direct threat to the civic virtue that is the political backbone of democratic liberalism. Locke believed that a democratic government has the authority to address the threat to its basic values by legally regulating atheism. From Locke's perspective, one must first accept the dominion of religion to obtain the fruits of religious tolerance. "[T]hose that by their atheism undermine and destroy all religion, can have no pretence of religion whereupon to challenge the privilege of a toleration."[8]

Whatever the rationale justifying intolerance of atheists, legal persecution of atheists was widespread in the early modern liberal states. In

England, for example, atheists continued to suffer severe legal disabilities until the end of the nineteenth century. There were several notorious public episodes that illustrate the government's discriminatory treatment of atheists. The poet Shelley, for example, was expelled from Oxford in 1811 after publishing a pamphlet entitled "The Necessity of Atheism." This tract also contributed to the British courts' decision to deny Shelley custody of his two children after the death of his first wife Harriet, a decision that was not an uncommon experience for avowed atheists. In addition to denying atheists custody of their children, British courts also denied atheists the right to give evidence in court. This legal disability was finally abandoned in 1869, with the passage of the Evidence Amendment Act.

Perhaps the most notorious instance of legal discrimination against an atheist during the nineteenth century was the exclusion of Charles Bradlaugh from the British Parliament. Bradlaugh was an avowed atheist and one of the founders of the National Secular Society. In 1880, Bradlaugh was elected to the House of Commons to represent Northampton. The House voted to deny Bradlaugh the right to affirm rather than swear on the Bible his oath of office, and expelled him from Parliament. Bradlaugh unsuccessfully attempted to take his seat in Parliament on several other occasions during the next decade. He was forcibly expelled from the House numerous times, fined for voting illegally, and once even imprisoned in the Tower of London. He was reelected three times – in 1881, 1882, and 1884 – and was finally seated in 1886 when the new Speaker of the House refused to interfere with his affirmation.

John Locke's reasons for refusing to extend legal toleration to atheists provided a common theoretical justification for the persecution of atheists in England during the nineteenth century. But in many ways, these official attacks on religious disbelief could not be sustained within the broader philosophical atmosphere created by the Enlightenment. The empiricism, intellectual skepticism, and scientific upheaval engendered by the Enlightenment, along with its larger social and economic context, made it increasingly difficult to sustain the strong legal protection of religious authority. Even during Locke's day, some of the philosophical literature reflected this tension.

Pierre Bayle was a contemporary of Locke's who wrote widely disseminated philosophical tracts on many of the same subjects of tolerance and religious liberty. Bayle went significantly beyond Locke, however, in applying the emerging Enlightenment intellectual framework to critique the legal protection of religious belief. Unlike Locke, Bayle argued that the government should not enforce religious belief through law, nor should the government refuse to extend theories of social and intellectual toleration to religious disbelief. Bayle argued that the same concept of individual autonomy that protects Protestants from oppression by Catholic political regimes (and vice versa) should also protect atheists from governments controlled by religious believers.

According to Bayle's version of tolerance theory, if one assumes that individuals are autonomous beings and that each individual has the right to make decisions about moral obligation and religious belief, then governments have a corresponding political duty to respect individual decisions about matters of religious faith. The government's duty to tolerate every citizen's interpretation of personal morality applies even if the individual arrives at the conclusion that God does not exist. Although Bayle's approach to religious liberty was characterized as a position of tolerance, it owed much more than Locke did to a modernist sensibility of intellectual skepticism rather than paternalistic forbearance. This sensibility inevitably produces a liberalizing effect on society. If the spirit of skepticism provides the intellectual framework of the modern world, then no collective entity (such as a government) has the intellectual authority to undercut that framework by imposing through law a particular set of debatable (and unprovable) precepts about the existence of God.

2. ATHEISM AND THE EARLY AMERICAN RELIGIOUS EXPERIENCE

It would take England and most other European countries over two hundred years after Locke wrote his "Letter Concerning Toleration" to extend religious tolerance to nonbelievers. In the United States, on the other hand, the situation was somewhat different. The differences were in some ways more favorable to the protection of atheists and in other ways less so. With the ratification of the U.S. Constitution in 1788 and the ratification of the Bill of Rights in 1791, the United States adopted the broadest possible articulation of the principle of religious liberty. The form of this protection logically extended to atheists. Indeed, the phrasing of the U.S. Constitution leaves religious decisions entirely to individual citizens and places religion outside the scope of the government's concern.

One of the enduring paradoxes of the American approach to religious liberty is that the country is both constitutionally secular and politically religious. On one hand, the United States was one of the first nations to adopt constitutional provisions explicitly insulating the government from religious influence. On the other hand, the United States also has a greater tendency than almost every other Western country to officially embrace religion and thereby politically ostracize atheists. The ostracism of atheists in the United States is social as well as political in nature, which is not surprising in a country in which the citizens have one of the highest rates of religious affiliation in the West. The political system in the United States directly reflects the religious beliefs and prejudices that prevail among the population at large. This phenomenon seems to contravene the constitutional prohibition on any government action "respecting" an establishment of religion. Despite the phrasing of the Constitution, however, the U.S. government frequently includes overt religious endorsements in many of its official pronouncements. Disputes over the legality of the government's endorsement of religious faith have been common throughout the country's history and continue to this day.

In many ways, the current conflicts over whether the U.S. government is primarily secular or religious reflect disputes that have defined the nation's political structure since its founding. The nation was founded in between two so-called Great Awakenings, during which religious devotion and fervor ran high. When the Constitution was ratified in 1788, six of the original thirteen states had some form of religious establishment. These state establishments usually took the form of mandatory tithes. In these states, citizens were required to pay a mandatory religious tax, which the state would collect and then forward to religious organizations. By the time the Constitution was adopted, all of the American states had abandoned European-style systems in which the government established a single church. In place of single establishments, the six American states that had some form of establishment had adopted so-called multiple establishments. Under this system, the states that maintained religious establishments would collect the religion taxes and then distribute the revenues to a church chosen by the taxpayer or on a proportional basis to every religious organization within the state based on the percentage of the population that belonged to each denomination. Atheists were automatically precluded from benefiting from this system of multiple establishments because atheists did not worship and therefore did not participate in formalized exercises of the sort that was financed by the religion taxes.

In contrast to the six states that still had some form of established religion, seven of the original thirteen states had abandoned any form of religious establishment by the time the Bill of Rights was ratified in 1791. Some of these states never had an official religious establishment at any time in their existence. Some states were founded by religious groups and persisted in their religious character, other states had never been religious, and still other states had been religious but had moved toward a secular model of governance. Thus, the United States had within its own borders a wide continuum of perspectives on religious liberty and the proper role of religion in public life.

One of the most important battles over religious establishments came in 1784–85 in the state of Virginia. This battle concerned Virginia Governor Patrick Henry's proposal to revive the Virginia system of multiple religious establishments.[9] James Madison was in the Virginia legislature at the time, and opposed the proposal. During the political battle over this legislation, Madison produced a document entitled the "Memorial and Remonstrance against Religious Establishments," which remains one of history's most forceful arguments against the alliance of religion and government. In the "Memorial," Madison reiterated the theory that religion is a private affair that is a protected aspect of individual autonomy, and should therefore be "exempt from [government's] cognizance."[10] Madison argued that multiple establishments were just as oppressive as single establishments because "Who does not see that the same authority which can establish Christianity, in exclusion of all other Religions, may establish with the same ease any particular sect of Christians, in exclusion of all other Sects?"[11] He also expressed in very harsh terms the tendency of religiously based governments to debase both religion and government:

During almost fifteen centuries has the legal establishment of Christianity been on trial. What have been its fruits? More or less in all places, pride and indolence in the Clergy, ignorance and servility in the laity, in both, superstition, bigotry and persecution.... What influence in fact have ecclesiastical establishments had on Civil Society? In some instances they have been seen to erect a spiritual tyranny on the ruins of the Civil authority; in many instances they have been seen upholding the thrones of political tyranny: in no instance have they been seen the guardians of the liberties of the people. Rulers, who wished to subvert the public liberty, may have found an established Clergy convenient auxiliaries.[12]

The effect of the "Memorial" was immediate. Within a year, the Virginia legislature rejected the governor's proposal to collect a religion tax, and instead enacted Thomas Jefferson's "Act for Establishing Religious Freedom." The operative provision of this act states:

[N]o man shall be compelled to frequent or support any religious worship, place, or ministry whatsoever, nor shall be enforced, restrained, molested, or burthened in his body or goods, nor shall otherwise suffer on account of his religious opinions or belief; but that all men shall be free to profess, and by argument to maintain, their opinion in matters of religion, and that the same shall in no wise diminish, enlarge, or affect their civil capacities.[13]

The Virginia experience and its strong articulation of religious liberty would greatly affect the legal landscape of the nation as a whole. It also provided a theoretical justification for extending religious liberty protections to atheists. Unlike many earlier arguments for religious liberty, the "Memorial" phrased the concept in terms of freedom *from* religion as well as freedom *of* religion. A few years later James Madison would move on to Congress in Washington, where he would draft the Bill of Rights. The Virginia battle provided Madison with a rich backdrop (and some specific language) for the religion clauses of the First Amendment.

Thomas Jefferson would also play a large role in the development of American religious liberty, and its extension to atheists. When Jefferson campaigned for President in 1800, his political opponents focused a great deal of attention on his religious beliefs. Jefferson was not an atheist, but he had very liberal views for the time. He was a deist; he believed in a naturalistic God who did not intervene directly in human affairs. Jefferson even composed a version of the Bible that excluded all references to miracles, the virgin birth, the divinity of Jesus, and the resurrection. Jefferson's political opponents routinely alleged that Jefferson was an atheist, and Jefferson's religious views were a focal point of political attacks on him. One set of slogans used by Jefferson's opponents in the presidential election of 1800 urged voters to choose "God – and a Religious President ... [or] Jefferson, and no God."[14] Another opponent, who was also a Dutch Reformed minister, issued a pamphlet in which he argued, "On account of his disbelief in the Holy Scriptures, and his attempts to discredit them, [Jefferson] ought to be rejected from the Presidency."[15]

Jefferson won the presidency despite these attacks, and while serving as President he made several efforts to enshrine his views of religious liberty in the law. Unlike other Presidents, Jefferson steadfastly refused to issue religious proclamations or proclaim official days of prayer or thanksgiving. His most famous pronouncement on the subject of religion and government was contained in a letter sent to the Danbury, Connecticut, Baptists, in which Jefferson argued that the Constitution had built "a wall of separation between Church and State."[16] Almost a century later, the Supreme Court would write that this statement "may be accepted almost as an authoritative declaration of the scope and effect of the [First] amendment."[17]

It seems clear that the two major figures in the development of the American constitutional guarantees of religious freedom intended to create a secular government, which neither advanced religion nor discriminated against it. Under such a regime, atheists would be granted full political rights and allowed to participate in public life on equal terms with religious believers. But in contrast to Jefferson's and Madison's detailed theoretical approach to the issue of religious liberty, the country continued to be divided along religious lines. It is telling that Jefferson's political opponents believed that it would be an effective political tactic to assert that Jefferson was an atheist. These attacks indicate that a substantial part of the American political constituency viewed atheism as a disqualification for political office. These attacks also indicate the depth of feeling among members of the religious majority in the United States during the early years of the country's existence, and reveal how reluctant the religious majority was to concede political power to those outside the religious fold. These debates have not yet abated.

The continuing debate over the relative merits of religious and secular politics produces contrasting paradoxes in the United States and other Western countries. In many ways, the debate in Western countries other than the United States has been definitively settled in favor of greater effective freedom for atheists. In the United States, on the other hand, the political context is much the same as it was in 1800, with the country bitterly divided along religious lines. Those on the religious side of the dividing line continue to assert that the government is "under God" and that atheism is incompatible with the nation's basic spirit. The paradox is that the U.S. Constitution contains some of the strongest secular mandates of any governing document in a modern Western democracy. Thus, the strong protection of religious liberty for atheists in the legal culture contrasts sharply with the effective exclusion of atheists from the political culture. The following passage from Alexis de Tocqueville's early nineteenth-century book *Democracy in America* provides a remarkably accurate description of modern America:

In the United States it is not only mores that are controlled by religion, but its sway extends even over reason. Among the Anglo-Americans there are some who profess Christian dogmas because they believe them and others who do so because they are afraid to look as though they did not believe in them. So Christianity reigns without obstacles, by universal consent; consequently, as I have said elsewhere, everything in the moral field is certain and fixed, although the world of politics seems given over to argument and experiment.[18]

The contrasts between the treatment of atheists in the United States and other Western countries is explored below using a framework that divides the legal protection of nonbelievers into two categories. The first category describes the legal protection of atheistic beliefs, expressions, and practices. The second category describes the legal constraints on incorporating religion into the government's structure and legal policies.

3. ATHEISM AND THE PROTECTION OF INDIVIDUAL RELIGIOUS LIBERTY

Legal protection of atheism and atheists is now the norm in modern Western constitutional democracies, at least in the sense that courts do not permit governments to impose legal sanctions on individuals simply for expressing atheistic ideas or denying the existence of God. This broad legal protection of nonbelievers is a relatively recent phenomenon. As noted above, the British government routinely discriminated against atheists in a range of different legal contexts as recently as the nineteenth century. Until the latter part of the century, atheists could not give evidence in court or be seated in Parliament. The American experience was similar. Tocqueville reports witnessing a trial in New York in 1831, for example, in which a witness "did not believe in the existence of God and denied the immortality of the soul. The judge refused to allow him to be sworn in, on the ground that the witness had destroyed beforehand all possible confidence in his testimony."[19]

Such episodes are rare in most Western countries today, in large part because of the profusion of constitutional provisions that explicitly prohibit governments from punishing individuals for their beliefs and expression about religious ideas, including atheistic ideas. The U.S. Constitution, for example, states that "no religious Test shall ever be required as a Qualification to any Office or public Trust."[20] The First Amendment to the Constitution also denies government the authority to "prohibit the free exercise" of religion.[21] European constitutions have similar provisions. Article 9 of the European Convention of Human Rights states, "Everyone has the right to freedom of thought, conscience and religion; this right includes freedom to change his religion or belief and freedom . . . to manifest his religion or belief, in worship, teaching, practice and observance." Article 14 of the convention prohibits discrimination on the basis of religion.

Both the U.S. Constitution and the European Convention refer to religion and religious adherents, without specifying whether the same rights and freedoms extend to atheists. In contrast, some domestic constitutions governing individual European countries specifically mention the freedom to be nonreligious. Article 4 of the German Basic Law (which is the German Constitution) recognizes that "Freedom of creed, of conscience, and freedom to profess a religious or nonreligious faith are inviolable."[22] Article 136 of the Basic Law states that civil and political rights may not depend on the exercise of religion and that no one is bound to reveal his or her religious affiliations or perform any religious act or oath. Similarly, the Hungarian Constitution protects both the "freedom of conscience and freedom of religion," and specifically protects the "freedom to publicly or privately express or decline to express, exercise and teach such religions and beliefs."[23] The Belgian Constitution states, "No one can be obliged to contribute in any way whatsoever to the acts and ceremonies of a religion, nor to observe the days of rest."[24] The Russian Constitution guarantees "the right to profess, individually or jointly with others, any religion, or to profess no religion."[25]

Each of these constitutional provisions, including the provisions that do not specifically mention the freedom to practice atheism, is broad enough to protect atheists from the sorts of overt legal sanctions or legal disabilities that were common prior to the twentieth century. It should be noted, however, that there are very few reported instances in which atheists have attempted to enforce these constitutional rights in judicial proceedings. Cultural factors may have made judicial enforcement of these rights unnecessary in many jurisdictions. These factors include the growing secularization of European culture and various aspects of globalization, which has resulted in increased migration across national borders and the diversification of formerly homogeneous societies. As a result, overt legal discrimination against atheists is no longer common in most industrialized Western countries.

The more common source of legal action against atheists occurs when atheistic or antireligious ideas are expressed in a fashion that offends the sensibilities of the dominant religious culture. Great Britain, for example, maintains the common-law crime of blasphemy. This crime applies to any publication that contains "any contemptuous, reviling, scurrilous or ludicrous matter relating to God, Jesus Christ or the Bible, or the formularies of the Church of England as by law established."[26] The crime applies to the manner and form of antireligious speech, rather than the content. Thus, religion may be criticized, but only in "decent and temperate language."[27] The House of Lords upheld a conviction for this crime in 1979,[28] and in 1996 the European Court for Human Rights ruled in another case that British blasphemy law does not violate the free speech protections of Article 10 of the European Convention of Human Rights.[29]

British blasphemy law applies only to expressive attacks on Christianity. Other laws in Britain and continental European countries provide for criminal sanctions for expressing religious hatred generally. The problem with all these laws is that they are so vaguely phrased that they could easily be used (as in the British blasphemy prosecutions) to suppress abstract beliefs about religion in general as well as direct threats against particular religious practitioners. Atheistic speech – which often denies the coherence or rationality of religious belief – may be susceptible to criminal sanctions under such a legal regime. Thus, public discussion of religious ideas is subtly skewed in favor of religion by legally mandating deference to religious ideas to which a nonbeliever strenuously objects.

The proliferation of speech regulations that encompass religious speech indicates that the religious exercise protections in most modern constitutions may be less important in protecting the liberty of atheists than the generic free speech and free expression protections of the same constitutions. The First Amendment to the U.S. Constitution contains such a provision, which has been interpreted to prohibit any government censorship of the viewpoint of those speaking on religious topics. European constitutions contain similar provisions, although as the recent British blasphemy decision indicates, these provisions are not yet as protective of religiously antagonistic speech as the American First Amendment. The general principle nevertheless has been recognized. As a concurring opinion in a recent European Court decision recently noted, the "religious dimension" of freedom of expression constitutes "one of the most vital elements that go to make up the identity of believers and their conception of life, but it is also a precious asset for atheists, agnostics, skeptics and the unconcerned."[30]

4. ATHEISM AND GOVERNMENTAL ENDORSEMENT OF RELIGION

A second aspect of religious liberty in modern Western legal systems involves constitutional and other legal constraints preventing governments from incorporating religion into their policies and laws. In many respects, these structural constraints are even more important than direct protections from religious coercion. Structural constraints prevent governments from subtly reinforcing patterns of religious favoritism and discrimination against atheists that are prevalent in civil society. Structural constraints also prevent governments from comprehensively incorporating religion into public affairs in a manner that effectively denies atheists full participation in the political culture.

A brief example from the American constitutional jurisprudence will illustrate the last point. The First Amendment to the U.S. Constitution prohibits the government from passing any law "respecting an establishment of religion."[31] For many years the Supreme Court has interpreted this phrase to prohibit the government from passing any law or engaging in any activity that has the purpose or effect of endorsing religion. This broad rule is justified by the need to protect the political process from religious domination. "Endorsement sends a message to nonadherents that they are outsiders, not full members of the political community, and an accompanying message to adherents that they are insiders, favored members of the political community. Disapproval sends the opposite message."[32] These messages of inclusion and exclusion are problematic from a political standpoint because they impermissibly "make religion relevant, in reality or public perception, to status in the political community."[33]

In many ways, the insulation of the political process from religion is the single most important legal mechanism for the protection of religious liberty. The incorporation of religious principles into government policies or the use of religious overtures or symbolism in official pronouncements or insignia inevitably distorts the intellectual marketplace in a way that subtly undercuts the equality between religion and atheism that is the sine qua non of religious liberty. Separation of church and state can thus be viewed as an indispensable prerequisite to a system of religious liberty.

Most European constitutions now mandate the separation of church and state. The most recent example of the trend in Europe is the new draft of the European Constitution. The drafters of the proposed Constitution rejected calls from the Catholic Church and other religious groups to recognize Europe's Christian roots. God and religion were omitted from the document, as was any mention of a state church. The various national constitutions throughout Europe are mostly to the same effect. According to the German Basic Law, for example, "There is no state church."[34] The French Constitution begins by noting that "France is an indivisible, secular, democratic and social Republic."[35] The principle of *laïcité* – or "secularism" – has been central to the French political self-conception for at least a century, and the same principle now defines the political landscape throughout Europe.

Despite these formal renunciations of religious establishments, many European countries continue to involve the state in religion, especially religious education. Although it does not have a state church, for example, the Belgian government finances religious education, and the Belgian Constitution states, "All pupils of school age have the right to moral or religious education at the Community's expense."[36] Likewise, although the German Basic Law renounces the concept of an established church, it is common for German schools in some *Länder* (states) to teach explicitly Christian values in state schools. Even the French government, which has probably the most secularized political structure of any European country, provides state financing for the maintenance of certain religious structures and permits Catholic priests and nuns to engage in religious counseling on the premises of state schools.

None of these deviations from the norm of governmental secularism comes close to disenfranchising atheists, as was common prior to the twentieth century. Nevertheless, these instances of governmental assistance to religion place gentle pressure on the social scale in favor of religion and against the values of those who reject religious faith. More important, government financial support of religious schools and other enterprises directly coerces atheists, in that nonreligious citizens are being forced to support financially (through their taxes) religious enterprises whose primary objectives are anathema to atheists. Under any analysis this involves a direct affront to the religious liberty of atheists.

Perhaps these examples are merely the residue of an earlier political era in which church and state were complementary institutions. Today almost every Western country has accepted the principle of modern constitutional democracy, which requires the complete secularization of government. Determining how the principle of secularism should be applied to particular social or educational programs will require revisiting longstanding social practices in light of the new secular political reality. This may lead to the elimination of many political benefits that governments have historically bestowed upon the church.

In many ways the Europeans face a simpler task than those in the United States in reconciling their traditions of support for religion with new secular constitutions. In contrast to Europe, the United States operates in a political atmosphere that is deeply contradictory. On the one hand, the United States operates under one of the oldest constitutional mandates of religious disestablishment, has a specific constitutional provision prohibiting religious tests for public office, and draws on an honored legacy of constitutional theory articulating the need for a "wall separating church and state." In these respects, atheists are afforded religious liberty on a par with traditional religious adherents. On the other hand, the political culture in the United States is infused with obligatory expressions of public piety, much of the population views atheism as antisocial if not unpatriotic, and the government has responded to the religious views of the population by overtly endorsing religious values. The government has gone so far as to insert the words "under God" in the official Pledge of Allegiance and place "in God we trust" on its currency. In these respects, atheists are effectively precluded from participating fully in the public life of their country, which is another way of saying that atheists do not yet possess the full measure of religious liberty granted to their fellow citizens.

CONCLUSION

The religious liberty of atheists has come a long way since the days in which serious political theorists could argue that atheists should be put to death, denied the ability to give evidence in court, or prohibited from becoming a Member of Parliament. But as the experience in the United States illustrates, protecting atheists from criminal punishments or other legal sanctions is not sufficient to protect their liberty. Atheists will not enjoy the same religious liberty as religious adherents unless the government under which they live is comprehensively secularized. This does not mean enshrining atheism as the new state religion. As the U.S. Supreme Court once observed, "A secular state, it must be remembered, is not the same as an atheistic or antireligious state. A secular state establishes neither atheism nor religion as its official creed."[37] Only a government defined in terms of collective agnosticism can ensure the conditions of liberty in which individual believers and nonbelievers can coexist peacefully in order to pursue their own personal visions of the ultimate good.

NOTES

1. See, e.g., Plato's extensive discussion of the proper treatment of the impious in Book X of *The Laws*. Plato, *The Laws of Plato*, ed. Thomas L. Pangle (New York: Basic Books, 1980), pp. 280–311.

2. More's utopians believed that anyone denying the immortality of the soul "has degraded the sublimity of his own soul to the base level of a beast's wretched body. Still less will they count him as one of their citizens, since he would openly despise all the laws and customs of society, if not prevented by fear." Thomas More, *Utopia*, ed. George M. Logan and Robert M. Adams (Cambridge: Cambridge University Press, 1975), p. 95.

3. See David A. J. Richards, *Toleration and the Constitution* (Oxford: Oxford University Press, 1989).

4. John Locke, *A Letter Concerning Toleration*, ed. Mario Montuori (The Hague: Martinus Nijhoff, 1963), pp. 91–93.

5. Christopher Hill, *Milton and the English Revolution* (London: Penguin, 1977), p. 155.

6. Locke, *A Letter Concerning Toleration*, p. 93.

7. For the classic discussion of the linkage between Locke's political and economic theories of classical liberalism, see C. B. MacPherson, *The Political Theory of Possessive Individualism* (Oxford: Oxford University Press, 1964).

8. Locke, *A Letter Concerning Toleration*, p. 93.

9. For a succinct account of the battle in Virigina, see Leonard Levy, *The Establishment Clause: Religion and the First Amendment* (New York: Macmillan, 1986), pp. 51–62. The book also contains one of the best surveys of the different approaches to religious establishment taken by the various states in the early republic.

10. James Madison, *Memorial and Remonstrance against Religious Establishments* (1785), para. 1, reprinted in *Everson v. Bd. of Educ.*, 330 U.S. 1, 63 (1947).

11. Ibid., para. 3.

12. Ibid., paras. 7–8.

13. Thomas Jefferson, "A Bill for Establishing Religious Freedom," in Merrill D. Peterson (ed.), *The Portable Thomas Jefferson* (New York: Penguin, 1975), p. 253.

14. Frank Lambert, *The Founding Fathers and the Place of Religion in America* (Princeton: Princeton University Press, 2003), pp. 276–77.

15. Ibid., p. 265.

16. Thomas Jefferson, "Letter to Nehemiah Dodge and Others, a Committee of the Danbury Baptist Association, in the State of Connecticut," in Peterson (ed.), *The Portable Thomas Jefferson*, p. 303.

17. *Reynolds v. United States*, 98 U.S. 145, 164 (1878).

18. Alexis de Tocqueville, *Democracy in America*, ed. J. P. Mayer, trans. George Lawrence (New York: Perennial, 1969), p. 292.
19. Ibid., p. 293.
20. U.S. Constitution, article VI, sec. 3.
21. U.S. Constitution, amendment I.
22. German Basic Law, article 4.
23. Hungarian Constitution, article 60.
24. Belgian Constitution, article 20.
25. Russian Constitution, article 28.
26. *Regina v. Lemon* [1979] Appeal Cases 617, 665.
27. Ibid.
28. The 1979 case involved a poem published in the London tabloid *Gay News*, which suggested that Jesus had engaged in sexual relations with his disciples and the Roman Centurions who presided over his crucifixion.
29. See *Wingrove v. United Kingdom*, 24 Eur. H.R. Rep. 1 (1997). This case involved the video *Visions of Ecstasy*, which contained a fictional depiction of a nun's erotic fantasies, including one with the figure of the crucified Christ.
30. *Kokkinakis v. Greece*, 17 Eur. H.R. Rep. 397, 418 (1994) (Mr. Loucaides, concurring).
31. U.S. Constitution, amendment I.
32. *Wallace v. Jaffree*, 472 U.S. 38, 68 (1985) (O'Connor, J., concurring).
33. Ibid.
34. German Basic Law, article 137.
35. French Constitution, article 1.
36. Belgian Constitution, article 24 (3.2).
37. *County of Allegheny v. ACLU*, 492 U.S. 573, 610 (1989).

16 Atheism, A/theology, and the Postmodern Condition

"Postmodernism" seems for all the world to religious believers as a continuation of Nietzsche by another means, the latest version of the idea that God is dead and everything is permitted. It has been vigorously attacked by the Christian right as a diabolical enemy of religion, a frivolous skepticism that undermines the possibility of any absolute – God, truth, or morality – and leaves us exposed to the wolves of relativism.[1] When Jean-François Lyotard described postmodernism as "incredulity toward grand narratives (*grands récits*),"[2] to take a famous example, he pitted it against the consolations of religious faith in divine providence, in a God who keeps an omnipotent and omniscient watch over the world, working all things wisely and to the good, which must surely be the grandest of the old, grand narratives. We just do not believe that sort of thing any more, Lyotard thinks; the old faith has become unbelievable.

But while it is perfectly true that in some of its incarnations postmodernism makes life difficult for traditional believers, it is no less true that it complicates the life of modern atheism. For, as Jacques Derrida says, we must keep a watchful eye for "theological prejudices" not only in theology, where they are overt, but no less in "metaphysics in its entirety, even when it professes to be atheist."[3] So Derrida warns us about the theologians of atheistic metaphysics! Theology reaches further than the divinity schools; it has to do with the very idea of a fixed center. That is why, on closer examination, postmodernism turns out to be not a particularly friendly environment for atheism, either, not if atheism is a metaphysical or an otherwise fixed and decisive denial of God. Thus a version of postmodern thinking has emerged recently that unnerves the religious right and a lot of secularizing postmodernists alike, neither of whom saw it coming, one that identifies "modernity" with "secularization" and sees in "postmodernity" an opening to the "postsecular" and even to a "postmodern theology."

Those complex interweavings are what I hope to sort out in what follows.

But first a word about the word: "postmodern." Originally coined in architecture to signify a mélange of modernism and historical citation, it was given philosophical currency by Lyotard in *The Postmodern Condition*. Derrida himself rejects the word both because it suggests an easy historical periodization and something *anti*-Enlightenment instead of a *new* Enlightenment, a continuation of the Enlightenment by another means.[4] For better or for worse the word has established itself, and while we can agree that it has been beaten senseless by overuse, we can for the purposes of this study locate its strictly philosophical content in a cluster of three ideas: (1) the affirmation of radical and irreducible pluralism (of what Lyotard calls "paganism"), (2) the rejection of an overarching, metaphysical, or foundational schema (of what Lyotard calls "monotheism" and Derrida calls "theology"), and (3) a suspicion of fixed binary categories that describe rigorously separable regions (typically characteristic of "structuralism"[5]).

(1) Although the American historian and philosopher of science Thomas Kuhn had nothing to do personally with the movement, Kuhn's seminal idea of scientific change as a series of holistic switches among "incommensurable" paradigms that resist one-to-one comparison is highly congenial to postmodern ways of thinking. This shows up in the use of Kuhn's ideas by Richard Rorty,[6] the foremost American philosopher associated with the postmodern style of thinking. By the same token, Wittgenstein's theory of an irreducible complex of "language games," which is also important to Rorty, was also adapted by Lyotard. (Generally speaking, as a philosophical idea, French and Franco-American postmodern thought corresponds to what in Anglo-America is called "nonfoundationalism.")

(2) Hegel is no doubt the high-water mark of modern "metaphysics" for postmodernists. Postmodernists share Hegel's critique of Enlightenment rationality as an abstract and ahistorical principle in favor of the complex, concrete rationality of social existence (*Sittlichkeit*); and they are (like Derrida) impressed enough by Hegel to look for ways to read Hegel against the grain. But in the end they see the Hegelian critique of the Enlightenment as one form of modernism being criticized by another. Like Kierkegaard before them – in this regard Kierkegaard is the first postmodernist – they reject Hegel's idea of absolute knowledge, of history and nature as the unfolding of a single absolute principle making its way through time and space. From an epistemological point of view they are, as Lyotard says, "incredulous" about such an overreaching meta-narrative, but from an ethical point of view they view it as obscene, since it is implicated in finding some sort of rationale for "Auschwitz," taken both as the historical reality and an emblem for genocide, for any "unthinkable" evil.

(3) Inasmuch as Hegelian metaphysics is premised on a logic of opposition, of categories that contradict and mutually exclude each other (such as "being" and "nonbeing"), the reconciliation of which generates the movement of dialectical logic ("becoming"), postmodern thinkers set about eroding such neat binary oppositions to begin with, thus preventing dialectical logic from ever engaging its gears of reconciliation in the first place. This strategy was put forth in 1962 by Gilles Deleuze in his *Nietzsche* book. Deleuze, seeing that simply to oppose Hegel is grist for the mill of dialectics, which turns on a logic of opposition,[7] formulated a logic of difference. The model for this is found in de Saussure's account of linguistic difference. Signifiers function just in virtue of the discernible difference, the phonic and graphic "space" or "play" between "signifiers." Thus the differences among ring/sing/king are discernible and significant, but not binary or contradictory, and neither require nor inspire any reconciliation.

While the postmodern critique of these assumptions produces results that are very antagonistic to traditional religious beliefs, the results are no less damaging for the atheistic critique of religion, which is why Derrida warns us about the theology of atheistic metaphysics. In fact, classical atheism comes under fire on all three points. (1) Given a plurality of incommensurable discourses, there is nothing to stop religious discourse from reasserting its rights as an irreducible discursive form against nineteenth-century modernist critiques of religion, a point made by Wittgenstein, among others.[8] (2) Given the demise of sweeping metaphysical meta-narratives, the simple atheistic dissolution or dogmatic reduction of religion to one big idea, such as the sigh of the oppressed (Marx), a psychotic fantasy (Freud), or the resentment of the weak against the strong (Nietzsche), is sheer overreaching. (3) Finally, the doubt thrown by postmodernists on binary pairs, which affects theological oppositions such as God/world, soul/body, or eternity/time, has no less an erosive effect on any clean distinction between theism and atheism or the religious and the secular. The characteristic postmodern move is made in what Mark C. Taylor calls "a/theology," something situated on the slash between theism and atheism, in a space of undecidability before things are definitively settled one way or the other, in the milieu in which any such decision can be made.[9]

Whence the dilemma of theism/atheism in a postmodern setting. "Modernity" is marked by a strict sense of boundaries – the rigorous discriminations in Kant's three critiques are exemplary of modernity in this regard – in which religious faith is cordoned off as something subjective, not objective, and private, not public, and finally reduced to something irrational or devoid of cognitive worth, the effect of which is summarized under the notion of "secularization," the disenchantment of the world, in Max Weber's phrase. But the postmodern view of things is to distrust such neat borders. So if modernity culminates in a decisive "death of God," in "the end of an illusion," then postmodernists expose the "illusion of the end," the end of big stories about the end, the death of the death of God. But then the question is, if postmodernists make trouble for both religious belief and antireligious disbelief, where does that leave us?

The place to start in any account of the fortunes of God in postmodern thought is Friedrich Nietzsche's notion of the "death of God,"[10] for Nietzsche more than anyone else is responsible for the atheistic side of postmodern thought. In the narrowest sense, Nietzsche was referring to what Kierkegaard complained about under the term "Christendom": in the increasingly secular and bourgeois world of the nineteenth century, religious faith had become, or was fast becoming – the statement was as much predictive as descriptive – moribund. Kierkegaard and Nietzsche are the two nineteenth-century background figures of contemporary postmodern thought, which is why it (like existentialism before it) has both religious and antireligious versions. Of this great event Nietzsche will have been the prophet. But as with most prophecies, the results have been uneven. While something like that might be happening in Western Europe, nothing of the sort has happened in the United States, not to mention South America, the Middle East, Asia, Africa, or the post-Soviet Eastern Bloc. Sociologists who wrote about the "secularization" of America in the 1960s were soon sent scurrying back to the drawing board to write about its "desecularization."[11]

More broadly, the death of God meant the demise of the "ascetical ideal," of belief in any sort of absolute center or unshakable foundation. This ideal includes not only theology but also metaphysics, and not only metaphysics but also physics, which is also an "interpretation," and even grammar (we shall not be rid of God until we are rid of grammar).[12] That is what Derrida meant when he spoke of the "theology" of atheistic metaphysics, which turns on the "theological" idea of an absolute center – even if the center is physics or grammar, both of which are menaced by a thinly disguised theological absolutism. To be sure, this very Nietzschean critique of God (of metaphysical theology) provides an opening for postmetaphysical religion, for by denying metaphysical knowledge, Nietzsche (like Kant) unavoidably makes room for faith. In the place of anything absolute and a priori Nietzsche himself put a kind of animal faith in fictions (hypotheses) that we produce to promote and enhance life, to push the drive to life (conatus essendi), the "will-to-power," to ever new heights. Each thing has its own drive or local force – its "perspective" – and the world is a multiplicity of competing perspectives. Ideas have not "truth" but "value," that is, an effectiveness that is measured by their capacity to enhance life. The idea of "God" is a spent perspective, an idea once vital – it played a role in disciplining the will – that has turned inward and become destructive ("bad conscience"), life-denying, a longing for death and another world outside the strife of time and corporeality.

Insofar as we fail to recognize that the Platonic-Christian idea of God is a decadent perspective, a value that has lost all value, nihilism (the devaluation of all values) reigns. Nietzsche's prescription is an active nihilism, the active destruction of the preachers of death, in order to permit the joyous affirmation of becoming and bodily life in the very face of its mutability. Nietzsche is indeed a strident "atheist" and a prophet of the death of God, if that means the God of Paul and Augustine, of Luther and Calvin, which are morbid expressions of death and decay. But as a perspectivist he is not an atheist about the gods of Greek and Roman mythology, or even about a warlike tribal Yahweh, which are for him so many healthy fictions, ways that ancient poets have invented to honor the earth and give thanks for life. Indeed Nietzsche's entire thought is emblematized under the name of a god – Dionysus – whom he opposes to "The Crucified."

Nietzsche's point about God, grammar, and the ascetic ideal may be seen in the work of Gilles Deleuze's philosophy of sheer becoming, of the "plane of immanence." When we say "it's raining," do not be seduced by grammar into positing some "it" that is the subject of the action; do not separate the doer from the deed. To adhere rigorously to the plane of immanence thus is to affirm the "univocity of being" (Scotus) as a play of differences (Nietzsche) of infinitely varying intensities, of surfaces without depth. Philosophy must avoid the illusion of positing some transcendent point beneath difference that stabilizes becoming, like a substance, or above difference that imposes difference on some indifferent substrate below, like God, or that produces differences as mental constructs, as in epistemological representationalism, or as systemic effects of the opposing signifiers, as in structuralism. Those are just so many variations on the idea of a stabilizing center. Becoming demands not transcendent explanations, like God or mind, but transcendental ones, cultivated immanently from within the "events" or differences themselves. However, Deleuze adds a twist: we can willingly embrace the illusionary link of God and grammar with our eyes wide open, miming it and enjoying the play of simulacra. Our age has "discovered theology" as "the science of nonexisting entities that animate language and give our lives a buzz or glow, like reading *Alice in Wonderland*.[13]

The pivotal figure for any discussion of God in the twentieth century continental thought is Martin Heidegger whose project of "overcoming metaphysics" stakes out the space within which twentieth-century continental thought takes place. In his early writings, culminating in *Being and Time* (1927), Heidegger constructed an existential ontology that is a "formalization" of both Aristotle's man of practical wisdom (*Nichomachean Ethics*) and the early Christian experience of time contained in the Pauline letters. In this ontology, Heidegger said, we must practice a "methodological atheism,"[14] a systematic suspension, or *epoche*, of the data of revelation and faith in God, in order to isolate the formal structure of the "factical life" of Dasein. While the account of "authentic Dasein" in *Being and Time* is drawn from a reading of Paul, Augustine, and Kierkegaard, Heidegger insists that it is methodologically neutral, providing an existential ontological ground on whose basis one may make the "ontic" choice either for or against God, or immortalty, or a particular ethical ideal. The latter are matters to be decided by each existing individual, not by a formal ontology.

In his later writings, Heidegger shifts to the point of view of what he calls the "history of Being." Being was originally illuminated for but a moment in the "early Greek" (pre-Socratic) experience embodied in words of elemental power, such as *logos*, *physis*, and *aletheia*, and then gradually occluded by the rising tide of metaphysics. In metaphysics, the "subject" represents an "object" (*Gegenstand*), which is a latent tendency of Greek and medieval metaphysics that awoke explicitly in Descartes and modernity. Accordingly, eighteenth-century "onto-theo-logic," a science of God as the *causa sui* (like Pascal's "the God of the philosophers"), is a typically modern creation in which God is already as good as dead. Metaphysics is finally unleashed in all its fury in the essence of contemporary technology, in which the world and human being itself have become the raw material (*Bestand*) for the technological domination of the earth. Technology brings to completion what Nietzsche's called the "death of God" and "nihilism," now redefined as the time of need in which Being has been emptied of its true power. To this state of extreme depletion and oblivion, Heidegger opposes the possibility of another beginning. This he characterizes in terms of a new coming of the "holy" and the gods, so that an "atheism" about the God of onto-theo-logic (metaphysics) is in fact closer to the "truly divine God," by which he means dwelling poetically as mortals, on the earth, under the skies, and before the gods, a portrait drawn chiefly from the poetry of Hölderlin.[15]

By the death of God, then, Heidegger understands the technological darkening of the earth, and by the return of the holy a purely poetic experience that is closer to German Romanticism than to biblical faith. About the God of the Jewish and Christian scriptures one could observe a perfect "atheism" were one so minded, declaring this God to be part and parcel of the history of metaphysical oblivion, as secular Heideggerians do. But by the same token, what the later Heidegger says about language, meditative thinking, the holy, and overcoming onto-theology, is so evocative that Derrida was able to construct a fictional dialogue of Christian theologians with the later Heidegger, in which the theologians confess that this is just what they have been saying all along.[16]

Heidegger's most strident critic is Emmanuel Levinas whose thought is mobilized around a massive critique of "ontology," the paradigmatic representatives of which are Hegel and Heidegger. Levinas's critique is cast – contra Heidegger – in language that has such an unmistakably biblical resonance that it occasioned Dominique Janicaud to complain about the "theological turn" it precipitated in French phenomenology.[17] By ontology Levinas understood a thinking that remains "riveted" to Being, trapped inside the categories of being, almost claustrophobically, against which he posed the necessity to "escape" by thinking what is "otherwise than being."[18] "Being" means the brutal order of reality, the way things are done in the world (paganism), what he and Nietzsche following Spinoza called the *conatus essendi*. But what is "otherwise than Being" is the Good, *epekeinas tes ousias*, although definitely not in the strictly Platonic sense of an eternal transcendent metaphysical structure, in a world beyond this world, about which Levinas was as atheistic as Nietzsche.

By the Good he means something rather more Kantian than Platonic, the ought rather than the is; but all this is developed with a markedly biblical tone. Because God hides his face from us, we are turned to the face of the neighbor, which is marked by the trace of the withdrawn God, who is said to be "wholly other" (*tout autre*). Now the perplexing thing about Levinas is how closely his thought approaches what might be called a "death of God theology."[19] Like Kant's Enlightenment critique of religion, Levinas thinks that religion is ethics and the rest is superstition.[20] God is nothing more than the very order that orders us to the neighbor. To turn to God is to be returned to the neighbor. God is the law, the moral order of things, a kind of *ordo ordinans*, but not a being outside time and space, lest God be "contaminated" by being. God is an imperative issued from the depths of the face of the neighbor, but God is neither being itself nor some sort of higher being or person beyond the persons and beings we encounter in reality (being). Our being turned to God (*à-Dieu*) is our being returned to the neighbor, and that is all the God there is. God commands but God does not exist. About the separate and supreme being of classical theology, Levinas (the most theological resource of postmodern thinkers) is no less than Nietzsche (their most antitheological resource) an atheist.

Things certainly do not get less complicated with Jacques Derrida, who is to all appearances a secularized Jew and leftist intellectual who thinks that religion is a neurosis, and who says of himself that he "rightly passes for an atheist."[21] But it is in Derrida, more than in any other postmodern figure, that the undecidability between theism and atheism is the most intense and the distinction the most porous and unstable. For Derrida says that he prays all the time; he speaks of his faith in the pure "messianic" and of a "religion without religion," and he adds that while he "rightly passes" for an atheist, he has no way to know if he really *is* one.

In his earlier writings Derrida criticized the idea of God as a dream of plenitude, of "presence without difference" that brings the "play of signifiers" to rest in an absolute foundation, as an attempt to find refuge in "the encyclopedic protection of theology." All this seems to implicate his critique of the "metaphysics of presence" in religious skepticism and perhaps outright atheism.[22] At the very same time, Derrida was being accused of (or congratulated for) being a negative theologian. When he described *différance* as itself neither a word nor a concept, but the quasi-transcendental condition of possibility of words and concepts, that sounded to some a lot like the *deus absconditus* of negative theology. Both implications are incorrect. *Différance* withdraws from view not because it is a being beyond being (*hyperousios*), or a Godhead beyond God, in the manner of classical negative theology.[23] It is elusive not because it is transcendent but because it is a transcendental condition of possibility, a *Bedingung* not a *Ding*, a *quo* not a *quod*, a neutral condition that makes it possible either to affirm or deny or to withhold judgment about a God. But please note, it is a *quasi*-transcendental (not a new metaphysical center), which means it makes these things possible in just such a way as to see to it that whatever we say on behalf of or against God, we may have to unsay. Hence, our atheism may be inhabited from within by theological assurances and our theology may be a disguised form of atheism. In short, there is no negative ontological argument against God implied in *différance* nor is *différance* to be confused with God.

In his later writings, in which Derrida spoke of the affirmation of the "undeconstructible," deconstruction began to look like itself a certain kind of a/theological religion. In a now famous 1989 talk at the Cardozo Law School he made a distinction between the law, which is a contingent, positive, historical construction and hence deconstructible (revisable, repealable), and justice in itself, which, if there is a such a thing, is not deconstructible.[24] Without this revisability, the law would be an unyielding tyrant. So being able to deconstruct a law is a condition of its justice while justice is that undeconstructible affirmative something in the light of which laws get deconstructed. Justice, if there is such a thing (s'il y en a), is not deconstructible. In a sense, there never *is* justice, since whatever *is* is a conditioned positive law, and justice is what we desire, not what exists. Like Levinas's God, justice calls but justice does not (quite) exist, except insofar as it acquires the force of law in those deconstructible things we call more-or-less-just (positive) laws.

After 1989, Derrida analyzed a series of undeconstructible structures: the gift and forgiveness, hospitality and friendship, and most notably the "democracy to come." Furthermore, the name of God, hitherto criticized as a "theological" term, the absolute center, the show-stopper that arrests the play of signifiers and brings discourse to a full stop, a full presence, a "transcendental signified,"[25] is taken as the name of a desire beyond desire, of a memory and a promise, a self-effacing name that tries to erase its own trace, and is as such precisely unarrestable. The name of God evokes endless substitution and translation, and is caught up in ineradicable undecidability. When the scripture says that God is love, we will never know whether that means that love is the best name we have for God or that God is the best name we have for love, the latter being the "atheistic" position taken by Luce Irigaray, who often casts her accounts of love in the attributes of religion and divinity.[26]

When Derrida was asked why he says he "rightly passes" for an atheist instead of (simply!) saying "I am" an atheist, he said it is because he does not know.[27] By this he did not mean that he is personally confused about what he thinks. He meant, first of all, that there is always a number of competing voices within the self that says "I" believe or "I" do not believe, some of which are unconscious, so that we never achieve that kind of self-identity and self-transparency required by a simple egological assertion. We never know to what extent our belief or disbelief is a disguised form either of its opposite or of some third thing. But beyond that point of self-questioning, he meant that the object of radical affirmation, the undeconstructible, is subject to an undecidable fluctuation and an open-ended future, a certain promise/threat in virtue of which we have no way to monitor the real distance between an "atheist" who affirms the justice to come and a religious believer who affirms the coming of a messianic age. Derrida distinguished the structural "messianic," an indeterminate affirmation of the "to come" (à venir), from the determinate belief systems of the concrete messianisms, such as Christianity, which awaits the second coming of Jesus. The structural messianic is built into deconstruction as the affirmation of the undeconstructible, which gives deconstruction the formal structure of a certain religion without (concrete, confessional) religion. The operative distinction therefore in deconstruction is not between theism and atheism but between determinate and indeterminate objects of affirmation, the words "theism" or "atheism" being rather too simple to describe what is going on.[28] That is why, when asked about the "death of God," Derrida said he does not believe in the simple death of anything.[29]

The permutations of which postmodern thought is capable are also strikingly illustrated by the paradox of the *theological* form atheism assumed in the 1960s and thereafter, principally in the Anglo-American world.[30] In "death of God *theology*," in which we recognize a certain continuation of Feuerbach's "transformational criticism" of Hegel, the perplexing idea is to produce not a simple atheism in the manner of a David Hume or Bertrand Russell, but an atheistic theology, one with historical roots in theology itself. By this was meant an analysis of how the transcendence of God had become immanent in the world, so that the secular world could be sounded in terms of echoes left behind by the "dead" or immanentized God, for which one would require a theological ear.

The British version of the movement was marked by the appearance of Bishop John Robinson's best-seller *Honest to God*, which begins with citations of Paul Tillich, Dietrich Bonhoeffer, and Rudolph Bultmann. For Robinson, following Tillich, the Christian is today called on to recognize that God is neither a being "up there" (pre-Copernican astronomy) nor something "out there" (metaphysical transcendence). God is here amidst the joys and trials of human life, in the very ground of our being, and the only real atheist is one who denies that life has depth and seriousness.[31] The movement's most sophisticated philosophical expression is the "theological nonrealism" of Don Cupitt. For Cupitt, the word "God" does not pick out either Tillich's ground of being or some entity in reality who answers to that name but instead constitutes a *"focus imaginarius,"* as George Pattison puts it, around which the strictly human project of autonomously configuring our spiritual values may be organized. In his later writings, under the influence of Derrida, Cupitt gravitated away from the language of an autonomous human subject as too modernist a formulation and adopted instead the postmodern, deconstructionist idea of a disseminated subject.[32]

The same shift from a modernist to a postmodernist version of death of God theology, again under the influence of Derrida, can also be found in the United States. The best known of the older atheistic theologies in the United States is Thomas J. J. Altizer's *The Gospel of Christian Atheism*,[33] which follows Hegel's view that the Jewish God is an alien and pure being (the religion of the father) that is first negated by the incarnation (the religion of the son) and then superceded when the empirical reality of the son (Jesus) breaks up (the crucifixion) in order that the divine principle may be distributed among everyone (the post-Easter religion of the spirit). While Hegel regarded Christianity as a picture story (*Vorstellung*), like a series of stained windows, of a conceptual truth that could be stated only in the metaphysics of absolute idealism, Alitzer holds in some more literal way that in an act of divine self-sacrifice, God abdicated transcendence, became flesh in Christ and died on the cross, making purchase on an unspecified "apocalyptic future." The baffling thing is that Altizer rejects both the Hegelian explanation that Christianity is simply a picture story needing to be demythologized by philosophy and the distinctions introduced by orthodox theology that the son underwent a death in his human but not in his divine nature.

Altizer's position was criticized and reworked by Mark C. Taylor in the light of deconstruction. Taylor argued that Altizer was serving up another version of the metaphysics of presence, a dialectical presence/absence system in which everything is either simply dead or alive, simply absent or present, in which total death is the purchase price of "total presence." In *Erring: An A/theology* (1984), the book that was for many the first introduction of the work of Derrida into theology, Taylor describes deconstruction as the "hermeneutics of the death of God," by which he meant not the black-or-white modernist dialectics of Altizer but the nuanced undecidability of the "a/theological," in which the clean distinction between the theological and the atheistic is disrupted. Taylor's critique of Altizer is a parallel to the way a Deleuzian would describe as still too theological (or modernist) Robinson's Tillichian affirmation of the depth or ground of being, where even if God is no longer transcendent, God is still being deployed as a way to stabilize becoming, as a grounding center of our being.

But Taylor was in turn criticized for failing to adhere rigorously to the demands of the "a/theological" program, for not maintaining the slash, or undecidability, between theology and atheism, and for simply allowing the theological to dissipate without remainder in a world of random play and bottomless chessboards.[34] Taylor has gone on to write creatively about art, architecture, and the revolution in information technologies, about everything it seems except religion (since, on his thesis, religion is present where it is not) and consequently to be read less and less by people who are interested in religion where it actually is present. Taylor's use of deconstruction in theology was guided largely by a certain reading of Derrida that was dominant in the United States in the 1960s and 1970s, whereas recent work on deconstruction and religion takes its lead from Derrida's writings in the last two decades of his life. There deconstruction is described in terms not of the endless play of signifiers but of

an affirmation of the impossible, of a desire beyond desire for the undeconstructible, so that deconstruction is structured like a certain faith or
religion without religion.[35]

The "secular theology" of Charles Winquist was associated with the
early death of God movement, but in seizing on the idea of "theological
desire" in his later writings Winquist entered into an interesting alliance
with Deleuze and the later post-*Erring* deployment of deconstruction in
theology.[36] Gianni Vattimo, who earlier had been tracing the hermeneutics of nihilism or of the death of God, in his recent writings has come
to see in the breakup of the God of the old ontotheology a new life for
Christianity as the religion of love, peace, and justice on earth, on the
basis of which Vattimo has entered into a dialogue with Rorty's idea of
democratic hope.[37]

The most recent chapter in the story of postmodern atheism is found in
a reaction against the specific postmodern tendencies I have singled out.
Slavoj Zizek complains that postmodernism is a kind of permissiveness
in which anything is possible under the rubrics of identity politics, political correctness, liberalism, or capitalism. One of its most deplorable
developments, he says, is the return of religion – not only fundamentalist religion and New Age religion, but even the religion without religion to be found within deconstruction itself and hence the whole idea
of "postsecularism" that we have been discussing.[38] As an atheist, a
Leninist, and a Lacanian, Zizek warns that the best way to combat all
this obscurantism (religion) is not to attack it frontally but to employ the
kind of Trojan horse strategy found in Alain Badiou's reading of St. Paul,
which infiltrates the religious camp and boldly affirms the lineage from
Christianity to Marxism. Zizek sees Badiou's defense of Christianity
against its postmodern corruptions as a model for the radical left, which
must defend a hardy and radical Marxist-Leninism against its wimpish
liberal humanist corruption. Badiou's St. Paul exhibits, albeit in a strictly
formal way, all the marks of a militant Marxist: personally galvanized
by a singular life-transforming event, Paul sets out with apostolic zeal to
declare its truth, undertaking a worldwide mission to turn that singular
event into a universal truth. For whatever is true is true for everyone,
Greek or Jew, master or slave, male or female. Of course, Badiou's point is
that Paul's truth (the resurrection) is a pure fable, that Paul is telling the
(Marxist) truth in a mystified manner. In his own work Zizek dialogues
with Christian orthodoxy, both the older one of G. K. Chesterton and
the more recent "radical orthodoxy" of John Milbank. Militant Christian
orthodoxy is vastly to be preferred to deconstruction's religion without
religion, as decision is to be preferred to undecidability, as substance to
froth, as firmly affirmed truth to historical relativism, as real faith to

skeptical dilly-dallying. As in Hegel and Feuerbach, Christianity is the real truth but in mythological form, and it needs only to clear its head with a few sessions on the couch with Lacan and a stirring speech by Lenin about the need to be hard, with whose help the theistic myth can be demythologized into concrete social truth. But as critical of postmodernism and deconstruction as Badiou and Zizek are, they do not challenge the postmodernist claim that religion and atheism communicate with each other and share a common form of life.

Taken in strictly philosophical terms, postmodernism is a sustained attempt to displace a fixed categorial opposition of theism and atheism, to make trouble for both traditional religious faith and modern atheism. Postmodernists identify the ways these opposites turn on a common structure and explore the possibility of a certain region or even an affirmation that is indifferent to the difference between the theistic and the atheistic, or the religious and the secular. If critics like Zizek think this arises from an anemic refusal to make decisions, thinkers like Derrida seem inspired by a kind of "learned ignorance," believing that we are not hard-wired to some metaphysical verity, hesitating – in the name of peace – before making determinate and militant declarations of belief or unbelief. They are moved, I think, by a hope or suspicion that there might be some other possibility (Derrida's "perhaps," *peut-être*), something a/theological, beneath or beyond this dichotomy, some hidden future that is concealed from all of us today.[39]

NOTES

1. See Brian Ingraffia, *Postmodern Theory and Biblical Theology* (Cambridge: Cambridge University Press, 1995), and Douglas Groothuis, *Truth Decay: Defending Christianity against the Challenges of Postmodernism* (Downers Grove, Ill.: InterVarsity Press, 2000), for rather strident evangelical critiques of postmodern thought. Brian D. McLaren – see, esp., *A New Kind of Christian* (San Francisco: Jossey-Bass, 2001) – is an astute defender of the positive implications of postmodernism for evangelical faith.
2. Jean-François Lyotard, *The Postmodern Condition*, trans. Geoff Bennington and Brian Massumi (Minneapolis: University of Minnesota Press, 1984), pp. xxiii–xxv; this is the most well-known philosophical definition of postmodernism.
3. Jacques Derrida, *Of Grammatology*, corrected ed., trans. Gayatri Spivak (Baltimore: Johns Hopkins University Press, 1997), p. 323 n3.
4. Jacques Derrida, *Points... Interviews, 1974–94*, ed. Elisabeth Weber, trans. Peggy Kamuf (Stanford, Calif.: Stanford University Press, 1995), p. 428. For a commentary, see John D. Caputo, *Deconstruction in a Nutshell: A Conversation with Jacques Derrida*, edited with a commentary (New York: Fordham University Press, 1997), pp. 50–60.

5. That is why it would be more accurate to call the core philosophical idea "poststructuralism."

6. For the sake of economy, I refer only to Richard Rorty, *Contingency, Irony and Solidarity* (Cambridge: Cambridge University Press, 1989), as the most representative.

7. Gilles Deleuze, *Nietzsche and Philosophy*, trans. Hugh Tomlinson (New York: Columbia University Press, 1983).

8. See D. Z. Philips, *Wittgenstein and Religion* (New York: Palgrave Macmillan, 1984).

9. Mark C. Taylor, *Erring: A Postmodern A/theology* (Chicago: University of Chicago Press, 1984), p. 12.

10. See Friedrich Nietzsche, *The Gay Science*, trans. Walter Kaufmann (New York: Vintage Books, 1974), secs. 125 and 343.

11. Both Peter Berger, *The Desecularization of the World: Resurgent Religion and World Politics* (Grand Rapids, Mich.: Eerdmanns, 1999), and Harvey Cox, *Religion in a Secular City: Toward a Postmodern Theology* (New York: Simon and Schuster, 1984), have been forced by the facts to recast their earlier pronouncements on secularization and the secular city.

12. Friedrich Nietzsche, *Beyond Good and Evil*, trans. Walter Kaufmann (New York: Vintage Books, 1989).

13. Gilles Deleuze, *The Logic of Sense*, trans. Mark Lester (New York: Columbia University Press, 1990), p. 281. Among his many works, Gilles Deleuze (with Felex Guattari), *What Is Philosophy?* trans. Hugh Tomlinson and G. Burchill (London: Verso, 1994), is not a bad place to start.

14. Martin Heidegger, *Being and Time*, trans. John Macquarrie and Edward Robinson (New York: Harper & Row, 1962); see Istvan Feher, "Heidegger's Understanding of the Atheism of Philosophy," *American Catholic Philosophical Quarterly* 64 (May 1995): 189–228.

15. A great deal of this argument can be found in the essays collected in *Martin Heidegger Basic Writings*, ed. David F. Krell, 2nd ed. (New York: Harper & Row, 1993), and in the crucial essay "The Onto-Theological Constitution of Metaphysics," in Martin Heidegger, *Identity and Difference*, trans. Joan Stambaugh (New York: Harper & Row, 1969). Heidegger gives a brilliant account of his later view of the genesis of modernity in *The Principle of Reason*, trans. Reginald Lilly (Bloomington: Indiana University Press, 1991).

16. Jacques Derrida, *Of Spirit: Heidegger and the Question*, trans. Geoffrey Bennington and Rachel Bowlby (Chicago: University of Chicago Press, 1989), pp. 109–13. See John D. Caputo, "Heidegger and Theology," in Charles Guignon (ed.), *The Cambridge Companion to Heidegger* (Cambridge: Cambridge University Press, 1993), pp. 270–88.

17. Dominique Janicaud et al. (eds.), *Phenomenology and the "Theological Turn": The French Debate* (New York: Fordham University Press, 2000).

18. The problem that Levinas first poses to himself in 1935 in *On Escape*, trans. Bettina Bergo (Stanford, Calif.: Stanford University Press, 2003), reaches its highest resolution in the 1970s in *Otherwise Than Being or Beyond Essence*, trans. Alphonso Lingis (Pittsburgh, Pa.: Duquesne University Press, 1998).

19. See the interesting "Annotations" by Jacques Rolland in *On Escape*, esp. no. 10, pp. 89–90.

20. Merold Westphal, "Levinas's Teleological Suspension of the Religious," in Adriaan T. Peperzak (ed.), *Ethics as First Philosophy: The Significance of Emmanuel Levinas for Philosophy, Literature, and Religion* (London/New York: Routledge, 1995), pp. 151–60.

21. Jacques Derrida, "Circumfession: Fifty-nine Periods and Periphrases," in Geoffrey Bennington and Jacques Derrida, *Jacques Derrida*, trans. Geoffrey Bennington (Chicago: University of Chicago Press, 1993), p. 155.

22. Derrida, *Of Grammatology*, pp. 18, 47, 84, 131, 135, 139.

23. See Jacques Derrida, "How to Avoid Speaking: Denials," in Howard Coward and Toby Foshay (eds.), *Derrida and Negative Theology* (Albany: SUNY Press, 1992), pp. 73–142.

24. "The Force of Law: 'The Mystical Foundation of Authority,'" trans. Mary Quantaince, in Drucilla Cornell et al. (eds.), *Deconstruction and the Possibility of Justice* (New York: Routledge, 1992), pp. 68–91.

25. Derrida, *Of Grammatology*, p. 71.

26. Luce Irigaray, *An Ethics of Sexual Difference*, trans. Carolyn Burke and Gillian C. Gill (Ithaca, N.Y. Cornell University Press, 1993), and "Belief Itself," in *Sexes and Genealogies* (New York: Columbia University Press, 1993). For a commentary, see Grace Jantzen, *Becoming Divine: Towards a Feminist Philosophy of Religion* (Manchester and Bloomington: Manchester University Press and Indiana University Press, 1998).

27. See Jacques Derrida, "The Becoming Possible of the Impossible: An Interview with Jacques Derrida," in Mark Dooley (ed.), *A Passion for the Impossible: John D. Caputo in Focus*, ed. (Albany: SUNY Press, 2003), pp. 21–33.

28. While Michel Foucault appears to reduce religion to a set of confessional and disciplinary practices that constitute the religious subject, there is a growing and comparable interest in finding his religious side. See James Bernauer and Jeremy Carrette (eds.), *Michel Foucault and Theology: The Politics of Religious Experience* (Burlington, Vt.: Ashgate, 2004).

29. Jacques Derrida, *Positions*, trans. Alan Bass (Chicago: University of Chicago Press, 1972), p. 6. See Hugh Rayment-Pickard, *Impossible God: Derrida's Theology* (Hampshire, England: Ashgate, 2003), pp. 18–19, 134–43.

30. This is the atheistic form of theology – as opposed to the theological (dogmatic, metaphysical) form of atheism.

31. John Robinson, *Honest to God* (London: SCM Press, 1963), p. 22.

32. Don Cupitt, *Taking Leave of God* (London: SCM Press, 1980), and *Is Nothing Sacred?* (New York: Fordham University Press, 2002). For a good commentary on the British movement, see George Pattison, *Thinking about God in an Age of Technology* (Oxford: Oxford University Press, 2005), ch. 1, "The Long Goodbye."

33. Thomas J. J. Altizer, *The Gospel of Christian Atheism* (Philadelphia: Westminster Press, 1966); *The New Gospel of Christian Atheism*, rev. ed. (Aurora, Colo.: Davies Publishing, 2002); and T. J. J. Altizer and William Hamilton, *Radical Theology and the Death of God* (Indianapolis: Bobbs-Merrill Press, 1966).

34. See my review of *Erring* in *Man and World* 21 (1988): 108–26.

35. John D. Caputo, *The Prayers and Tears of Jacques Derrida: Religion without Religion* (Bloomington: Indiana University Press, 1997); Hent de Vries, *Philosophy and the Turn to Religion* (Baltimore, Md.: Johns Hopkins University

Press, 1999); Kevin Hart, *The Trespass of the Sign* (New York: Fordham University Press, 2000); and Richard Kearney, *The God Who May Be* (Bloomington: Indiana University Press, 2001).

36. Charles Winquist, *Desiring Theology* (Chicago: University of Chicago Press, 1995).

37. Gianni Vattimo, *Belief*, trans. Luca D'Isanto and David Webb (Stanford, Calif.: Stanford University Press, 1999), and Richard Rorty and Gianni Vattimo, *The Future of Religion* (New York: Columbia University Press, 2005).

38. Alain Badiou, *Saint Paul: The Foundations of Universalism*, trans. Roy Brassier (Stanford, Calif.: Stanford University Press, 2003); Slavoj Zizek, *The Fragile Absolute* (New York and London: Verso Books, 2000); and Giorgio Agamben, *A Time That Remains: A Commentary on the Letter to the Romans*, trans. Patricia Dailey (Stanford, Calif.: Stanford University Press, 2005).

39. See Gavin Hyman's suggestive chapter in this volume, which demonstrates both the inner link between modernity and atheism and the relativity of atheism to the theism it is denying. If modern atheism is the rejection of a modern God, as Hyman says, then the delimitation of modernity opens up another possibility, less the resuscitation of premodern theism than the chance of something beyond both the theism and the atheism of modernity.

17 Anthropological Theories of Religion

I. INTRODUCTION

Anthropological theories of religion are diverse. They are based variously on ideas human social structures, emotions, or cognition. Most concentrate on one of these, but some combine them. A few look beyond human nature to that of other animals, for analogues or precursors to religion. A few theories are indigenous to anthropology, but many have been borrowed. Thus any review must be similarly wideranging and include material that is not solely anthropological. I offer a brief historical overview and a look at a promising contemporary approach.

No sharp break or any single feature separates anthropological explanations of religion from their forebears or from those of other disciplines. However, a few common features do tend to set them apart. Of these, humanism, evolutionism, and cross-cultural comparison are primary. Humanism in anthropology means simply that explanations of religion (as of other human thought and action) are secular and naturalistic. They account for religions as products of human culture and human nature, not as manifestations of anything transcendental, supernatural, or otherwise *sui generis*.

Darwinian evolutionism – the view that all forms of life are products of natural selection – also is basic to anthropology and somewhat distinguishes it from other disciplines that study religion. Evolutionism is unsurprising, of course, in biological anthropology, a major subfield. But even in cultural anthropology, founded shortly after Darwin, natural selection is foundational. Indeed, cultural evolutionism was the "perspective with which anthropology started life" (Carneiro 2003: 287). Partly in consequence, a search for origins and long-term trends characterized the early discipline and persists today. One such long-term trend, for example, is the tendency of stratified societies, unlike unstratified ones, to ascribe their moral systems to religious mandates. Another partial consequence of evolutionism is a degree of ostensible support for functionalism, the explanation of features of organisms and of societies

283

by their positive effects. Thus religion sometimes is explained, for example, by the social cohesion it is said to produce.

The third and last principal feature of anthropological theory of religion is cross-cultural comparison. Although the comparative method was not original to anthropology, it has become especially important there. In cross-cultural perspective, the ultimate object of study is not religion in any particular place or time but religion everywhere and at all times.[1] Such study reveals a gamut of beliefs and practices, almost to the exclusion of any common denominator (Saler 2000 [1993]). The variety seems to preclude ecumenism as well as any shared "perennial philosophy" (Huxley 1990 [1945]).

Thus issues of definition come to the fore. These issues are difficult even for scholars within the few, relatively similar societies providing most of the anthropologists. When we try to compare religions globally, definition becomes both central and daunting. Arguably, this situation leads to further humanism, much as news of non-Western religions did in the Enlightenment. Darwinian evolutionism tends to lead in the same direction. Hence these three features of anthropology are mutually reinforcing.

Given the great variety of thoughts and actions called religion, and given that most languages do not have a word for it, the question arises whether religion is universal. The answer, of course, depends on one's definition. The more abstract the definition, the more widespread that which it defines. If one accepts a definition as abstract as Tillich's (1948: 63), that religion is an engagement with some "ultimate concern," then presumably people everywhere are religious, since all judge some concern more important than others. If, however, one stipulates belief in God, together with a morality sanctioned by an afterlife, then the religious are a smaller group. In any case, most anthropologists believe that religion may be defined broadly enough that it is virtually universal (Rappaport 1999; Crapo 2001; Atran 2002: 264).

2. A BRIEF HISTORY

Anthropological theories of religion usefully may be divided into three groups: social-solidarity (or social-glue) theories, wishful-thinking theories, and intellectualist (or cognitivist) theories. Social-solidarity theories take the needs of society as primary and explain religion by how it caters to them, especially by its supposed promotion of harmony and cohesion. Wishful-thinking theories take the emotions of individuals as primary and explain religion by its mitigation of negative feelings, such as fear and loneliness, and by its promotion of confidence or serenity. Finally, intellectualist theories take as primary the human need to comprehend the world. In this last view, the religious interpretation of the world is, first and foremost, an attempt at understanding. Each of these three may be combined with either or both of the others.

The social-solidarity theory has been the principal approach in anthropology since the latter began in the late nineteenth century. It is a form of functionalism, since it explains religion by its nominal inculcation of allegiance to a society. Religion does this by symbolic means, displaying special clothing, architecture, song, dance, and verbal formulae to augment communal feelings. Indeed, the social-solidarity theory sometimes is called symbolism, meaning that it holds that religion is entirely a symbolic activity that does not engage the world as a whole (as its performers or casual observers may think), but only human social relations. Its symbols may be covert and grasped only unconsciously.

That religious symbolism unifies society is not a new idea. In East Asia, for example, the use of religion by the state goes back at least to 1,027 B.C.E., when the new Chou dynasty cited its conquest of subject peoples as a sign that it had received the mandate of heaven. Later dynasties continued the claim. In addition, they enlisted Confucius as a quasi-religious figure supporting the state, as did governments in Japan and Korea. In Japan, both Shinto and ancestor worship also were made to serve national unity. In the West as well, the social-solidarity view (and use) of religion appeared early and has persisted. Starting at least with Polybius in the first century B.C.E. and followed by Bodin, Vico, Comte (Preus 1987), and Freud (e.g., 1964 [1927]), among others, and most recently Wilson (2002) and Roes and Raymond (2003), many scholars have held that religion maintains the social order.

The social-glue theory, however, owes most to Durkheim (1965 [1915]), who was preoccupied with how societies cohere. He said that they do it largely through religion, which comprises beliefs and practices that are "relative to sacred things" and which organizes followers into solidary groups. Sacred things need not include gods (Buddhism, Durkheim writes, is a religion without them) but are anything representing the essential elements of society. Profane things, in contrast, constitute a residual category of all that is not sacred. The distinction that religion makes between sacred and profane is its signal characteristic.

Relying on ethnographers of Australian aboriginal religion, Durkheim concluded that the chief object of worship for members of Australian clans, the "totem," actually stands for the clan itself, and that it is the clan that is sacred. The same principle holds for complex, modern societies. The explicit object of worship, whether totem, flag, or God, represents all that is vital and hence sacred in society. By formulating and expressing the sense that members of a society have of their mutual dependence, a feeling that otherwise is only sporadic, religion consolidates and augments that sense. This helps to make members behave ethically toward their fellows and rallies them to the society's defense.

The social-solidarity theory of religion has several strengths, principally that religions do appear often to have produced solidarity (Wilson 2002) and that leaders in varied societies have used this capacity. However, the theory has weaknesses as well. Durkheim's claim that religion's central feature is its dichotomy of sacred and profane, for example, met immediate objection from ethnographers who reported that no such distinction was made in the cultures they studied (Guthrie 1996).

Another problem is that if the claim that religions unite societies is to be more than the tautology that religions unite their own members, then one must show that they arise out of groups with some other basis, which the religion then strengthens. But in fact there are many kinds of groups – families, villages, ethnic communities, states – that are split, not joined, by religion. A corollary is that, whereas social groupings allegedly are preserved by religion, many instead have been destroyed by it. Examples are the T'ai-p'ing Tao of second-century China and the People's Temple at Jonestown.

Finally, a problem for all functionalism must be addressed: why is the feature (religion) adopted in the system (a society) that it benefits? Functionalists often ignore this question or appear tacitly to endorse something like a Darwinian account: societies with a given trait are more successful and therefore survive longer or spread wider. The trait survives with them.

The more basic question of how the traits arise usually is ignored as well. One might surmise that they arise randomly, on the model of genetic mutation. Randomness, however, though adequate to describe mutation, is an impoverished account of the genesis of culture. Too much is known of human mental process to abandon it for blind chance.

Moreover, cultural traits, unlike genetic ones, are not passed on biologically, but must be learned and often must actively be taught as well. Therefore the question arises, what motivates people to teach or learn particular doctrines or behavior? This question is sharpened by the fact that the people doing so often appear unaware of the social benefit attributed by the observer. In the case of religion, for example, few say they pray because it makes their society cohere.

The fact that functionalism vis-à-vis religion (and other features of societies and organisms) persists is due, perhaps, not to its strength under analysis but to an intuitive but misleading appeal. This appeal is that functionalism jibes with the human proclivity, noted at least since Hume (1957 [1757]) and detailed experimentally by Kelemen (2004), to find design and purpose in the world generally. This proclivity,

Kelemen shows, emerges spontaneously in young children ("clouds are for raining") and remains powerful throughout life. She shows that this tendency readily takes a religious form. Some current religionists believe, for example, that they see an "intelligent design" that rivals evolutionism as a scientific account of biology. However, this belief seems to reveal more about human perceptual susceptibilities than about biology.

Thus the social-glue theory of Durkheim and others seems to founder on objections to a core concept (the sacred-profane distinction), on counterexamples in which religion is not a glue but a dispersant, and finally on its failure to provide a credible dynamics of religion's genesis and transmission. Although religion often welds groups together and may be deliberately used for that purpose, that is not why people adopt it. Moreover, religion often sunders groups as well.

A second collection of theories may be called the wishful-thinking approach. According to these, religion serves as a palliative for human anxiety and discontent by imagining a more satisfactory condition, in either the present or the future. By postulating a world in which we can better ourselves by appealing to gods, or in which life's suffering will be compensated by a better life to come, religion makes life bearable.

These theories, too, have an ancient lineage. Writers have noted that religiosity correlates with anxiety, at least since Euripides' observation that stress leads us, because of "our ignorance and uncertainty," to worship the gods (*Hecuba* 956, in Hume 1957 [1757]: 31). Similarly, the first-century Diodorus Siculus wrote that disaster chastises us into a "reverence for the gods" (Hume 1957 [1757]: 31). Spinoza (1955), Feuerbach (1957 [1873]), Marx (Marx and Engels 1957: 37–38), and the twentieth-century anthropologists Malinowski (1955 [1925]) and Kluckhohn (1942) made comparable observations.

The wishful-thinking theorist most widely read, however, doubtless is Freud (e.g., 1964 [1927]). Anthropologists following Freud include Kardiner and Linton (1945), Spiro (1966), Wallace (1966), and La Barre (1972). As Freud is discussed elsewhere in this volume (by Beit-Hallahmi), I shall describe his ideas only briefly. For Freud, religions are delusions, "born from man's need to make his helplessness tolerable" and are "illusions, fulfillments of the oldest, strongest, and most urgent wishes of mankind" (1964: 25 and 47). Their particular features are "projections" of emotions and experiences.

The notion of projection, however, is a misleading metaphor, probably based on a folk theory of vision as touching (Guthrie 2000b). Among other problems, it implies that there are two kinds of perception: projection, which is subjective and fallacious, and nonprojective perception, which is objective and accurate. This implication is contradicted by the facts that all perception reflects the perceiver's interests and that there is no neutral point of view.

Many religions, moreover, fit any wish-fulfillment theory badly because they have features for which no one is likely to wish. The deities of some are cruel or angry, and often complemented by devils or frightening ghosts. In others the afterlife either is absent or fleeting, or is a Hades or other unpleasant place. Such religions may threaten as much as they promise. As one anthropologist remarked (Radcliffe-Brown 1979 [1939]: 55), one could equally hold that religions afflict people with "fears and anxieties from which they would otherwise be free."

Even if the balance of religious ideas tipped toward comfort rather than affliction, one would need to explain what makes them believable. We do not appear simply to believe whatever might comfort us. As Pinker (1997: 555) notes, opposing the comfort theory of religion, people freezing to death do not seem to comfort themselves with the thought that they really are warm.

The third group of theories is called intellectualism, cognitivism, or (occasionally) neo-Tylorianism. These hold that religion is primarily an attempt at understanding the world and at acting in accordance with that understanding. One such theory, in Tylor (1871), led the earliest anthropological approaches to religion. Tylor, who is classically humanistic, evolutionary, and comparative, describes religion as a universal attempt to explain certain puzzling human experiences.

Tylor's theory, like the social-solidarity and wishful-thinking theories, has predecessors. Its comparativism and apparently its humanism date back to Xenophanes (6th century B.C.E.), whose fragments report that humans form their varied gods in their own varied images (Freeman 1966: 22). Ethiopians, for example, make their gods black, whereas Thracians give theirs red hair. Much later, Spinoza (1955) and Hume (1957 [1757]), whom Tylor credits with forming modern opinion on religion, more closely anticipated Tylor in writing that popular religion, at least, consists in our attributing human characteristics to the nonhuman world, in order to interpret our otherwise-inscrutable surroundings.

Tylor added to these earlier ideas an emphasis on cultural evolution, which, coupled with a more wide-ranging comparativism, strengthened the naturalistic view of religion as one more product of human mental activity. As a comparativist, he drew systematically on the reports of travelers, administrators, missionaries, and early ethnographers for descriptions of beliefs and practices around the world, in order to find a common denominator of religions. He saw differences in culture, including religion, as reflecting not genetics but forms of society, since a "psychic unity" of shared mental process exists among all humans. These emphases became part of the anthropological canon.

Tylor concluded that religion may be defined as animism, a belief in spirit beings, and that this belief arises universally from two experiences: dreams and the deaths of other people. Dreams, he said, everywhere are interpreted as visits from what is dreamed of (he termed the visitor the "phantom"). Death, in contrast, almost everywhere is conceived as the departure of something (the "life"). The phantom and the life then are conceived as a single thing, the "spirit." This is a

thin unsubstantial human image, in its nature a sort of vapor, film, or shadow; the cause of life and thought in the individual it animates; independently possessing the personal consciousness and volition of its corporeal owner, past or present; capable of leaving the body far behind, to flash swiftly from place to place; mostly impalpable and invisible, yet also manifesting physical power, and especially appearing to men waking or asleep as a phantasm. (1979: 12)

Critics soon charged Tylor with telling a "just-so" story, with little evidence either that the notions of phantom and life arise as he claimed or that the notion of the spirit being originates in their conjunction. Despite his broad ethnographic sources, his evidence of such a genesis does seem circumstantial. He also was charged, perhaps with some justification, with having turned ordinary people into philosophers concerned with explanation, and with having slighted emotion. Still other critics have noted that while a key assumption that Tylor makes is that all deities are spirit beings and hence insubstantial, in fact the deities of some religions are embodied and substantial – for example, the God of early Christianity (Teske 1986).

Tylor's thesis about dreams and death, and his emphasis on religion as cognition, were adopted by other anthropologists for a time, but then were largely abandoned. His term "animism" has lived on, though its meaning is somewhat changed. Whereas Tylor meant by it a belief in any spirit beings, including monotheistic gods, current users mean belief in multiple spirits. Tylor's doctrine of the psychic unity of humankind also has survived. His view that religion should be understood as cognition, moreover, reappeared in the 1960s with Robin Horton and again from 1980 to the present, in the work of varied writers drawing from cognitive science.

Horton, an anthropologist of the Kalabari people of Niger and of religion and its relation to other thought, gives a careful intellectualist account of religion (1960, 1967, 1973, 1982, 1993), emphasizing its similarities to, and continuities with, science. An early publication (1960: 211), following Tylor's suggestion that deities resemble humans, defines religion as the "extension of the field of people's social relationships beyond the confines of purely human society." That is, people model aspects of the nonhuman world as significantly humanlike and as capable of social relationships.

Subsequently, Horton argued (e.g., 1967) that religious thought and action are not sharply different from scientific thought and action. Both are "second-order" theoretical schemes once removed from the first-order theories of common sense. The central aim of both is to unify experience by reducing complexity and disorder to order and simplicity; and both work by analogy and metaphor. The fact that religion models the world by analogy with humans, while science tries to avoid this, is superficial and mere idiom.

Horton is influential as a forerunner of what now is called the cognitive approach to religion, though he draws more on philosophy of science and on fieldwork than on cognitive science. Recent cognitive psychology and related research add to and modify his work by emphasizing unconscious, nonrational processes and by showing that our tendency to model the world on humans is neither superficial nor mere idiom, but is pervasive and deeply rooted (Lakoff and Johnson 1999; Carey 2000; Heberlein 2004; Kelemen 2004; Hassin, Uleman, and Bargh 2005).

A final figure in this brief history is Clifford Geertz, who to some degree synthesizes the three groups above. Most relevant is his widely cited "Religion as a Cultural System." This is an unpacking of his extended definition of religion as "(1) a system of symbols which acts to (2) establish powerful, pervasive and long-lasting moods and motivations in men by (3) formulating conceptions of a general order of existence and (4) clothing these conceptions with such an aura of factuality that (5) the moods and motivations seem uniquely realistic" (1966: 4). This defines religion by its function, namely, to motivate and hearten its adherents by presenting an ordered world of meaning. It fulfills a deep-seated human wish for meaning and unifies society with a shared symbol system, by interpreting the world as having a general order of existence.

However, the essay does not specify clearly what *kind* of meaning religion offers, other than as "ultimate," nor precisely why this meaning convinces. These omissions allow Geertz's description wide applicability, but leave little motivation for religion as a cultural system. The most important silence concerns the "general order of existence" at the heart of the definition. What – or who – is involved in this general order, that it should encourage us? We learn only that the specifics of the order are highly variable and, apparently, arbitrary. The order remains, finally, a black box (Guthrie 1993: 28–29). Into it go our existential problems, and out come, if not solutions, at least reassurances. We learn not how the order works, but only that it provides the meaning we need.

Both reassurance and meaning, however, are characteristically human phenomena. Thus a possible, more-specific description of this general order of existence would be that it is created or inhabited by a human-like being or beings – that is, by something like a deity or deities. If so, then its content would be neither arbitrary nor infinitely variable but, as Tylor and Horton urged, modeled on human persons. Thus constrained, Geertz's system would become narrower (though still broad enough to include virtually all cultures) but also on sounder psychological footings.

3. RECENT COGNITIVISM

Over a century after Tylor gave anthropological form to the intellectualist view of religion, and almost a century since that form lost most of its followers, new versions of intellectualism have arisen. Most emphasize unconscious processes (whereas Tylor dealt with conscious ones) and draw on the new field of cognitive science, and accordingly are termed "cognitivist." Currently, these seem the most energetic theories.

Cognitivists at present generally agree with Tylor and Horton that what we mean by religion includes dealings with humanlike, yet not human beings. Nonetheless, their theories can be divided roughly into two approaches. One approach maintains that religious ideas arise regularly and inevitably, because they are intuitive (Guthrie 1980, 1993, 2002; Burkert 1996; Bering 2002; Kelemen 2004). Intuitive ideas are products of "spontaneous and unconscious perceptual and inferential processes" (Sperber 1996: 89). We have such ideas without knowing why, or even that we have them. They transmit easily because they strike chords that already are familiar.

Most important, this approach provides a new explanation for the intuitive phenomena most central to religious ideas, namely, animism and anthropomorphism. This explanation is that they constitute apparent but mistaken discoveries – that is, false positives – of animals or people, and are inevitable products of our chronic search for important agents in an ambiguous world. This search in turn is part of an evolved strategy for finding the most important features in our uncertain perceptual environment. Perceptual uncertainty is heightened by natural deception in the form of camouflage. Hence our sensitivities to possible important agents and traces of agents (predator or prey, friend or enemy) are on a hair trigger, and we cannot help often thinking we have detected them when we have not.

The other cognitivist approach sometimes is called cultural epidemiology, for the notion (Sperber 1996) that culture spreads like a disease. Its adherents hold that religious ideas arise only randomly and sporadically, but are widespread because they are memorable and thus easily transmitted. They are memorable because they are "counterintuitive" and therefore novel (Medin and Atran 1999; Barrett 2000; Boyer 2001; Pyysiäinen 2001).

Boyer (2001) is representative of this second approach. He says his central term, "counterintuitive," is "technical" and does not "mean strange . . . exceptional or extraordinary" but rather "contradicting some information provided by ontological categories" (2001: 65). For example, he says, the categories *animal, person,* and *plant* are ontological. They tell us that their members have distinct biological properties: they are alive, need nutrition, grow, become old, and die. Counterintuitive ideas, according to Boyer, include beings that are not animal, person, or plant yet have one or more of these biological properties. They also include animals, persons, or plants that lack one or more of these properties. To be remembered best, concepts should be "minimally counterintuitive," meaning that in some ways they should be familiar, but in other ways not. A ghost, for example, is a human being with ordinary desires, intentions, and feelings, who also is insubstantial.

Several problems seem to beset this account. Centrally, the meaning of "counterintuitive" is not clear. Boyer writes that its ordinary sense is misleading and that the "neologism *counterontological* may be a better choice" (2001: 65). As noted, he defines counterintuitive as that which contradicts ontological categories by mixing their properties, particularly those of animate and inanimate beings. However, the categories he calls ontological and intuitive, especially biological ones, are themselves controversial. Some researchers (Carey 1985, 1995, 2000; Cherry 1992; Johnson and Carey 1998) say that biology is learned, not intuitive. Until that issue is resolved, we will not know whether religious concepts violate ontological categories, however defined.

In addition, because Boyer does not clearly define the term "ontological categories," his definition of counterintuitive in terms of them is circular. One might suppose that ontological categories have some independent basis in science or in nature, but Boyer says they are not "always true or accurate. . . . They are just what we intuitively expect, and that's that" (2001: 68). Thus ontological categories are defined as whichever categories are intuitive, and counterintuitivity is defined as whatever conflicts with them. Later Boyer and Barrett (2005) write that "intuitive" ontological categories differ from "real" ontological categories, but their criteria remain unclear.

The epidemiologists also characterize the supernatural as counterintuitive and make it a hallmark of religion. But the very notion of the supernatural is Western and again controversial (Lohmann 2003). (To add to the confusion, Boyer elsewhere (2001: 158–59) says that we represent supernatural agents intuitively.) Although the epidemiologists claim to explain religion by explaining what makes it memorable, a more parsimonious approach to memory would be that of information theory. This holds simply that an event is memorable to the degree that it is unusual, thus making moot the fraught question of what is and is not counterintuitive.

A last problem with the epidemiological theory of religion is that it is inconsistent with Darwinian evolution. According to Darwin, major features of organisms, including perception and cognition, are selected for their usefulness. Accordingly, perception and cognition have evolved so as to provide useful information – which is to say, veridical information that meets specific needs. The cultural epidemiologists, in contrast, claim that the human mind has evolved to favor information that is paradoxical and false ("counterfactual," as they put it). Some evidence, in addition to the putative example of religion, is needed that this is so, and some explanation is needed for such an odd evolutionary turn. Occam's razor recommends that we look instead for a more economical explanation of religion.

Such an explanation is offered by the first cognitivist approach mentioned above. This maintains that religious ideas, and especially three particular conceptual features, are widespread because they are intuitive. The first two features are distinct, though related, senses of "animism": that of concepts of spirit beings (humanlike beings who may be invisible and/or more or less insubstantial) and that of attributing life to phenomena that biologists consider nonliving. The third feature is anthropomorphism (the attribution of human characteristics to non-human phenomena). These three are linked and, to a degree, arise from related dispositions and processes. They frequently or always are present in religion.

The belief in spirit beings that Tylor said defines religion still is central to it for many Westerners. Although some deities such as the early Christian God are embodied and substantial, many others often are invisible and more or less insubstantial. The epidemiologists, as noted, find such beings counterintuitive. However, recent ethology, psychology, and philosophy suggest that these beings are not counterintuitive for most people.

Ethology indicates that, as an evolved response to our biological world, we are more sensitive to behavior (to spontaneous or irregular motion, for example) than to form. Hence the questions of whether and how an agent is embodied are secondary. For example, young infants try to interact with mobiles as though they were social beings (Carey 1995: 279). This flexibility concerning embodiment reflects a real world in which animals conceal their form in many ways. How they look, therefore, is less important than how they act. Moreover, many animals obscure their location and direction of movement, for example, by complex schooling or flocking. In addition, such minute forms of life as viruses and bacteria have been both invisible and intangible throughout most of human history, yet their effects on us often have been perceived as the effects of agents – of demons, for example. Thus unconscious perception of agency without definite shape or location has a basis in experience over the course of human evolution.

Further, a subjective reason why disembodied agency is intuitive is that we conceive our selves and the selves of others as immaterial. A contemporary philosopher (Leder 1990) argues that in most of our self-awareness, the body is absent unless we are in some discomfort. Normally, our attention is, instead, to our external environment. Hence normal experience is disembodied.

Moreover, the human theory of mind holds that minds – phenomena that we intuitively regard as of greatest importance – are by nature unobservable (Malle 2005: 225). They are postulated behind events rather than on the surface. Fueled, perhaps, "by our deep appreciation of the idea of mind" (Wegner 2005: 22), we even imagine an unseen controller behind the processes of our own minds. This controller is the self that Lakoff and Johnson (1999: 268) call the "Subject," which cross-culturally is the "locus of consciousness, subjective experience, reason, will and our 'essence.'" People everywhere unconsciously conceive it, Lakoff and Johnson hold, as immaterial and disembodied. Being disembodied, it survives death and, in some religions, is called "the Soul or Spirit" (563).

Recent experimental evidence also indicates that we intuitively see our deepest selves both as disembodied and as surviving death. Work in cognitive psychology (Bering 2002; Bering and Bjorklund 2004) suggests that young children (and, to a large extent, adults) default to a model of postmortem continued sentience because they have no model for mental nonexistence. Using puppets to tell children a story in which a mouse is eaten by an alligator, Bering (2002) found that while young children understood that the mouse's death ended its capacity to run and to eat, they supposed that it still could be hungry or sad. Thus their conception of the mind remains the same, although the body now is missing. Hence their assumption of continued mental functioning does not appear as an extra hypothesis, but rather as the absence of one. Bering and Bjorklund conclude that the virtual universality of afterlife beliefs reflects "innate cognitive biases" about the mental state of dead agents. Thus several kinds of evidence converge to suggest that animism in the first sense, a belief in humanlike but disembodied agents, is intuitive.

A second sense of animism, advanced notably by Piaget (1929, 1933) and now standard among psychologists, is the tendency to "consider things as living and conscious" (1933: 537), that is, to attribute sentient life to nonliving things. Evidence from varied sources suggests that animism in this sense, too, is intuitive (Tiedemann 1927 [1787]; Cherry 1992; Guthrie 1993, 2002). One kind of evidence will suffice here. This is our multimodal group of special sensitivities (several of which we share with other animals) to features of our environments that may reveal the presence of complex animals, such as insects, fishes, reptiles, birds, and mammals. We react automatically to such features as spontaneous motion (Darwin 1871; Heider and Simmel 1944; Michotte 1950; Poulin-Dubois and Heroux 1994), eyespots (Ristau 1998: 141), bilateral symmetry (Washburn 1999), and faces (Johnson 2001), each of which we tend to interpret as a sign of life.

The third conceptual feature of religion, anthropomorphism – the attribution of human characteristics to nonhuman things or events – appears intuitive as well. Evidence includes its sheer diversity and pervasiveness at varied levels of perception and cognition (Cherry 1992; Guthrie 1993, 2002, forthcoming; Mitchell, Thomas, and Miles 1997, Kelemen 2004), including anthropomorphic linguistic (Cherry 1992) and visual (Guthrie 2000a) structures of which speakers and viewers are unaware, and our "intentional stance" and related teleology (Dennett 1987; Kelemen 2004).

Animism and anthropomorphism are by-products of a general cognitive stance. This strategic stance (which includes the intentional one) constitutes a good bet in the face of perceptual uncertainty. It assumes that unidentified phenomena – sights, sounds, smells, and so on – that may reflect the presence of life, including human life, in fact do so. Put another way, it is a stance in which sensitivity to possible signs of life is high and the threshold for accepting them as such is low.

This strategy has been produced by natural selection (in us and in other animals) because, as I have argued at length (1980, 1993, 1996, 1997, 2001, 2002, forthcoming), our perceptual world is inherently ambiguous and because where highly organized life is present, it is important that we detect it. Moreover, the ambiguity of perception is exacerbated by natural deception, including camouflage and mimicry. Because most of our predators, prey, and social others (including our fellow humans) have a highly evolved capacity to hide themselves, it is good strategy to assume that any given ambiguous shape or sound we encounter indicates their presence.

The most important information we can detect usually is that some animal – especially some human – is at hand. Under chronic perceptual uncertainty, our default assumption therefore is that irregular or spontaneous motions, face- or eye-like shapes, novel sounds, symmetries, "design," and other salient phenomena are signs that some animate being is present. If we assume that one is present, we can prepare for flight, fight, or social overtures. When that assumption is correct, we benefit by our readiness. When it is mistaken, as it often is, we lose little. In retrospect, we call the mistake animism or anthropomorphism.

Thus these mistakes are not themselves motivated, but rather are the by-products of a cognitive system that is motivated. This system necessarily has evolved to detect significant organisms wherever they may exist.

4. CONCLUSION

Despite over a century of anthropology of religion, its theories remain diverse and contentious. In the last two decades, however, cognitivism has reemerged as the leading theoretical orientation. Of its two main subdivisions, I have advocated that which considers religious thought and action intuitive.

In this view, the animism and anthropomorphism central to religious thought and action are not unique but are subsets of our general animism and anthropomorphism. They are distinguished from the general set only by their relative systematization and gravity. No clear line distinguishes religions from other thought and action. They are not themselves selected for, nor are they a unitary phenomenon. Rather, they are a family of side effects of our perceptual and cognitive proclivities, linked to each other by our search for order and meaning.

Religions, like other animism and anthropomorphism, may be put to varied uses. However, these uses neither account for their existence nor guarantee that they are beneficial. Ultimately, religions are products of evolutionary chance: unintended consequences of prior evolutionary products. Looking for a function in them, our intuitive bent, is an aspect of our teleology. That teleology, which assumes meaning and purpose in the world in general, is itself one more component of our anthropomorphism.

NOTE

1.   Postmodern anthropologists, however, decry comparativism and maintain that one can interpret only a culture at a time.

REFERENCES

Atran, Scott. 2002. *In Gods We Trust*. New York: Oxford University Press.
Barrett, Justin. 2000. "Exploring the Natural Foundations of Religion." *Trends in Cognitive Sciences* 4, no. 1: 29–34.
Bering, Jesse. 2002. "Intuitive Conceptions of Dead Agents' Minds: The Natural Foundations of Afterlife Beliefs as Phenomenological Boundary." *Journal of Cognition and Culture* 2: 263–308.
Bering, Jesse, and David Bjorklund. 2004. "The Natural Emergence of 'Afterlife' Reasoning as a Developmental Regularity." *Developmental Psychology* 40: 217–33.
Boyer, Pascal. 2001. *Religion Explained*. New York: Basic Books.

Boyer, Pascal, and Clark Barrett. 2005. "Domain Specificity and Intuitive Ontology." In David Buss (ed.), *Handbook of Evolutionary Psychology*. Hoboken, N.J.: Wiley, pp. 96–118.

Burkert, Walter. 1996. *Creation of the Sacred*. Cambridge, Mass.: Harvard University Press.

Carey, Susan. 1985. *Conceptual Change in Childhood*. Cambridge: MIT Press.

Carey, Susan. 1995. "On the Origin of Causal Understanding." In D. Sperber, D. Premack, and A. J. Premack (eds.), *Causal Cognition*. Oxford: Oxford University Press, pp. 268–302.

Carey, Susan. 2000. "Science Education as Conceptual Change." *Journal of Applied Developmental Psychology* 1: 37–41.

Carneiro, Robert. 2003. *Evolutionism in Cultural Anthropology*. Boulder, Colo.: Westview Press.

Cherry, John. 1992. "Animism in Thought and Language." Ph.D. thesis, University of California, Berkeley.

Crapo, Richley H. 2001. *Cultural Anthropology*. Boston: McGraw-Hill.

Darwin, Charles. 1871. *The Descent of Man, and Selection in Relation to Sex*. London: Murray.

Dennett, Donald. 1987. *The Intentional Stance*. Cambridge: MIT Press.

Durkheim, Emile. 1965 [1915]. *The Elementary Forms of the Religious Life*. New York: Free Press.

Feuerbach, Ludwig. 1957 [1873]. *The Essence of Christianity*. New York: Harper and Row.

Freeman, Kathleen. 1966. *Ancilla to the Pre-Socratic Philosophers*. Oxford: Basil Blackwell.

Freud, Sigmund. 1964 [1927]. *The Future of an Illusion*. Garden City, N.Y.: Anchor.

Geertz, Clifford. 1966. "Religion as a Cultural System." In M. Banton (ed.), *Anthropological Approaches to the Study of Religion*. London: Tavistock, pp. 1–46.

Guthrie, Stewart. 1980. "A Cognitive Theory of Religion." *Current Anthropology* 21, no. 2: 181–203.

Guthrie, Stewart. 1993. *Faces in the Clouds*. New York: Oxford University Press.

Guthrie, Stewart. 1996. "The Sacred: A Skeptical View." In Thomas Idinopulos and Edward Yonan (eds.), *The Sacred and Its Scholars*. Leiden: Brill, pp. 124–38.

Guthrie, Stewart. 1997. "Anthropomorphism: A Definition and a Theory." In R. Mitchell, N. Thompson, and L. Miles (eds.), *Anthropomorphism, Anecdotes, and Animals*. Albany: SUNY Press, pp. 50–58.

Guthrie, Stewart. 2000a. "Bottles Are Men, Glasses Are Women." *Anthropology News* 41, no. 4: 20–21.

Guthrie, Stewart. 2000b. "Projection." In Russell McCutcheon and Willi Braun (eds.), *Guide to the Study of Religion*. London: Cassell, pp. 225–38.

Guthrie, Stewart. 2001. "Why Gods? A Cognitive Theory." In Jensine Andresen (ed.), *Religion in Mind*. Cambridge: Cambridge University Press, pp. 94–111.

Guthrie, Stewart. 2002. "Animal Animism." In Ilkka Pyysiänen and Veikko Anttonen (eds.), *Current Approaches in the Cognitive Science of Religion*. London: Continuum, pp. 38–67.

Guthrie, Stewart. Forthcoming. "Gambling on Gods." In David Wulff (ed.), *Handbook of the Psychology of Religion*. New York: Oxford University Press.

Hassin, Ran R., James S. Uleman, and John A. Bargh. 2005. *The New Unconscious*. New York: Oxford University Press.

Heberlein, Andrea. 2004. "Impaired Spontaneous Anthropomorphizing Despite Intact Perception and Social Knowledge." *Proceedings of the National Academy of Sciences* 101, no. 19: 7487–91.

Heider, Fritz, and Marianne Simmel. 1944. "An Experimental Study of Apparent Behavior." *American Journal of Psychology* 57: 243–59.

Horton, Robin. 1960. "A Definition of Religion, and Its Uses." *Journal of the Royal Anthropological Institute* 90: 201–26.

Horton, Robin. 1967. "African Traditional Thought and Western Science." *Africa* 37: 50–71, 155–87.

Horton, Robin. 1973. "Lévy-Bruhl, Durkheim, and the Scientific Revolution." In Robin Horton and Ruth Finnegan (eds.), *Modes of Thought*. London: Faber and Faber, pp. 249–305.

Horton, Robin. 1982. "Tradition and Modernity Revisited." In Martin Hollis and Steven Lukes (eds.), *Rationality and Relativism*. Cambridge: MIT Press, pp. 201–60.

Horton, Robin. 1993. *Patterns of Thought in Africa and the West*. Cambridge: Cambridge University Press.

Hume, David. 1957 [1757]. *The Natural History of Religion*. Stanford, Calif.: Stanford University Press.

Huxley, Aldous. 1990 [1945]. *The Perennial Philosophy*. New York: HarperCollins.

Johnson, Mark H. 2001. "The Development and Neural Basis of Face Recognition: Comment and Speculation." *Infant and Child Development* 10 (March–June): 31.

Johnson, S. C., and Susan Carey. 1998. "Knowledge Enrichment and Conceptual Change in Folkbiology: Evidence from Williams Syndrome." *Cognitive Psychology* 37: 156–200.

Kardiner, Abram, and Ralph Linton. 1945. *The Psychological Frontiers of Society*. New York: Columbia University Press.

Kelemen, Deborah. 2004. "Are Children 'Intuitive Theists'? Reasoning about Purpose and Design in Nature." *Psychological Science* 15, no. 5: 295–301.

Kluckhohn, Clyde. 1942. "Myths and Rituals: A General Theory." *Harvard Theological Review* 35: 1.

La Barre, Weston. 1972. *The Ghost Dance: Origins of Religion*. New York: Dell.

Lakoff, George, and Mark Johnson. 1999. *Philosophy in the Flesh*. New York: Basic Books.

Leder, Drew. 1990. *The Absent Body*. Chicago: University of Chicago Press.

Lohmann, Roger Ivar, ed. 2003. "Special Issue: Perspectives on the Category 'Supernatural.'" *Anthropological Forum* 13, no. 2.

Malinowski, Bronislaw. 1955 [1925]. *Magic, Science and Religion*. Garden City, N.Y.: Doubleday.

Malle, Bertram F. 2005. "Folk Theory of Mind: Conceptual Foundations of Human Social Cognition." In Ran Hassin, James Uleman, and John Bargh (eds.), *The New Unconsciousness*. New York: Oxford University Press, pp. 225–55.

Marx, Karl, and Friedrich Engels. 1957. *On Religion*. Moscow: Progress.

Medin, D., and S. Atran. 1999. *Folk Biology*. Cambridge: MIT Press.

Michotte, A. 1950. *The Perception of Causality*. New York: Basic Books.

Mitchell, R., N. Thomas, and H. Miles, eds. 1997. *Anthropomorphism, Anecdotes, and Animals*. Albany: SUNY Press.

Piaget, Jean. 1929. *The Child's Conception of the World*. London: Routledge and Kegan Paul.

Piaget, Jean. 1933. "Children's Philosophies." In *A Handbook of Child Psychology*, 2nd ed. Worcester, Mass.: Clark University Press, pp. 505–16.

Pinker, Steven. 1997. *How the Mind Works*. New York: Norton.

Poulin-Dubois, D., and G. Heroux. 1994. "Movement and Children's Attribution of Life Properties." *International Journal of Behavioral Development* 17, no. 329: 47.

Preus, J. Samuel. 1987. *Explaining Religion*. New Haven: Yale University Press.

Pyysiäinen, Ilkka. 2001. *How Religion Works*. Leiden: Brill.

Radcliffe-Brown, A. R. 1979 [1939]. "Taboo." In William Lessa and Evon Vogt (eds.), *Reader in Comparative Religion*. New York: Harper and Row, pp. 46–56.

Rappaport, Roy. 1999. *Ritual and Religion in the Making of Humanity*. Cambridge: Cambridge University Press.

Ristau, C. 1998. "Cognitive Ethology: The Minds of Children and Animals." In D. Cummins and C. Allen (eds.), *The Evolution of Mind*. New York: Oxford University Press, pp. 127–61.

Roes, Frans, and Michel Raymond. 2003. "Belief in Moralizing Gods." *Evolution and Human Behavior* 24: 126–35.

Saler, Benson. 2000 [1993]. *Conceptualizing Religion*. Leiden: Brill.

Sperber, Dan. 1996. *Explaining Culture*. Oxford: Blackwell.

Spinoza, Benedict de. 1955. *The Chief Works of Benedict de Spinoza*. New York: Dover.

Spiro, Melford. 1966. "Religion: Problems of Definition and Meaning." In Michael Banton (ed.), *Anthropological Approaches to the Study of Religion*. London: Tavistock, pp. 85–126.

Teske, Roland, S. J. 1986. "The Aim of Augustine's Proof That God Truly Is." *International Philosophical Quarterly* 26: 253–68.

Tiedemann, D. 1927 [1787]. "Observations on the Development of the Mental Faculties of Children." *Journal of Genetic Psychology* 34: 205–30.

Tillich, Paul. 1948. *The Shaking of the Foundations*. New York: Scribner's.

Tylor, E. B. 1871. *Primitive Culture*. London: John Murray.

Tylor, E. B. 1979 [1871]. "Animism." In William Lessa and Evon Vogt (eds.), *Reader in Comparative Religion*. New York: Harper and Row, pp. 9–19.

Wallace, Anthony F. C. 1966. *Religion: An Anthropological View*. New York: Random.

Washburn, Dorothy. 1999. "Perceptual Anthropology: The Cultural Salience of Symmetry." *American Anthropologist* 101, no. 3: 547–62.

Wegner, Daniel. 2005. "Who Is the Controller of Controlled Processes?" In R. Hassin, J. Uleman, and J. Bargh (eds.), *The New Unconscious*. New York: Oxford University Press, pp. 19–36.

Wilson, David. 2002. *Darwin's Cathedral*. Chicago: University of Chicago Press.

18   Atheists

A Psychological Profile

Those who have shaped the modern human sciences have been preoccupied with explaining the phenomena of religion and religiosity. Accounting for the absence of religious faith has never been of much concern to them. The reasons for the neglect of atheism as a phenomenon in need of explanation are twofold. First, religion, and religiosity, seem to be adhered to by the majority of humans, and thus explaining their existence and survival is called for. Second, explaining religious beliefs is urgently called for if those doing it do not share those beliefs. And this indeed has been the case. Most of the great names in the history of modern human sciences have been atheists or agnostics, and we can recall Karl Marx, Sigmund Freud, Emile Durkheim, Bronislaw Malinowski, and Max Weber. They looked at religion from the outside, and explaining why they did not believe in any of it was unnecessary.

ATHEISTS AS DEVIANTS

Most theories of religion assume that it stems from universal aspects of the human condition or the human mind. Classical explanations used the notions of such universal and automatic psychological processes as projection, animism, or anthropomorphism. In some more recent theoretical formulations (Boyer 2001; Atran 2002) the framework is cognitive-evolutionary and assumes that the brain is a machine operating according to rules developed through evolution. The question is that of the seeming plausibility of religious ideas for most humans. Religion uses the basic and ordinary cognitive processes that are the evolutionary endowments of every human. The belief in supernatural agents is a by-product of naturally selected cognitive mechanisms. This useful evolutionary machinery makes costly, but acceptable, errors inevitable. Religion is one of the most important errors we make, but if indeed religiosity is natural, "hard wired," how do you avoid it? If religion is indeed natural and universal, what does it say about atheists? Do they go against "human nature"? Boyer (2001) and Atran (2002), continuing the Enlightenment tradition, would state that human nature and the human brain allow us to correct our cognitive errors, just as we have overcome similar anthropocentric errors in physics.

LOOKING FOR THE DATA

What can we say, at the psychological level, about individuals who are atheists or agnostics, those who do not share in the human tendency to believe in the world of the spirits and in some spirits that are greater than others and control our destiny?

For the past one hundred years, social science researchers have looked at the correlates of religiosity (Argyle and Beit-Hallahmi 1975; Beit-Hallahmi 1989; Beit-Hallahmi and Argyle 1997). The research has been based on regarding religiosity as a continuous, rather than discrete, variable. That means that each individual's level of religiosity is conceived of as lying on a scale, let us say, from 0 to 100. An atheist would get a score of 0; the most devout, 100. This body of findings contains much of the relevant information we need, as the psychology of religion is also the psychology of irreligion. If our findings about the correlates of religiosity make any sense, then atheists should be to some extent the psychological mirror image of highly religious people.

WHO ARE THEY? DEMOGRAPHICS

In representative surveys of the U.S. population in the 1970s and 1980s, the unaffiliated were found to be younger, mostly male, with higher levels of education and income, more liberal, but also more unhappy and more alienated in terms of the larger society (Hadaway and Roof 1988; Feigelman, Gorman, and Varacalli 1992). According to 2004 Gallup data, based on 12,043 interviews, the 9 percent of Americans who say they do not identify with any religion whatsoever or who explicitly say they are atheist or agnostic tended to be politically liberal, Democrats, independents, younger, living in the West, students, and those who are living with someone without being married (Newport 2004).

In Australia, secularists are much better educated than the rest of the population, socially liberal, independent, self-assertive, and cosmopolitan. In Canada, census data and national surveys show that those reporting "no religion" are younger, more male than female, more urban than rural, as well as upwardly mobile (Beit-Hallahmi and Argyle 1997).

Being an atheist overwhelmingly means being male. Data from all cultures show women to be more religious than men (Beit-Hallahmi 2005b). Recent polling data from the United States show that the statement "there is a god" was endorsed by 72.5 percent of men and 86.8 percent of women. The statement "I don't believe in any of these" was endorsed by 7.0 percent of men and only 1.3 percent of the women (Rice 2003).

PARENTS AND THE MAKING OF ATHEISTS

Some atheists have been raised without any religious teaching; others have chosen to reject what they have been taught as children. Apostasy is defined as disaffection, defection, alienation, disengagement, and disaffiliation from a religious group. Apostasy means not switching to another group, but declaring no allegiance to any religious tradition (Caplovitz and Sherrow 1977). Thus, it is a general disillusionment with religion, a private secularization. Caplovitz and Sherrow (1977) state, "It indicates not only loss of religious faith, but rejection of a particular ascriptive community as a basis for self-identification" (p. 31).

Continuity and discontinuity in any identity may be a function of interpersonal networks, especially involving intimate relations. Apostasy and conversion can both be seen as a rejection of parental identity and parental beliefs. It "might well be symptomatic of familial strain and dissociation from parents ... apostasy is to be viewed as a form of rebellion against parents" (Caplovitz and Sherrow 1977: 50). The Christian psychoanalyst Stanley A. Leavy (1988) suggested that atheism may be an expression of the liberation from the dominance of one's parents.

Findings regarding those who come from religious homes and then give up religion show that they have had more distant relations with their parents (Hunsberger 1980, 1983; Hunsberger and Brown 1984). Caplovitz and Sherrow (1977) found that the quality of relations with parents was a crucial variable, as well as a commitment to intellectualism. Hunsberger and Brown (1984) found that lesser emphasis placed on religion in home, especially by the mother, and self-reported intellectual orientation had a positive impact on rejecting the family's religiosity as a young adult. Dudley (1987) found that alienation from religion in Seventh-Day Adventist adolescents was correlated (0.72) with the quality of their relationship with their parents and other authority figures. Alienation was tied to authoritarianism and harshness on the part of the parents. But parents may also have a more consonant effect on their children's religiosity. Sherkat (1991), analyzing large-scale U.S. surveys in 1988, found that parents' religious exogamy and lapses in practice led to their children's apostasy. Thus, children may be following in their parents' footsteps or acting out their parents' unexpressed wishes.

Attachment theory (Kirkpatrick 2005) assumes that interpersonal styles in adults, the ways of dealing with attachment, separation, and loss in close personal relationships, stem directly from the mental models of oneself and others that were developed during infancy and childhood. Attachment styles can be characterized as secure, avoidant, or anxious/ambivalent. Secure adults find it relatively easy to get close to others. Avoidant adults are somewhat uncomfortable being close to others. Anxious/ambivalent adults find that others are reluctant to get as close as they would like. Kirkpatrick (2005) reports that in a study of 400 adults in the United States, those having an avoidant attachment style were most likely to identify themselves as either atheist or agnostic.

Does losing a parent early in life lead one to atheism? Vetter and Green (1932–33) surveyed 350 members of the American Association for the Advancement of Atheism, 325 of whom were men. Among those who became atheists before age twenty, half lost one or both parents before that age. A large number in the group reported unhappy childhood and adolescence experiences. (The twenty-five women reported "traumatic experiences" with male ministers. We can only wonder about those today.) Vitz (1999) presents biographical information from the lives of more than fifty prominent atheists and theists as evidence for his theory that atheism is a reaction to losing one's father.

The problem with this early deprivation hypothesis is that we find that losses and problems in early life may lead to serious pathology, but also to religious conversion and great personal achievements (cf. Eisenstadt 1989; Beit-Hallahmi 2005a). This discussion demonstrates that apostates are in some ways similar to religious converts. One major difference is the absence of testimonials and reports of visions and apparitions (cf. Shaffir 1991; Beit-Hallahmi 2005a).

ATHEISTS ARE LIBERAL AND TOLERANT

"While some studies did not find a connection between religious orthodoxy and political attitudes, no empirical study has ever found a relation between doctrinal orthodoxy and political liberalism or radicalism" (Argyle and Beit-Hallahmi 1975: 107). One general hypothesis assumes that religiosity would be linked to support for nondemocratic ideology, because religion has always been connected to tradition, authority, and hierarchy. Nelson (1988) found that in surveys using representative samples of the U.S. population between 1973 and 1985, disaffiliation from religious denominations contributed to greater political liberalism. Hartmann and Peterson (1968) studied 1,500 freshmen at thirty-seven American colleges. A "liberalism" factor was extracted, consisting of support for a welfare state, organized labor, and social change toward greater equality. The nonreligious and Jews scored highest, Protestants lowest.

In a classical study of ethnocentrism and anti-Semitism, those respondents reporting no religious affiliation were found to be much lower in prejudice (Adorno et al. 1950). The authors summarized the findings as follows: "[I]t appears that those who reject religion have less ethnocentrism that those who seem to accept it" (1950: 213). These findings have been confirmed many times since.

Much research was done in the United States during the politically turbulent 1960s. In a 1966 sample of U.S. students at nine Midwestern private colleges, an inverse relationship was found between religiosity and support for the civil rights movement active then. During the Vietnam War, studies in the United States showed that religious orthodoxy was tied to hawkish attitudes in support of U.S. involvement. Among participants in a demonstration against the Vietnam War, 61 percent reported no religious affiliation, and among American students in the 1960s, participation in protest demonstrations against the war was positively correlated with having no religious affiliation or a Jewish ancestry. It was negatively correlated with the practice of praying. A survey of 1,062 American students in 1968 found that Catholic students showed most acceptance of modern war and that students with no religious affiliation were most opposed to it (Beit-Hallahmi and Argyle 1997). Hamilton (1968) showed that in both 1952 and 1964, when the United States was involved in foreign wars, those having no religious affiliations were most opposed to military measures.

The correlation between rejection of religious beliefs and radical political views for individuals has been clearly demonstrated in several studies. Spray and Marx (1969) showed that the degree of political radicalism was directly related to the degree of irreligiosity. Self-identified atheists were more radical than self-identified agnostics.

Using a representative sample of the U.S. population between 1973 and 1977, Hadaway and Roof (1988) found that individuals raised as "nones" who remained unaffiliated were more liberal in politics and morals than those who later in life became religiously affiliated. Smidt and Penning (1982) found that in representative samples of the U.S. population in 1974, 1977, and 1980, religious commitment was inversely related to political tolerance. In a 1994 public opinion survey in the United States, it was found that opposition to the death penalty was highest (34%) among those reporting no religious affiliation, and lowest (9%) among Mormons. The overall figure was 25 percent, and it was 26 percent among Jews, 27 percent among Protestants, and 25 percent among Catholics.

One way of looking at the relationship between religious and political beliefs is to examine closely members of radical political groups. Grupp and Newman (1973) studied, in 1965, two activist groups in the United

States: the John Birch Society, a radical right-wing group, and Americans
for Democratic Action (ADA), a left-wing group within the Democratic
Party. Among the Birchers, 16 percent belonged to liberal Protestant
groups or had no affiliation, while among ADA members, 80 percent
were in that category or were Jewish. Nassi (1981) reported that radical
students who were members of the students' free speech movement at
the University of California, Berkeley, in 1964 (which started the 1960s
upheavals on U.S. campuses) were more likely (compared with controls)
to come from families that were identified as Jewish, agnostic, or atheist.
Fifteen years later, they were likely to report the same affiliations.

Since the 1940s, numerous studies in the United States have investigated attitudes to deviates of various kinds. The results have shown
that the more religious are less tolerant; Jews and the irreligious are
most tolerant. Kirkpatrick (1949) found that people who scored high on
his "religionism" factor had more punitive attitudes toward criminals,
homosexuals, unmarried mother and conscientious objectors, though
the relationship was very weak. Stouffer (1955) found that churchgoers
were more intolerant of political dissent than nonchurchgoers: "There
would appear to be something about people who go to church regularly
that makes fewer of them, as compared with non-churchgoers, willing
to accord civil rights to nonconformists who might be communists, sus-
pected Communists, or merely Socialists" (p. 142). Jewish respondents,
noted for secularity, were more tolerant than the others.

MENTAL HEALTH: ARE ATHEISTS NEUROTIC?

Marie Bonaparte (1958), a close associate of Freud, stated that atheism
represents realism, but also sadism. Atheists are able to adapt to reality,
and psychoanalysis, being "that outstanding school for adaptation to
reality," naturally leads to atheism. At the same time, it is pointed out
that such realism is also a form of sublimated sadism (Ambrose Beirce
and H. L. Mencken?).

Rollo May, a well-known advocate of existential psychology and religion, claimed that all atheists demonstrate "unmistakable neurotic tendencies" (in Wulff 1997: 625). Julia Kristeva, a well-known advocate of
both psychoanalysis and religion, states that "the depressed person is a
radical, sullen atheist" (Kristeva 1991: 5) and that atheism is "deprived
of meaning, deprived of values" (p. 14). This description should then
be applied to both of her mentors, Sigmund Freud and Jaques Lacan,
wellknown for their atheism.

When we turn to systematic studies of mental health and religiosity,
the picture is more complex. Schumaker (1992), in a literature survey,
reports a correlation between irreligiosity and psychological problems.

Ventis (1995), after surveying the literature, concludes that the non-religious are psychologically healthier than religious individuals and hypothesizes that this may be related to "a sense of personal competence and control, self-acceptance and self-actualization, and perhaps open-mindedness and flexibility." At the same time, such individuals may suffer from "existential anxiety and guilt" (p. 43). Feigelman et al. (1992), using a representative sample of the U.S. population, noted that disaffiliation does not contribute to happiness. Ross (1950) reported that individuals with no religious affiliation in the United States enjoyed low levels of psychological distress, just like highly religious individuals, despite their marginal status in society. Maslow (1970) reported that of the fifty-seven individuals he judged to be self-actualized, that is, having achieved the highest level of personality development, very few were religious.

So it seems that while the findings are not clear-cut, and religiosity may contribute to individual adjustment (Beit-Hallahmi and Argyle 1997), atheists do appear to cope just as well with reality.

MORALITY AND CRIME

The claim that atheists are somehow likely to be immoral or dishonest has long been disproven by systematic studies. In studies that looked at readiness to help or honesty, it was atheists that distinguished themselves, not the religious. Early in the twentieth century, a survey of 2,000 associates of the YMCA found that those identifying themselves as atheists or agnostics were more willing to help the poor than those who called themselves religious (Ross 1950).

When it comes to the more serious matter of violence and crime, ever since the field of criminology got started and data were collected of the religious affiliation of criminal offenders, the fact that the unaffiliated and the nonreligious had the lowest crime rates has been noted (Lombroso 1911; Bonger 1943; von Hentig 1948). According to von Hentig, being unaffiliated is the best predictor of law-abiding behavior. There is no reason to doubt the validity of this generalization today.

ATHEISTS AND THE INTELLECTUAL ELITE

To reach the intellectual elite, you have to start with a very high IQ (in addition to other qualities). Starting in 1925, L. M. Terman and his colleagues studied 1,528 gifted youth with IQs greater than 140 who were approximately twelve years old. At midlife, 10 percent of the men and 18 percent of women held strong religious beliefs. Some 62 percent of the men and 57 percent of the women claimed "little religious inclination," while 28 percent of the men and 23 percent of the women claimed it was "not at all important" (Terman and Oden 1959).

Beyond intelligence, leading academics and scientists display intellectuality and intellectualism, a commitment to scholarship. In a study of 2,842 graduate students in the United States, Stark (1963) found that church attendance was negatively associated with self-identification as an intellectual, and with positive attitudes toward creativity, occupational freedom, and professional ambition. Thus, those who were more conforming religiously appeared to place less value on intellectual achievement. Other studies have shown rather consistent patterns of decreased involvement in institutional religion among those who move on through graduate school, particularly among those who identify with intellectualism as a value (Caplovitz and Sherrow 1977). A study by Lehman (1972) shows inverse relationships between scholarly perspective and religiosity. It has often been shown that universities in the United States that are dominated by religious organizations have a lower reputation (cf. Mixon, Lyon, and Beaty 2004).

Students with ability and commitment to the academic life reach elite colleges and universities. Goldsen et al. (1960) carried out in 1950–51 a survey of a 6 percent sample ($n = 2,975$) of male students at eleven campuses across the United States. The percentage of students who believed in God was at Harvard 30; at UCLA 32; at Dartmouth 35; at Yale 36; at Cornell 42; at Wayne State 43; at Wesleyan 43; at Michigan 45; at Fisk 60; at Texas 62; and at North Carolina 68. Caplovitz and Sherrow (1977) found that apostasy rates rose continuously from 5 percent in low-ranked universities to 17 percent in high-ranked universities. Zelan (1968) analyzed data from U.S. arts and science graduate students in 1958, and found 25 percent religious "nones," 80 percent of whom had been raised in some religion. The pattern was accentuated in elite universities. Niemi, Ross, and Alexander (1978) reported that at elite colleges, organized religion was judged important by only 26 percent of their students, compared with 44 percent of all students.

ACADEMIA AND SCIENCE AS THE ATHEIST BASTIONS

Studies on the religiosity of scientists and academics have been carried out since early in the twentieth century. Their findings have been consistent, showing them to be quite irreligious (Ament 1927; Lehman and Witty 1931). Moreover, early on researchers found that the more eminent scientists were less religious than others. In the best-known early surveys, starting in 1914, James L. Leuba mailed a questionnaire to leading scientists asking about their belief in "a God in intellectual and affective communication with humankind" and in "personal immortality." "I do not see any way to avoid the conclusion that disbelief in a personal God and in personal immortality is directly proportional to abilities making for success in the sciences in question" (Leuba 1916: 279). Later on, Leuba (1934) found that only 32 percent of "greater" scientists believed in God, compared with 48 percent of "lesser" ones; the figures for belief in immortality were 37 percent and 59 percent, respectively.

Roe (1952) interviewed sixty-four eminent scientists, nearly all members of the prestigious National Academy of Sciences or the American Philosophical Society. She reported that, while nearly all of them had religious parents and had attended Sunday school, only three were seriously active in church. All the others had long since dismissed religion as any guide to them, and the church played no part in their lives. A few were militantly atheistic, but most were just not interested.

Since early in the twentieth century, large differences have been found between the religious and nonreligious, and also among religious denominations, in the numbers of scientists they produced. Bello (1954) studied research scientists under the age of forty judged by senior colleagues to be outstanding. Of the eighty-seven respondents, 45 percent claimed to be "agnostic or atheistic," and an additional 22 percent claimed no religious affiliation. For the twenty most eminent, "the proportion who are now a-religious is considerably higher than in the entire survey group." He also found a massive overrepresentation of "nones" and secularized Jews, and underrepresentation of Roman Catholics among in American scientists. There was a great deal of apostasy, as 45 percent of scientists were "nones," but only 8 percent of their parents were.

Vaughan, Smith, and Sjoberg (1966) polled 850 U.S. physicists, zoologists, chemical engineers, and geologists listed in *American Men of Science* (1955) on church membership, attendance, and belief in afterlife. Of the 642 replies, 38.5 percent did not believe in an afterlife, whereas 31.8 percent did. Belief in immortality was less common among major university staff than among those employed by business, government, or minor universities. They found that 54 percent of their group had religious affiliations different from those of their parents. Larson and Witham (1997) reported 60 percent believers in a random sample taken from *American Men and Women of Science* in 1996.

ATHEISTS AND THE HUMAN SCIENCES

A finding that goes against the common-sense view and calls for an explanation is the greater degree of religiosity among physical scientists, as compared with social scientists, especially psychologists. This was reported already by Leuba (1916). What should be noted is that the differences among academic field vanished with growing eminence.

Consistently, studies have reported that social scientists are among the least religious, most often with an overrepresentation of "nones" or Jews (who are highly secularized), together with some liberal Protestants, but a paucity of Catholics (Glenn and Weiner 1969; Thalheimer 1973).

A 1989 large-scale survey in the United States (Politics of the Professoriate 1991) found that the percentage of faculty members answering "none" in response to "What is your present religion?" was 65 percent in anthropology, 55 percent in philosophy, 53 percent in zoology, 52 percent in physiology/anatomy, 51 percent in other biological fields, 50 percent in education (foundations), 50 percent in psychology, 49 percent in electrical engineering, 49 percent in sociology, 47 percent in French, 47 percent in molecular biology, 44 percent in art, 44 percent in Spanish, 41 percent in English, 35 percent in mathematics/statistics, 33 percent in physics, and 26 percent in medicine. The lowest percentages (possibly because of the majority of faculty being female were in dentistry (16%), library science (13%), nursing (12%), civil engineering (11%), social work (9%), and home economics (4%).

Lehman and Shriver (1968; Lehman 1974) proposed the "scholarly distance" hypothesis: those in subjects remote from the study of religion, such as physics, were more religious than those whose academic fields studied religion, such as psychology and sociology. Subjects such as education and economics were scored as intermediate. Those at a greater distance were more religious.

The reason, in psychological terms, is that natural sciences apply critical thinking to nature; the human sciences ask critical questions about culture, traditions, and beliefs. The mere fact of choosing human society or behavior as the object of study reflects a curiosity about basic social beliefs and conventions and a readiness to reject them. Physical scientists, who are at a greater scholarly distance, may be able to compartmentalize their science and religion more easily.

The same scholarly distance effects were found among students. One factor may be that of self-selection in terms of unconventionality. Thalheimer (1965) found that the relative secularization of faculty members in the United States took place earlier than their college years. Bereiter and Freedman (1962) found that social science majors take a more liberal and less conventional stand on most issues, while students in the applied fields are more conservative in their attitudes. Jones (1970) also found that among university freshmen, those majoring in natural science were the most favorable to religion, those studying psychology the least. Hoge (1974) found natural sciences university students to be higher on orthodoxy. It seems likely that individuals choose their fields in terms of their own curiosity, whether about nature or about culture. This curiosity, in turn, may be related to personality factors and early experiences.

GREAT PSYCHOLOGISTS AS ATHEISTS

Among celebrity atheists with much biographical data, we find lead-
ing psychologists and psychoanalysts. We could provide a long list,
including G. Stanley Hall, John B. Watson, Carl R. Rogers, Albert Ellis,
James Leuba, Abraham Maslow, B. F. Skinner, Hans Jurgen Eysenck, and
Raymond B. Cattell, and among psychoanalysts Ernest Jones, Melanie
Klein, Jaques Lacan, and William Alanson White (Beit-Hallahmi 1992).
Maslow was a second-generation atheist, and his father was a militant
freethinker (Wulff 1997). Homans (1982) presented the case of Sigmund
Freud, together with those of Carl Rogers and Carl Gustav Jung, as exam-
ples of personal secularization and its effects on psychological theories.
What becomes clear from this analysis was that Freud's early life was
much less affected by religion than those of Rogers and Jung. He never
experienced an apostasy crisis, which the other two did.

Rank and file psychologists are also irreligious. Ragan, Malony, and
Beit-Hallahmi (1980) studied a random sample including 555 members
of the American Psychological Association. There were 34 percent atheists, compared with 2 percent in the general U.S. population; the least
religious were the experimental psychologists, the most religious were
in counseling and research on personality.

ARE PSYCHOTHERAPISTS ATHEISTS?

Research has shown that most psychotherapists remain less religious
than the general population. In medicine, psychiatrists are by far the
least religious (Kosa 1969). Henry, Sims, and Spray (1971) found that out
of 1,387 American clinical psychologists, 50 percent came from Jewish
families, but only 30 percent described themselves as currently Jewish.
Only 20 percent of the clinical psychologists described themselves as
Protestant, 8 percent as Catholic, and 42 percent as unaffiliated. With
psychoanalysis, the picture is similar. Lally (1975) reported that among
psychiatrists in New York City in 1960, some 7 percent were Catholic,
13 percent Protestant, 62 percent Jewish, and 18 percent had no religion;
of those who were are also psychoanalysts, the respective figures are
2 percent, 12 percent, 62 percent, and 25 percent.

A study of 113 aging (over fifty) psychoanalysts in the United States
reported that 42 percent of the group were of Jewish background, and
the group as a whole showed a high degree of irreligiosity, with most
respondents listing no religious affiliation (Tallmer 1992). Weintraub and
Aronson (1974) found that among individuals undergoing psychoanalysis
in the United States, those of Jewish origin were overrepresented (42%),
while Roman Catholics were underrepresented (16%).

ATHEISTS AS THE MOST EMINENT SCIENTISTS

In an unpublished study, I have used the book by Sherby and Odelberg (2000) to determine the religious affiliation and religiosity of Nobel laureates between 1901 and 2001. The book contains the most reliable biographical information on 696 laureates, who in terms of nationality represent mainly the United States (282, or 41%), Britain (77, or 11%), Germany (68, or 9.7%), and France (51, or 7.3%). Behind are Sweden (26 laureales), Switzerland (14), Austria (13), Denmark (13), the Netherlands (13), and Italy (12). Other nations have smaller representations.

The Nobel Memorial Prize is awarded each year in physics, chemistry, physiology or medicine, peace, and literature. Since 1968, the Bank of Sweden Award in Economic Science has provided an entrée for the social sciences. Sherby and Odelberg (2000) tried to provide a nominal affiliation for each laureate, not looking at the level of individual religiosity, but the attempt to do that showed that the issue was religiosity. As they reported, it was most difficult to locate information regarding affiliation in most cases, and this is for individuals who are public celebrities!

Only 49 percent of laureates could be classified (as Roman Catholic, Protestant, Jewish, Unitarian, or other). For the remaining 51 percent, 20.26 percent were classified as "none," apostates (e.g., "from Christian background"), or "no record." For almost 35 percent of laureates, the classification was speculative, ambiguous, and generic, such as "Protestant" (no denomination), "Christian," or "most probably Christian." This was an indication of how reluctant these individuals were to align themselves with any denominations. To appreciate this, it should be noted that five of the economics laureates, who received the award fairly recently and are world famous, are listed as "no record." In addition, the 18 percent of the Nobel laureates who were listed as Jewish do not represent a religious group, but an ethnic label. We know that the vast majority of them are thoroughly secular. As to those openly identifying themselves as "nones," two things should be noted. First, they are the largest group among the literature laureates (31 out of 97). Second, they were found among the laureates as early as the first decade of the twentieth century.

When it comes to Nobel laureates, the "eminence effect" (Leuba 1916), showing a lower level of religiosity among scientists of renown, as compared with lesser ones, has been demonstrated again. What this study of the most eminent scientists of the century has shown is that eminence accentuates differences in both religious affiliation and religiosity between scientists and the general population, so that eminence in natural and social sciences (and even in literature) is clearly tied to a personal distance from religion.

If there were any doubts about the irreligiosity of eminent scientists after looking at the biographical, secondary data in the Sherby and Odelberg (2000) book, they were laid to rest thanks to the survey done in 1996 by Larson and Witham. Larson and Witham (1997, 1998) performed an exact replication of the 1914 and 1933 surveys by James H. Leuba. Larson and Witham used the same wording and sent questionnaires to 517 members of the United States National Academy of Sciences from the biological and physical sciences (i.e., mathematicians, physicists, and astronomers; many members of the National Academy of Sciences are Nobel laureates). The return rate was slightly over 50 percent. The results showed that the percentage of believers in a personal God among eminent scientists in the United States was 27.7 in 1914, 15 in 1933, and 7.0 in 1998. Belief in personal immortality was slightly higher (35.2% in 1914, 18% in 1933, and 7.9% in 1998).

The findings demonstrate, first, that the process of turning away from religion among the most eminent scientists has been continuing over the past century, and, second, that in the United States, eminent scientists, with only 7 percent believing in a personal God, present a mirror image of the general population, where the corresponding percentage hovers around 90 percent in various studies. Larson and Witham state that "disbelief in God and immortality among NAS biological scientists was 65.2% and 69.0%, respectively, and among NAS physical scientists it was 79.0% and 76.3%. Most of the rest were agnostics on both issues, with few believers. We found the highest percentage of belief among NAS mathematicians (14.3% in God, 15.0% in immortality). Biological scientists had the lowest rate of belief (5.5% in God, 7.1% in immortality), with physicists and astronomers slightly higher (7.5% in God, 7.5% in immortality)." The article concludes with the following remarks: "As we compiled our findings, the NAS issued a booklet encouraging the teaching of evolution in public schools.... The booklet assures readers, 'Whether God exists or not is a question about which science is neutral.' NAS president Bruce Alberts said: 'There are many very outstanding members of this academy who are very religious people, people who believe in evolution, many of them biologists.' Our survey suggests otherwise."

What the findings regarding the Nobel laureates and the U.S. National Academy of Sciences show is that since the nineteenth century, an international intellectual elite, made up of creative and highly secular individuals, committed to the life of the mind, has been in existence. (Those studied by Leuba in 1914 and those awarded the Nobel Prize in the early years, between 1901 and 1950, had their formative years in the nineteenth century. Among those awarded the Nobel Prize before 1920, most were born before 1850.) Academics and scientists are expected to excel in critical thinking, innovation, and independence. If I may be allowed to offer a psychodynamic interpretation, what these individuals had, in addition to their creativity and high intelligence, was a strong wish to create distance between themselves and their parents.

JEWISH ANCESTRY AS A FACTOR

Throughout this chapter, Jewish self-identification or background has been consistently reported as being similar or identical to atheism or irreligiosity. In many cases the reader of research articles is led to believe that "Jewish" and "no religion" are almost interchangeable. Here is how one U.S. sociologist interpreted the "no affiliation" and "Jewish" labels in research: "'No religious affiliation' was assumed to indicate a low value on conformity and an individualistic approach. 'Jewish' was considered a liberal designation because of the high level of education of this group, its low degree of organized religion, and its political liberality" (Reiss 1967: 122). In the research literature we have surveyed, the label "Jewish" has been mentioned in all the contexts in which atheists are likely to be active: liberal or radical politics, social issues, and the global intellectual elite, as represented by Nobel laureates. Jewish secularization has been vigorous and thorough ever since it started in the eighteenth century. It meant that Jewish identity was maintained by individuals who completely stopped the practice of Jewish religion, and that Jewishness became separated from Judaism (Beit-Hallahmi 1993). Indeed, modern Jews are highly secularized, scoring low on every measure of religious belief and religious participation in every known study. What should also be recalled is that apostasy, if it took place, was in many cases not very recent, a part of the experience of earlier generations.

SUMMARY

What we are able to conclude about the modal atheist in Western society today is that that person is much more likely to be a man, married, with higher education. Can we speak about a modal atheist personality? A tentative psychological profile can be offered. We can say that atheists show themselves to be less authoritarian and suggestible, less dogmatic, less prejudiced, more tolerant of others, law-abiding, compassionate, conscientious, and well educated. They are of high intelligence, and many are committed to the intellectual and scholarly life. In short, they are good to have as neighbors.

REFERENCES

Adorno, T. W., E. Frenkel-Brunswik, D. J. Levinson, and R. N. Sanford. 1950. *The Authoritarian Personality*. New York: Harper & Row.

Ament, W. S. 1927. "Religion, Education, and Distinction." *School and Society* 26: 399–406.

Argyle, M., and B. Beit-Hallahmi. 1975. *The Social Psychology of Religion*. London and Boston: Routledge & Kegan Paul.

Atran, S. 2002. *In Gods We Trust: The Evolutionary Landscape of Religion*. New York and Oxford: Oxford University Press.

Beit-Hallahmi, B. 1989. *Prolegomena to the Psychological Study of Religion*. Lewisburg, Pa.: Bucknell University Press.

Beit-Hallahmi, B. 1992. "Between Religious Psychology and the Psychology of Religion." In M. Finn and J. Gartner (eds.), *Object Relations, Theory and Religion: Clinical Applications*. New York: Praeger.

Beit-Hallahmi, B. 1993. *Original Sins: Reflections on the History of Zionism and Israel*. New York: Interlink.

Beit-Hallahmi, B. 1996. *Psychoanalytic Studies of Religion: Critical Survey and Annotated Bibliography*. Westport, Conn.: Greenwood Press.

Beit-Hallahmi, B. 2005a. "Religious Conversion." In D. M. Wulff (ed.), *Handbook of the Psychology of Religion*. Oxford University Press.

Beit-Hallahmi, B. 2005b. "Women, Psychological Feminity, and Religion." In D. M. Wulff (ed.), *Handbook of the Psychology of Religion*. Oxford University Press.

Beit-Hallahmi, B., and M. Argyle, 1997. *The Psychology of Religious Behaviour, Belief, and Experience*. London: Routledge.

Bello, F. (1954). "The Young Scientists." *Fortune* 49: 142–43.

Bereiter, C., and M. B. Freedman, 1962. "Fields of Study and the People in Them." In N. Sanford (ed.), *The American College*. New York: Wiley.

Bonaparte, M. 1958. "Psychoanalysis in Relation to Social, Religious and Natural Forces." *International Journal of Psychoanalysis* 39: 513–15.

Bonger, W. A. 1943. *Race and Crime*. New York, New York: Columbia University Press.

Boyer, P. 2001. *Religion Explained: The Human Instincts That Fashion Gods, Spirits and Ancestors*. London: William Heinnemann.

Caplovitz, D., and F. Sherrow, 1977. *The Religious Drop-outs: Apostasy among College Students*. Beverly Hills, Calif.: Sage.

Dudley, R. L. 1987. "Alienation from Religion in Adolescents from Fundamentalist Religious Homes." *Journal for the Scientific Study of Religion* 17: 389–98.

Eisenstadt, M. 1989. *Parental Loss and Achievement*. New York: International Universities Press.

Feigelman, W., B. S. Gorman, and J. A. Varacalli. 1992. "Americans Who Give Up Religion." *Sociology and Social Research* 76: 138–44.

Glenn, N. D., and D. Weiner. 1969. "Some Trends in the Social Origins of American Sociologists." *American Sociologist*, 4: 291–302.

Goldsen, R. K., M. Rosenberg, R. M. Williams, Jr., and E. A. Suchman. 1960. *What College Students Think*. Princeton, N.J.: D. Van Nostrand.

Grupp, F. W., Jr., and W. M. Newman. 1973. "Political Ideology and Religious Preference: The John Birch Society and Americans for Democratic Action." *Journal for the Scientific Study of Religion* 12: 401–13.

Hadaway, C. K., and C. D. Roof. 1988. "Apostasy in American Churches: Evidence from National Survey Data. In D. G. Bromley (ed.), *Falling from the Faith*. Newbury Park, Calif.: Sage.

Hamilton, R. F. (1968), "A Research Note on the Mass Support for 'tough' Military Initiatives." *American Sociological Review* 33: 439–45.

Hartmann, R. T., and R. E. Peterson. 1968. "Religious Preference as a Factor in Attitudinal and Background Differences among College Freshman." *Sociology of Education* 41: 227–37.

Henry, E. R., J. H. Sims, and S. L. Spray. 1971. *The Fifth Profession*. San Francisco: Jossey-Bass.

Hoge, D. 1974. *Commitment on Campus: Changes in Religion and Values over Five Decades*. Philadelphia: Westminster Press.

Homans, P. 1982. "A Personal Struggle with Religion: Significant Fact in the Lives and Work of the First Psychologists." *Journal of Religion* 62: 128–44.

Hunsberger, B. E. 1980. "A Reexamination of the Antecedents of Apostasy." *Review of Religious Research* 21: 158–70.

Hunsberger, B. E. 1983. "Apostasy: A Social Learning Perspective." *Review of Religious Research* 25: 21–38.

Hunsberger, B. E., and L. B. Brown. 1984. "Religious Socialization, Apostasy, and the Impact of Family Background." *Journal for the Scientific Study of Religion* 23: 239–51.

Jones, V. (1970). "Attitudes of College Students and Their Changes: A 37-Year Study." *Genetic Psychology Monographs* 81: 3–80.

Kirkpatrick, C. (1949). "Religion and Humanitarianism: A Study of Institutional Implications." *Psychological Monographs*, 63, no. 309.

Kirkpatrick, L. A. 2005. *Attachment, Evolution, and the Psychology of Religion*. New York: Guilford Publications.

Kosa, J. 1969. "The Medical Student: His Career and Religion." *Hospital Progress* 50: 51–53.

Kristeva, J. 1991. *Black Sun: Depression and Melancholia*. New York: Columbia University Press.

Lally, J. J. (1975). "Selection as an Interactive Process: The Case of Catholic Psychoanalysts and Psychiatrists." *Social Science and Medicine* 9: 157–64.

Larson, E. J., and L. Witham. 1997. "Scientists Are Still Keeping the Faith." *Nature* 386: 435–36.

Larson, E. J., and L. Witham. 1998. "Leading Scientists Still Reject God." *Nature* 394: 313.

Leavy, S. A. 1988. *In the Image of God: A Psychoanalyst's View*. New Haven: Yale University Press.

Lehman, E. C., Jr. 1972. "The Scholarly Perspective and Religious Commitment." *Sociological Analysis* 33: 199–216.

Lehman, E. C., Jr. 1974. "Academic Discipline and Faculty Religiosity in Secular and Church-Related Colleges." *Journal for the Scientific Study of Religion* 13: 205–20.

Lehman, E. C., Jr., and D. W. Shriver. 1968. "Academic Discipline as Predictive of Faculty Religiosity." *Social Forces* 47: 171–82.

Lehman, H. C., and P. A. Witty. 1931 "Scientific Eminence and Church Membership." *Scientific Monthly* 33: 544–49.

Leuba, J. H. 1916. *Belief in God and Immortality: A Psychological, Anthropological and Statistical Study*. Boston: Sherman & French.

316   BENJAMIN BEIT-HALLAHMI

Leuba, J. H. 1934. "Religious Beliefs of American Scientists." *Harper's* 169: 292–300.

Lombroso, C. 1911. *Crime: Its Causes and Remedies*. London: Heinemann.

Maslow, A. H. 1970. *Motivation and Personality*. New York: Harper & Row.

Mixon, S. L., L. Lyon, and M. Beaty. 2004. "Secularization and National Universities: The Effect of Religious Identity on Academic Reputation." *Journal of Higher Education* 75: 400–419.

Nassi, A. 1981. Survivors of the Sixties: Comparative Psychosocial and Political Development of Former Berkeley Student Activists." *American Psychologist* 36: 753–61.

Nelson, L. D. 1988. "Disaffiliation, Desacralization, and Political Values." In D. G. Bromley (ed.), *Falling from the Faith: Causes and Consequences of Religious Apostasy*. Newbury Park, Calif.: Sage, 122–39.

Newport, F. "America's Religious Identification 2004." Http://www.gallup.com/poll/content/?ci = 14446, accessed January 6, 2006.

Niemi, R. G., R. D. Ross, and J. Alexander. 1978. "The Similarity of Political Values of Parents and College-Age Youths." *Public Opinion Quarterly* 42: 503–20.

Politics of the Professoriate. 1991. "Public Perspective." *The American Enterprise* 2, no. 4 (July–August): 86–87.

Ragan, C. H., H. N. Maloney, and B. Beit-Hallahmi. 1980. "Psychologists and Religion: Professional Factors and Personal Belief." *Review of Religious Research* 21: 208–17.

Reiss, I. L. 1967. *The Social Context of Premarital Sexual Permissiveness*. New York: Holt, Rinehart and Winston.

Rice, T. W. 2003. "Believe It or Not: Religious and Other Paranormal Beliefs in the United States." *Journal for the Scientific Study of Religion* 42: 95–106.

Roe, A. 1952. *The Making of a Scientist*. New York: Dodd, Mead.

Ross, M. 1950. *Religious Beliefs in Youths*. New York: YMCA.

Schumaker, J. F., ed. 1992. *Religion and Mental Health*. New York: Oxford University Press.

Shaffir, W. 1991. "Conversion Experiences: Newcomers to and Defectors from Orthodox Judaism." In Z. Sobel and B. Beit-Hallahmi (eds.), *Tradition, Innovation, Conflict: Jewishness and Judaism in Contemporary Israel*. Albany: SUNY Press.

Sherby, L. S., and W. Odelberg. 2000. *Who's Who of Nobel Prize Winners 1901–2000*. Phoenix, Az.: Oryx Press.

Sherkat, D. E. 1991. "Leaving the Faith: Testing Theories of Religious Switching Using Survival Models." *Social Science Research* 20: 171–87.

Smidt, C. E., and J. M. Penning. 1982. "Religious Commitment, Political Conservatism, and Political and Social Tolerance in the United States: A Longitudinal Analysis." *Sociological Analysis* 43: 231–46.

Spray, S. L., and J. H. Marx. 1969. "The Origins and Correlates of Religious Adherence and Apostasy among Mental Health Professionals." *Sociological Analysis* 30: 132–50.

Stark, R. 1963. "On the Incompatibility of Religion and Science: A Survey of American Graduate Students." *Journal for the Scientific Study of Religion* 3: 3–20.

Stouffer, S. A. 1955. *Communism, Conformity and Civil Liberties*. New York: Doubleday.

Tallmer, M. 1992. "The Aging Analyst." *Psychoanalytic Review* 79: 381–404.

Terman, L. M., and M. H. Oden. 1959. *The Gifted Group at Mid-life: Thirty-five Years' Follow-up of the Superior Child*. Stanford, Calif.: Stanford University Press.

Thalheimer, F. 1965. "Continuity and Change in Religiosity: A Study of Academicians." *Pacific Sociological Review* 8: 101–8.

Thalheimer, F. 1973. "Religiosity and Secularization in the Academic Professions." *Sociology of Education* 46: 183–202.

Vaughan, T. R., D. H. Smith, and G. Sjoberg. 1966. "The Religious Orientations of American Natural Scientists." *Social Forces* 44: 519–26.

Ventis, W. L. 1995. "The Relationships between Religion and Mental Health". *Journal of Social Issues* 51: 33–48.

Vetter, G. B., and M. Green, 1932–33. "Personality and Group Factors in the Making of Atheists." *Journal of Abnormal and Social Psychology* 27: 179–94.

Vitz, P. C. 1999. *Faith of the Fatherless: The Psychology of Atheism*. Dallas, Tex.: Spence Publishing.

von Hentig, H. 1948. *The Criminal and His Victim*. New Haven: Yale University Press.

Weintraub, W., and H. Aronson. 1974. "Patients in Psychoanalysis: Some Findings Related to Sex and Religion." *American Journal of Orthopsychiatry* 44: 102–8.

Wulff, D. M. (1997). *Psychology of Religion: Classic and Contemporary Views*, 2nd ed. New York: John Wiley & Sons.

Zelan, J. 1968. "Religious Apostasy, Higher Education, and Occupational Choice." *Sociology of Education* 41, no. 4: 370–79.

INDEX

Abbruzzese, John, 209
Abonouteichos, Pontus, Asia Minor, 20
abstract object, defined, 188
Adeimantus, 161
Adler, Rachel, 237
Africa, 61
agnosticism, 30; cancellation, 3; defined, 2; (Huxley), 44; and positive atheism (Martin), 2–3; skeptical, 3
Alberts, Bruce, 312
Albright, Carol Rausch, 61
aletheia, 272
Alexander, J., 307
Alliez, Eric, 41
Alston, William, 98–100, 217–219, 221, 230
Altizer, Thomas J. J., 276–277
American Religious Identification Survey (CUNY, 2001), 60
Americans for Democratic Action (ADA), 305
analogy, 37, 42
Analogy of Names, The (Cajetan), 42
Anaxagoras, 13–14
Anderson, Pamela, 234
angels, 170
animism, 293, 300; of Piaget, 294–295; of Tylor, 289
Anslem, Saint, 87–89
anthropic principle, 144
anthropomorphism, 293, 295, 300
Antiphon, 17
Apollodorus, 18
Apologeticus (Tertullian), 21
Apology (Justinus), 21

Apology (Plato), 14
apostasy, 302
Aquinas, Thomas, 2, 33, 37–38, 40–42, 90–92, 116, 141, 152, 200, 252
arahat, 224
argument: cosmological, types of, 182; evidential, a posteriori, or inductive, 167, 170–180; Liebniz cosmological, 182; logical, a priori, or deductive, 167–170; Thomistic, 182
Aristophanes, 14, 15, 16, 18
Aristotle, 140, 161, 187, 272
Aronson, H., 310
Ashbrook, James, 61
Asia, 61
astral projection, 128
atheism, 1; and the American experience, 255–259; Christian period of, in antiquity, 21–22; classical, 269; classical period of, in antiquity, 12–19; coercive, 57–59; defined, 28–29; in early seventeenth century France, 29; feminist argument for, 233–243, 246; and governmental endorsement of religion, 262–265; Greek roots of the word, 1; Hellenistic period of, in antiquity, 19–21; historical development of the concept of, 1; and individual religious freedom, 259–262; Kalam cosmological argument for, 188–191; methodological (Heidegger), 272; mind/body positions of, 119; modern, as a rejection of a specific